OFFICIAL MICROSOFT® SITE SERVER 2.0 ENTERPRISE EDITION TOOLKIT

Farhad Amirfaiz

PUBLISHED BY
Microsoft Press
A Division of Microsoft Corporation
One Microsoft Way
Redmond, Washington 98052-6399

Library of Congress Cataloging-in-Publication Data
Amirfaiz, Farhad, 1959-
    Official Microsoft Site Server 2.0 Enterprise Edition Toolkit / Farhad Amirfaiz.
       p. cm.
   Includes index.
   ISBN 1-57231-622-5
   1. Client/server computing. 2. Microsoft Site server. I. Title.
QA76.9.C55A525 1998
658.8'4--dc21   97-43124
                                                 CIP

Printed and bound in the United States of America.

1 2 3 4 5 6 7 8 9 MLML 3 2 1 0 9 8

Distributed to the book trade in Canada by Macmillan of Canada, a division of Canada Publishing
Corporation.

A CIP catalogue record for this book is available from the British Library.

Microsoft Press books are available through booksellers and distributors worldwide. For further
information about international editions, contact your local Microsoft Corporation office. Or contact
Microsoft Press International directly at fax (425) 936-7329. Visit our Web site at mspress.microsoft.com.

Acquisitions Editor: David Clark
Project Editors: Tory McLearn, Ron Lamb
Technical Editor: Lang Zerner
Manuscript Editor: Chrisa Hotchkiss

This book is dedicated to Diana and Alexandria.

Contents

Introduction

If you are curious about what Microsoft is doing in the areas of online commerce, Web content management, and site management, let me introduce you to Microsoft Site Server. Site Server Enterprise Edition is Microsoft's premier electronic commerce platform. This new, secure, and robust technology is the key to planning, creating, and managing a world-class online commercial site.

This toolkit is a collection of architectural information, design samples, development examples, and deployment and maintenance experiences from participation in the architecture, design, development, deployment, and maintenance of over 50 Web sites using Microsoft electronic commerce technologies over the past two years.

This book primarily serves two classes of audiences:

- Internet service providers (ISPs) such as people who may or may not provide content, but who host sites and provide technical services.

- Internet content providers (ICPs) such as financial institutions, publishers, media content providers, and educational and training institutions and specialty retailers who host their sites internally.

This book's secondary audience includes Internet Web professionals in general, such as Management Information System directors, Web consultants, Web database developers, Web application developers, Web designers, small business managers, and individuals who are considering an electronic commercial presence on the Net.

This toolkit features a complete, step-by-step approach to understanding Microsoft Site Server technology, and the companion disc contains fully functional evaluation versions of all of the required software. Add hardware and a bit of interest to test drive the technology.

There is more for the Web developer on the companion CD. It also contains a full development environment including Microsoft Visual InterDev and Visual Basic

Control Creation Edition, to facilitate development and customization. This CD contains complete and fully functional evaluation versions of the following software:

■ Microsoft Site Server Enterprise Edition version 2.0

■ Microsoft SQL Server version 6.5

■ Microsoft Visual Basic Control Creation Edition version 5.0

■ Microsoft Visual InterDev Web development environment version 2.0

Refer to *default.htm* in the root directory of the CD and Appendix A.

Eight chapters cover the different technologies of Site Server, beginning with Commerce Server. Some technical sections of this book assume familiarity with HTML, knowledge of a programming language, and general familiarity with the Internet and related technologies.

Chapter 1 starts with an introduction to Site Server and enumerates its components. It then begins a discussion of a core component of Site Server: Commerce Server. Some of the discussion takes a visual approach. A tour of a sample Commerce Server store follows. The remainder of the chapter covers management and the Commerce Server build concept.

Chapter 2 discusses Commerce Server's stores in more detail.

Chapter 3 introduces the programming concepts of Site Server Active Server Pages, including scripting, built-in objects, and components. This chapter requires understanding of a programming language. VB Scripting is used for examples.

Having understood the basic concepts of Active Server Pages, Chapter 4 introduces the Visual InterDev development environment and provides some standard store customization examples.

Chapter 5 is about Component Object Model (COM) components and building COM skeletons in a language-neutral manner. Visual Basic Control Creation is one tool featured in this chapter, and other tools are also discussed.

Having covered one core technology of Site Server as a template, Chapter 6 covers other major technologies of Site Server, as well as a number of complementary servers, tools, and technologies that help you get the most from your Site Server.

Chapter 7 discusses security and performance topics and techniques. The associated tools are covered in Appendix J.

Chapter 8 is a preview of Site Server Enterprise Edition version 3.0.

The following conventions are used in this book:

■ Lines of code continuing onto the next lines are delimited with a "↵" character as the last character of the line.

■ Reserved names are italicized.

■ The names of methods, parameters, and options for a component or API are in boldface.

I am happy to receive feedback on topics related to this book. You can e-mail me at *sitesvr@classic.msn.com*. Please enter *siteserver2* in the subject box for any recommendations you have for the next version of this book.

ACKNOWLEDGMENTS

Special thanks goes to David Clark, Kim Field, Ron Lamb, and John Pierce of Microsoft Press for their help.

Thanks also to Chrisa Hotchkiss, Beverly McGuire, Tory McLearn, Curtis Philips, and Lang Zerner at Labrecque Publishing. Special thanks also goes to Gytis Barzdukas, Vince Orgovan, and Subbrao Vedula for their contributions to this book.

I would like to express my appreciation for the input of the following teams and individuals on this book. Microsoft Developer Relations group: Morris Beton, Brad Chase, Hans Hugli, Sundar Krishnamurthy, Todd Merrel, Todd Nielsan, Tal Saraf, Naseem Taffaha, and Sara Williams. Commerce Server product unit managers: Mark Kroese and Satya Nadella. Commerce Server development: Josh Axelrod, Arnold Blinn, Greg Burns, Michael Cohen, Mike Daly, Dipan Dewan, Don Gillett, Gary Halstead, Kris Iverson, Vijay Kolli, Michael Lorton, Kanchan Mitra, Daryl Olander, Greg Stein, Marc Whitman, and Vincent Yu. Commerce Server test: Eric Askilsrud, Vijay Gajjala, C. W. Jones, Clifford Mosley, William Nagle, Ken Oien, David Rohwer, Lidia Schwarz, James Visintainer, and Luanne Warden. Commerce Server user education: Linn Compton, Seth Manheim, Cristal Weber, Audrey Wehba, and Steven Wood. Commerce Server program managers: Phivos Aristides, Graham Astor, Derrick Bazlen, Jeff Bell, Michael Cockrill, Thomas Grate, Pierre Jammes, Rick Johnson, Bjorn Levidow, Vince Orgovan, David Tuniman, and Tom Zebroski. Commerce Server product support services: Jay Jaacks, Ken Jones, and Subbarao Vedula.

The following groups also contributed. Microsoft Visual InterDev group: Karin Anderson and Greg Leak. Microsoft NT group: Lee Fisher. Microsoft Commerce Server group, Microsoft SQL Server group, Microsoft MCIS and ISBU Server group, Microsoft Visual Basic group, and Microsoft marketing group. And many thanks to those who contributed to this book whose names I may have failed to mention.

Chapter 1

Microsoft Commerce Server

This chapter provides a brief history of Microsoft Site Server and the major features of Microsoft Commerce Server, one core component of Site Server. After this overview, you will take a short shopping journey that showcases one of Commerce Server's starter stores. Having installed Site Server Enterprise Edition,[1] you will be able to generate the same store for your purposes by following the steps. Finally, this chapter shows Commerce Server store administration and build processes. For serious planning, Appendix B outlines a more formal planning process for a commercial online store. Appendix C illustrates Building a BuyNow type of store.

Chapter 2 discusses Commerce Server design concepts and lays a foundation for development and customization. Chapter 3 covers Active Server Pages (ASP) in detail and explains ASP concepts and components.

Chapter 4 covers the Visual InterDev development environment and includes actual code samples and listings.

Chapter 5 is devoted to components and building custom components. Both Chapters 4 and 5 discuss components and objects that perform certain tasks, but these components and objects are not covered in detail until Chapter 5.

Electronic commerce may expand faster if the cost and risk of conducting commerce on the Net were reduced to a manageable level. This includes, but is not

---

1. The CD in the back of the book includes an evaluation copy of Site Server Enterprise Edition version 2.0 to jump-start your online commercial store. Please see Appendix A.

limited to, the total cost of developing and maintaining a virtual presence on the Net, and the risk of carrying out a secure transaction on the Net.

The set of tools, technologies, and components Microsoft Site Server Enterprise Edition provides reduces the risk and cost of electronic commerce on the Internet. This does not mean that Microsoft Site Server Enterprise Edition solves every problem of the Internet and removes all associated business risks.[2] However, it does mean that a solid foundation and a set of tools and technologies exist to reduce the cost and risk of development and to streamline deployment and management of commercial Web sites.

What is Microsoft Site Server Enterprise Edition in a nutshell?

1. A Windows NT–based set of server technologies and client components to facilitate electronic commerce on the Internet

2. A full life cycle workbench for developing, managing, maintaining, and growing an Internet commercial presence

    This chapter concentrates on the first point and is organized to provide

- History and evolution of Microsoft Site Server

- Major features of Commerce Server 2.0 (a core component of Site Server)

- An online shopping experience scenario

- Commerce Server store administration and build processes

HISTORY AND EVOLUTION OF MICROSOFT SITE SERVER

Today's Site Server incorporates at least five technology cycles, as shown in Figure 1-1.

1. HTML plus CGI

    Commerce Server technology's origins lie in HTML static content augmented with CGI[3] programming. This model served well for a while; however, development of a new store was a long process of modifying both the HTML content and all the CGI programs.

    The purchasing process was tailored specially for the needs of an individual online store. Business rules and store fronts were hard-coded and designed, more or less, from scratch. A number of commercial sites

---

2. Some Internet risks are solved with technology. Others yet may need business acumen or legal savvy.

3. CGI stands for Common Gateway Interface, a method of adding processes to HTML documents.

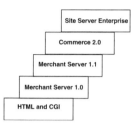

Figure 1-1. *Evolution of Site Server technology.*

exist on the Net today that employ these earlier technologies. Because of the large effort required to build a minimal system, most of these sites do not have an easy-to-use set of administrative functionality built into the base store.

Working with the online stores required knowledge of HTML and CGI programming. Contrast this approach to an ideal world where you only need to update assets such as products (product description) and images to modify or build a store.

Stores based on these early technologies were typically stand-alone, meaning they had few (or no) interfaces to other systems and applications. Contrast this approach to one of leveraging the predeveloped technologies to work coherently with other existing systems.

2. Microsoft Merchant Server 1.0

Microsoft introduced Merchant Server 1.0 in 1997 and it featured the following:

❑ A set of sample stores to speed up new development

❑ A model of the online sales process and a flexible set of sales process stages

❑ A software developer's kit (SDK) for customization and interfacing

These features helped reduce the total cost of owning an online store. However, the language of Merchant Server 1.0 remained proprietary in nature.

3. Microsoft Merchant Server 1.1

In early 1997, Microsoft announced Merchant Server 1.1, built based on the experience with Merchant 1.0. The new version's major enhancements included the following:

❑ Used Active Server Pages (ASP) as the server's internal programming language

❑ Added remote build of store foundation through the Web browser

- ❑ Added remote configuration of store through the Web browser
- ❑ Added remote administration of the store through the Web browser
- ❑ Invented migration tool for 1.0 to 1.1
- ❑ Aeditor for pipeline (purchase process) modification and customization
- ❑ Improved database performance (cached queries)
- ❑ Included development environment and set of tools to provide a platform for developing commercial Web sites rather than just a single Web site application

4. Commerce Server 2.0[4]

Based on the experience with Merchant 1.1, in mid-1997 Microsoft announced Commerce Server (MSCS) 2.0. The name change reflected a scope change to the wider electronic commerce audience, in addition to retailers. The major enhancements were as follows:

- ❑ Added performance enhancements to store pages
- ❑ Improved database performance
- ❑ Introduced SDK enhancement

5. Site Server Enterprise Edition

Commerce Server was an excellent electronic commerce system but lacked in administrative, reporting, site management, and development tools. To further strengthen the product, Microsoft augmented Commerce Server with administrative, reporting, site management, and development tools from the Microsoft family of tools and technologies. This package is called Site Server Enterprise Edition. The major areas of enhancements were as follows:

- ❑ Included a number of servers under the same umbrella (For example, Personalization and Content Replication were added.)
- ❑ Included an enhanced development environment and set of tools such as Visual InterDev (VI), Site Analyst, and Usage Analyst
- ❑ Enhanced management tools
- ❑ Added remote build of stores

---

4. Depending on the packaging decisions, Commerce Server may also be marketed under the name Site Server Enterprise Edition, which includes Commerce Server and a number of related technologies.

Chapter 4 covers Visual InterDev, and Chapter 6 covers Site Analyst and Usage Analyst. While there are many components to Site Server, the remainder of this chapter concentrates on Commerce Server 2.0, one major component of Site Server Enterprise Edition 2.0 (see Figure 1-2).

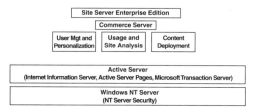

Figure 1-2. *Major components of Site Server Enterprise Edition.*

The Major Features of Commerce Server 2.0

The major features of the Commerce Server 2.0 platform are discussed below and are shown in Figure 1-3.

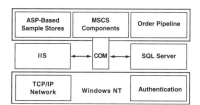

Figure 1-3. *Components of Commerce Server technology.*

Runs on the Windows NT and Internet Information Server (IIS) platform

Commerce Server runs under the Windows NT server operating system version 4.0 and later, and on the Intel and DEC Alpha platforms. NT server also includes an integrated Web server called Internet Information Server (IIS). IIS provides comprehensive, secure Web-site administration for Internet sites running Commerce Server. Chapter 7 covers IIS administration and security details of the platform. IIS version 3.0 also includes Open Database Connectivity (ODBC) version 3.0 for connection to databases such as SQL server, Oracle, or Informix. (Chapter 7 discusses ODBC.) In addition, IIS version 3.0 and later supplies the Active Server Pages (ASP) environment for developing Web-based stores and applications. For more information on ASP, see Chapter 3.[5]

---

5. Active Server Pages (ASP) is an open, extensible application environment. It supports the use of virtually any scripting language and components written in any programming language. The functionality of a Web application built with ASP is component-based, so pieces can be reused in other Web and client-server applications.

Commerce Server handles heavy processing loads efficiently, extends by means of published application program interfaces (APIs), integrates with other Microsoft technologies and products, and presents a flexible architecture that supports diverse system configurations. This means that companies can readily translate their existing applications and information-technology infrastructure into Internet-based marketing. It also means that any third-party service provider can easily build a component that plugs in to the system.

Personalizes to individual user

Just as the ability to customize offers and promotions helps a retailer target markets effectively, the same functionality produces a beneficial effect on the shopper as well. Customers are generally pleased to receive offers and promotions that take their individual needs and preferences into account. This tells them that you have their interests in mind, and often it means they do not have to search through information to find exactly what they want. Generally, shoppers are pleased to learn about associated products offered through cross-selling, or superior products offered through up-selling. With Commerce Server, you can offer customers additional personal services that are order-specific, such as

- A gift message or special greeting to accompany an order shipped as a gift

- The ability to give specific instructions for delivery

- A guarantee that an order will arrive on a specified date (for example, December 24)

Through a customizable HTML form, retailers can collect any details they want about individual customers: age, gender, address, hobbies, and so on. The system can also keep track of an individual shopper's purchase record and number of visits to the online store. This information forms the basis of individual consumer profiles and in turn can be used for compiling mailing lists and making personalized promotional offers. Microsoft Site Server includes Personalization Server, described in Chapter 6.

Site Server provides a means of collecting and storing shopper data, managing membership accounts, and creating customized site reports. A company can quickly create targeted discount promotions based on detailed user tracking and analyze the promotion results for future planning. This new technology improves a merchant's ability to offer customers attractive sales opportunities, improve product introduction strategy, and provide a customized environment for each individual shopper. Imagine if the marketing manager could test how it plays in Peoria, overnight.

Integrates optionally with a membership component

As an option, you can offer shoppers membership in the online store. Site Server supports membership accounts and password login. An optional membership component is also available for Commerce Server. Chapter 6 also describes the Membership Server.

Supports all major credit cards

The system supports all major credit cards as well as private-label card payment, with the additional option of live credit-card authorization. By using online real-time credit authorization schemes, retailers can immediately route credit-card transactions to their own choice of acquiring bank(s). Using Secure Electronic Transaction (SET) technology allows for authentication of accounts through card-issuing companies and ensures that retailers can route information directly to the card issuers. Commerce Server installation can simply integrate this function into their existing credit authorization department.

Commerce Server doesn't require credit cards to be authorized online. Sensitive retailers, such as high-ticket items retailers, can choose to simply post authorization requests from the server to their existing credit department or credit authorization application. At the end of a purchase (after a shopper has selected a method of payment and the credit payment is approved), Commerce Server sends the shopper a confirmation. The retailer can assign tracking numbers to orders so that the customer can inquire about the status of the order and the retailer can track the order information readily.

Includes built-in tools for collecting and reporting user data and events

The system's reporting features allow a store manager to use any standard reporting tool for generating data on sales, traffic, demographics, and other statistics. These graphical tools present the data in easy-to-understand forms. As mentioned before, Microsoft Site Server includes the Site Analyst tool, which generates site reports.

Implements a complete sales cycle

Commerce Server presale services perform the following specific tasks:

- Supply descriptions and cross-reference information on products offered for sale

- Check the availability of the items ordered and report whether they are in stock, back-ordered, and so on

- Determine prices for the items a shopper selects, applying promotional sale prices, member discounts, or other factors as appropriate

- Calculate the cost of shipping and handling for items selected

■ Calculate the tax due

Commerce Server sale services include the following:

■ Order capture: Processing customers' orders, totaling prices, authorizing and accepting payment

■ Order routing: Routing orders to the appropriate service providers and delivery carriers

Postsale services primarily involve order and customer status, enabling both the retailer and the customer to check, audit, and track account and order status after a purchase.

Presents an unlimited number of offerings and variations

The system's database management functions allow for an unlimited number of product attributes. You can offer individual products or services in any number of variations, from colors and sizes to languages. You can also prompt shoppers for add-on options ranging from personal monograms to optional warranty services.

Includes a built-in promotional engine

You can adjust product pricing instantly, and as often as necessary. Furthermore, dynamic page generation makes spotlighting a "featured product" possible every day or every hour of the day. You can offer special sales promotions to the entire online audience or to a particular set of shoppers based on customer personalized data. For example, sales promotions can be

■ Aimed at shoppers of a particular age range or living in specified ZIP code areas

■ Customized to reflect data on an individual customer's purchasing history

■ Configured to last for a limited time only ("Offer valid until December 31," or the like)

■ Geared for the quick sale of inventory that needs to be moved

You can design product presentation for cross-selling or up-selling. When a shopper selects an item for purchase, the system can automatically suggest a complementary item (cross-selling) that is available at a discounted price. For example, a shopper who selects a camera can be offered a tripod at 10 percent off. Alternatively, the system can suggest a similar item of better quality (up-selling). For example, a similar but superior product can be offered to position the product and its features compared for comparison and contrast.

Provides real-time pricing

Commerce Server features real-time pricing including applicable tax, shipping, and handling charges. Customers can choose from among a variety of payment methods. VPos[6] software from VeriFone is available for checking a shopper's credit in real time.[7] As an option, a retailer can choose from several types of inventory management.

Integrates into existing business processes

Extensible APIs enable a company to integrate commerce system incoming Internet orders with other kinds of inventory management, tax, shipping, and fulfillment systems. Shipping and order-tracking steps might integrate into existing processes where a business process already exists. Alternatively, Microsoft and other third-party providers offer several additional options, including electronic data interchange (EDI) components, e-mail, and fax capabilities.

Additionally, you can use Visual InterDev to develop a Web-based application in a matter of hours to allow your shipping department or vendor to view, track, audit, and process Commerce Server shipping requests.

Supports multiple levels of inventory management

Commerce Server's extensible inventory-management features accommodate multiple levels of inventory status integration. A retailer can decide, for example, among

- No inventory-management control
- Dedicated inventory control for online orders that work by decrementing the database for each order
- Inventory control integrated with existing inventory-management systems

Reaches all browsers in local or international markets

Commerce Server is browser-agnostic. The HTML it generates relies only on the <TABLE> HTML tag, as all base processing is performed on the server side and only the resulting HTML is sent to the browser.

Commerce Server gives retailers a truly international market potential. Web users located anywhere in the world can have access to an online store 24 hours a day and seven days a week. You can denominate product prices in a variety of currencies such as U.S., Canadian dollars, French francs, pounds sterling, Japanese yen, German marks, and others. A simple tax component shipped with Commerce Server

---

6. VPos is a third-party clearing software that facilitates real-time credit-card authorization for the major providers.

7. *http://www.verifone.com/products/software/icommerce/html.*

calculates Japanese tax charges and European value-added taxes (VAT). You can extend European VAT support by using third-party tax software.

Provides a strong suite of management HTML-based tools

Commerce Server provides the following management tools (all tools are Web-based and none requires knowledge of programming or HTML):

- Product management pages: for laying out the products in an online store (Department and Product pages) and adjusting information, including pricing information, while the store is open

- Order management pages: for viewing orders sorted by day, month, product, or shopper

- Shopper management pages: for viewing information about shoppers

- Promotion management pages: for establishing merchandise promotions such as item discounts, order discounts, shopper discounts, cross-sells and up-sells

Commerce Server store administration and build processes and associated tools are discussed later in this chapter in the "Commerce Server Store Administration and Build Processes" section.

Commerce Server utilities include tools for administering the services of the server and integrating and managing services developed by third parties. This makes it easy to create and update data used by services or service providers, and to replace services with compatible third-party solutions as the retailer's operational needs change.

Provides a choice of development tools

Commerce Server supports all standard HTML and HTML-related tools. Designers of online stores can use their favorite software tools for creating Web pages and including media enhancements, pictures, sound, or video. Additionally, the Microsoft Visual InterDev (VI) development environment, which is also now part of Microsoft Visual Studio's integrated toolset, is one excellent development environment available for authoring Commerce Server stores and applications.

Provides a choice of databases and schema

Starter stores propose database schema, but the Commerce Server will work with a variety of possible schemas. You can design any schema to reflect the specific needs of the business as long as any Commerce Server templates that access information from the database understand the schema. A retailer can readily integrate existing assets databases with the Commerce Server system. This means that there is no theoretical limit to the number of products and product attributes that Commerce Server can list and access. Commerce Server requires a database for a store running on the system. Conformity to the open database connectivity (ODBC) standard allows retailers to use existing, familiar databases. Commerce Server makes use of the ODBC standard, which means that the system can be combined with existing databases containing product information or customer data. Existing product schemas do not have to be changed, but rather are adapted for online commerce.

Features Dynamic HTML technology

Dynamic page generation affords flexibility of product presentation and up-to-the-moment pricing. Thus, the online store can keep pace with special sales promotions and changing product specifications. This feature simplifies implementation and reduces costs by creating HTML pages on the fly, including the latest information from the product database.

Personalizes to your existing business sales model

Commerce Server processes orders in a sequence of stages called the Order Processing Pipeline. After the shopper places an order, the order is passed through the Order Processing Pipeline, each stage of which consists of zero or more components that are specified by business needs. Three types of components can be used in each stage depending on make versus buy decision:

- BUY: Components supplied by Microsoft with the Commerce Server System, such as SimpleTax

- BUY: Components supplied by third parties, such as VPos and Taxware

- MAKE: Components developed by the merchant or mall operator using Visual Studio development language and environments

All components are optional: businesses can use whichever ones fit their needs, or they can create their own. For example, a tax stage in the Order Processing Pipeline computes the relevant taxes for an order. Multiple tax components are available for this stage, including several from Microsoft for use in different tax jurisdictions, and other sophisticated components available from third-party providers. Alternatively, the business may choose to develop its own or to interface to an existing application or process.

Provides in-house or remote host sites and management

If you have a commercial Web site without the technical infrastructure, you can choose to use a service provider to run your store. In this case, the administrator of the host site handles the preliminary stages of store setup by running the Commerce

Host Administrator application.[8] Using the Store Builder Wizard, you can build a store on an existing store foundation or build from the foundation up. In the Store Foundation Wizard pages, the administrator sets up the store foundation by creating a file system structure for the store pages, creating virtual directory aliases for the store, and specifying a data source name (DSN) for connecting to the store database. (The store database is created when you run the Store Builder Wizard.)

The service provider notifies the merchant of the URL for connecting to the Store Builder Wizard. Using this URL, the merchant can run the wizard as many times as necessary, selecting store features to include, until the merchant achieves the appropriate store functionality. Then the merchant's designer performs the finishing touches that produce an appealing and effective Web presence for the merchant. If the merchant wants to use any audio, video, or image files in the store, these should be transferred to the host service provider. This can be done by means of a file transfer protocol (FTP) server such as the one Internet Information Server provides or by other appropriate methods. After testing, the store site is ready for use.

Some merchants may wish to run Commerce Server–based stores on their own server hardware in their organization. Typically these merchants are large organizations with in-house staff who are experienced in administering a Web server, working with HTML design, and managing a database. Like host service providers, administrators or store managers in these organizations begin the store creation process by running the Store Foundation Wizard to set up a store foundation. After determining which components the store will need to run, based on existing systems and business practices, the administrator can configure the store Order Processing Pipeline using the Pipeline Editor. (Otherwise, the administrator can select the built-in pipeline when the Store Builder Wizard is run.) At this point, the store designer can take over. Using the URL provided by the service provider, the designer runs the Store Builder Wizard. With this wizard, the designer can determine how the store will be organized and how the pages will appear. In either case, the designer will probably make HTML modifications to add special effects or other features as needed. In addition, the store manager or administrator might want to update the database schema and queries, using existing database tools for more advanced functionality. After satisfactory testing of the site, the store is ready to go "live." Thereafter, the store manager updates products or promotions and reviews store traffic statistics using the store's Management pages. These two alternative approaches are covered later in this chapter.

---

8. Merchants who plan to integrate credit-card authorization components will need to register with an acquiring bank to authorize Internet transactions and install bank-specific authorization software along with the component.

Provides a scalable and secure platform

Because Commerce Server runs on Windows NT servers, scales based on multiple ODBC database servers, and runs on a number of standard and scalable hardware platforms, it provides a high degree of scalability and portability. As a company's business grows, its Internet commercial capacity can grow simultaneously. Commerce Server is scalable to large numbers of transactions, customers, and merchants. A company can host hundreds of thousands of products. Internet malls and commercial Internet service providers can host multiple stores on a single server, optimizing their hardware investment and simplifying systems management without compromising security. Chapter 7 discusses scalability in detail in the section called "Site Server Scalability."

Customers must be confident that their transactions are safe from fraud and that purchases will reach them expeditiously. Their ability to charge purchases against their existing credit-card accounts gives them a familiar method of payment, but it is just as important that their transactions be tamper-proof. Commerce Server has built-in features that help answer these security needs.

Commerce Server uses Internet-standard Secure Sockets Layer (SSL) channel encryption to protect sensitive information as it is transmitted. SSL encryption is built into standard Web browsers, including Netscape Navigator and Microsoft Internet Explorer. Commerce Server also supports the Secure Electronic Transactions (SET) protocol through third-party credit-card authorization applications such as VPos. For shopper authentication, Commerce Server takes advantage of the security mechanisms IIS provides. Security details of the platform are covered in Chapter 7.

Features the BuyNow technology

This feature allows any page on any Web server to carry out commerce. Here are some applications of this feature:

- To increase the server reach

- To promote the site on other Web sites (This may or may not be a Commerce Server installation.)

- To allow for a very quick shopping cycle for short-purchase-cycle items

- To allow for impulse purchases

A scenario of this technology is included later under the heading "BuyNow Process."

Supports the full life cycle of business from development through maintenance at a lower total cost of ownership

Using Commerce Server, you can quickly set up a store on the World Wide Web, customize the system to meet specific marketing needs, and participate in selling to an international base.

Commerce Server includes a number of starter stores with its installation to serve as examples for developing your online store. You can think of a starter store as a kit for constructing a prefabricated electronic retail outlet, complete with basic building blocks. Starter stores, HTML templates for the development of an online "storefront," make it possible to build a retail-oriented Web site without having to design the site layout, or individual pages, from scratch. These building blocks save a great deal of time and resources. The starter stores shipped with Commerce Server are in part basic templates, and in part operational samples that you can modify to fit a specific model. They provide formats for a home page, product pages, company information pages, and other typical structures of a Web site designed for retailing. Templates consist of HTML as well as ASP-generation commands that specify what data should be inserted in a page, what queries should be run against the database, and so on. The "Online Shopping Experience Scenario" section later in this chapter provides a brief tour of a starter store called Adventure Works. No additional development was required for this sample.

Without needing advanced programming skills, retailers can put product data online and administer or modify the contents of their store. This is one feature that helps reduce roll-out, training, and ongoing management costs of doing business online. The "Store Administrator Process" section covers Commerce Server administration later in this chapter.

Chapters 1 through 5 cover Commerce Server. Chapter 6, "Getting the Most from Your Site Server," covers the remaining Site Server tools and services that help reduce the long-term operational and maintenance costs of an online store. These tools include Personalization, Usage and Site Analyst, and Content Replication, as well as other complementary tools and servers.

AN ONLINE SHOPPING EXPERIENCE SCENARIO

The previous section discussed the major features of Commerce Server. In this section you will test drive an online store. This section is a scenario of how you can experience Commerce Server.

Imagine you are a shopper who loves the outdoor life. You have worn out your rock-climbing shoes and wish to replace them. A friend tells you that you can buy a great pair from Adventure Works,[9] an online store specializing in clothing and equipment for camping and mountaineering. If you would like to follow along with this demonstration on your own server, please see Appendix A first. The illustrations will help you visualize in the absence of an installed server.

1. Start up your browser and connect to the Adventure Works Web site (see Figure 1-4).

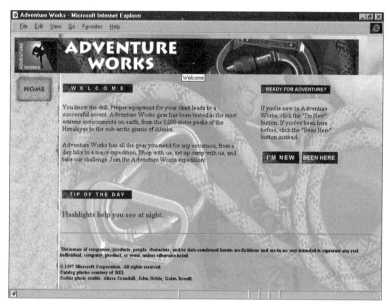

Figure 1-4. *Adventure Works welcome page.*

The Adventure Works welcome page opens, and it will take you an instant to see the I'm New button. Starting from accessing the welcome (main) page, the customer's request for pages within the store pages is optionally logged using the Traffic object of Commerce Server. Even if the consumer never makes a purchase, the merchant can gain useful information about the site hits as well as visits to the store using the Traffic object.

2. Click the I'm New button to find the registration page (see Figure 1-5). This store allows for both membership-based and nonmembership-based shopping. Members are provided with discounts and special deals. The nonmember's experience is similar to the member's, except the price may not include these special discounts or other arrangements. I registered as myself and entered as a member.

---

9. A fictitious camping and climbing gear manufacturer and marketer, and one of the MSCS sample stores.

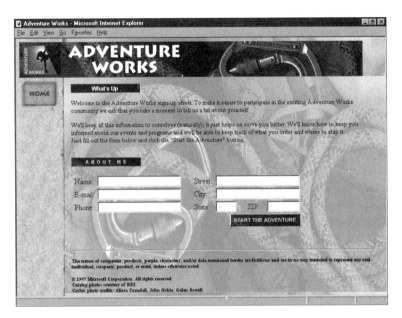

Figure 1-5. *Adventure Works registration page.*

3. Type your name, address, phone number, and e-mail address on the simple form.

4. Click the Start The Adventure button and move on to the Adventure Works main store lobby page, shown in Figure 1-6.

   The store is based on a simple three-frame approach. The top frame includes logo and navigation buttons. The main frame features the store and any featured products for this month. The left frame is also navigational. As you can see under the Special Deal heading in the lower right, there is a hiking boot special going on right now. This store features products in its lobby. You click the link next to the image to get additional information on this product. You are now in an information-gathering stage and visiting departments and offerings. Variations are built into this store. You may add more items or remove them before you arrive at the checkout.

   From there, you are only one click away from the Rock Shoes department, where you discover a special sale on one of the brands you know to be among the best.

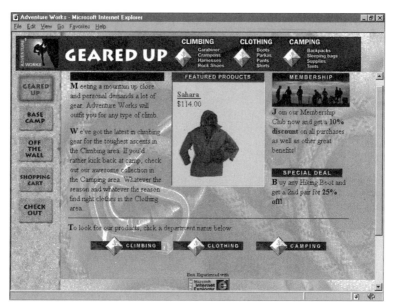

Figure 1-6. *Adventure Works main store lobby page.*

5. In the top navigational frame, click Rock Shoes under the Climbing section (see Figure 1-7).

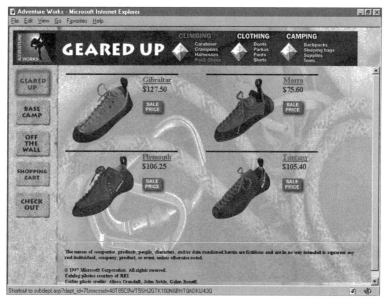

Figure 1-7. *Adventure Works Rock Shoes department.*

6. Select a pair of shoes that you like and that is on sale (see Figure 1-8).

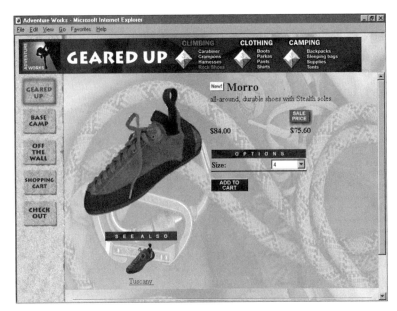

Figure 1-8. *Adventure Works product showcase page.*

7. Select your size from the drop-down list.

8. Click the Add To Cart button. As shown in Figure 1-9, the display changes to a page representing your Shopping Cart, with the details about the item you just selected.

Satisfied with your choice, you think about your mountaineering parka, which is almost as old as your shoes.

9. Click the Geared Up link to go back to the store's main page.

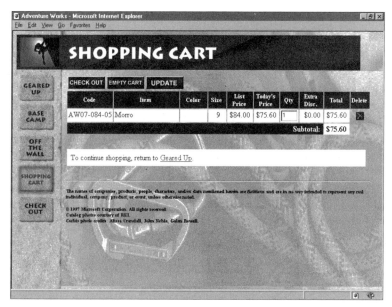

Figure 1-9. *Adventure Works Shopping Cart page.*

10. In the upper navigational frame, click Clothing (see Figure 1-10).

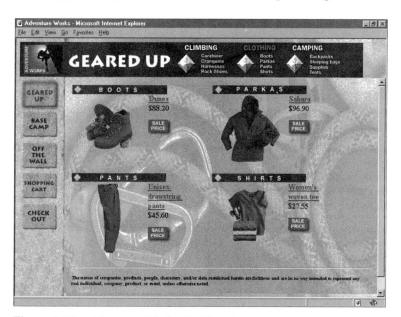

Figure 1-10. *Adventure Works Clothing department.*

11. There you find several attractive parkas on sale. Choose one.

12. Specify your size and preferred color.

13. Add this item to your Shopping Cart. The Shopping Cart page now displays details about both items, as shown in Figure 1-11.

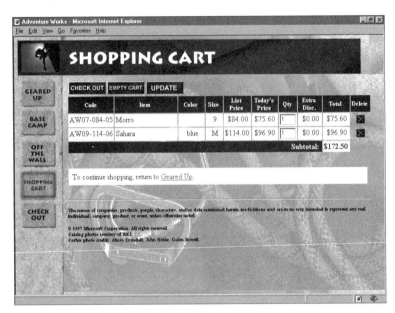

Figure 1-11. *Adventure Works Shopping Cart page, two items.*

14. This is fun, but you can't think of anything else you need now. Click the Check Out button and proceed to the address form and payment form (Figure 1-12).

15. Fill in your shipping address and select the type of credit card. Do not type in your account number; use 424242424242 or a test account number per the documentation for the evaluation copy of the product in the back of this book. Having entered a test number, double check all information to make sure it's accurate (see Figure 1-13).

WARNING Do not perform the following steps on a live Commerce Server site, or you will wind up purchasing a new pair of shoes and a parka! Just follow along by examining the figures.

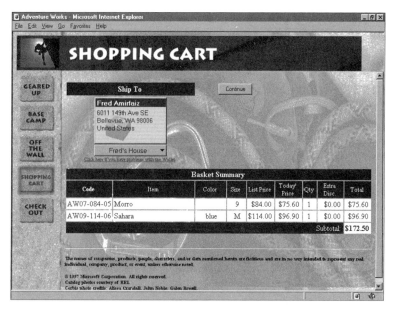

Figure 1-12. *Adventure Works Check Out page.*

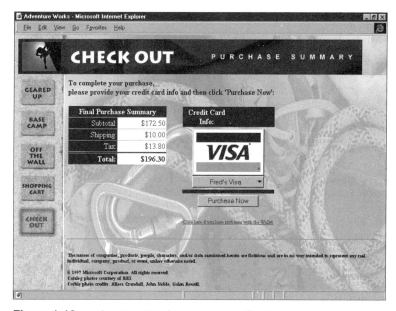

Figure 1-13. *Adventure Works payment verification.*

You have one more chance to change your order before committing to the purchase. If you were actually ordering the merchandise, you would open the Final Approval page, which shows a statement of the total bill, including tax and shipping costs. If you were satisfied that all was in order, you would click the Purchase Now button. You would type in your credit-card authorization password[10] and click OK (see Figure 1-14).

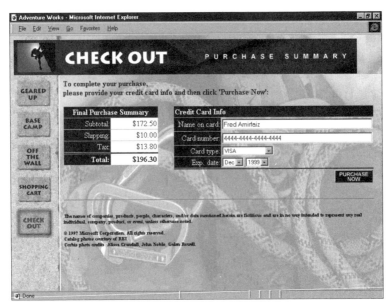

Figure 1-14. *Credit-card authorization.*

Then the confirmation page would appear, confirming your purchase and giving you an order reference number should you care to inquire about the order (see Figure 1-15).

That concludes our quick tour of an online store. We next cover the administration and build processes of Commerce Server to give administrators and managers a tour of the platform.

---

10. You can choose your credit-card authorization password the first time you use the Wallet (discussed in more detail later in this chapter). The first time you want to purchase using a credit card, a wizard gathers your credit-card information and stores it in encrypted format locally on your machine. This card information is also password-protected to guard against unauthorized use of your credit card information by others who may also have access to your computer system. Having entered the card information and password once, you simply select the card and enter the password to validate subsequent use of your card, but you do not need to reenter this information again and again.

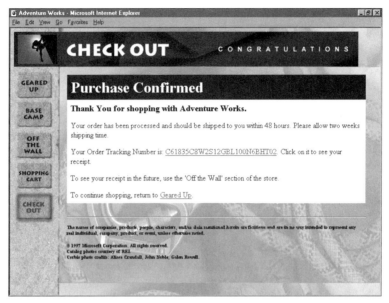

Figure 1-15. *Adventure Works Check Out confirmation page.*

COMMERCE SERVER STORE ADMINISTRATION AND BUILD PROCESSES

The major features of Commerce Server 2.0 store administration and build processes are discussed below:

- BuyNow process
- Host Administrator process
- Store Administrator process
- Build process
- Foundations store process

BuyNow Process

Perhaps the best way to talk about the BuyNow feature is to walk through a Buy-Now process together. For example, imagine you were working online, browsing the Net, or interacting with a broadcast PC/TV, when you remembered that you did not send any roses to your significant other for Valentine's Day. You happen to be viewing a page and notice the A Dozen Roses button on this page. You can send roses from this page.

1. You click the A Dozen Roses button and a second window pops up to let you shop for roses without leaving the page that you were viewing. The page recommends a dozen roses at $29.95, but you decide for only three.

2. Next you are asked for the shipping address, so you enter shipping address information. This is quicker than spelling the information over the telephone and perhaps more accurate.

3. Then you enter a personalized message to accompany the flowers.

4. Next you enter the credit-card information.

5. Finally you are asked to confirm all information, and you commit to the purchase.

6. The Wallet (discussed later in this chapter) requires a password when you use a credit card, so you enter your password.

The order is confirmed back to you. You are still on the original page. In fact, the page you are viewing is on a different server than the Commerce Server that carries out the completed request.

Host Administrator Process

Store managers and site administrators use Commerce Host Administrator, an application based on Active Server Pages (ASP), to open, close, or delete stores running on a Commerce Server installation. Additionally, from the Commerce Host Administrator's page, the site administrator or store manager can create a new store by starting the Starter Store Copy Wizard or the Store Foundation Wizard (see Figure 1-16).

Commerce Host Administrator is especially useful for service providers who host stores, or for large organizations that host their own stores and wish to offer stores to other complementary businesses and organizations. This tool separates the tasks of store site administration from store creation and management. Commerce Host Administrator separates the technical tasks—such as selecting a data source name (DSN) or setting permissions on the file system—from the administrative activities, such as store-merchandising activities, loading product data, or designing pages. This ensures that the right people have access to the resources they need.

Commerce Host Administrator offers two options for creating a store. First the user can create a store foundation, which defines some of the necessary structure of the store. This foundation is not a functional or a complete store until you run the Store Builder Wizard. The foundation consists of

■ A set of directories for storing ASP files and assets for the store

■ The Web server virtual directory aliases

Figure 1-16. *Commerce Host Administrator page.*

■ A DataSource name (DSN) for database access

■ The user and administrator accounts for the new store

The Store Foundation Wizard generates a store foundation; after you run this wizard, you use the Store Builder Wizard to complete store design.

Once you build a store, you may wish to generate another store based on that design and not start over. As an alternative, you can create a complete store that is a copy of an existing starter store. This copy is identical to the starter store except that you change the store's name and DSN to those the administrator specifies. The resulting store has all the features of the starter store that you copied. You use the Starter Store Copy Wizard to generate a copy of a starter store.

If removing a store is necessary, Commerce Host Administrator provides this capability, removing store elements including the store's files, database, and virtual directory aliases.

Store Administrator Process

What is the shop owner's experience? How do you open the store, close it, promote merchandise, manage pricing, etc.? You do this in the main administration page of the store, the Adventure Works Store Manager page, shown in Figure 1-17. This page is password-protected and an error is returned after three unsuccessful attempts to log on.

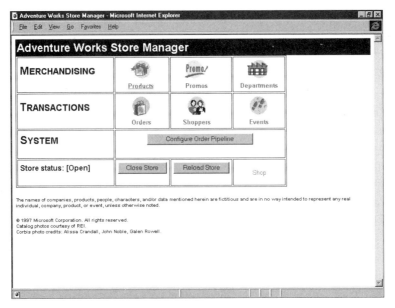

Figure 1-17. *Adventure Works Store Manager page.*

This page executes three main categories of tasks:

1. Merchandise management

2. Department management

3. Report management

Merchandise management

Merchandise management includes two categories of tasks: product management and price promotion management.

Product management This view provides a complete list of all offerings. You can easily add, update, or delete products from this view.

Price promotion management Figure 1-18 shows how the hiking boot special was created. You can update or delete price promotions at any time.

Figure 1-19 illustrates how member discounts are created. All members receive a 10 percent discount on every purchase.

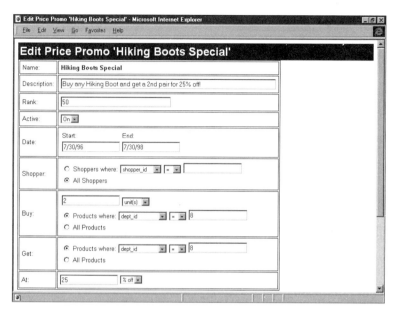

Figure 1-18. *Adventure Works price promotion example: Buy one and get second pair at discount.*

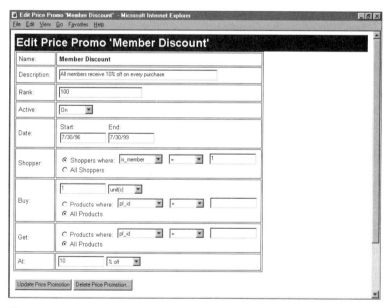

Figure 1-19. *All members receive a 10 percent discount on every purchase.*

Department management

Commerce Server stores can be organized into departments. Products are categorized into departments for a large store. For smaller stores, each department can be a store and the server is really a small mall in which you can carry the shopping basket from one store to the other. Each individual department for a store can be managed from the Departments management page, such as the Rock Shoes department.

Report management

Figure 1-20 illustrates how orders are managed. This view is useful for customer service personnel.

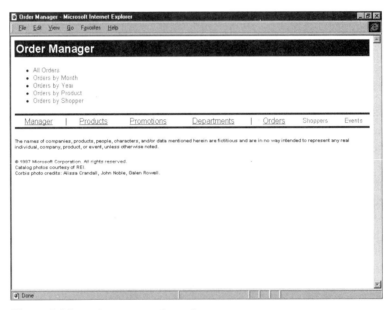

Figure 1-20. *Adventure Works Order Manager page.*

You can view every order in the All Orders page, and you can view each order in complete detail if needed.

We now move to the process of building a store.

Build Process

This section covers

- Using the Store Builder Wizard

- Building a store from foundation up

- Copying an existing store

Using the Store Builder Wizard

The Store Builder Wizard offers a step-by-step approach to designing a store. The wizard hides the complexity of database schema editing, scripting, and HTML coding from the designer and instead presents a series of streamlined forms that the designer completes to plan the structure and operation of the store.

Run the Store Foundation Wizard before the Store Builder Wizard in order to create the foundation on which the store is built—the DSN, the virtual directories, the file structure, and the necessary user accounts. Figure 1-21 shows the architecture of the Store Builder Wizard.

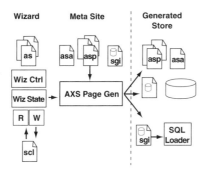

Figure 1-21. *Using metafiles together with store-specific information, a completed store is generated.*

The architecture of the Store Builder Wizard is composed of the following:

1. A wizard for input processing and as an aid to store generation. I produced most illustrations in this section with the wizard and they show the steps and actual dialogs carried out to build a store. The wizard gathers information about a store's presentation and operation from the designer.

2. A Store Configuration File (SCF) the wizard generates. A Store Configuration File contains information about the configurations and customizations for a store.

3. The metafiles for translating the SCF file into an actual store. Metafiles are store-page templates and database templates. Using metafiles together with store-specific information, a completed store is generated.

As the wizard presents each form in sequence, the designer specifies the following aspects of store presentation and operation:

■   Merchant information such as address and telephone information

■   Style of the store pages, including fonts, colors, use of company logo, and the appearance of selection buttons and navigation bar

- Store browsing features such as turning shopper registration and search capability on or off, and defining shopper authentication methods

- Product characteristics such as whether or not products have selectable attributes (such as size or color), and merchandising options such as whether to enable sale pricing

- Product fields that describe how product data is organized in the store database (the names and data types of the columns) so that the database schema can be integrated to function with the store pages

- Shipping methods, and shipping and handling charges

- Tax collection criteria such as state and amount

- Accepted payment methods

At any time before clicking the Finish button, the designer can go back through the forms and change any options previously selected. When he or she has entered all options, the designer completes a final page similar to a checklist, summarizing the steps the Store Builder Wizard will perform. Depending on features and selections, clicking the Finish button creates the following:

- All store pages and files

- Definition of the store's database schema

- Definition of the store's Order Processing Pipeline[11]

- Sample store data including loading the data directly into the database

You can run the Store Builder Wizard repeatedly with different options each time to vary the selected store features. When you achieve the appropriate store configuration, you use HTML editors or other tools to customize the look and feel of the store pages. The wizard is not designed for modifying existing production stores because it overwrites the original store files, including any editing or design changes made after you last used the wizard.

The Store Builder Wizard is an ASP-based application and is accessed from within a Web browser operating over the Internet or an intranet. The next section provides more information about the Store Builder Wizard.

Foundations Store Process

There are two main approaches to building a store: building it from foundation up, and copying an existing store.

---

11. Chapter 2 covers the Order Processing Pipeline.

Building a store from the foundation up

Follow the steps to build a store from foundation up.

1. Start the Store Foundation Wizard.

2. Enter the store name and nickname, as shown in Figure 1-22.

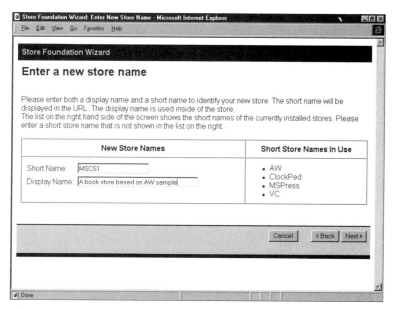

Figure 1-22. *Store Foundation Wizard, Enter a new store name page.*

3. Choose a database driver page. Specify a database server (SQL server, in this case) here.

4. Next specify an ODBC data source name (DSN), in this case, *LocalServer*. The database is SQL server and is installed on the same machine.

5. Next specify an existing or a new user id as the store's management account. If you specify an existing user id, you would select it here. If you specify a new user id, you add it here. This user id and password will have access to store management pages illustrated in the last section. For development purposes, use the NT administrator account. For malls and ISPs, a new account for each store is recommended.

6. Click Finish to create the store foundation building.

The process takes just a few minutes. You then receive a positive confirmation from the store build process once the store foundation creation process is completed successfully (see Figure 1-23). Check database name, database device existence, database server status, and ODBC DSN name supplied, should you have build difficulties.

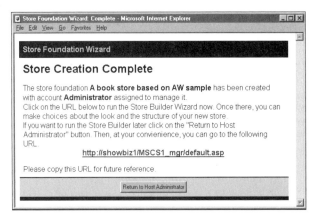

Figure 1-23. *Store Foundation Wizard, Store Creation Complete page.*

Having built the store foundation, you are now ready to use the Store Builder Wizard to build the store.

1. Open the Store Builder Wizard.

2. Enter the store's basic information, as shown in Figure 1-24.

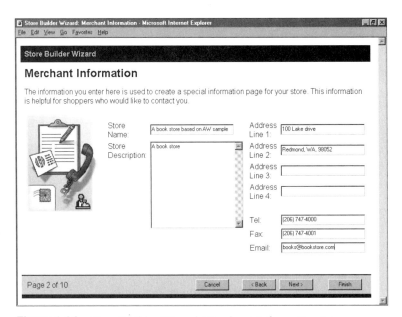

Figure 1-24. *Store Builder Wizard, Merchant Information page.*

3. Enter the store's locale information.

4. Enter the store's basic styling information.

5. Next enter the store's basic features, such as registration requirements and search capabilities. This example requires registration from the store entry page and enables product search capabilities for ease of locating products and services.

6. Next enter product features of the store. If you are a soft good manufacturer, these next few screens allow for application of Commerce Server to non–hard goods areas. Please add attributes as desired. These attributes help extend the Commerce Server functionality into the soft goods arena.

7. For example, you might want to keep manufacturer information on each product. If you did not find Manufacturer as a preexisting product attribute, add the field in this step. As shown in Figure 1-25, custom database columns are automatically added to the store's schema.

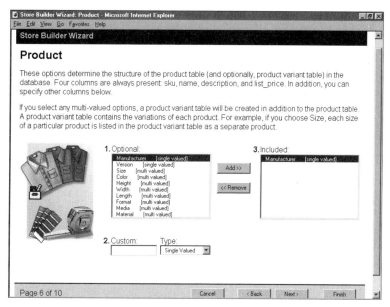

Figure 1-25. *Store Builder Wizard, Product page with custom column.*

8. Next select the different types of shipping and handling that your new store will offer.

9. Now agree to take all major credit cards, as in Figure 1-26. Please note that many more options exist for credit processing and many third-party vendors that support them. The figure shows the simplest case here to illustrate.

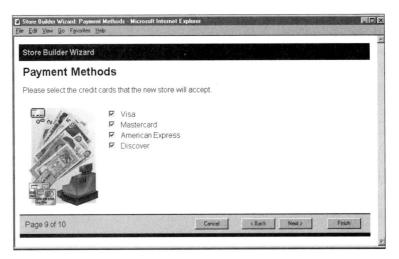

Figure 1-26. *Store Builder Wizard, Payment Methods page.*

You are ready to build your store. For the first few attempts, do not be concerned with the exact details of the final store. You may delete a store and create a new store in a matter of minutes.

10. Set all options for debugging and loading of test data if you are planning on further development and modifications of the store's pages and schema after generation.

11. In the last step, check the boxes next to *Load schema* and *Load sample data*. The build process returns positive acknowledgment of successful completion.

Here is the site that you created (see Figure 1-27). At this point the designer can take over the basic store just created and add logo and design elements. The developer can add additional functionality, customize the store, and develop assets, audio, and video functionality.

Now you can begin entering the store's inventory, department, products, and services. You should be ready to use the wizard to experiment on your own with the different options to get as close as possible to the store that you have in mind.

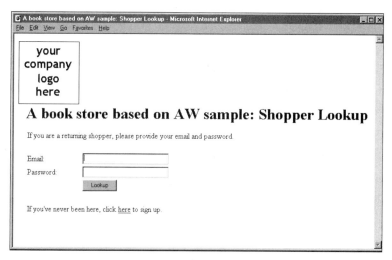

Figure 1-27. *Sign-up page of a store created by the Store Builder Wizard.*

Copying an existing store

The alternative to creating a store from the foundation up is to copy an existing store. This alternative is quicker in operation but less flexible in terms of store attributes that you can change. This alternative is also useful in propagating a newly developed and customized store to support a number of merchants with similar needs. For example, an ISP or Web consultant may develop the first few stores from the foundation up and then copy the store to build others based on this new design.

1. Open the Starter Store Copy Wizard.

2. Select a template for your store from existing store sites (see Figure 1-28).

3. Enter the name of the store you want to create.

4. Just as with the Store Builder Wizard, select a database driver page for the store.

5. Also select a DSN for database connection to the store's database.

6. Now select an administrative account for the new store.

7. Finish creating the store.

8. Finally, look for successful completion of the build process.

Figure 1-28. *Starter Store Copy Wizard, Choose a store template page.*

Client Controls: The Wallet

Most processing is performed on the server side; however, Commerce Server ships with two client-side controls collectively called the Wallet for integration into a store. Available either as ActiveX controls or as Netscape plug-ins, the Wallet provides functionality to improve the convenience and security of a consumer's shopping experience. The Wallet consists of the Payment Selector control and the Address Selector control.

The Payment Selector control provides for the entry, secure storage, and use of various types of payment methods for online shopper purchases. The Payment Selector control also provides a programmatic interface for the Client Payment Components (CPCs), which support third-party development of plug-ins for payment methods such as digital or electronic cash, private-label credit cards, and so on. The Commerce Server Software Developer's Kit contains an interface reference, sample code, and documentation for the CPCs. The Address Selector control provides for the entry, storage, and use of shipping and billing information.

This concludes our overview and features section. Next we look at the programming concepts of Commerce Server.

Chapter 2

Microsoft Commerce Server Stores

In this chapter, we delve deeper into Commerce Server architecture and design concepts to look at what is behind the curtain. We will not be putting pressure suits on and diving deep into development and customization here. Rather, this chapter lays a foundation for development and customization. Chapters 3, 4, and 5 cover the actual mechanics.

COMMERCE SERVER ARCHITECTURE

Although the build process appears deceptively simple to the administrator, and the shopping processes easy and convenient to the shopper, presenting product information and generating and executing order forms are complex tasks. During the shopping process, the store is using Commerce Server's functionality to read data from and write data to the store database, passing data among Commerce Server's pages, stages, and components for presentation, calculation, and validation of information.

Figure 2-1 illustrates Commerce Server architecture.

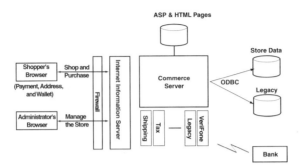

Figure 2-1. *Commerce Server architecture.*

Commerce Server stores include the following major architectural components:

■ Active Server Pages

■ Objects

■ Order Processing Pipeline

Each of these components is further discussed below.

Active Server Pages

Commerce Server pages are written in ASP language. Most pages of a typical store have a .ASP extension, which allows for addition of programming commands to the HTML tags to turn static content into dynamic. ASP includes a language engine such as JavaScript or Visual Basic Scripting Edition (VBScript), and a set of components that implement the Component Object Model (COM) interfaces. ASP is further discussed in Chapter 3 and COM in Chapter 5. For now, think of COM as a way to ask an application or applet: What is your name and what do you do? Think of ASP as a preparser that executes any programming language's commands and returns the pure HTML generated, or as a language-neutral CGI environment.

Objects

One set of Commerce Server components specializes to support retrieval of product data, storage of shopper data, creation of order forms that the Order Processing Pipeline uses, and report of diagnostic data. These exclusive Commerce Server components are called objects. Commerce Server objects are also COM components (objects[1]), and are registered on your server system just the same way as Active Server components.

---

1. Commerce Server components implement the basic COM interfaces, as well as Commerce Server–specific interfaces.

Figure 2-2 illustrates Commerce Server's exclusive objects.

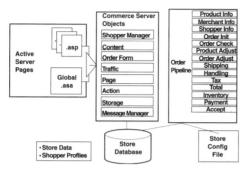

Figure 2-2. *Commerce Server run-time objects.*

Commerce Server objects include, in alphabetical order,

- Action

- Content

- Context

- Data Source

- DB Storage

- Message Manager

- Order Form

- Order Pipeline

- Page

- Shopper Manager

- Traffic

The Commerce Server run-time environment consists of both long-lived and short-lived objects. Long-lived objects load and stay in memory for better performance. The Content object is an example of a long-lived object. In contrast, short-lived objects load and execute each time a shopper visits a store, and these objects maintain state information specific to the shopper's current session. The Page and Action objects are examples of short-lived objects.

The objects you will use the most during development and customization are Page, Content, Order, and Order Pipeline. This chapter discusses the Order Processing Pipeline in detail later. For further description of objects, including their methods and properties, see Appendix F. Here we cover two concepts only: the concept of lists and dictionaries and the concepts of the order form.

Lists and Dictionaries

Commerce Server supports two other objects that hold the interim commerce data: SimpleList, and Dictionary.

A SimpleList is just a list object implemented for Commerce Server's use. This concept is no different than lists developed in any other languages or for any other purpose. A SimpleList object holds a list of variants. Regular languages have data types such as integer, floating-point, character, string, and so on. Think of a variant as a generic data type. You can use an index to retrieve the values in a list, and where a list consists of string values, you can use the string value between parentheses to reference a list element. The SimpleList object supports the AddItem and the Delete methods. The AddItem method adds the specified item to the list; the Delete method deletes an item based on a specified index value.

Because a SimpleList consists of variants, a SimpleList will often consist of Dictionary objects, or a Dictionary will often contain a SimpleList as a value.

Dictionaries are name-value pairs that you use to access a parameter's value by reference to its name. For example, if you were to hold information about user age, you could use the Dictionary object to store and retrieve age of users by their name: Fred = 10, Evita = 11. The Dictionary object consists of name-value pairs separated by a period.

Order Form

The Order Form, another COM object similar to the Dictionary, is essentially a collection of name-value pairs that contain attributes pertaining to an order. The components in each stage of the Order Processing Pipeline write values to the name-value pairs on the Order Form beginning with an underscore, then the name of the stage. For example, all name-value pairs set and read during the Shopper Information stage (see below) are prefixed with shopper.[2] The next section expands on the Order Processing Pipeline and its stages.

Order Processing Pipeline

Think of the pipeline stages as the process steps your virtual store clerk follows to walk a shopper through an on-line sales process. Commerce Server's order processing system consists of a series of distinct stages called the Order Processing Pipeline. After the shopper places an order, the order passes through the Order Processing Pipeline, each stage of which consists of some number of components that you specify and configure. These components are optional; you can include one or more of the components that fit your needs. Alternatively, you can specialize the order processing by creating your own custom components. This section describes

---

2. This is a convention that all components (and any custom components that you write) should follow; however, it is not enforced by the system.

the pipeline and all of the components Commerce Server version 2.0 includes. Custom components are covered in Chapter 5.

Figure 2-3 illustrates Commerce Server's Order Processing Pipeline.

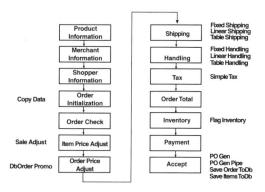

Figure 2-3. *Commerce Server Order Processing Pipeline.*

After a shopper has placed an order with a Commerce Server–based store, Commerce Server retains the order data in the Order Form. The Order Form is carried from stage to stage and component to component. Like a real order, each component modifies the contents of the Order Form by reading data from it and writing data to it.

The sequence of stages through which the order passes is determined by the pipeline configuration file, typically the file PIPELINE.PCF in the store's CONFIG directory. A pipeline configuration file is created using the Pipeline Editor, one of Commerce Server's tools (more on the Pipeline Editor later in this chapter). For example, in order to transfer Order Form data to a legacy system for further handling, the store developer may configure the pipeline to run a component that captures Order Form data for the transfer.

To extend the pipeline's functionality, developers can create custom pipeline components. This chapter presents a few samples. For additional information about developing custom components, see the Commerce Server Software Development Kit (SDK) on the Evaluation CD, under the DOC directory. This CD contains header files, libraries, sample components, and documentation describing the pipeline component interfaces. Also, please see Appendix I, "Using MFC to Create Order Processing Components."

The Order Processing Pipeline has two important concepts: stages and execution modes. Each stage consists of "required" and "default" components.

Order processing stages

Stages are collections of related components. The pipeline is essentially a set of stages, each of which is a set of components. Attached to these stages are additional attributes such as stage name. Commerce Server's order processing components are described later in the "Order Processing Components" section of this chapter. The stages of the Order Processing Pipeline, in order of execution, are as follows:

Product Information This stage retrieves product information from long-term storage and writes it to the Order Form. You will use this information a lot in the product and department pages of a store.

Commerce Information This stage retrieves merchant information from a database and writes it to the Order Form. It currently has no required or default components; it is a placeholder for a customized merchant information component. You can insert additional components into this stage.

Shopper Information This stage retrieves shopper information from a database. If nonmembers can shop from a store, there will be no existing shopper data, but no error is produced in this case, and the purchasing process continues for a nonmember.

Order Initialization This stage sets the initial order information on the Order Form. Typically, you will copy fields and set initial name-value pairs during this stage. This stage is also of interest when writing custom components to set initial or default variables and parameters that the custom component uses.

Order Check This stage verifies that the order can be processed and contains all the required elements. Include additional business components to validate your store orders in this stage.

Item Price Adjust This stage calculates the regular and current prices for each item on the order. The component for this stage can use shopper information, store information, or system status (time, for instance) to determine the current price or handle promotions at an item level. This stage is the heart of the promotion management. Include additional components to extend the promotional capabilities beyond those offered out of the box.

Order Price Adjust This stage sets the adjusted price of each item in the order. It can use any of the information Item Price Adjust uses, as well as information about the order. You can specify more than one Order Price Adjust component. This order processing stage also handles some promotions, such as discounts on individual items.

Shipping This stage calculates the total shipping charge for the order. Use third-party modules or interface components for legacy systems in this stage.

Handling This stage calculates the total handling charge for the order. Use third-party modules or interface components for legacy systems in this stage.

Tax This stage calculates the sales tax for each item of the order and sums the tax for the entire order. Use third-party modules or interface components for legacy systems in this stage.

Order Total This stage sums the subtotal, tax, shipping, and handling values (less any discount) and writes the total to the Order Form. You can include business rules, frequent flyer miles, membership price adjustments, and discount components in this stage.

Inventory This stage verifies that every item ordered is in stock.

Payment This stage handles payment details for the order, including credit-card authorization. Use third-party modules or interface components for legacy systems in this stage.

Accept This stage handles the completed order, including initiating order tracking, generating purchase orders, and inventory.

Order processing execution mode

The second important concept of the Order Processing Pipeline is the execution mode. To the client, a single pipeline is called in various modes. Depending on the mode, you execute different stages with different error constraints. In particular, a pipeline can perform any one or all of the following functions:

- Update product information in the order object (product mode)

- Check the information in the order object for correctness (plan mode)

- Attempt to commit the order (purchase mode)

Every Order Processing Pipeline component is written to operate in one of the following three execution modes:

Product mode This mode runs components in the Product Information, Commerce Information, Shopper Information, and Item Price Adjust stages; tolerates warnings.

Plan mode This mode runs components from the Product Information through the Inventory stages; tolerates warnings.

Purchase mode This mode runs components in all stages. It tolerates warnings from the Product Information through the Inventory stages, but requires complete success for the Payment and Accept stages.

The mode determines which components run in a particular stage, and what level of failure is tolerated. Details of order processing components and their name-value pairs are included both in Appendix F, "Commerce Server Component Reference Documentation," and is also available in the back of the book with the product CD.

Using the Order Processing Pipeline, companies can enforce business rules that direct the processing of orders through a specified sequence of stages and procedures. Think of the Order Processing Pipeline as the order processing manual for your online business. Please take a moment to review the Component Reference appendix and note the stages in which each component is used.

Order processing components

The components in each stage are responsible for the actual work of reading or writing name-value pairs to and from the Order Form. Each stage has a set of components that perform specific functions. Some stages have two additional components: a default component (called *DefaultComponent*) that can be run if no other components are specified; and a required component (called *RequiredComponent*) that will always be executed after all other components for that stage have run (to enforce system consistency rules). You cannot modify or rewrite these two components. For example, a stage such as Tax might also have one or more predefined optional components, as shown in the Order Processing Pipeline, Figure 2-3. You cannot modify or rewrite these optional components either, though you can configure them by passing arguments to them. You can also write your own customized order processing components and plug them into the Order Processing Pipeline. Please see Chapter 5.

COMMERCE SERVER CUSTOMIZATION

Chapter 1 included steps for copying an existing sample store as an alternative to building a store from foundation. Having built a store from foundation or copied a an existing store, the task of customizing the store to your business needs begins.

Appendix B also included steps to plan for a Commerce Server store. Given the requirements gathered, you can perform Gap Analysis[3] or the equivalent to map out a set of changes and customizations required to transform the out-of-the-box store into the final deliverable online site.

The three main Commerce Server store customizations are database customizations, store page customizations, and pipeline customizations. Familiarizing yourself with the different ways that a store can be enhanced and extended so the set of changes and customizations required may be translated into one or more of the following customizations tasks as schedules and resources required for the enhancements depends on the type of customization needed.

Database Customization

Database customization is the first step to customizing a store to meet your business needs. If you need to add product features and attributes, refer to the "Building a Store from Foundation" section in Chapter 1, and add additional attributes for the soft and hard goods offered in step 7 of the Store Foundation Wizard process. An example of a database customization is the product manufacturer attribute.

---

3. Gap Analysis is the process of taking a snapshot of the current implementation or environment and contrasting this to the desired future current implementation or environment. Consultants or those familiar with planning methodologies may use their own equivalent methods.

The sample stores include functional but minimal schema. Another more fundamental database customization is addition of tables. Use Microsoft Visual InterDev (VI) for this type of work. Integrate the newly created tables into the existing store schema. This step requires some ASP and HTML knowledge to add the functionality around the newly added table(s). Please see Chapter 3 and Chapter 4.

A third kind of database customization is to extend the schema with a set of tables and relationships.[4] If the tables and relationships are not disturbed, this is similar to addition of tables above. View the store in VI's data view to review and document the store's tables, schema, and relationships. However, if the relationships are changed, store pages and stored queries may be affected. To view store pages, use VI's editor. To view links among pages to follow a program thread, use VI's Link View feature. To gain an understanding of the stored queries of a store, view the GLOBAL.ASA file in the root directory of the store.

Remember to add database triggers to your new tables for cascading inserts and deletes, and build the enforcement triggers for these relationships.

Store Page Customization

Examples of store page customization are inclusion or exclusion of store sign-in requirements, changes to frames, and minor programming logic changes. Use the include files in a store's *Include* sub-directory for the following:

- Logo addition, header and footer information changes that appear in all pages of the store
- Changes to the store colors and frames
- Inclusion of links to other store pages or other Web application pages

Use VI editor for programming and debugging. Chapter 4 covers VI and related techniques.

Pipeline Customization

An example of a pipeline customization is changes to discount rates for members and nonmembers. For instance, you might want to add 100 frequent-flyer miles to a member's account for every $100 spent in the store. Before modifying the pipeline, ask if this feature can be added using a table trigger or database stored procedure.

For example, a client may wish to allow everyone to purchase from the store but would like to give a 15 percent across-the-board discount to members only. The membership itself might be an item in the product database that can be purchased. For this change, you can add a trigger to the shopper database, and add a Boolean

---

4. Relationships among tables typically are foreign-key based.

column called *is_member* to the shopper database. The *is_member* value is 0 by default and reset to 1 by a trigger on the Shopping Cart table that is fired if the membership product is placed in the Cart.[5] This chapter includes two samples, one in VBScript for use with the Scriptor component, and one in C++ for addition to a pipeline stage.

The next two sections cover two important tools that allow for customization and extension of the Order Processing Pipeline: the Scriptor component and the Pipeline Editor.

Scriptor component The Scriptor component is an optional component that you can add to any stage of an order pipeline. The Scriptor is programmable in VBScript or languages. This is an alternative to C++ or Visual Basic component creation options, which take longer to develop and require a second language other than ASP. The Scriptor is easily inserted at one or more stages of the pipeline to customize it. You can insert one or more instances at each stage. Some instances may run a debug script to display (dump) the information at a given point in the order processing during development. Finally, the Scriptor is a wrapper around a script file. A Scriptor component opens a text file and executes the script language contents of the file as though the script code were really a component.

Pipeline Editor The Pipeline Editor is installed with the Commerce Server installation.

To run the Pipeline Editor,

1. Select Start.

2. Select Programs from the list.

3. Select Commerce Server.

4. Select Pipeline Editor. The following screen is displayed, as in Figure 2-4. Open the Pipeline Configuration file for the store of your choice.

---

5. In addition, there should be a trigger to set the value back to 0 when the membership is removed, or set the value permanently to 1 if the membership is actually purchased.

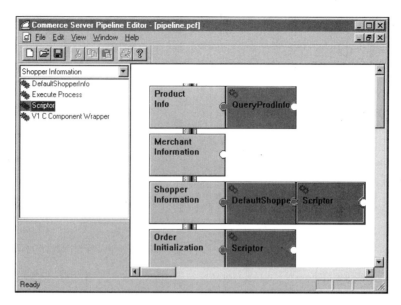

Figure 2-4. *Commerce Server Pipeline Editor.*

5. Select and drag-and-drop the Scriptor component onto a stage that you want to modify or debug (see Figure 2-5).

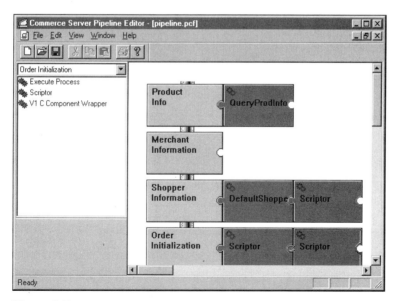

Figure 2-5. *Commerce Server Pipeline Editor with additional Scriptor component.*

Note You can enter any JScript or VBScript code as the script file or directly type into the Scriptor component, as long as it is Commerce Server knowledgeable, meaning it understands Commerce Server Lists and Dictionaries and the representation of the order data in the pipeline.

6. Double-click the Scriptor component to configure the VBScript file used (see Figure 2-6).

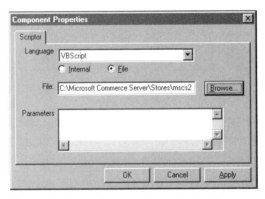

Figure 2-6. *Configuring the VBScript file property for a Scriptor component.*

7. Select the language of choice and browse to find the VBScript file. You can also use JScript.[6]

8. Click OK and test the pipeline by entering an order, adding an item to the Shopping Cart, or checking out. The complete list of variable information from the specific stage of the pipeline is dumped to a file on your root directory for review.

6. JScript is a JavaScript implementation. Minor differences exist only in implementation of the two. Refer to JScript and JavaScript implementation differences in this book.

Chapter 3

Site Server Active Server Pages

Site Server is developed based on the Active Server Pages (ASP) environment of IIS. This chapter provides you with an understanding of ASP by defining it, explaining its features, and discussing Active Server Pages scripting languages.

To give you a firm grounding of how to use ASP, this chapter also covers selected examples of ASP, under the heading "Active Server Pages Tutorial." In Chapter 4, we will build upon these concepts and examples to understand, enhance, customize, and extend Commerce Server.

ACTIVE SERVER PAGES DEFINITION

What is Active Server Pages (ASP)? Let's take a look at what an Active Server Page is from a number of perspectives.

An Open Application Environment

ASP is an open application environment that supports active scripting, allowing virtually any scripting language to be used. Native support is provided for Visual Basic Scripting Editions and Microsoft JScript. It allows Web developers to write scripts that are executed on the server. We will look at Basic and Java scripting examples in more detail later in this chapter.

An Environment That Supports Code Reuse

Active server components support the Microsoft Component Object Model (COM), and these components can be written in virtually any programming language, including Visual Basic, C++, COBOL, and Java. COM objects are related to object linking and embedding (OLE) automation servers and can be called upon from a Web page (or other applications) to access and reuse prepackaged functionality. Please refer to the COM chapters in this book or other publications on COM for a fuller description of COM.

ASP ships with a core set of components, including Browser Capabilities, Ad Rotator, and the Active Data Object (ADO). For example, ASP provides easy access to all HTTP server variables such as browser type and referring page through another component: Browser Capabilities. This makes developing pages that are customized to the user easy.

To read records from a database, a script passes the request to the ADO component that handles all the details of accessing the database. Another script may retrieve the result from the ADO component and display it in the resulting HTML page. Another ASP component, ADO provides standardized access to any ODBC-compatible data source, including Microsoft Access and Microsoft SQL server, as well as other popular databases from Oracle, Informix, and Sybase. Therefore, developers use one ASP component to access virtually any kind of data. For example, several independent software vendors provide ODBC drivers to access information on IBM mainframe and Unix server databases. In this case, the ASP script is never changed. It still executes the same ADO commands, but replacing the ODBC driver enables ASP/ADO to target a different server's database.

A Compile-Free Environment

ASP provides the flexibility of CGI programs and scripts without the significant performance tradeoff. Unlike CGI, ASP runs in-process with the server process (no heavy *fork* and *exec* overhead), is multi-threaded, and is optimized to handle large numbers of users.

An ASP script is only compiled once and then it is cached. All subsequent requests to the same page use the cached, precompiled results. A changed script is automatically recompiled the next time it is requested based on comparison of the script's last modification date and the compiled version. This is similar to using the make utility in Unix or NT, comparing the date of the *.o file to the *.c file.

A Key Component of the Active Server

With the release of IIS 3.0 with Active Server Pages, Microsoft ships a key component of IIS. Other related IIS Server technologies include the Distributed Component Object Model (DCOM), Microsoft Transaction Server, and Message Queue technology. Visit *http://www.microsoft.com* for additional information on these related technologies. In addition to components discussed in this chapter, ASP is used to leverage all Microsoft server components.

In synergy with other Microsoft components, Active Server Pages is the technology that enables developers to easily build and deploy component-based server applications without the complexities generally associated with traditional programming.

An HTML Page with an .ASP Extension

Another perspective is that Active Server Pages is simply an HTML page with the extension renamed to .ASP. For example, *default.html* becomes *default.asp.* While *default.html* can only contain HTML commands and tags, *default.asp* can also contain language-type commands.

In this example, *default.html* is a set of browser commands and display tags. There is no notion of a FOR loop or an IF clause. A programmer may wonder how to loop, or how to decide to execute some command based on a variable. One view of ASP is that it is a set of HTML commands augmented with a powerful programming language. The options range from a derivative of Basic to Rexx, JavaScript, and Perl. The list of language options is growing.

An Active Server Page file is a simple text file. You can edit ASP files with any text editor, including Microsoft Visual InterDev (VI). The next section discusses the features of ASP.

ACTIVE SERVER PAGES FEATURES

ASP's main features include the following:

- Offering intrinsic objects for all HTTP requests

- Offering server components

- Protecting intellectual property

- Maximizing browser reach

- Maintaining state and user information

Each of these features is discussed below.

Offering Intrinsic Objects for All HTTP Requests

You may leverage these objects to jumpstart your development. ASP includes the following intrinsic objects for handling all aspects of HTTP and state management:

- Request
- Response
- Server
- Session
- Application

As examples, the Request object is used to reference HTML form variables in a Web page and the Response object is used to send HTML back to the client. Adventure Works example, discussed earlier, uses all five intrinsic objects. These objects and examples of their usage and discussed in the Active Server Pages tutorial later in this chapter.

Offering Server Components

I mentioned that ASP can be extended by the use of components that perform specific tasks such as ADO objects, advertisement rotation, and browser checking capabilities.

ASP includes a number of such server components. Third parties may develop and market their own ASP custom components. Components either provide the developer with access to the underlying operating system, Web server, and database, or are used as a wrapper for business rules. In this latter usage, components are much more powerful, flexible, and maintainable than SQL triggers and stored procedures. For a complete description of components and techniques to build components, please see Chapter 5.

Protecting Intellectual Property

In the client browser world, anyone can use a browser's View Source function to see the what and how of any page, save the page, and use it with or without modification. Whether or not this is good practice depends on your thoughts and philosophy. But what if you wanted to keep the work, embedded data, any access codes, embedded logons, and so forth, secret and protected?

You could wrap your code, creativity, and intellectual property in a CGI application or alternatively, use ASP. ASP has better performance, easier maintenance, and lower development costs. The price of ASP is definitely right. It comes free with installation of IIS.

Maximizing Browser Reach

When considering the different browsers with which you can access Web pages, ignorance is indeed bliss. Keep in mind that only the result of the processed code (HTML commands after language processing) is ever sent down to the browser. With ASP, the complicated work happens at the server before the browser receives the resulting HTML. From the browser's point of view, the only requirement is supporting basic HTML tags, namely, the <TABLE> tag. Chances are a lot higher that whatever you use to access Web pages supports tables rather than any of the newer, fancier, or specialized tags. The server processes scripts and components, and the output of an ASP file is always standard HTML, so ASP works with any Web browser.[1] With Active Server Pages, the information and content can live in any form on any server, and be made available to any World Wide Web browser that supports simple table tags.

Alternatively, you can customize your content to the capabilities of each browser to provide more compelling results (using the Browser Capabilities component, for example). From the same page, using simple IF statements, Java, objects, and frames may be selectively sent to the browser, depending on its additional capabilities.

Maintaining State and User Information

Historically, Web applications have been difficult to write because of the stateless nature of HTTP. ASP makes it very easy to keep state information for a particular user across pages within the same Web application. For example, using Session and Application objects, an array of variables may be maintained for a user, so that every subsequent Web page can access it.

ACTIVE SERVER PAGES
SCRIPTING LANGUAGES

Scripting languages are an intermediate stage between HTML and programming languages such as C, C++, and Visual Basic. HTML is generally used for formatting and hypertext linking purposes. Programming languages are generally used for giving complex instructions to computers. Scripting languages fall somewhere in between, although scripting languages function more like programming languages than

---

1. ASP works with any browser that supports the <TABLE> tag. However, store developers may use other advanced features such as frames and custom components to make a more powerful presentation.

simple HTML. The primary difference between scripting languages and programming languages is that the syntax and rules of scripting languages are less rigid and intricate than those of programming languages.

Scripting engines are the COM objects that process scripts. ASP provides a host environment for scripting engines and distributes .ASP files to these engines for processing. For each scripting language that is used in coordination with ASP scripting, the related scripting engine must be implemented in Active Server Pages. For example, VBScript is the default host language of Active Server Pages, so the VBScript scripting engine resides as a COM object within ASP so that it may process VBScript scripts. Likewise, ASP can provide a scripting environment for a number of other scripting engines, such as (but not limited to) JScript, Rexx, and Perl.

ASP enables the Web developer to use a variety of scripting languages. In fact, you can use several scripting languages within a single .ASP Web page. You can do this by identifying the script language in a simple tag at the beginning of the script sequence.

For example, the following script indicates that the upcoming script sequences are to be processed by ASP as JScript code and VBScript code, respectively:

```
<HTML>
<SCRIPT LANGUAGE=JScript RUNAT=Server>
JScript code here...
<SCRIPT LANGUAGE=VBScript RUNAT=Server>
VBScript code here...
</HTML>
```

In addition, because scripts are read and processed on the server side, the client browser that you use to read the .ASP file can be of any type.

Setting the Primary Scripting Language

ASP enables you to use any scripting language as the primary scripting language. VBScript is the default language that is used for primary scripting. In addition, you can set the primary scripting language on a page-by-page basis or on all pages within your application.

The procedure for setting the primary scripting language depends on whether the chosen language supports the Object.Method syntax or not. The procedures are detailed below.

For languages that support the Object.Method syntax and use parentheses to enclose parameters, you can change the primary scripting language for a single page by adding a command line to the beginning of your .ASP file. The syntax for this command is

```
<%@ LANGUAGE = ScriptingLanguage %>,
```

where *ScriptingLanguage* = the language that you want to set for that page.

Follow these guidelines when setting the primary scripting language for a particular page:

- Set the primary scripting language on the first line of the file.

- Do not set the page's primary scripting language in an INCLUDE file.

- Place a space between @ and LANGUAGE.

- Do not place any elements other than @ and LANGUAGE = *[Language-Name]* between the scripting delimiters (<% %>).

To change the primary scripting language for all pages in your application, you must change the value of the *DefaultScriptLanguage* entry in the registry to that language. For more information about editing registry entries, see the "Registry Editor Tool" section of Appendix J.

In order to use a language that does not support the *Object.Method* syntax as the primary scripting language, you must first create the *LanguageEngines* registry key with the corresponding language name subkey and values:

```
HKEY_LOCAL_MACHINE\SYSTEM\CurrentControlSet\Services\W3SVC\ASP↵
   \LanguageEngines  \<LanguageName>
Value: Write REG_SZ: Response.WriteEquiv |
Value: WriteBlock REG_SZ: ResponseWriteBlockEquiv |,
```

where *LanguageName* = the name of the chosen language, *Response.WriteEquiv* = the language's equivalent of *Response.Write*, and *ResponseWriteBlockEquiv* = the language's equivalent of *Response.WriteBlock*. The pipe symbol (|) is an insertion ASP uses to send expressions and HTML blocks that are normally processed with *Response.Write* and *Response.WriteBlock* methods.

Writing Procedures with Multiple Languages

An attractive feature of ASP is the capability to incorporate several scripting languages within a single .ASP file. One example of this feature is the ability to create procedures of different scripting languages within a single script.

A procedure is a group of script commands that perform a specific task. You can define your own procedures and call them repeatedly in your scripts. Procedure definitions must appear within <SCRIPT> and </SCRIPT> tags and must follow the rules for the declared scripting language. You cannot define a procedure within scripting delimiters (<% %>).

You can place procedure definitions in the same ASP page that calls the procedures, or you can put commonly used procedures in a shared .ASP file and use a server side include statement (<!—#INCLUDE FILE= ...) to include it in other .ASP files that call the procedures. Alternatively, you could package the functionality in a component.

Using VBScript and JScript

ASP scripting supports VBScript's syntax, method and property calls, and statements with two exceptions. Because ASP scripts are executed on the server, the VBScript statements that present user-interface elements, *InputBox* and *MsgBox*, are not supported. Use of these statements will cause an error.[2] You are not required to use the Dim statement to explicitly declare VBScript variables in your scripts. You can implicitly declare variables by using their names somewhere in your script.

For a list and description of all VBScript operators, functions, statements, objects, properties, and methods, refer to the *Microsoft VBScript Language Reference* at *http://www.microsoft.com/iis/usingiis/resources/ASPdocs/roadmap.asp* or consult Microsoft ASP documentation installed online, under Start Programs, Microsoft Internet Server, Active Server Roadmap. For a list and description of all JScript operators, functions, statements, objects, properties, and methods, refer to the *Microsoft JScript Language Reference* at *http://www.microsoft.com/iis/usingiis/resources/ASPdocs/roadmap.asp*

Including comments

Because the processing of all ASP scripts occurs on the server side, you don't need to include HTML comment tags to hide the scripts from browsers that do not support the scripting language being used.

VBScript comments VBScript supports Basic REM and apostrophe-style comments. Unlike HTML comments, these are removed when the script is processed and are not sent to the client.[3]

```
<%
REM This line and the following two are comments
'The PrintTable function prints all
'the elements in an array.
Call PrintTable(myarray())
%>
<% i = i +1 'this increments i. This script will work. %>

<%= name 'this prints the variable name. This script will fail. %>
```

JScript comments JScript supports Basic // tags. Use these tags on each line in which comments appear.

```
<% Call PrintDate %>
// This is a VBScript call of the JScript procedure PrintDate.
```

---

2. VBScript provides error-handling functionality through the OnError statement. You will sometimes find it helpful when debugging to iterate through all elements of a collection by using VBScript's For...Each statement.

3. Technical note: You cannot include a comment in a line that begins with the opening delimiter and an equal sign. For example, the first line that follows works, but the second line does not, because it begins with <%=.

```
<SCRIPT LANGUAGE=JScript RUNAT=Server>
function PrintDate()
{
// This is a definition for the procedure PrintDate.
// This procedure will send the current date to the client-side browser
var x
x = new Date()
Response.Write(x.getDate())
}
</SCRIPT>
```

This concludes our brief overview of ASP features.

ACTIVE SERVER PAGES TUTORIAL

In this section, we will use scripting examples and discuss ASP objects and components. This section assumes familiarity with HTML and one or more programming languages and is intended for more technical readers. Here you will delve deep into ASP and scripting. Most of the examples are in Visual Basic Script. You could just as easily use JScript. For that matter, you could use a number of scripting engines. First a word about including code in HTML.

The three ways to include programming language code in the HTML page are

- Using <% and %> tags

- Using "<SCRIPT>" tags[4]

- Using <Function> tags (more on these a bit later)

Scripts call on components and objects. ASP has five built-in objects: Request, Response, Server, Session, and Application. ASP also provides components that can be customized or replaced, such as the ADO, the TextStream file access object, and the Browser Capabilities object.

Request Object

The Request object deals with input from the browser. This includes page parameters, cookies, and forms parameters. The Request object retrieves the values that the client browser passed to the server during an HTTP request. Typical syntax is Request[.Collection](variable), where collections is one of the following:

- ClientCertificate: client certificate sent in the HTTP request

- Cookies: cookies sent in the HTTP request

---

4. With EXECUTE AT SERVER, remember, a variant of Visual Basic allows for scripting the browser. This variant is called VBScript as opposed to ASP (server side VB). Once you understand one version, the other should become intuitive.

- ■ Form: HTTP request body

- ■ QueryString: HTTP query string

- ■ ServerVariables: environment variables

If the specified variable is not in one of these four collections, the Request object returns the string *EMPTY*.

You can access all variables directly by using calling Request(variable) without the collection name. In this case, the Web server searches the collections in the following order:

1. ServerVariables

2. Form

3. Cookies

4. QueryString

5. ClientCertificate

Each collection is further discussed below.

ServerVariables

One interesting collection is ServerVariables. The ServerVariables collection retrieves the values of environment variables. It can be one of the following values:

- ■ AUTH_TYPE: The authentication method that the server uses to validate users when they attempt to access a protected script

- ■ CONTENT_LENGTH: The length of the content as given by the client

- ■ CONTENT_TYPE: The data type of the content (Used with queries that have attached information, such as HTTP POST, PUT queries, and custom content.)

- ■ GATEWAY_INTERFACE: The revision of the CGI specification used by the server (Format: CGI/revision.)

- ■ HTTP_<HeaderName>: The value stored in the header *HeaderName* (Any header other than those listed in this table must be prefixed by "HTTP_" in order for Request.ServerVariables to retrieve its value.)

- ■ LOGON_USER: The Windows NT account that the user is logged into, useful in authentication.

- ■ PATH_INFO: Extra path information as given by the client (Access scripts by using their virtual path and the PATH_INFO server variable. If this information comes from a URL it is decoded by the server before it is passed to the script.)

■ PATH_TRANSLATED: A translated version of PATH_INFO that takes the path and performs any necessary virtual-to-physical mapping

■ QUERY_STRING: Query information stored in the string following the question mark (?) in the HTTP request, useful in parsing parameters.

■ REMOTE_ADDR: The IP address of the remote host making the request, useful in authentication.

■ REMOTE_HOST: The name of the host making the request (If the server does not have this information, it will set REMOTE_ADDR and leave this field empty.)

■ REQUEST_METHOD: The method used to make the request (For HTTP, this is GET, HEAD, POST, and so on.)

■ SCRIPT_MAP: Gives the base portion of the URL, useful in accessing image subdirectories.

■ SCRIPT_NAME: A virtual path to the script being executed (This is used for self-referencing URLs.)

■ SERVER_NAME: The server's host name, DNS alias, or IP address as it would appear in self-referencing URLs

■ SERVER_PORT: The port number to which the request was sent

■ SERVER_PORT_SECURE: A string that contains either 0 or 1 (If the request is being handled on the secure port, then this will be 1. Otherwise, it will be 0.)

■ SERVER_PROTOCOL: The name and revision of the request information protocol (Format: protocol/revision.)

■ SERVER_SOFTWARE: The name and version of the server software answering the request and running the gateway (Format: name/version.)

■ URL: Gives the base portion of the URL

If a client sends a header other than those specified above, retrieve the value of that header by prefixing the header name with *HTTP_* in the call to Request.ServerVariables. For example, if the client sent the header NewHeader: NewValue, retrieve SomeNewValue by using the following syntax:

```
<% Request.ServerVariables("HTTP_NewHeader") %>.
```

Example 1: You may loop through all server variables. For example, the following script prints out all of the server variables in a table.

```
<TABLE>
<TR><TD><B>Server Variable</B></TD><TD><B>Value</B></TD></TR>
    <% For Each name In Request.ServerVariables %>
    <TR><TD> <%= name %> </TD><TD> <%= Request.ServerVariables(name) ⤸⁵
        %> </TD></TR>
    </TABLE>
    <% Next %>
```

Example 2. The following example uses the Request object to display several server variables:

```
<HTML>
<!--This example displays the content of several ServerVariables.-->
    ALL_HTTP server variable =
    <%= Request.ServerVariables("ALL_HTTP") %> <BR>
    CONTENT_LENGTH server variable =
    <%= Request.ServerVariables("CONTENT_LENGTH") %> <BR>
    CONTENT_TYPE server variable =
    <%= Request.ServerVariables("CONTENT_TYPE") %> <BR>
    QUERY_STRING server variable =
    <%= Request.ServerVariables("QUERY_STRING") %> <BR>
    SERVER_SOFTWARE server variable =
    <%= Request.ServerVariables("SERVER_SOFTWARE") %> <BR>
    </HTML>
```

Example 3. The next example uses the ServerVariables collection to insert the name of the server into a hyperlink:

```
<A HREF = "http://<%= Request.ServerVariables("SERVER_NAME") %>⤸
/scripts/MyPage.asp">Link to MyPage.asp</A>
```

Form

The Form collection retrieves the values of form elements passed to the script by the HTTP request body. The syntax is *Request.Form*(parameter)[(index)|.Count]. The parameter specifies the name of the form element from which the collection is to retrieve values.

The index parameter is optional; it enables access to one of multiple parameter values. It can be any integer in the range 1 to *Request.Form*(parameter).Count. The Form collection is indexed by the names of the parameters in the request body. The value of *Request.Form*(parameter) is an array of all of the parameter values that occur in the request body. Determine the number of values of a parameter by calling *Request.Form*(parameter).Count. If a parameter does not have multiple values associated with it, the count is 1. If the parameter is not bound, the count is 0.

---

5. The ⤸ symbol indicates a line that had to be broken for the printed page. Treat it as a single line when typing or editing it.

To reference a single value of a form element that has multiple values, specify a value for the index parameter. The index parameter may be any number between 1 and *Request.Form*(parameter).Count. When referencing one of multiple form parameters without specifying a value for the index parameter, the data is returned as a comma-delimited string.

When using parameters with *Request.Form*, the Web server parses the HTTP request body and returns the specified data. If the application requires unparsed data from the form, access it by calling *Request.Form* without any parameters.

Example 1: You may loop through all the data values in a form request. For example, if a user filled out a form by specifying two values, *Chocolate* and *Butterscotch*, for the FavoriteFlavor parameter, retrieve those values by using the following script:

```
<%
  For Each item In Request.Form("FavoriteFlavor")
    Response.Write item & "<BR>"
    Next
    %>
```

This script would display the following:

```
Chocolate
Butterscotch
```

Example 2: The same output can be generated with a For...Next loop, as shown in the following script:

```
<%
  For I = 1 To Request.Form("FavoriteFlavor").Count
    Response.Write Request.Form("FavoriteFlavor")(I) & "<BR>"
    Next
    %>
```

Loop to display the parameter name, as shown in the following script:

```
<% For Each x In Request.From %>
Request.Form( <%= x %> ) = <%= Request.Form(x) %> <BR>
    <% Next %>
```

This will display

```
FavoriteFlavor = Chocolate
FavoriteFlavor = Butterscotch
```

Example 3: Consider the following form:

```
<FORM ACTION = "/scripts/submit.asp" METHOD = "post">
<P>Your first name: <INPUT NAME = "firstname" SIZE = 48>
    <P>What is your favorite ice cream flavor: <SELECT NAME = "flavor">
    <OPTION>Vanilla
    <OPTION>Strawberry
    <OPTION>Chocolate
    <OPTION>Rocky Road</SELECT>
    <p><INPUT TYPE = SUBMIT>
    </FORM>
```

From that form, you might send the following request body:

```
firstname=James&flavor=Rocky+Road
```

Then you can use the following script:

```
Welcome, <%= Request.Form("firstname") %>.
```

The following output results:

```
Your favorite flavor is <%= Request.Form("flavor") %> .
Welcome, James. Your favorite flavor is Rocky Road.
```

Cookies

The Cookies collection enables retrieval of the values of cookies sent in an HTTP request. The syntax is *Request.Cookies(cookie)[(key) | .attribute]*.

The parameters are the following:

Cookie	Specifies the cookie whose value should be retrieved.
Key	An optional parameter used to retrieve subkey values from cookie dictionaries
Attribute	Specifies information about the cookie itself.

Cookies uses the following method:

HasKeys	Specifies whether the cookie contains keys.

Access the subkeys of a cookie dictionary by including a value for key. If you access a cookie dictionary without specifying key, all of the keys are returned as a single query string. For example, if MyCookie has two keys, First and Second, neither of these keys is specified in a call to *Request.Cookies*, and the following string is returned:

```
First=firstkeyvalue&Second=secondkeyvalue
```

If the client browser sends two cookies with the same name, *Request.Cookies* returns the one with the deeper path structure. For example, if two cookies had the same name but one had a path attribute of */WWW/* and the other of */WWW/home/*, the client browser would send both cookies to the */WWW/home/* directory, but *Request.Cookies* would only return the second cookie.

To determine whether or not a cookie is a cookie dictionary (whether the cookie has keys), use the following script:

```
<%= Request.Cookies("myCookie").HasKeys %>
```

If myCookie is a cookie dictionary, this value evaluates to TRUE. Otherwise, it evaluates to FALSE.

Example 1: You may loop through all the cookies in the Cookie collection, or all the keys in a cookie. However, iterating through keys on a cookie that does not have keys will not produce any output. Avoid this condition by first checking to see whether a cookie has keys (using the *.HasKeys* syntax). This is demonstrated in the following example:

```
<%
'Print out the entire cookie collection.
For Each cookie in Request.Cookies
    If Not cookie.HasKeys Then
        'Print out the cookie string
%>
        <%= cookie %> = <%= Request.Cookies(cookie)%>
<%
    Else
        'Print out the cookie collection
        For Each key in Request.Cookies(cookie)
%>
        <%= cookie %> (<%= key %>) = <%=Request.Cookies(cookie)(key)%>
<%
        Next
    End If
Next
%>
```

Example 2: The following example prints the value of myCookie in a Web page. Here is the value of the cookie named myCookie:

```
<%= Request.Cookies("myCookie") %>
```

QueryString

The QueryString collection retrieves the values of the variables in the HTTP query string; that is, it retrieves the values encoded after the question mark ("?") in an HTTP request.

The syntax is *Request.QueryString(variable)[(index)|.Count]*

The QueryString parameters are

Variable	Specifies the name of the variable in the HTTP query string to retrieve
Index	An optional parameter that enables retrieval of one of multiple values for variable. It can be any integer value in the range 1 to *Request.QueryString*(variable).Count.

The QueryString collection is a parsed version of the QUERY_STRING variable in the ServerVariables collection. It enables retrieval of the QUERY_STRING variables by name. The value of *Request.QueryString*(parameter) is an array of all of the values of parameter that occur in QUERY_STRING. Determine the number of values of a parameter by calling *Request.QueryString*(parameter).Count. If a variable does not have multiple data sets associated with it, the count is 1. If the variable is not found, the count is 0.

To reference a QueryString variable in one of multiple data sets, specify a value for the index. The index parameter may be any value between 1 and *Request.QueryString*(variable).Count. Referencing one of multiple QueryString variables without specifying a value for the index returns the data in a comma-delimited string. If the application requires unparsed QueryString data, retrieve by calling *Request.QueryString* without any parameters.

Example 1: You may loop through all the data values in a query string. For example, if the following request is sent,

```
http://NAMES.ASP?Q=Fred&Q= Diana
```

and NAMES.ASP contained the following script,

```
<%
  For Each item In Request.QueryString("Q")
    Response.Write item & "<BR>"
  Next
%>
```

NAMES.ASP would display the following:

```
Fred
Diana
```

Example 2: You could also write this script using Count:

```
<%
  For I = 1 To Request.QueryString("Q").Count
    Response.Write Request.QueryString("Q")(I) & "<BR>"
  Next
%>
```

Example 3: Or you could write it by iterating through the keys in *Request.QueryString*:

```
<% For Each x In Request.QueryString %>
  Request.QueryString( <% = x %> ) = <% = Request.QueryString(x) %>
%>
    <% Next %>
```

Example 4: The client request

```
/scripts/directory-lookup.asp?name=fred&age=22
```

results in the QUERY_STRING value

```
name=fred&age=22.
```

The QueryString collection would then contain two members, name and age:

```
Welcome, <%= Request.QueryString("name") %>.
Your age is  <%= Request.QueryString("age") %>.
```

The output would be

```
Welcome, Fred. Your age is 22.
```

ClientCertificate

The ClientCertificate collection retrieves the certification fields (specified in the X.509 standard) from the request issued by the Web browser.

If a Web browser uses the SSL3/PCT1 protocol (in other words, it uses a URL starting with *https://* instead of *http://*) to connect to a server and the server requests certification, the browser sends the certification fields. If no certificate is sent, the ClientCertificate collection returns EMPTY.

The syntax is *Request.ClientCertificate*(Key[SubField]).

The parameter is

Key   Specifies the name of the certification field to retrieve.

A client certificate consists of the following fields:

Subject	A string that contains a list of subfield values that themselves contain information about the subject of the certificate. If this value is specified without a subfield, the ClientCertificate collection returns a comma-separated list of subfields. For example, "C=US, O=Msft, …."
Issuer	A string that contains a list of subfield values containing information about the issuer of the certificate. If you specify this value without a subfield, the ClientCertificate collection returns a comma-separated list of subfields. For example, "C=US, O=Verisign, …."
ValidFrom	A date specifying when the certificate becomes valid. This date follows VBScript format and varies with international settings. For example, in the U.S.: 9/26/96 11:59:59 PM.
ValidUntil	A date specifying when the certificate expires.
SerialNumber	A string that contains the certification serial number as an ASCII representation of hexidecimal bytes separated by hyphens ("-"). For example, 04-67-F3-02.
Certificate	A string containing the binary stream of the entire certificate content in ASN.1 format.

SubField	An optional parameter. Use this parameter to retrieve an individual field in either the Subject or Issuer keys. This parameter is added to the key parameter as a suffix. For example, IssuerO or SubjectCN. The following list gives some common SubField values:

C: Specifies the name of the country of origin

O: Specifies the company or organization name

OU: Specifies the name of the organizational unit

CN: Specifies the common name of the user (Used with the Subject key.)

L: Specifies a locality

S: Specifies a state or province

T: Specifies the title of the person or organization

GN: Specifies a given name

I: Specifies a set of initials

SubField values other than those listed in this table can be identified by their ASN.1 identifier. The format of the ASN.1 identifier is a list of numbers separated by a period ("."). For example, 3.56.7886.34.

Example 1: Loop through the keys of the ClientCertificate collection as demonstrated in the following example:

```
<%
For Each key in Request.ClientCertificate("key")
   Response.Write( key & ": " & Request.ClientCertificate("key"))
Next
%>
```

Example 2: The following example retrieves the common name of the company that issued the client certificate:

```
<%= Request.ClientCertificate("IssuerCN") %>
```

Example 3: The following example checks the organization name of the subject of the client certification:

```
<%
If (Request.ClientCertificate("SubjectO")="Msft")
   Response.Write("Good Choice!")
End if
%>
```

Example 4: The following example displays the expiration date of the client certificate:

```
This certification will expire on
<%= Request.ClientCertificate("ValidUntil") %>
```

Response Object

The Response object deals with output to the browser. Writing HTML back to the browser, setting parameters, and making cookies are functions that the Response object provides. Use the Response object to send output and cookies to the client. The syntax is Response.collection|property|method.

The Response object uses the collections listed below. However, only the Cookies, ContentType, and Status collections are covered here.

■ Cookies: Specifies cookie values (Use this collection to set cookie values.)

■ Buffer: Indicates whether to buffer page output (Use flush to send the buffer.)

■ ContentType: Specifies the HTTP content type for the response

■ Expires: Specifies the length of time before a page cached in a browser expires

■ ExpiresAbsolute: Specifies the date and time on which a page cached in a browser expires

■ Status: The value of the status line returned by the server

Cookies

The Cookies collection sets the value of a cookie. If the specified cookie does not exist, it is created. If it exists, it takes the new value and the old value is discarded.

The syntax is *Response.Cookies(cookie)[(key)|.attribute] = value.*

The parameters are as follows:

Cookie	The name of the cookie.
Key	An optional parameter. If key is specified, cookie is a dictionary, and key is set to value.
Attribute	Specifies information about the cookie itself.

The attribute parameter can be one of the following:

Expires	The date on which the cookie expires.
Domain	If specified, the cookie is sent only to requests to this domain.
Path	If specified, the cookie is sent only to requests to this path. If this attribute is not set, the application path is used.
Secure	Specifies whether the cookie is secure.
HasKeys	Specifies whether the cookie contains keys.
Value	Specifies the value to assign to key or attribute.

If a cookie with a key is created, for example,

```
<%
Response.Cookies("mycookie")("type1") = "sugar"
Response.Cookies("mycookie")("type2") = "ginger snap"
%>
```

The following header is sent:

```
Set-Cookie:MYCOOKIE=TYPE1=sugar&TYPE2=ginger+snap
```

A subsequent assignment to myCookie without specifying a key would overwrite type1 and type2. This is shown in the following example:

```
<% Response.Cookies("myCookie") = "chocolate chip" %>
```

In this example, the keys type1 and type2 are overwritten. The myCookie cookie now has the value *Chocolate Chip*.

Conversely, calling a cookie with a key overwrites any other nonkey values it might have contained.

Example 1: For example, if after this code, a call to Response.Cookies is made such as the following,

```
<% Response.Cookies("myCookie")("newType") = "peanut butter" %>
```

the value *Chocolate Chip* is overwritten and *newType* would be set to *peanut butter*.

Example 2: To determine whether a cookie has keys, use the following syntax:

```
<%= Response.Cookies("myCookie").HasKeys %>
```

If myCookie is a cookie dictionary, this value evaluates to TRUE. Otherwise, it evaluates to FALSE.

Example 3: To set all of the cookies to expire on a particular date, use the following syntax:

```
<%
For Each cookie in Response.Cookies
    Response.Cookie(cookie).ExpiresAbsolute = #July 4, 1997#
Next
%>
```

Example 4: Use the .HasKeys syntax to check to see whether a cookie has keys. This is demonstrated in the following example:

```
<%
'Set the value for the entire cookie collection
For Each cookie in Response.Cookies
    If Not cookie.HasKeys Then
        'Set the value of the cookie
        Response.Cookies(cookie) = ""
    Else
        'Set the value for each key in the cookie collection
```

```
        For Each key in Response.Cookies(cookie)
            Response.Cookies(cookie)(key) = ""
        Next key
    End If
Next cookie
%>
```

Example 5: The following example demonstrate how to set a value for a cookie and assign values to its attributes:

```
<%
Response.Cookies("Type") = "Chocolate Chip"
Response.Cookies("Type").Expires = "July 31, 1997"
Response.Cookies("Type").Domain = "corporate.com"
Response.Cookies("Type").Path = "/www/home/"
Response.Cookies("Type").Secure = FALSE
%>
```

ContentType

The ContentType property specifies the HTTP content type for the response. If no ContentType is specified, the default is *text/HTML*.

The syntax is Response.ContentType [= ContentType].

The ContentType property has only one parameter:

ContentType   A string describing the content type. This string is usually formatted type/subtype, where type is the general content category and subtype is the specific content type. For a full list of supported content types, see the Web browser's documentation.

Example 1: The following example sets the content type to non-HTML encoded text. This means that the browser will not interpret any HTML tags in the file; instead, they will be displayed on the screen.

```
<% Response.ContentType = "text/plain" %>
```

Example 2: The following examples set ContentType to other common values:

```
<% Response.ContentType = "text/HTML" %>
<% Response.ContentType = "image/GIF" %>
<% Response.ContentType = "image/JPEG" %>
```

Status

The Status property specifies the value of the status line returned by the server. Status values are defined in the HTTP specification.

The syntax is Response.Status = StatusDescription.

Status has one property:

StatusDescription A string that consists of both a three-digit number that indicates a status code and a brief explanation of that code. An example would be *310 Move Permanently*.

Use this property to modify the status line returned by the server.

Example 1: The following example sets the response status:

```
<% Response.Status = "401 Unauthorized" %>
```

Now that we've looked at some of the the Response object properties, let's turn to the methods. The Response object has the methods listed below:

- AddHeader: Sets the HTML header name to value.

- AppendToLog: Adds a string to the end of the Web server log entry for this request.

- BinaryWrite: Writes the given information to the current HTTP output without any character-set conversion.

- Clear: Erases any buffered HTML output.

- End: Stops processing the .ASP file and returns the current result.

- Flush: Sends buffered output immediately.

- Redirect: Sends a redirect message to the browser, causing it to attempt to connect to a different URL.

- Write: Writes a variable to the current HTTP output as a string.

AddHeader

The AddHeader method adds an HTML header with a specified value. This method always adds a new HTTP header to the response. It will not replace an existing header of the same name. Once you add a header, you cannot remove it.

The syntax is *Response.AddHeader name, value*

The AddHeader method has the following parameters:

Name	The name of the new header variable.
Value	The initial value stored in the new header variable.

Because HTTP protocol requires that all headers be sent before any content is sent, call AddHeader before you send any output to the client. The exception is when the output is buffered: the Buffer property is set to TRUE. Call the AddHeader method preceding calls to Flush.

Example 1: In the following example, the page is not buffered:

```
<% Response.AddHeader "WARNING", "Error Message Text" %>
<HTML>
```

Some text on the Web page.

```
</HTML>
```

The script works, however, because the AddHeader method is called before the server sends the output—some text on the Web page—to the client. If the order were reversed, the call to the AddHeader method would generate a run-time error.

Example 2: In this example the page is buffered, and as a result, the server will not send output to the client until all the ASP scripts on the page have been processed or until the Flush method is called.

```
<% Response.Buffer = TRUE %>
<HTML>
```

Here's some text on your Web page.

```
<% Response.AddHeader "WARNING", "Error Message Text" %> ⏎
    Here's some more interesting and illuminating text.
<% Response.Flush %>
<%= Response.Write("some string") %>
</HTML>
```

With buffered output, calls to AddHeader can appear anywhere in the script as long as they precede any calls to Flush. If the call to AddHeader appeared below the call to Flush in this example, the script would generate a run-time error since the header was already sent off.

Use this method to send multiple copies of the same header with different values, as with WWW-Authenticate headers.

Example 3: This example uses the AddHeader method to request that the client use BASIC authentication:

```
<% Response.Addheader "WWW-Authenticate", "BASIC" %>
```

This script merely informs the client browser which authentication to use. If you use this script in a Web application, ensure that the Web server has BASIC authentication enabled.

AppendToLog

The AppendToLog method adds a string to the end of the Web server log entry for this request. Each time the method is called, the specified string is appended to the existing entry.

The syntax is *Response.AppendToLog string*.

The AppendToLog method has only one parameter:

String — The text to append to the log file. Because fields in the IIS log are comma-delimited, this string cannot contain any comma characters (","). The maximum length of this string is 80 characters.

BinaryWrite

The BinaryWrite method writes the specified information to the current HTTP output without any character conversion. This method is useful for writing nonstring information such as binary data required by a custom application. The syntax is Response.BinaryWrite data.

The BinaryWrite method has only the following parameter:

Data   The data to write to the HTTP output.

Example: The following example uses the BinaryWrite method to send an array of bytes to a custom application:

```
<%
set bg = CreateObject(BinaryGenerator)
pict = bg.MakePicture
Response.BinaryWrite pict
%>
```

Redirect

The Redirect method causes the browser to attempt to connect to a different URL. The syntax is *Response.Redirect URL.*

The Redirect method has only the following parameter:

URL   The Uniform Resource Locator that specifies the location to which the browser is redirected.

Any response body content set explicitly in the page is ignored. However, the method does send to the client other HTTP headers set by this page. An automatic response body containing the redirect URL as a link is generated. The Redirect method sends the following explicit header, where URL is the value passed to the method:

```
HTTP/1.0 302 Object Moved
Location URL __
```

Write

The Write method writes a specified string to the current HTTP output. The syntax is *Response.Write variant.*

The Write method has only the following parameter:

Variant   The data to write. This parameter can be any data type supported by the Visual Basic Scripting Edition variant data type; this includes characters, strings, and integers. This value cannot contain the character combination "%>"; use the escape sequence "%\>" if needed. The Web server translates the escape sequence when it processes the script.

If Visual Basic Scripting Edition is the primary scripting language, the variant cannot be a string literal that contains more than 1022 characters. This is because VBScript limits static strings to 1022 bytes. However, the name of a variable that contains greater than 1022 bytes can be specified.

For example, this VBScript, in which *a* is repeated 1023 times in the string literal, will fail:

```
<% Response.Write "aaaaaaaaaaaa…aaaaaaaaaaaaaaaaaa"
```

But this VBScript will succeed:

```
<%
AVeryLongString = String(4096, "a")
Response.Write(AVeryLongString)
%>
```

Example. The following example uses the Response.Write method to send output to the client:

```
I just want to say <% Response.Write "Hello World." %>
Your name is:  <% Response.Write Request.Form("name") %>
```

This example adds an <HTML> tag to the Web page output. Because the string returned by the Write method cannot contain the character combination, "%>", the escape, "%\>", has been used instead:

```
<% Response.Write "<TABLE WIDTH=100 %\>" %>
```

Server Object

The Server object provides access to methods and properties on the server. Most of these methods and properties serve as utility functions.

The Server object has the following property:

ScriptTimeout   The amount of time that a script can run before it times out.

The Server object has the following methods:

CreateObject   Creates an instance of a server component. This one is the workhorse for creating all other objects like ADO described below.

HTMLEncode   Applies HTML encoding to the specified string.

MapPath   Maps the specified virtual path, either the absolute path on the current server or the path relative to the current page, into a physical path.

URLEncode   Applies URL encoding rules, including escape characters, to the string.

Session Object

Use the Session object to store information needed for a particular user-session. Variables stored in the Session object are not discarded when the user moves between pages of the application; instead, these variables persist for the entire user-session.

A session is defined as the set of consecutive requests, from the same user, to view pages that are organized under a set of related pages (comprise an application). In this way, the server can cache information, objects, connections, and resources for the user without storing it on the user's machine because the server knows when the user first browsed this directory and its content.

The Web server automatically creates a Session object the first time a user requests a Web page from the application. The server releases the Session object when the session expires or is abandoned.

The Session object properties are as follows:

SessionID	Returns the session identification for this user.
Timeout	The timeout period for the session state for this application, in minutes. Used for setting session timeout for a user.

The Session object method is

Abandon	This method destroys a Session object and releases its resources.

Store values in the Session object by using the following syntax:

```
<%
    Session("username") = "Janine"
    Session("age") = 24
%>
```

However, if you store an object in the Session object using VBScript as your primary scripting language, you must use the following syntax (note the use of the Set keyword in the second line):

```
<%
Set MyObj = Server.CreateObject("MyComponent")
Set Session("Obj1") = MyObj
%>
```

Next, call the methods and properties of MyObj on subsequent Web pages, using the following syntax:

```
<% Session("Obj1").MyObjMethod %>
```

Example 1: Note that you cannot store a built-in object in a Session object. For example, each of the following lines would return an error:

```
<%
Set Session("var1") = Session
Set Session("var2") = Request
Set Session("var3") = Response
Set Session("var4") = Server
Set Session("var5") = Application
%>
```

Example 2: However, parameters and components may be stored.

```
<%
Session("name") = "MyName"
Session("year") = 96
Set Session("myObj") = Server.CreateObject("someObj")
 %>
```

Scripting events

Scripts for the following events are declared in the GLOBAL.ASA file:

```
Session_OnEnd
Session_OnStart
```

The Session_OnEnd event occurs when a session is abandoned or times out. Of the server built-in objects, only the Application, Server, and Session objects are available.

```
<SCRIPT LANGUAGE=ScriptLanguage RUNAT=Server>
Sub Session_OnEnd
. . .
End Sub
</SCRIPT>
```

ScriptLanguage specifies the scripting language used to write the event script. It may be any supported scripting language, such as VBScript or JScript. If more than one event uses the same scripting language, they can be combined under a single set of <SCRIPT> tags.

The Session_OnStart event occurs when the server creates a new session. This event is processed prior to executing the requested page. You must set any session-wide variables during the Session_OnStart event. All the built-in objects (Application, Request, Response, Server, and Session) are available and can be referenced in the Session_OnStart event script.

```
<SCRIPT LANGUAGE=ScriptLanguage RUNAT=Server>
Sub Session_OnStart
. . .
End Sub
</SCRIPT>
```

Although the Session object persists if the Session_OnStart event contains a call to the Redirect or End methods, the server stops processing the script in both the GLOBAL file and in the file that triggered the Session_OnStart event.

Call the Redirect method in the Session_OnStart event to ensure that users always start a session at a particular Web page. When the user enters the application, the server creates a session for that user and processes the Session_OnStart event script. Include script in this event to check whether the page the user opened is the starting page and, if not, direct the user to the starting page by calling the Response.Redirect method. This is demonstrated in the following example:[6]

```
<SCRIPT RUNAT=Server Language=VBScript>
Sub Session_OnStart
    ' Make sure that new users start on the correct
    ' page of the ASP application.

    ' Replace the value given to startPage below
    ' with the virtual path to your application's
    ' start page.

    startPage = "/MyApp/StartHere.asp"
    currentPage = Request.ServerVariables("SCRIPT_NAME")

    ' Do a case-insensitive compare, and if they
    ' don't match, send the user to the start page.

    if strcomp(currentPage,startPage,1) then
        Response.Redirect(startPage)
    end if
End Sub
</SCRIPT>
```

Any Session_OnStart event script that follows a call to the Redirect method is not executed. For this reason, you should call the Redirect method last in your event script. This is demonstrated in the following example:

```
<SCRIPT LANGUAGE=VBScript RUNAT=Server>
    Sub Session_OnStart
        ' Session initialization script
        Response.Redirect "http:/server/app/StartHere.asp"
    End sub
</SCRIPT>
```

In the preceding example the Redirect method hides any text displayed to the client during the session-initialization script.

Use the Session object to store state information needed for a particular user and session. Variables stored in the Session object are not discarded when the user jumps between pages in the application; instead, these variables persist for the entire user-session or after 20 minutes has passed after the user has left the session.

---

6. Currently, the following example only works for browsers that support cookies. Because a noncookie browser does not return the SessionID cookie, the server creates a new session each time the user requests a page. Thus for each request, the server processes the Session_OnStart script and redirects the user to the starting page. If you use the following script, you should put a notice on your starting page to inform users that the site requires a cookie-enabled browser.

Application Object

Use the Application object to share information among all users of a given application. An ASP-based application is defined as all the .ASP files in a virtual directory and its subdirectories.

The Application object uses the following methods:

Lock   The Lock method prevents other clients from modifying Application object properties.

Unlock   The Unlock method allows other clients to modify Application object properties

Scripting events

Scripts for Application object events are declared in the GLOBAL.ASA file. Similar to Session but in a more restricted space of pages belonging to an application within a session, the Application object can store values using the following script:

```
Application_OnEnd
Application_OnStart
```

Example 1: Store values in the Application object by using the following syntax:

```
<%
    Application("greeting") = "Welcome to ..."
    Application("num") = 25
%>
```

Example 2: Similarly, you cannot store ASP built-in objects. The following lines each generate an error:

```
<%
Set Application("var1") = Session
Set Application("var2") = Request
Set Application("var3") = Response
Set Application("var4") = Server
Set Application("var5") = Application
%>
```

Example 3: This example implements a visit counter.

```
<%
Application.Lock
Application("NumVisits") = Application("NumVisits") + 1
Application.Unlock
%>
```

This example uses the application variable *NumVisits* to store the number of times that a particular page has been accessed. In this example, the Lock method is called to ensure that only the current client can access or alter *NumVisits*. Calling the

Unlock method then enables other users to access the Application object. Be careful of integer overflow! Use Long integers.

You may print the counter from another page. This application page has been visited:

```
<% Application("NumVisits") = Application("NumVisits")  + 1 %>
<%= Application("NumVisits") %> times!
```

Components

A large number of components are available for ASP. Some are shipped with IIS, and others you can add. Three of the shipped objects are covered here: the Active Data object, the TextStream and File Access object, and the Browser Capabilities object. (Documentation shows more basic objects; however, these three are the workhorses.)

Active Data Object (ADO)

The ADO component is used for accessing and editing data that resides in a local or remote database. ODBC technology is built into this base component; therefore, access to any database, remote or local, for which an ODBC driver is available is permitted. Using ADO, for example, with the correct version of an ODBC driver or OLEDB provider, the server code can access a General-Ledger table residing in an Oracle or Informix database, locally or remotely.

Complete list of ADO commands and properties

This list includes all ADO methods in alphabetical order. Please refer to product documentation for up-to-date details of all ADO commands and object properties.

ADO command list

AddNew	Append	AppendChunk
BeginTrans	CancelBatch	CancelUpdate
Clear	Clone	Close
CommitTrans	CreateParameter	Delete
Execute	GetChunk	GetRows
Move	MoveFirst	MoveLast
MoveNext	MovePrevious	NextRecordset
Open	Refresh	Requery
Resync	RollbackTrans	Supports
Update	UpdateBatch	

ADO property list

AbsolutePage	AbsolutePosition	ActiveConnection
ActualSize	Attributes	BOF
Bookmark	CacheSize	CommandText
CommandTimeout	CommandType	ConnectionString
ConnectionTimeout	Count	CursorType

DefaultDatabase	DefinedSize	Description
Direction	EditMode	EOF
Filter	HelpContext	HelpFile
IsolationLevel	LockType	MaxRecords
Mode	Name	NativeError
Number	NumericScale	OriginalValue
PageCount	PageSize	Precision
Prepared	Provider	RecordCount
Size	Source	SQLState
Status	Type	UnderlyingValue
Value	Version	

ADO programming model

The Active Data Objects (ADO) programming model represents the best of the existing Microsoft data access programming models. If you are familiar with Data Access Objects (DAO) or Remote Data Objects (RDO), you will recognize the interfaces and will be able to work with them very quickly. Otherwise, use existing samples to come up to speed. This component bridges Web and database servers.

The ADO objects provide the fastest, easiest, and most productive means for accessing a variety of data sources. The ADO model strives to expose everything that the underlying data provider can do, while adding value by making shortcuts available for most common operations.

The command interface is optional and may not be supported with some OLE/ODBC drivers, since some unstructured data providers are not capable of processing text-based command syntax or providing parameterized statements. Since the Recordset object is creatable and the Source property of the Recordset interface may be set to a simple text command, you can still create Recordsets, even if the provider does not support the Command interface.

ADO is an aggregate of five objects, working together to deliver seamless access to databases: Connection, Command, Error, Parameter, and Recordset. All objects in the implementation can be created on their own with the exception of the Error and Field objects. The ADO model deemphasizes the hierarchy of objects found in previous models. This allows greater flexibility in reusing objects in different contexts. For example, you can create a Command object, execute it against one connection, then associate it with a different connection and execute a second command.

Connection object summary

A Connection object represents an open connection to an OLE DB data source. You can create Connection objects independently of any other previously defined object. A Connection object represents a unique session with a data source. In the case of a client/server database system, it may be equivalent to an actual network connection to the server. Depending on the functionality the provider exposes, some collections, methods, or properties of a Connection object may not be available.[7]

Using the collections, methods, and properties of a Connection object, you can

■ Set the default database for the connection with the DefaultDatabase property

■ Set the level of isolation for the transactions opened on the connection with the IsolationLevel property

■ Select an OLE DB provider with the Provider property

■ Establish, and later break, the physical connection to the data source with the Open and Close methods

■ Execute a command on the connection with the Execute method and configure the execution with the CommandTimeout property

■ Manage transactions on the open connection, including nested transactions if the provider supports them, with the BeginTrans, CommitTrans, and RollbackTrans methods and the Attributes property

■ Examine errors returned from the data source with the Errors collection

■ Read the version from the ADO implementation in use with the Version property

ADO's connection object includes: connection string, connection timeout mode, default database, isolation level, provider, open method, and close method. Properties of the connection object are described below.

ConnectionString property The ConnectionString property contains the information used to establish a connection to a data source. Use the ConnectionString property to specify a data source by passing a data source name (DSN) or a detailed connection string containing a series of parameter = value arguments separated by semicolons. If the property value contains an equal sign ("="), ADO assumes that a connection string was provided rather than a DSN.

ADO supports five arguments for the ConnectionString property; any other arguments pass directly to the provider without any processing by ADO. The arguments ADO supports are as follows:

Provider	Specifies the name of a provider to use for the connection
Data Source	Specifies the name of a data source for the connection, for example, an SQL Server database registered as an ODBC data source

7. For information on Microsoft OLE DB providers including the Microsoft ODBC Provider for OLE DB, see the documentation for the Microsoft OLE DB SDK or visit the Microsoft OLE DB Web page (*http://www.microsoft.com/oledb*).

User	Specifies the user name to use when opening the connection
Password	Specifies the password to use when opening the connection
File Name	Specifies the name of a provider-specific file containing preset connection information (Used for OLEDB providers versus ODBC drivers.)

After the ConnectionString property is set and the Connection object is opened, the provider may alter the contents of the property.

The ConnectionString property automatically inherits the value used for the ConnectionString argument of the Open method. Override the current Connection-String property during the next Open method call. Because the File Name argument causes ADO to load the associated provider, do not pass both the Provider and File Name arguments. The ConnectionString property is read/write when the connection is closed, and read-only when it is open. Also note that if you specify userid and password, the database is opened using this user and password, or else in the context of IUSR_*machinename* user.

ConnectionTimeout property This property indicates how long to wait while establishing a connection before terminating the attempt and generating an error.

Sets or returns a Long value that indicates, in seconds, how long to wait for the connection to open. Default is 15.

Use the ConnectionTimeout property on a Connection object if delays from network traffic or heavy server use make it necessary to abandon a connection attempt. If the time elapses prior to the database returning a successful opening result for the requested connection, an error occurs and ADO cancels the connection attempt. If the property is set to 0, ADO will wait indefinitely until the connection is opened. Make sure the provider (driver) targeted supports the ConnectionTimeout functionality. The ConnectionTimeout property is read/write when the connection is closed and read-only when it is open.

Mode property This property indicates the available permissions for modifying data in a connection. It sets or returns a Long value that can be one of the following constants:

Constant	*Value*	*Description*
AdModeUnknown	0	The permissions have not yet been set or cannot be determined. (Default)
AdModeRead	1	Read-only permissions
AdModeWrite	2	Write-only permissions
AdModeReadWrite	3	Read/write permissions
AdModeShareDenyRead	4	Prevents others from opening connection with read permissions
AdModeShareDenyWrite	8	Prevents others from opening connection with write permissions

AdModeShareExclusive	12	Prevents others from opening connection with read/write permissions
AdModeShareDenyNone	16	Prevents others from opening connection with any permissions

Use the Mode property to set or return the access permissions in use by the provider for the current connection. Set the Mode property before the Connection object is opened, or set after a close and before a reopen.

DefaultDatabase property This property indicates the default database for a Connection object. It sets or returns a string that evaluates to the name of a database available from the provider.

Use the DefaultDatabase property to set or return the name of the default database on a specific Connection object. If you don't specify a default database, the default database assigned to the user on the SQL server is opened by default. Secondly, SQL strings can use an unqualified syntax to access objects in that database. In other words, select * from table rather than select * from owner.database.table. To access objects in a database other than the one specified in the DefaultDatabase property, qualify object names with the desired database name as shown. Upon successful connection, the provider will set the DefaultDatabase property. Some providers allow only one database per connection, in which case the DefaultDatabase property cannot be changed after it is set. Other providers allow the DefaultDatabase property to be reset on the fly.

IsolationLevel property This property indicates the level of isolation for a Connection object. It sets or returns a Long value equal to one of the following constants:

Constant	Value	Description
adXactUnspecified	−1	If the provider is using a different IsolationLevel than specified but which one cannot be determined, the property returns this value
AdXactChaos	16	Indicates that pending changes from more highly isolated transactions cannot be overwritten
AdXactBrowse	256	Indicates that from one transaction, uncommitted changes in another transactions can be viewed
adXactReadUncommitted	256	Same as adXactBrowse
AdXactCursorStability	4096	Indicates that from one transaction you can view changes in other transactions only after they've been committed (Default)
AdXactReadCommitted	4096	Same as adXactCursorStability

AdXactRepeatableRead	65536	Indicates that from one transaction you cannot see changes made in other transactions, but that requerying can bring new Recordsets
AdXactIsolated	1048576	Indicates that transactions are conducted in isolation of other transactions
adXactSerializable	1048576	Same as adXactIsolated

Use the IsolationLevel property to set the isolation level of a Connection object. The IsolationLevel property is read/write. The setting does not take effect until the next time we call the BeginTrans method. If the level of isolation requested is unavailable, the provider may return the next greater level of isolation. Consult SQL language specifications for a more detailed discussion of isolation levels and transactions.

Provider property Indicates the name of the provider for a Connection object. Use the Provider property to set or return the name of the provider for a connection. This property can also be set by the contents of ConnectionString property or the ConnectionString argument of the Open method. If no provider is specified, the property will default to MSDASQL (Microsoft ODBC provider for OLE DB).

The Provider property is read/write when the connection is closed and read-only when it is open. The setting does not take effect until either the Connection object is opened or the Properties collection of the Connection object is accessed. If the setting is invalid, an error occurs.

For information on Microsoft ODBC Provider for OLE DB and OLE DB providers in general, see the documentation for the Microsoft OLE DB SDK or visit the Microsoft OLE DB Web page (*http://www.microsoft.com/oledb*).

Open Method property This property opens a connection to a data source. The syntax is

```
connection.Open ConnectionString, User, Password.[8]
```

The properties include the following:

ConnectionString	A String containing connection information (Optional). See the ConnectionString property for details on valid settings.
User	A String containing a user name to use when establishing the connection (Optional).
Password	A String containing a password to use when establishing the connection (Optional).
Source	A variant that evaluates to a valid Command object variable name, an SQL statement, a table name, or a stored procedure call (Optional).

8. *Open* also applies to a Recordset object. For a Recordset object: recordset.Open Source, ActiveConnection, CursorType, LockType, Option.

ActiveConnection A variant that evaluates to a valid Connection object variable name or a String containing a definition for a connection (Optional).

CursorType A Long expression that determines the type of cursor that the provider should use when opening the Recordset (Optional). Can be one of the following constants:

adOpenForwardOnly, 0 (Default): adOpenKeyset, 1

adOpenDynamic, 2: adOpenStatic, 3

LockType A Long expression that determines what type of locking (concurrency) the provider should use when opening the Recordset (Optional). Can be one of the following constants:

adLockReadOnly, 1: adLockPessimistic, 2

adLockOptimistic, 3: adLockBatchOptimistic, 4

Option A Long expression that indicates how the provider should evaluate the Source argument if it represents something other than a Command object (Optional). Can be one of the following constants:

adCmdUnknown, 0: The type of command in the CommandText argument is not known

adCmdText, 1: Evaluate CommandText as a textual definition of a command

adCmdTable, 2: Evaluate CommandText as a table name

adCmdStoredProc, 4: Evaluate CommandText as a stored procedure

Use the Open method on a Connection object or a Recordset object to activate the object for use. When the operations over an open Connection object or in an open Recordset object have been concluded, use the Close method to free any associated system resources. Closing an object does not remove it from memory. You can use the Open method to reopen a closed Connection object. To completely eliminate an object from memory, set the object variable to Nothing or wait until session time expires.

Using the Open method on a Connection object establishes the physical connection to a data source. After this method successfully completes, the connection is live. Execute commands against it and access results.

Use the optional ConnectionString argument to specify a data source name (DSN) or a detailed connection string containing a series of parameter = value arguments separated by semicolons. If the argument contains an equal sign ("="), ADO assumes that a connection string is provided rather than a DSN. The ConnectionString property automatically inherits the value used for the ConnectionString argument. Therefore, either set the ConnectionString property of the Connection object before opening it, or use the ConnectionString argument to set or override the current connection parameters at the time the call to Open method is made.[9]

Close Method property This method closes an Open object and any dependent objects. Use the Close method to close a database connection. To completely eliminate an object from memory, set the object variable to Nothing.

Using the Close method to close a Connection object also closes any active Recordset objects associated with the connection. A Command object associated with a closed Connection object will persist, but it will no longer be associated with a Connection object; that is, its ActiveConnection property will be set to Null. Also, the Command object's Parameters collection will be cleared.

Call the Open method again to reestablish the connection to the same or another data source. While the Connection object is closed, calling any methods that require an open connection to the data source generates an error. In other words, if the connection is closed and a result set is then accessed or a command executed, an error is reported.

Closing a Connection object while Recordset objects are open on the connection rolls back any pending changes in all of the Recordset objects. Closing a Connection object while a transaction is in progress generates an error.

Command object summary

A Command object is a definition of a specific command for execution. With the collections, methods, and properties of a Command object, you can do the following:

- Associate an open connection and the Command object with the ActiveConnection property

- Define the text version of the command (for example, an SQL statement) with the CommandText property

- Create a Command object independently of a previously defined Connection object

To create a Command object independently of a previously defined Connection object, set its ActiveConnection property to another valid connection string. ADO still creates a Connection object, but it doesn't assign that object to an object variable. If you want to associate multiple Command objects with the same connection, you should explicitly create and open a Connection object and use this for all Command objects. If not all Command objects' ActiveConnection properties are set to this same object variable, ADO creates a new Connection object for each Command object, even if you use the same connection string.

---

9. For most data sources, you can use the optional User and Password arguments to override any user or password information provided in the ConnectionString parameter.

Use Command objects to obtain records and create a Recordset object, to execute a bulk operation, or to manipulate the structure of a database. If you are using a third-party provider, consult the documentation for the collections, methods, and properties that the Command object makes available.

The Command object contains several collections, methods, and a property (CommandType), discussed below.

CommandTimeout property

The Command object uses the property to

■ Set the number of seconds a provider will wait for a command to execute

■ Specify the type of command described in the CommandText property with the CommandType property prior to execution in order to optimize performance

■ Determine whether or not the provider prepares a command prior to execution with the Prepared property

■ Manage arguments passed to and from the provider with the Parameters collection

■ Execute a command and return a Recordset object if appropriate with the Execute method

Collections

A Command object has a Parameters collection made up of Parameter objects including the following: Parameters (default), Properties, Methods, CreateParameter, and Execute. Command objects include a number of collections such as parameters and properties. These two collections are discussed below.

Parameters collection A Parameters collection contains all the Parameter objects of a Command object. Using the Refresh method on a Command object's Parameters collection retrieves provider parameter information for the stored procedure or parameterized query specified in the Command object.

The collection will be empty for providers that do not support stored procedure calls or parameterized queries.

If you have not defined your own Parameter objects and you access the Parameters collection before calling the Refresh method, ADO will automatically call the method and populate the collection for you.

Create Parameter objects with the appropriate property settings and use the Append method to add them to the Parameters collection. This allows for setting of return parameter values without calling the provider for each parameter information.

To refer to a Parameter object in a collection by its ordinal number or by its Name property setting, use any of the following syntax forms:

```
command.Parameters(0)
command.Parameters("name")
     command(0)
     command("name")
     command!{name]
```

Properties collection A Properties collection contains all the Property objects for a specific instance of an object. Some ADO objects have a Properties collection made up of Property objects. Each Property object corresponds to a characteristic of the ADO object specific to the provider. To refer to a Property object in a collection by its Name property setting, use the following syntax form:

```
object.Properties("name")
```

Command object supports a number of methods such as CreateParameters and Execute. The Execute method has parameters of its own, including Active Connection, Command Text, Command Timeout, Command Type, and Prepared.

Methods The Command object uses the CreateParameter and Execute methods.

CreateParameter method This method creates a new Parameter object with the specified properties.

The syntax is: Set parameter = command.CreateParameter(Name, Type, Direction, Size, Value).

The parameters are the following:

Parameter	An object variable representing the Parameter object that you want to create
Command	An object variable representing the Command object for whose Parameters collection you want to create a new Parameter object
Name	A String representing the name of the Parameter object
Type	A Long value specifying the data type of the Parameter object. See the Type property for valid settings (Optional)
Direction	A Long value specifying the type of Parameter object (Optional). See the Direction property for valid settings
Size	A Long value specifying the maximum length for the parameter value in characters or bytes (Optional).
Value	A Variant specifying the value for the Parameter object (Optional)

Use the CreateParameter method to create a new Parameter object with the specified name, type, direction, and value. Any values passed in the arguments are written to the corresponding Parameter properties.

This method does not automatically append the Parameter object to the Parameters collection of a Command object. This allows setting of additional properties whose values ADO validates when a Parameter object is appended to the collection.

If a variable-length data type is specified in the Type argument, either pass a Size argument or set the Size property of the Parameter object before appending it to the Parameters collection. Similarly, when specifying a numeric data type, set the Precision property of the Parameter object before appending it to a collection to avoid an error.

Execute method Using the Execute method on a Command object executes the query specified in the CommandText property of the object. If the CommandText property specifies a row-returning query, any results the execution generates are stored in a new Recordset object. If the command is not a row-returning query, the provider does not create a Recordset object and only returns a Null object reference. Most application languages allow this return value to be ignored if no Recordset is needed.

The syntax is: *Set recordset = command.Execute(RecordsAffected, Parameters, Option)*.

The details are discussed below:

Recordset	An object variable representing the Recordset object in which the results of the query are stored.
Command	An object variable representing a Command object whose CommandText property contains the query to execute.
Connection	An object variable representing a Connection object on which the query is executed.
RecordsAffected	A Long variable to which the provider returns the number of records that the operation affected (Optional).
Parameters	A Variant array of parameter values passed with an SQL statement (Optional). (Output parameters are not allowed in this argument.)
CommandText	A string containing the SQL statement, query, or stored procedure to execute. CommandText argument can be one of the following constants:
	adCmdUnknown, 0: The type of command in the CommandText argument is not known.
	adCmdText, 1: Evaluate CommandText as a textual definition of a command.
	adCmdTable, 2: Evaluate CommandText as a table name.
	adCmdStoredProc, 4: Evaluate CommandText as a stored procedure.
Option	A Long expression that indicates how the provider should evaluate the __ (Optional).

If the query has parameters, the current values for the Command object's parameters are used unless these are overriden with parameter values passed with the Execute call. You can override a subset of the parameters by omitting new values for some of the parameters when calling the Execute method. The order in which the parameters is specified is the same order in which the method passes parameters to the database engine. For example, if there were four (or more) parameters and you wanted to pass new values for only the first and fourth parameters, you would pass varArray(var1,,,var4) as the Parameters argument.

Properties The properties of the Execute method are ActiveConnection, CommandText, CommandTimeout, CommandType, and Prepared.

Execute method: ActiveConnection property This property indicates to which Connection object the specified Command or Recordset object currently belongs. It sets or returns a String containing the definition for a connection or a Connection object variable. The default is Null.

Use the ActiveConnection property to set or return an open Connection object over which the specified Command object should execute or the specified Recordset should be opened. If you pass a connection string for this argument, ADO opens a new connection using the specified parameters.

For Command objects, the ActiveConnection property is read/write. If you attempt to call the Execute method on a Command object before setting this property to an open Connection object or valid connection string, an error occurs.

Setting this property to Nothing disassociates the Command object from the current Connection, clears the Parameters collection of the Command object, and causes the provider to release any associated resources on the data source. You can then associate the Command object with the same or another Connection object. If this property is currently set to an open Connection object and you change the setting to another open Connection object, the Parameters collection will remain intact.

Closing the Connection object with which a Command object is associated sets the ActiveConnection property to Nothing. Setting this property to a closed Connection object generates an error.

Execute method: CommandText property This property contains the text of a command that you want to issue against a provider. It sets or returns a string value containing an SQL statement, a table name, or a stored procedure call. The default is "" (zero-length string).

Use the CommandText property to set or return the text version of the query in a Command object. The contents of the CommandText property are specific to the provider and can be standard SQL syntax or any special command format that the provider supports.

If the Prepared property of the Command object is set to TRUE and the Command object is bound to an open connection when you set the CommandText property, ADO prepares the query when you call the Execute or Open methods. Depending on the CommandType property setting, ADO may alter the

CommandText property during preparation or execution. After you call the Execute method, you may read the CommandText property to see if its value has changed.

Execute method: CommandTimeout property This property indicates how long to wait while executing a command before terminating the attempt and generating an error. It sets or returns a Long value that indicates, in seconds, how long to wait for a command to execute. The default is 30.

Use the CommandTimeout property on a Connection object or Command object to allow the cancellation of a command due to delays from network traffic or heavy server use. If the time from the CommandTimeout property setting elapses prior to execution of the command, an error occurs and ADO cancels the command. If you set the property to 0, ADO will wait indefinitely until the execution is complete. Make sure the provider and data source to which you are writing code supports the CommandTimeout functionality.

For Connection objects, the CommandTimeout property is read/write. When you use CommandTimeout on a Connection object, you set a global value for all commands executed and all recordsets opened on that connection. You can override this value for a specific command by setting the CommandTimeout property of the appropriate Command object.

Execute method: CommandType property This property indicates the type of a Command object. It sets or returns a Long value equal to one of the following constants:

Constant	Value	Description
AdCmdUnknown	0	The type of command in the CommandText property is not known (Default)
AdCmdText of a command	1	Evaluates CommandText as a textual definition
adCmdTable	2	Evaluates CommandText as a table name
adCmdStoredProc	4	Evaluates CommandText as a stored procedure

Use the CommandType property to optimize evaluation of the CommandText property. If the CommandType property value equals adCmdUnknown (0), you might experience diminished performance because ADO must make calls to the provider to determine if the CommandText property is an SQL statement, a stored procedure, or a table name. If you know what type of command you're using, setting the CommandType property instructs ADO to go directly to the relevant code. If the CommandType property does not match the type of command in the CommandText property, an error occurs when you call the Execute method.

Execute method: Prepared property This property indicates whether or not to create a prepared statement from the command before execution. It sets or returns a Boolean value.

Use the Prepared property to have the provider create a temporary stored representation of the query specified in the CommandText property before a Command object's first execution. Setting this property to TRUE requests the provider to compile a command on its first execution. This may slow a command's first execution, but once the provider compiles a command, the provider will use the compiled version of the command for any subsequent executions, which will result in improved performance.

If the property is FALSE, the provider will execute the Command object directly without creating a compiled version. If the provider does not support command preparation, it ignores any requests to prepare the command and sets the Prepared property to FALSE. Next Error objects are discussed.

Error object summary

The ADO Error object contains details about data access errors pertaining to a single operation involving ADO. You can read an Error object's properties to obtain specific details about each error, including the following:

- The Description property, which contains the text of the error alert

- The Number property, which contains the Long integer value of the error constant

- The Source property, which identifies the object that raised the error (This is particularly useful when you have several Error objects in the Errors collection following a request to a data source.)

- The HelpFile and HelpContext properties, which indicate the appropriate Microsoft Windows Help file and Help topic, respectively (if any exist), for the error

- The SQLState and NativeError properties, which provide information from ODBC data sources

When a provider error occurs, it is placed in the Errors collection of the Connection object. If there is no valid Connection object, you will need to retrieve error information from the Visual Basic for Applications Error object. ADO supports the return of multiple errors by a single ADO operation to allow for error information specific to the provider.

ADO can return the following specific errors:

Constant Name	Number	Description
AdErrInvalidArgument	3001	Invalid argument
AdErrNoCurrentRecord	3021	No current record for the operation
AdErrIllegalOperation	3219	Invalid operation
AdErrInTransaction	3246	Transaction error

AdErrFeatureNotAvailable	3251	Operation is not supported for this type of object
AdErrItemNotFound	3265	Item not found in this collection
AdErrObjectNotSet	3420	Object is invalid or not set
AdErrDataConversion	3421	Data type conversion error
AdErrObjectClosed	3704	Object is closed
AdErrObjectOpen	3705	Object is open
AdErrProviderNotFound	3706	Provider could not be found
AdErrBoundToCommand	3707	Recordset object has a Command object as its source: ActiveConnection property cannot be changed

The Errors collection on the Connection object is cleared and populated only when ADO or the provider generates a new error.

Some properties and methods return warnings that appear as Error objects in the Errors collection but do not stop a program's execution. Before calling the Delete, Resync, UpdateBatch, or CancelBatch methods on a Recordset object, or before setting the Filter property on a Recordset object, call the Clear method on the Errors collection so that the Count property of the Errors collection can be read to test for any returned warnings. The ADO Parameter object is discussed next.

Parameter object

The ADO Parameter object represents a parameter or argument associated with a Command object based on a parameterized query or stored procedure. Parameter objects represent parameters associated with parameterized queries, or the in/out arguments or return values of stored procedures. Depending on the functionality the provider exposes, some collections, methods, or properties of a Parameter object may not be available.

With the collections, methods, and properties of a Parameter object, you can do the following:

- Set or return the name of a parameter with the Name property

- Set or return the value of a parameter with the Value property

- Set or return parameter characteristics with the Attributes and Direction, Precision, NumericScale, Size, and Type properties

- Pass long binary or character data to a parameter with the AppendChunk method

If you know the names and properties of the parameters associated with the stored procedure or parameterized query, you can create Parameter objects with the appropriate property settings. Use the Append method to add Parameter objects to the Parameters collection. The ADO Recordset object is discussed next.

Recordset object summary

An ADO Recordset object represents the entire set of records from a base table or the results from an ADO command executed.

When opening multiple Recordset objects over the same connection, create and open a Connection object and explicitly set the Recordset property. Otherwise, ADO creates a new Connection object for each new Recordset object by default, even if the same connection string is used every time.

Use Recordset objects to manipulate data records. Recordset objects are constructed using rows and columns. You can use one of four different cursor types when opening a Recordset object:

- Dynamic cursor: Allows you to view additions, changes, and deletions by other users, and allows all types of movement through the Recordset that don't rely on bookmarks; allows bookmarks if the provider supports them

- Keyset cursor: Behaves like a dynamic cursor, except that it prevents you from seeing records that other users add, and prevents access to records that other users delete from your recordset; always allows bookmarks and therefore allows all types of movement through the Recordset. Data changes by other users will still be visible

- Static cursor: Provides a static copy of a set of records for you to use to find data or generate reports (Additions, changes, or deletions by other users will not be visible.)

- Forward-only cursor: Behaves identically to a static cursor except that it allows you to scroll only forward through records, which improves performance in situations where you need to make only a single pass through a Recordset

The CursorType property is useful in implementing operations such as editing in place, accesing texts and blobs, and so on. For most SQL query commands this discussion is overdone.

Set the CursorType property prior to opening the Recordset object to choose the cursor type of the Recordset object. You can also pass a CursorType argument with the Open method. If you don't specify a cursor type, ADO opens a forward-only cursor by default.

When you create a Recordset object, the current record is positioned to the first record (if any) and the BOF and EOF properties are set to FALSE. If there are no records, the RecordCount property setting is 0, and the BOF and EOF property settings are TRUE.

Use the MoveFirst, MoveLast, MoveNext, and MovePrevious methods, as well as the Move method, the AbsolutePosition, AbsolutePage, and Filter properties, to reposition the current record, assuming the provider supports the relevant functionality. Forward-only Recordset objects support only the MoveNext method. When you use the Move methods to visit each record (or enumerate the Recordset), you can use the BOF and EOF properties to see if you've moved beyond the beginning or end of the Recordset object.

Recordset objects can support two types of updating: immediate and batched. In immediate updating, all changes to data are written immediately to the underlying data source once you call the Update method. Pass arrays of values as parameters with the AddNew and Update methods and simultaneously update several fields in a record.

If a provider supports batch updating, you can have the provider cache changes to more than one record and then transmit them in a single call to the database with the UpdateBatch method. This applies to changes made with the AddNew, Update, and Delete methods. After you call the UpdateBatch method, you can use the Status property to check for any data conflicts in order to resolve them.[10]

This concludes our discussion of ADO objects. The next section covers using the ADO component.

Using the ADO component

ADO provides easy access to information stored in a database (or in another tabular data structure) that complies with the Open Database Connectivity (ODBC) standard. In this section, you will connect to a Microsoft Access customer database and display a listing of its contents. You will learn how to extract data using the SQL SELECT statement and create an HTML table to display the results.

Before using a database with the Database Access component, you must identify the database in the ODBC application in Control Panel. In this example, you will use an Access database that is provided with the ASP sample Web site.

To identify the database,

1. At the computer running Windows NT Server, open Control Panel.

2. Double-click the ODBC icon, and then click System DSN. There are two types of data sources: User, which is available only to you, and System, which is available to anyone using the computer. Data sources for use with the Web server need to be System.

3. Click Add, choose the Microsoft Access Driver, and then click Finish.

---

10. You should use batch updating only with either a keyset or static cursor.

4. In the Data Source Name box, type *AXTutorial*, and then click Select. Select the path to the sample database on the companion CD (AXTUTORIA.MDB) (in the INETPUB directory on the CD), and click OK.

5. Click OK to close the dialog boxes.

First, you need to create an instance of the ADO component in order to use it. To create the component instance,

1. Add the following code to your script in an ASP file:

```
<% Set DBConnObject = Server.CreateObject("ADODB.Connection")
```

2. For the Database Access component, you also need to specify the ODBC data source (the database from which you want data) by opening a connection to the database.

```
DBConnObject.Open "AXTutorial"
```

3. Use the Database Access component Execute method to issue an SQL Select query (SQLQuery) to the database and store the returned records in a result set (RSCustomerList).

4. Add the following code to your script below the DBConnObject.Open statement:

```
SQLQuery = "SELECT * FROM Customers"
Set RSCustomerList = DBConnObject.Execute(SQLQuery)
```

You could combine these two lines of script code by passing the literal Select string directly to the Execute method rather than assigning it to SQLQuery. When the query string is long, however, it makes the script easier to read if you assign the string to a variable name, such as SQLQuery, and then pass the variable name on to the Execute method.

To display the returned result set,

1. Think of the result set as a table whose structure is determined by the fields specified in the SQL SELECT query. Displaying the rows returned by the query, therefore, is as easy as performing a loop through the rows of the result set.

In this example, the returned data is displayed in table rows:

```
<% Do While Not RScustomerList.EOF %>
  <TR>
  <TD BGCOLOR="f7efde" ALIGN=CENTER>
    <FONT STYLE="ARIAL NARROW" SIZE=1>
      <%= RSCustomerList("CompanyName")%>
    </FONT></TD>
```

```
<TD BGCOLOR="f7efde" ALIGN=CENTER>
  <FONT STYLE="ARIAL NARROW" SIZE=1>
    <%=RScustomerList("ContactLastName") & ", " %>
    <%=RScustomerList("ContactFirstName") %>
  </FONT></TD>
<TD BGCOLOR="f7efde" ALIGN=CENTER>
  <FONT STYLE="ARIAL NARROW" SIZE=1>
  <A HREF="mailto:">
    <%=RScustomerList("ContactLastName")%>
  </A></FONT></TD>
<TD BGCOLOR="f7efde" ALIGN=CENTER>
  <FONT STYLE="ARIAL NARROW" SIZE=1>
    <%=RScustomerList("City")%>
  </FONT></TD>
<TD BGCOLOR="f7efde" ALIGN=CENTER>
  <FONT STYLE="ARIAL NARROW" SIZE=1>
    <%=RScustomerList("StateOrProvince")%>
  </FONT></TD>
</TR>
```

2. The Do...Loop statement repeats a block of statements while a condition is TRUE. The repeated statements can be script commands or HTML text and tags. Thus, each time through the loop, construct a table row (using HTML) and insert returned data (using script commands).

3. To complete the loop, use the MoveNext method to move the row pointer for the result set down one row. Because this statement still falls within the Do...Loop statement, it is repeated until the end of the file is reached.

4. Replace the comment with the words *Tutorial Lesson - Next Row* with the following code:

```
<%
RScustomerList.MoveNext
Loop
%>
```

This concludes the coverage of the ADO object. The next section discusses the TextStream object.

TextStream Object[11]

Using TextStream with the correct user rights, an HTML page can access a file on the server or the network.

The syntax is: *<% Set oVar = Server.CreateObject("MS.TextStream") %>*

---

11. This object may be superseded by the FileSystem object with similar properties. A seek method would be nice.

The TextStream object properties are as follows:

AtEnd	Indicates whether the file pointer is at the end of the file
Column property	The current column in characters. Returns Integer. On a new line, Column returns 1. After three characters have been written, Column returns 4. To add spaces, set Column to a higher number than the current value. If you set Column to a number less than the current value, a new line is started and enough spaces are written to match the Column setting.
Position property	The current file position in bytes. Position([value]). (Returns Integer.) When a file is initially opened, Position is 1. After one byte has been written, Position is 2, and so on.
Size property	Returns the size of the stream, in bytes. (Long integer.)

The TextStream object uses the following methods:

Read method	Reads characters from a file and returns them. (String.)
ReadAll method (Returns String)	Reads the entire file and returns it. Use this method with caution on large files. Other techniques, such as scanning the file line by line, are more efficient.
ReadLine method	Reads all characters (until a newline character appears) and returns them. (Returns String.) ReadLine consumes the newline character, but does not include it in the return value.
ReadLines method: ReadLines(Count)	Reads the specified number of lines and returns them in an array. (Returns array of strings.) The strings do not contain newline delimiters—these are consumed but not returned. If ReadLines cannot read Count lines, it reads as many as it can and returns them in the array.
Skip method	Skips characters in the file.
SkipLine method	Skips the next line in the file. The characters up to and including the next newline character are skipped. The file must be open for reading.
SkipLines method: SkipLines(Count)	Skips lines in the file. *Count* newline characters are consumed.
Write method	Writes the specified value to the file, with no separation among the items. Write(Value ___). Value of the string to write to the file.

Example: The following example writes the string *abcd* to the file:

```
s.Write("a")
s.Write("b")
s.Write("c")
s.Write("d")
```

WriteLine method	Writes a line to the file, followed by a newline character. WriteLine([Value]). Value the string to write to the file. WriteLine appends a newline character to the Value as it is added to the file. If Value is not specified, WriteLine writes a newline character to the file.
WriteLines method	Writes lines to the file, each followed by a newline character. WriteLines(Lines())
WriteBlankLines method	Writes blank lines to the file. WriteBlankLines(Count).
CloseTextFile method	Closes an open file on the server. Returns Object. The file must already be open.
CreateTextFile method	Creates and opens a new file on the server. CreateTextFile (filename,[openfor][,overwrite][,lockread][,lockwrite]). Returns Object. If the file already exists and overwrite is not set to TRUE, an error occurs.
OpenTextFile method	Opens an existing file on the server. OpenTextFile(filename, [openfor][,createfile][,lockread][,lockwrite]). Returns Object. If the file does not exist and createfile is not set to True, an error occurs.

The TextStream object parameters are as follows:

Filename	The name of the file to open or create
Openfor	Whether to open for reading (1), writing (2), or appending (8)
Overwrite	Whether to overwrite an existing file of the same name
Lockread	Whether to lock reading of the file
Lockwrite	Whether to lock writing to the file

Example: This example creates a file, writes a test line, and closes the file.

```
<HTML>
<BODY>
<H3>Textstream test</H3>
<%
Set OutStream = Server.CreateObject("MS.TextStream")
OutStream.CreateTextFile "c:\tsworks.txt", , True
OutStream.WriteLine "This is a test..."
OutStream.CloseTextFile
%>
</BODY>
</HTML>
```

Next we cover the Browser Capabilities component of ASP.

Browser Capabilities Object

When a browser connects to the Web server, it automatically sends a User Agent HTTP header. This header is an ASCII string that identifies the browser and its version number. The Browser Capabilities component compares this header to entries in a BROWSCAP.INI file. If the component does not find a match for the header in the BROWSCAP.INI file, it takes on the default browser properties. If the component does not find a match and default browser settings have not been specified in the Browscap.ini file, it sets every property to the string *Unknown*.

Example: The following example uses the Browser Capabilities component to display a table showing some of the capabilities of the current browser:

```
<% Set bc = Server.CreateObject("MSWC.BrowserType") %>
<table border=1>
<tr><td>Browser</td><td>  <%= bc.browser  %>
<tr><td>Version</td><td>  <%= bc.version  %>  </td></TR>
<tr><td>Frames</td><td>
<%  if (bc.frames = TRUE) then  %>  TRUE
<%  else  %>  FALSE
<%  end if  %> </td></TR>
<tr><td>Tables</td><td>
<%  if (bc.tables = TRUE) then  %>  TRUE
<%  else  %> FALSE
<%  end if  %> </td></TR>
<tr><td>BackgroundSounds</td><td>
<%  if (bc.BackgroundSounds = TRUE) then  %>  TRUE
<%  else  %> FALSE
<%  end if  %> </td></TR>
<tr><td>VBScript</td><td>
<%  if (bc.vbscript = TRUE) then  %>  TRUE
<%  else  %> FALSE
<%  end if  %> </td></TR>
<tr><td>JScript</td><td>
<%  if (bc.javascript = TRUE) then  %>  TRUE
<%  else  %> FALSE
<%  end if  %> </td></TR>
</table>
```

Add properties or new browser definitions to this component by updating the BROWSCAP.INI file. In the following example, the <parent> tag allows the second browser definition to inherit from the first, so that the Microsoft Internet Explorer 3.01 definition inherits all the properties of the Microsoft Internet Explorer 3.0 definition (for example, frames=TRUE, tables=TRUE, and cookies=TRUE). The definition adds platform-specific information by adding the line platform=Win95, and overwrites the version information in the line version=3.01.

```
;;ie 3.0
[IE 3.0]
browser=IE
Version=3.0
majorver=#3
minorver=#0
frames=TRUE
```

```
tables=TRUE
cookies=TRUE
backgroundsounds=TRUE
vbscript=TRUE
javascript=TRUE
ActiveControls=TRUE
Win16=False
beta=False
AK=False
SK=False
AOL=False

;;ie 3.01
[Mozilla/2.0 (compatible; MSIE 3.01*; Windows 95)]
parent=IE 3.0
version=3.01
minorver=01
platform=Win95

; Default Browser
[Default Browser Capability Settings]
browser=Default
frames=FALSE
tables=TRUE
cookies=FALSE
backgroundsounds=FALSE
vbscript=FALSE
javascript=FALSE
```

We close our tutorial at this point. In Chapter 4, having introduced the Visual InterDev development environment, we return to working on ASP in the context of a Commerce Server store.

Commerce Server Development Environment (Visual InterDev)

Chapter 3 discussed the concept of Active Server Pages and provided a tutorial with example usage of ASP commands and components. So far we have been talking only about the concepts. This chapter introduces the Visual InterDev development environment and proceeds to use this tool to view, enhance, customize, and extend Site Server Enterprise Edition with emphasis on the Commerce Server technology of Site Server. A client said to me once, "The development environment makes or breaks a platform."

Included with the Site Server Enterprise Edition is the Microsoft Visual Inter-Dev (VI) application development environment. While you are free to use any development environment, VI[1] increases developers' productivity by providing a

---

1. Not to be mistaken for the old Unix editor called VI.

visual, integrated development environment specialized for building Web applications.

This chapter is divided into three parts:

1. Visual InterDev Key Features for Site Server Developers: Provides a brief introduction to VI and its key features. This section does not require any software installation and serves as an evaluator's overview.

2. Visual InterDev Applications. Builds upon the concepts covered in the first part to showcase applications of VI to Commerce Server stores. This part requires Commerce Server and VI software installations and includes programming exercises for developers of Commerce Server sites. A few illustrations are provided to allow reviewers to see the end results of an exercise.

3. Commerce Server Store Customization Features: Builds upon the first two parts of the chapter. This final part includes a discussion of some common methods of customizing and enhancing Commerce Server stores.

VISUAL INTERDEV KEY FEATURES FOR SITE SERVER DEVELOPERS

This section briefly introduces Visual InterDev's key features for Site Server developers. Visual InterDev can be described as an integrated development/editor tool, a powerful database tool, and a complete and extensible system. Each of these is further discussed below.

An Integrated Development/Editor Tool

Visual InterDev increases developers' productivity by providing a visual, integrated development/editor environment for building Web applications. Visual InterDev's editor features include the following: Visual Basic Script and JScript (ASP) development languages for Web page and Web database application development; and color-coded lines to visually separate scripts, comments, HTML, and other tags and Internet components. The editor is equivalent to Front Page editor, which eases the learning curve and allows designers and developers to work on the same page concurrently.

Developers often have to use separate environments for application and database development. VI includes both.

A Powerful, Integrated Database Tool

Visual InterDev's database development features include the following:

- Open database connectivity (ODBC) for working with all leading database management systems on the market, including Microsoft SQL server, Microsoft Access, Microsoft FoxPro, Oracle, Sybase, Informix, IBM DB2, Borland dBASE, and others

- Query designers to visually construct and test SQL statements

- Database wizards such as the one used to build a Commerce Server customer data browser application. (Please see "Building a Commerce Server Customer Data Browser Application" later in this chapter.)

A Complete and Extensible System

VI includes a number of editors and technologies, such as Microsoft Image Composer, Microsoft Music Producer, and Microsoft Media Manager discussed here.

Microsoft Image Composer is useful for developers who wish to modify or create images for a Web site. It recognizes popular image file formats, including Adobe PhotoShop, GIF, and JPG formats. Microsoft Image Composer has a command that automatically saves images to the Microsoft Visual InterDev project. For detailed information on this tool, see the Microsoft Image Composer Web site at *http://www.microsoft.com/imagecomposer/*.

Visual InterDev also includes a music creation tool for creating sound effects used on Web sites and store pages, Microsoft Music Producer. It simplifies music creation with prebuilt musical styles. Styles (templates) define entire musical genres (such as samba or Texas swing), as well as musical moods and accompaniment of instruments. Over 100 predefined styles are included.

Finally, Media Manager is a utility for developers looking to manage dynamic and static media assets such as images, sound and video clips, HTML files, office documents, and so forth. Media Manager allows developers to search, preview, play, and retrieve media assets stored in Media Manager libraries. You can create Media Manager libraries either on a local machine or on a network server for multiple user access.

For a full set of product features, please refer to VI product documentation or visit *http://www.microsoft.com/vInterDev*.

VISUAL INTERDEV APPLICATIONS

This section requires Commerce Server and VI software installations. Commerce Server installation steps are provided with the CD in the back of the book, under

DOCS\COMMERCE\INSTALLATION.DOC, and are reprinted in Appendix A. This section includes programming exercises for Commerce Server site developers. The following sections are included:

- Developing an MSCS Sample Store with VI

- Moving a Store to a New Location

- Working with Active Server Pages

- Working with Objects

- Working with Store Database Schema

- Using Links to View Store Page Flow

- Building a Commerce Server Customer Data Browser Application

Developing an MSCS Sample Store with VI

Building a Commerce Server sample store such as Adventure Works or Microsoft Press is a straightforward process. These steps were outlined in Chapter 1, in the section "Build Process." Having created a store, follow these simple steps to prepare an existing sample store for customization and enhancement under VI.[2]

1. Create a Visual InterDev workspace. From the main menu of Visual InterDev, click File, New Workspace, and enter a name for the new workspace or open an existing workspace. The name of the newly created workspace appears in the upper left frame.

2. Create a Visual InterDev project. Right-click on the newly created workspace and select Add New Project to the workspace. Also, at this point, you have the option to open a brand new project or add to an existing one. Since this is your first, choose to open a brand new project here.

3. Enter a Commerce Server name (IIS) for the Web server name.

4. Insert store files into the project. Include all *.ASA files. Select *.* in the lower drop-down list to see all files in the store. Browse to the store directory, such as //COMMERCESERVER/STORES/STORENAME/SHOP, or in the corresponding directory path for the store management application, such as //COMMERCESERVER/STORES/STORENAME/MANAGEMENT. Substitute your site-specific parameters in above.

5. Add a DSN to the Visual InterDev project for the store when needed. This step is necessary only if the store database is modified or accessed during the session in VI. DSNs in VI also serve a second purpose, which

---

2. In later releases this process is automated.

is providing a session-level connection for database component use. For this reason, a DSN definition is automatically created at the project's session level when you insert a project DSN. Move the generated code to the application side by cutting and pasting the code into the *On_ApplicationStart* section of GLOBAL.ASA from *On_SessionStart*. Otherwise, if database components are not required, click Edit, Undo to remove the automatic addition.

6. Having completed the work on the enhanced store, copy the enhanced files back to the original Commerce Server directory.

Moving a Store to a New Location

Alternatively you may move your newly created store to a VI project directory. If you move a store out of the Commerce Server installation tree, Host Administrator will no longer list that store. Additionally, the Store Manager pages will not show whether the store is open or closed or whether it has changed from one state to the other. However, you may find that this alternative better suits your needs.

To make a store work in a new directory, you must specify a new path for the Order Processing Pipeline configuration (.PCF) file for both the shop and management applications. You must also use Internet Service Manager to change the three virtual directories associated with your store.

Before starting these procedures, move your store, including all its associated files, into a new directory.

To specify a new path for a relocated store,

1. After moving your store into a new directory, start your browser and type in the URL for your store.

2. Go to the Shop directory for the relocated store.

3. Open GLOBAL.ASA.

4. Locate the following line:

```
pathPipeConfig = Server.MapPath("/NewStoreName") & "\..\⤸3
    config\pipeline.pcf"
```

5. Duplicate this line and then comment the original out with a REM statement.

6. Create a new pointer by editing the duplicate line as follows:

```
pathPipeConfig = "NewStore_Path\config\pipeline.pcf"
```

---

3. The ⤸ symbol indicates a line that had to be broken for the printed page. Treat it as a single line when typing or editing it.

7. Save GLOBAL.ASA.

8. Go to the Manager directory for the relocated store.

9. Use Notepad (or another text editor) to open DEFAULT.ASP.

10. Repeat steps 4 and 5.

11. Save DEFAULT.ASP.

    To change virtual directory paths for your relocated store,

1. On the Start menu, point to Programs, point to Microsoft Internet Server, then click Internet Service Manager.

2. Open the WWW service and then click the Directories tab.

3. Edit the three directories associated with the relocated store. For example, the virtual directory C:\MICROSOFT COMMERCE SERVER\ STORES\NEWSTORE\ASSETS might become C:\NEWSTORE\ASSETS.

4. Apply changes.

5. To verify that you have moved the store successfully, point your browser at the store's management page (*http://hostname/store-name_mgr/default.asp*). A relocated store will not appear in the Commerce Server Host Administrator.

    Having prepared or moved the newly created store, you may view, enhance, and customize your site.

Working with Active Server Pages

The power of Commerce Server pages is derived from the mix of HTML, scripting, object tags, plug-ins, graphics, and a number of other elements. Figure 4-1 illustrates a store page viewed in VI editor. Note that ASP code is shown in gray in Figure 4-1.

Working with Objects

The exercise below demonstrates how to enhance an existing store page with a Calendar object.[4]

    To insert an Active object into a page, follow these simple steps.

1. Click on the page you want to enhance. The page appears in the right frame.

2. Click a line in the text where you want to add the object.

---

4. The process of inserting Java code is similar. You may also wish to experiment with other possible scenarios.

3. Right-click on this spot to line the menu for inserting objects.

Figure 4-1. *ASP color coding in VI editor.*

An ever-increasing number of objects are available for insertion into a page from this menu. BuyNow and Calendar controls are included on the list.[5] See Figure 4-2.

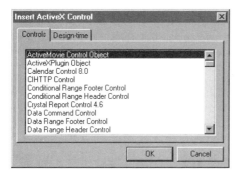

Figure 4-2. *ActiveX control selection box of VI.*

Simply selecting one of these objects from the selection box automatically inserts all HTML code and object tags required into the ASP page.

---

5. The product documentation includes a complete list of objects and their attributes.

Working with Store Database Schema

In the process of designing and developing a store, you will often view or modify the database tables and schema. The purpose may range from database design and development to adding a trigger for interface tables. This section covers the following exercises:

■ Editing data in store tables

■ Generating a Commerce Server sample store schema

■ Viewing a store's database schema

■ Modifying a store's table design

■ Building a database table trigger

Editing data in store tables

In a number of cases, you will want to edit a Commerce Server store database table for customizations. To edit a Commerce Server store database table using VI,

1. Switch to the Data View by clicking the Data View tab.

2. Locate and double-click the table, as illustrated for the table AW_dept, the department table of the Adventure Works sample store. These tables are part of this sample store's database schema. You can enter data directly into the table.

3. Close the table view to save.

Viewing a store's database schema

This exercise focuses on VI's database capabilities as applied to Commerce Server store schema. Commerce Server views VI as a database CASE tool as well as a development environment. For a store to function properly, both the pages and database schema have to be in sync.

The following graphical representation of the Adventure Works sample store's department table was generated using VI in approximately two minutes (see Figure 4-3). Figure 4-4 illustrates the schema of the Adventure Works sample store. Click to Data View, select the Adventure Works tables, and drag them to the left frame for a visual representation of the Adventure Works store schema.

Modifying a store's table design

To switch to design mode, select a table, right-click, and choose Design. The store table is modified visually from this window. Modifications include adding a table row, deleting a table row, updating a table row, and entering data directly into the row.

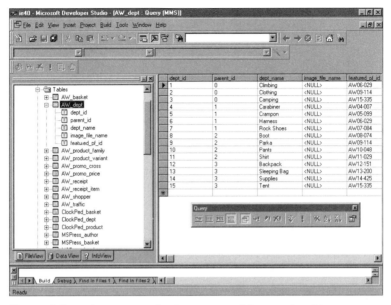

Figure 4-3. *Adventure Works department table viewed in VI.*

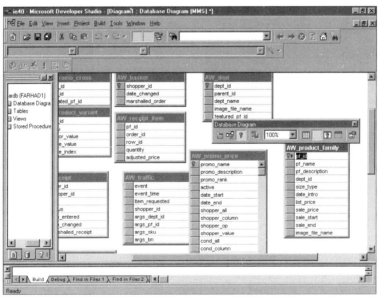

Figure 4-4. *Schema of Adventure Works viewed in VI.*

Building a database table trigger and stored procedure

Triggers[6] and stored procedures are two additional areas where VI can add value. By providing a more powerful and visual environment to develop triggers and stored procedures for stores than are available from the database toolset, VI helps increase developers' productivity. Stores may use triggers for database integrity, cascading inserts, deletes, and updates, or for interfacing or staging table population.

To create a trigger for a store, locate and right-click on the table in Data View and click Add Trigger. An editing view opens. See Figure 4-5. Notice the multiple views that allow a developer to code the trigger efficiently by providing all the views needed in one glance—from design and content, to the editor's view where the trigger is under development. Test data is entered into one view, column names looked up in the second, and code developed in the third. You may add other views as needed. Also note that all trigger header information is color-coded in green.

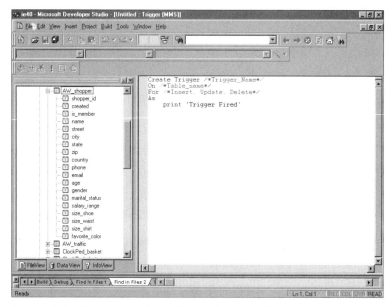

Figure 4-5. *Trigger edit view of VI for shopper table customization.*

A close relative of triggers, stored procedures greatly enhance the power, efficiency, and flexibility of SQL Server and dramatically improve the performance of SQL statements and batches. Stored procedures are preparsed and are compiled the first time SQL Server is started. Thereafter, the compiled version resides in memory, eliminating re-compilation overhead and increasing performance.

---

6. A trigger is a database program written in Standard Query Language. This program is executed when an insert, delete, or update operation is performed on the table. Stores may use triggers for database integrity, cascading inserts, deletes, and updates, or for interfacing or staging table population.

The process of creating a stored procedure is similar to the process of creating a trigger. For example, the Clock Peddler \SHOP\GLOBAL.ASA file contains the following query:

```
Call MSCSContent.AddQuery("department", "select * from↵
   ClockPed_dept where dept_id = :1")
```

In VI, you could create the following stored procedure named *clock_dep*:

```
create procedure clock_dept @id int as
select * from clockped_dept where dept_id=convert(numeric,@id)
```

Then modify the AddQuery statement in the Clock Peddler \SHOP\GOBAL.ASA file as follows:

```
Call MSCSContent.AddQuery("department", "exec clock_dept :1")
```

For more information about stored procedures and triggers, see "Using Stored Procedures and Triggers" in the *SQL Server Database Developer's Companion* of *SQL Server Books Online*.

Using Links to View Store Page Flow

Editing pages and schema are two valuable VI features. Among other features, the Link view is worth noting. Link view allows visual navigation of links from a page such that the customization or enhancement that spans many pages of a store may be easily followed through completely. To activate the Link view, click Tools, View Links on WWW, and enter a URL. See Figure 4-6.

Building a Commerce Server Customer Data Browser Application

VI includes powerful wizards capable of generating ASP applications as well. One such wizard, the FormWizard, is exemplified here. Let's take another example. Let's say you want to browse and edit the shopper information from a browser. Follow the steps to build such an application.

To launch the development environment,

1. Select the Programs folder and then the Visual InterDev folder.
   To create a new Web project using a wizard,

1. From the File menu, choose New.

2. Click the Projects tab and select the Web Project Wizard by single-clicking.

3. Enter *Customers* in the Project Name input box and click OK. Make sure Web Project Wizard is selected.

4. Now select your Internet Information Web server by typing in your Commerce Web server's name, and leave Connect Using SSL unchecked. Click Next.

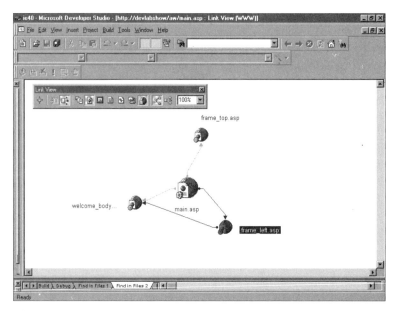

Figure 4-6. *The Link view of the MAIN.ASP page of the Adventure Works sample store.*

5. Leave the Create A New Web default option checked and click Finish. You can choose to have Visual InterDev automatically index your site for full text searches if you want to.

Upon completion, you have successfully created the Customers project. To add a database connection to the project,

1. Right-click on the newly created project and select Add Data Connection.

2. Select an existing ODBC DSN or create a new DSN.

3. Verify the properties for the database connection and close the Properties window.

Having created the project, we now move to create the application using the Data Form Wizard.

To create a data form using the Data Form Wizard,

1. From the File menu, choose New.

2. Click the File Wizard tab and select the Data Form Wizard by single-clicking.

3. Enter *browse* as the filename and click OK.

4. Select your database connection.

5. Enter a title for the page, such as Customer Support Browser Application. Click Next.

6. In Choose A Record Source, step 2 of 7 of the wizard, select Table as the source. Click Next.

7. Select columns of interest from the *AW_shopper* table or click the ">>" button to include all columns. Click Next.

8. Specify editing functions of interest for your application. Click Next.

9. Specify viewing options of interest. Click Next.

10. Specify the look and feel of pages. Click Next.

11. Finally, click Finish.

From this project, you could add a column to the database using the VI design features and regenerate the example above for your personalized table in Commerce Server. No HTML or scripting is required for generating typical Commerce Server applications in VI.

1. Right-click on the BROWSERLIST.ASP file generated by the wizard.

2. Select Preview in Browser.

Two views of this application are illustrated below. First, Figure 4-7 illustrates the All-Shoppers view of the application. This view is used to locate a shopper when calling in for customer support. Second, Figure 4-8 illustrates the page for editing individual shopper information.

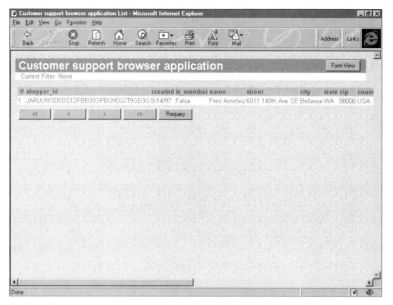

Figure 4-7. *The All-Shoppers view.*

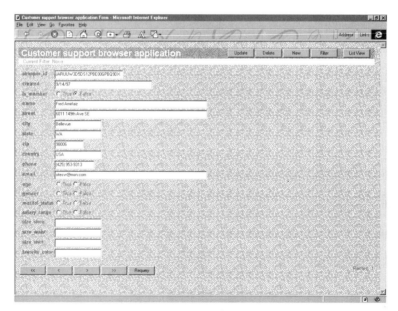

Figure 4-8. *Single Shopper view.*

COMMERCE SERVER STORE CUSTOMIZATION

VI is a powerful tool for implementing Commerce Server customization. You can implement a number of common customizations and enhancements to a Commerce Server store such as working with traffic data and implementing promotions. Some of these topics are discussed below. Use VI and NT/IIS tools discussed in Appendix J to implement these Commerce Server customizations.

Commerce Server's Component Reference documentation included on the companion CD of this book is a prerequisite for this section. An excerpt from this document is included below to give a flavor for the topics covered:

"The Commerce Server components are a group of ActiveX™ server components that provide the run-time environment for the presentation of online stores. These components are registered on your system as ActiveX server components when you install Commerce Server. Like the components included with Active Server Pages (ASP), Commerce Server components support methods and properties that you call and set from within the Visual Basic® Scripting Edition (VBScript) or JScript server-side code that runs your Commerce Server store."

Commerce Server components, however, provide an extensive set of services that Active Server Pages do not provide, services that simplify and automate many of the tasks that you would have to perform manually to build a working store with ASP components alone. Such tasks include the reliable maintenance of state data across multiple sessions, the easy access to and modification of content stored in a database, the logging of store traffic for marketing and diagnostic purposes, and the automated processing of order data through the Order Processing Pipeline (OPP). Commerce Server defines the server components listed in Table 4-1.

This chapter describes the Commerce Server components and includes definitions of the methods and properties that they support. For a tour of the online stores that use these components, see the section "Building a Store from the Foundation Up" in Chapter 1.

The remaining part of this chapter enumerates some common tasks, customizations, and enhancements to a Commerce Server store.

Table 4-1. *Alphabetical list of Commerce Server components.*

Component	Description
Content	Provides a cache in which to store string variables that you associate with data source names (DSNs) and SQL queries.
DataFunctions	Supports a collection of functions that validate the format of data for database storage or for processing by the OPP.
Datasource	Executes queries that you specify. These can be SQL queries that you construct at runtime, or that you have associated with string variables and stored in a Content component cache.
DBStorage	Supports flexible interaction with the database, primarily for the storage of receipt and order information.
Dictionary	Provides for the in-memory storage of name-value pairs.
MessageManager	Provides a cache in which to store shopper messages that the OPP uses to describe error conditions.
OrderForm	Supports the in-memory storage of shopper and purchase information for the current shopping session.
OrderPipeline	Loads the pipeline configuration (.PCF) file that contains the pipeline configuration information for your store.
Page	Simplifies the layout of HTML pages and the interaction between these pages and the data sources used by your store.
SimpleList	Includes a list of variants.
StandardsManager	Supports the creation, deletion, and retrieval of unique shopper identifiers.
TrafficLogFile	Supports logging store events to a text file.
TrafficTable	Supports logging store events to database tables.

Working with Traffic Data

Commerce Server can collect data about your store traffic that can provide useful information for performance tuning or merchandising. Commerce Server can send this traffic data either to a log file or to a database table. You specify the option you want by creating an instance of either the TrafficTable component or the TrafficLogfile component in the GLOBAL.ASA file.

Collecting traffic data in a database table

To collect traffic data in a database file, you create and initialize an instance of the TrafficTable component in the \SHOP\GLOBAL.ASA file. Also in the GLOBAL.ASA file, you store the object reference in the Application object under the name MSCSTraffic. On the page where you want to log traffic, you create a page variable that references the object, and then call the object's LogTraffic method.

To set up logging of traffic data to a database table,

1. In your database, create a table for storing traffic data. The columns you create in the database table determine what data is collected. The column names must exactly match those shown in Table 4-2 below (substitute your own argument names for *argname*).

Table 4-2. *Alphabetical list of Traffic Table column names and description.*

Column Name	Data Collected
args_*argname*	Logs a page or form argument.
event	Logs an identifier that specifies the source of the event.
event_time	Logs the time the event occurred.
http_*argname*	Logs environment variables, such as REFER and USER_AGENT (for example, *http_REFER*). Note that, in names containing hyphens, an underscore is used instead of a hyphen because database column names cannot contain hyphens.
item_requested	Logs the page being called.
remote_addr	Logs the IP address of the client machine.
remote_host	Logs the host name of the client machine (in some cases, this value may be an IP address).
shopper_id	Logs the shopper ID.
store_name	Logs the name of the store, which is obtained from the *StoreKey* specified when initializing the TrafficTable object.

2. In the \SHOP\GLOBAL.ASA file, create and initialize an instance of the TrafficTable component.

The following example is from the Adventure Works \SHOP\ GLOBAL.ASA file:

```
REM Database traffic server
Set MSCSTraffic = Server.CreateObject("Commerce.TrafficTable")
call MSCSTraffic.InitTraffic(MSCSDataSource, "AW", "AW_traffic")
```

3. The CreateObject method creates an instance of the TrafficTable object, which is given the variable name MSCSTraffic. The InitTraffic method initializes the instance with the data source (MSCSDataSource), the *StoreKey* (AW), and the name of the database table (AW_traffic) to be used for storing traffic data. The value of *StoreKey* is inserted into the database table in the *store_name* column.

Also in the \SHOP\GLOBAL.ASA file, store the MSCSTraffic object as a variable in the Application object. The following example is from the Adventure Works \SHOP\GLOBAL.ASA file:

```
Set Application("MSCSTraffic") = MSCSTraffic
```

4. On the page where you want to log traffic events, create a page variable that references the MSCSTraffic object in the Application object, and then call the LogTraffic method. In the Adventure Works store, this is done in the \SHOP\INCLUDE\SHOP.ASP file, which is included in every store template:

```
REM --Log a traffic event
Set Traffic = Application("MSCSTraffic")
call Traffic.LogTraffic(mscsShopperID, 1,↵
    CStr(Request.ServerVariables("SCRIPT_NAME")), Page.Context)
```

The page variable named Traffic references the MSCSTraffic object. The LogTraffic method logs events to the database table. The parameters to the LogTraffic method pass the shopper ID, the event number, the event requested (in this case, the URL of the current page), and the context.

Collecting traffic data in a log file

To collect traffic data in a log file, you create and initialize an instance of the Traffic-Logfile object in the \SHOP\GLOBAL.ASA file. Also in the GLOBAL.ASA file, you store the object reference in the Application object under the name MSCSTraffic. On the page where you want to log traffic, you create a page variable that references the object, and then call the object's LogTraffic method.

You can experiment with logging traffic data to a file by using the Adventure Works store. In the default installation, the log file code in the \SHOP\ GLOBAL.ASA file is commented out. However, you can remove the REM comments and experiment with the parameters as shown in the following example (additional code was added to illustrate its use).

```
REM Example file traffic server
Set MSCSTraffic = Server.CreateObject("Commerce.TrafficLogfile")
MSCSTraffic.ColumnDelimiter=":"
MSCSTraffic.RowDelimiter=chr(10)
MSCSTraffic.BlankSubstitution="-"
call MSCSTraffic.InitTraffic("AW", "c:\AW_traffic.log",↵
    "store_name", "shopper_id", "item_requested",↵
    "args_dept_id", "event_time")
```

To set up logging of traffic data to a file,

1. In the \SHOP\GLOBAL.ASA file, create an instance of the TrafficLogfile object.

```
REM Example file traffic server
Set MSCSTraffic = Server.CreateObject("Commerce.TrafficLogfile")
```

The CreateObject method creates an instance of the TrafficLogfile object, which is given the variable name MSCSTraffic.

2. Set the properties of the TrafficLogfile object to specify the formatting of the log file.

```
MSCSTraffic.ColumnDelimiter=":"
MSCSTraffic.RowDelimiter=chr(10)
MSCSTraffic.BlankSubstitution="-"
```

Table 4-3 shows the properties of the TrafficLogfile object that you can use to specify the formatting of the log file.

3. Initialize the TrafficLogfile object.

```
call MSCSTraffic.InitTraffic("AW", "c:\AW_traffic.log",↵
    "store_name", "shopper_id", "item_requested", ↵
    "args_dept_id", "event_time")
```

The InitTraffic method initializes the object with the store name (AW), the path to the file that is to be used to store traffic data, and arguments that specify what data is to be collected. If you specify store_name as one of the arguments, the store name that you specify is inserted into the log file (see Table 4-4).

4. In the \SHOP\GLOBAL.ASA file, store the MSCSTraffic object as a variable in the Application object, as shown in the following example:

```
Set Application("MSCSTraffic") = MSCSTraffic
```

5. On the page where you want to log traffic events, create a page variable that references the MSCSTraffic object in the Application object, and then call the LogTraffic method. The following example is from the Adventure Works \SHOP\INCLUDE\SHOP.ASP template, which is included in every store page template.

```
REM --Log a traffic event
Set Traffic = Application("MSCSTraffic")
call Traffic.LogTraffic(mscsShopperID, 1,↵
    CStr(Request.ServerVariables("SCRIPT_NAME")), Page.Context)
```

Table 4-3. *TrafficLogFile object's properties.*

Object Property	Description
BlankSubstitution = *"string"*	Specifies the character to be used when there is no data for a particular row or cell (for example, MSCSTraffic.Blank-Substitution = "").
ColumnDelimiter = *"string"*	Specifies the ASCII characters used to separate the columns in log file (for example, MSCSTraffic.ColumnDelimiter = "." specifies that a period is to be used as a column delimiter, and MSCSTraffic.ColumnDelimiter = chr(22) specifies the ASCII code for a tab character).
ColumnSubstitution = *"string"*	Specifies the character to be used as the column delimiter if the data itself contains the character previously specified as MSCSTraffic.ColumnDelimiter (using the previous example, MSCSTraffic.ColumnSubstitution = "," specifies that a comma is to be used if the data contains a tab character).
LocaleDate = *localeID*	Specifies the hexadecimal code for the locale, used for formatting dates in the log file (for example, LocaleDate = 0x0409).
LocaleTime = *localeID*	Specifies the hexadecimal code for the locale, used for formatting times in the log file (for example, LocaleTime = 0x0409).
RowDelimiter = *"string"*	Specifies the character used to separate the rows in log file (for example, MSCSTraffic.RowDelimiter = chr(10) specifies the ASCII code for a line break [newline character], which is to be used as the row delimiter).
RowSubstitution = *"string"*	Specifies the character to be used as the row delimiter if the data itself contains the character previously specified as MSCSTraffic.RowDelimiter. Using the previous example, MSCSTraffic.RowSubstitution = "|" specifies that a "pipe" character is to be used if the data contains a line break.

Table 4-4. *Alphabetical list of TrafficLogFile object's arguments and associated descriptions.*

Argument	Data Collected
args_*argname*	Logs a page or form argument.
event	Logs a number that specifies the source of the event.
event_time	Logs the time the event occurred.
http_*argname*	Logs environment variables, such as REFER (for example, *http_REFER*). Note that, in names containing hyphens, an underscore is used instead of a hyphen because database column names cannot contain hyphens.
item_requested	Logs the page template being called.
remote_addr	Logs the IP address of the client machine.
remote_host	Logs the host name of the client machine (in some cases, this value may be an IP address).
shopper_id	Logs the shopper ID.
store_name	Logs the name of the store, which is obtained from the store name specified when initializing the TrafficLogfile object.

The traffic log this example produced contains entries such as the following:

```
AW:---:/aw/default.asp:---:4/18/97 3 49 PM
AW:---:/aw/welcome_left.asp:---:4/18/97 3 49 PM
AW:---:/aw/welcome_top.asp:---:4/18/97 3 49 PM
AW:---:/aw/welcome_body.asp:---:4/18/97 3 49 PM
AW:---:/aw/welcome_top.asp:---:4/18/97 3 49 PM
AW:---:/aw/welcome_left.asp:---:4/18/97 3 49 PM
AW:---:/aw/welcome_lookup.asp:---:4/18/97 3 49 PM
AW:0GTP45N6P0S12H130GM00D01WEG8WHRV:/aw/main.asp:---:4/18/97 3 49 PM
AW:0GTP45N6P0S12H130GM00D01WEG8WHRV:/aw/frame_left.asp:---:4/18/97 3 49 PM
AW:0GTP45N6P0S12H130GM00D01WEG8WHRV:/aw/frame_top.asp:---:4/18/97 3 50 PM
AW:0GTP45N6P0S12H130GM00D01WEG8WHRV:/aw/lobby.asp:---:4/18/97 3 50 PM
AW:0GTP45N6P0S12H130GM00D01WEG8WHRV:/aw/product_frame.asp:---:4/18/97 3 50 PM
AW:0GTP45N6P0S12H130GM00D01WEG8WHRV:/aw/frame_top.asp:---:4/18/97 3 50 PM
AW:0GTP45N6P0S12H130GM00D01WEG8WHRV:/aw/frame_left.asp:---:4/18/97 3 50 PM
AW:0GTP45N6P0S12H130GM00D01WEG8WHRV:/aw/product_frame.asp:---:4/18/97 3 50 PM
AW:0GTP45N6P0S12H130GM00D01WEG8WHRV:/aw/subdept.asp:8:4/18/97 3 50 PM
AW:0GTP45N6P0S12H130GM00D01WEG8WHRV:/aw/frame_top.asp:---:4/18/97 3 50 PM
AW:0GTP45N6P0S12H130GM00D01WEG8WHRV:/aw/frame_left.asp:---:4/18/97 3 50 PM
```

Implementing Promotions

Commerce Server supports several types of promotions:

- Sale pricing: You can offer a sale price on any product and specify start and end dates for the sale.

- Cross-sell promotions: You can offer a related product for sale when a shopper selects a particular product.

- Price promotions: You can set up a number of different types of discount promotions, such as member pricing, quantity discounts, and so on.

Implementing sale pricing

Sale pricing uses the following elements:

- The store's Order Processing Pipeline must contain the *QueryProdInfo* and *SaleAdjust* components.

- The product table in the database must contain the following three columns, which are used by the pipeline: *sale_start*, *sale_price*, and *sale_end*.

- The .ASP template that generates the product page must contain the appropriate script to display the sale price.

In addition, you can configure the store's Manager application to easily start and stop the sale pricing.

Product table When you use the Store Builder Wizard or the Starter Store Copy Wizard, the new store's product table by default contains the three columns that are necessary to support sale pricing: *sale_start*, *sale_price*, and *sale_end*. If you build a store from scratch, the product table must contain these three columns with these exact names. The values in these columns are used by the pipeline to determine whether a sale price is currently in effect for the product.

Pipeline components The Product Information stage of the store's Order Processing Pipeline must contain the *QueryProdInfo* component. This component runs a query to retrieve information about the product from the product table in the database. For each column in the product table—including the three columns that support sale pricing—this component sets a name-value pair prefixed by *_product_* on the Order Form. When the *QueryProdInfo* component has run, the order form contains values for *_product_sale_start*, *_product_sale_price,* and *_product_sale_end*.

The Item Price Adjust stage of the pipeline must contain the SaleAdjust component. This component determines whether the current date is between the dates given for *_product_sale_start* and *_product_sale_end* on the Order Form. (Note that the sale ends at the beginning of the *_product_sale_end* date. Therefore, if the *_product_sale_end* date is April 27, the sale price is used until midnight on April 26.) If the sale price is currently in effect, the SaleAdjust component sets the *_iadjust_currentprice* property of the Order Form to the value of *_product_sale_price*.

Shop templates   The .ASP template or templates that display the product must contain the appropriate script to display the sale price. You can examine the Adventure Works store templates to see an example implementation of sale pricing. Figure 4-9 illustrates the templates that are used in Adventure Works.

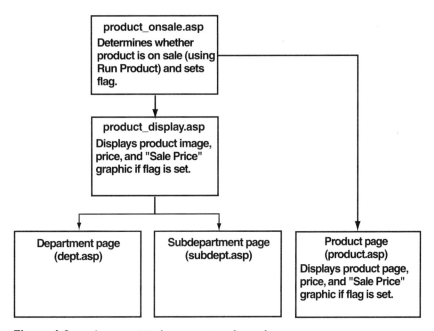

Figure 4-9.   *Adventure Works promotional template pages.*

In the Adventure Works store, the \SHOP\INCLUDE\PRODUCT_ONSALE.ASP template determines whether the product is on sale and sets a flag that is used by the PRODUCT_DISPLAY.ASP and PRODUCT.ASP templates to determine whether the Sale Price graphic should be displayed.

The script in the PRODUCT_ONSALE.ASP template executes the product-purchase query, which returns all the columns for the product. The value of the *list_price* column is added to the Order Form. The RunProduct method then processes the order form through the first few stages of the pipeline to set a value for *_iadjust _currentprice*. The template script then compares the value for _iadjust_currentprice_ with the value for _list_price_ and sets a flag named _is_on_sale_ to 1 if the product is on sale, and 0 if it isn't.

The PRODUCT_DISPLAY.ASP template displays the product image and the value of _iadjust_currentprice_. This template includes the PRODUCT_ONSALE.ASP template, which sets the _is_on_sale_ flag. The PRODUCT_DISPLAY.ASP template uses the _is_on_sale_ flag to determine whether to display the Sale Price graphic.

The product and its price are displayed to the shopper on the following pages:

- On the Department page (for example, Clothing), generated by the DEPT.ASP template

- On the Subdepartment page (for example, Boots), generated by the SUBDEPT.ASP template

- On the individual Product page (for example, Dunes boots), generated by the PRODUCT.ASP template

The PRODUCT_DISPLAY.ASP template is included in both the DEPT.ASP and the DUBDEPT.ASP templates. The PRODUCT_ONSALE.ASP template is included directly in the PRODUCT.ASP template.

In addition, the Shopping Cart page (ORDER_BASKET.ASP) and the Receipt page (RECEIPT.ASP) display the value of _iadjust_currentprice_ in a Today's Price column using the following script:

```
<% = MSCSDataFunctions.Money(CLng(lineItem.[_iadjust_currentprice])) %>
```

Manager templates The Adventure Works Manager application provides an example of an easy-to-use interface for modifying the values in the _sale_start_, _sale_price_, and _sale_end_ columns in the database. Clicking the Products link on the Adventure Works Store Manager page displays the Products page, from which you can either edit sale information for an existing product or add a new product. Clicking an SKU number displays the Edit Product page (PRODUCT_EDIT.ASP), on which you can modify the existing sale price and start and end dates. Clicking the Add New Product link displays the New Product page (PRODUCT_NEW.ASP), on which you can add a new product and its sale pricing information to the database.

Both the PRODUCT_EDIT.ASP and the PRODUCT_NEW.ASP templates display a form containing the fields that identify a product, including fields for _sale_price, sale_start,_ and _sale_end_. See these templates for the scripts used to edit an existing sale or add a new one.

Implementing cross-sell promotions

When a shopper selects a particular product, you can offer a related product for sale. The Volcano Coffee and the Adventure Works starter stores provide examples of two slightly different types of cross-sell promotions.

The Volcano Coffee store demonstrates an up-sell promotion. When the shopper adds a product to the basket, a message is displayed suggesting "Why not get something better for a change?" When the shopper clicks the link, the product page for the related product is displayed. If the shopper then clicks the Add To Basket button, the original product is removed from the basket and replaced with the up-sell product.

The Adventure Works store demonstrates a cross-sell promotion. When the shopper displays the Product page for a product that has a cross-sell promotion in effect, the image of the related product is displayed on the page under the heading See Also.

The Adventure Works store implements cross-sell promotions using the following elements:

- The database contains a cross-sell promotions table that specifies which related product is to be displayed when the original product is selected.

- Two queries are used to retrieve the data from the AW_promo_cross table and to retrieve data about the related product from the AW_product_family table.

- The Product page (PRODUCT.ASP) contains a script that displays the related product under the heading See Also.

- The Adventure Works Store Manager application provides several pages for viewing, editing, deleting, and adding new cross-sell promotions.

Database table The Adventure Works store identifies a particular product by a number called the product family ID (*pf_id*). Variations of a product are identified by an SKU number. For example, the *pf_id* for the Morro rock shoe is AW07-084, and the individual SKUs for the eight sizes of the shoe are AW07-084-01, AW07-084-02, and so on (the *pf_id* number plus 01, 02, 03...). For cross-sell promotions, the *pf_id* number is used to specify cross-sell between products.

The AW_promo_cross table in the database contains the following three columns:

- *pc_id*: A number uniquely identifying a particular cross-sell promotion

- *pf_id*: The product family ID that specifies the product for which the cross-sell promotion is in effect

- *related_pf_id*: The pf_id of the product that will be displayed under the heading See Also on the Product page

You might want to add other columns to your cross-sell table, such as a column to specify descriptive text to be displayed along with the related product. If you add a column defining the type of promotion, you can offer other kinds of cross-sell promotion, such as up-sell or replacement incentives.

Database queries A query named related-products is used in the PRODUCTS.ASP template to retrieve the data from the AW_promo_cross table. This query is defined and stored in the instance of the Content object in the \SHOP\GLOBAL.ASA file by the following statement:

```
Call MSCSContent.AddQuery("related-products", "select↵
    AW_product_family.pf_id from AW_promo_cross,↵
    AW_product_family where AW_promo_cross.pf_id = :1 and↵
    AW_promo_cross.related_pf_id = AW_product_family.pf_id", ↵
    0, adCmdText, 0, adOpenForwardOnly, 0)
```

If a cross-sell promotion is in effect, a second query (named *product-family*) is used to retrieve information about the related product from the AW_product_family table. This query is defined in \SHOP\GLOBAL.ASA by the following statement:

```
Call MSCSContent.AddQuery("product-family", "select * from↵
    AW_product_family where pf_id = :1", 0, adCmdText, 0,↵
    adOpenForwardOnly, 0)
```

Note that the *product-family* query is not specific to cross-sell promotions. It is used in any situation in which data about a product is required.

Product template When a shopper in the Adventure Works store selects a product for which a cross-sell promotion is in effect, the Product page (PRODUCT.ASP) displays the related product under the heading See Also. You can examine the PRODUCT.ASP template to see the scripts that are used.

The following script executes the *related-products* query, passing it the *pf_id* for the current product. The returned *pf_id* value is set as a property of the page variable named *relateds*:

```
set relateds = Datasource.Execute("related-products",↵
    Cstr(Request("pf_id")))
```

If there is a related *pf_id* for the current product, then the *product-family* query is executed to retrieve the data about that product from the database. The result set is assigned the variable name *related*:

```
if CBool(relateds.Count > 0) then
set related = Datasource.Execute("product-family", relateds(0).pf_id)
end if
```

The following script displays the image of the related product under the heading See Also, and generates a link to the product page for the related product:

```
<% REM related products: %>
<% if CBool(relateds.Count > 0) then %>
<TR>
```

```
      <TD ALIGN=CENTER VALIGN=TOP>
      <BR>
      <IMG SRC="/AW_assets/labels/seealso.jpg" ALT="See also" BORDER=0↵
         HEIGHT=19 WIDTH=155>
      <BR>
      <CENTER>
      <IMG SRC="/AW_assets/products/small/<% = Page.Encode(related(0).↵
         image_file_name) %>" ALT="related product" BORDER=0>
      </CENTER>
      <A HREF="<% = Page.URL("product.asp", "pf_id", related(0).pf_id) %>">↵
         <% = Page.Encode(related(0).pf_name) %> </A>
      </TD>
  </TR>
<% end if %>
```

Manager templates The Adventure Works Manager application provides an example of an easy-to-use interface for modifying the values in the AW_promo_cross table. Clicking the Promos link on the Adventure Works Store Manager page displays the Promo Manager page. Clicking the Cross Promotions link on the Promo Manager page displays the Cross Promotions page, from which you can either edit the information for an existing cross-sell promotion or add a new one. Clicking an SKU number displays the Edit Cross Promo page (PROMO-CROSS_EDIT.ASP), on which you can modify or delete the existing product relationship. Clicking the Add New Cross Promotion link displays the New Cross Promotion page (PROMO-CROSS_NEW.ASP), on which you can add a new cross-sell promotion to the database.

Both the PROMO-CROSS_EDIT.ASP and the PROMO-CROSS_NEW.ASP templates display a form containing drop-down lists for selecting the names of a product and a related product. See these templates for the scripts used to create the drop-down lists.

Implementing price promotions

Commerce Server supports a wide variety of discount promotions. If several promotions are in effect at the same time, you can specify the sequence in which they will be applied.

In the default installation, the Adventure Works store provides two price promotions: Member Discount, and Hiking Boots Special.

The Member Discount promotion offers 10 percent off all purchases for any shopper who signs up to be a member. In this promotion, the set of shoppers who can use the promotion is limited (members only), but the discount is available on all products to those shoppers.

The Hiking Boots Special promotion offers any shopper who purchases two pair of boots a 25 percent discount on the second pair. In this promotion, any shopper can use the promotion, but only a subset of products is available for the discount.

The Adventure Works Manager application provides a flexible framework that can be used to implement a number of different types of promotions, such as those shown in Table 4-5.

Table 4-5. *Adventure Works promotion types and associated descriptions.*

Type of Promotion	*Description*	*Example*
Cross-amount discount	Buy a specified dollar amount of one product and get another product at a discount.	"Buy at least $100 worth of Unisex Hiking Pants and get 25% off a Unisex long-sleeve button-down shirt."
Cross line-item discount	Buy one product and get another product at a discount.	"Buy a Galaxy tent and get a 15% discount on a Polar Star sleeping bag."
Cross-quantity discount	Buy a specified amount of one product and get another product at a discount.	"Buy two pair of Unisex Hiking Pants and get $10 off a Unisex long-sleeve button-down shirt."
General quantity discount	Buy a specified number of units of any product and get a discount on the order.	"Buy three of any product in the store and get $10 off the total order."
Line-item discount	Buy a specified product at a specified discount for a specified time.	"Buy a Starlight Tent between October 1st and October 10th and get 15% off."
Membership discount	Dollar or percentage discount for members.	"Register for the Frequent Shopper Club and receive 10% off all orders."
Targeted quantity discount	Buy a specified number of units of a specified product and get a discount on the order.	"Buy at least two Daytrip First Aid Kits and get 15% off the total order."

The Adventure Works store implements price promotions using the following elements:

- The AW_promo_price table in the database specifies the parameters of each promotion. For the Member Discount promotion, the *is_member* column in the AW_shopper table indicates whether the shopper is eligible for the promotion. For the Hiking Boots Special promotion, the *dept_id* column in the AW_product_family table is used to determine which products are involved in the promotion.

■ The Order Price Adjust stage of the pipeline contains the DBOrderPromo component, which uses the *price-promo-system* query to retrieve the data from the AW_promo_price table.

■ The Lobby page (LOBBY.ASP) contains a script that displays the Hiking Boots Special promotion under the heading Special Deal, and another script that allows the shopper to sign up for membership.

The Adventure Works Manager application provides several pages for viewing, editing, deleting, and adding new promotions.

Database tables The AW_promo_price table stores all the data about each promotion used in the store. The DBOrderPromo component in the pipeline uses data from this table to calculate and set several entries on the Order Form.

In addition, in the Adventure Works store, two other tables supply data used in the two default promotions:

■ The *is_member* column in the AW_shopper table specifies whether a shopper has registered for the Membership Discount promotion. This column is referenced in the *shopper_column* column in the AW_promo_price table.

■ The *dept_id* column in the AW_product_family table is used to specify which products are used in the Hiking Boots Special promotion. This column is referenced in the *cond_column* and *award_column* columns in the AW_promo_price table.

The columns marked as optional in Table 4-6 are used by the DBOrderPromo component if they exist, but they are not necessary for promotions to work.

An order promotion has three parts: the shopper criterion, the condition criterion, and the award discount. The shopper, the condition, and the award are each composed of a column name plus an operator plus a value. For example, the shopper criterion for the Adventure Works Member Discount promotion is determined by the following values, which specify that if the value in the *is_member* column of the AW_shopper table is one (1), then the shopper meets the criterion and the discount is applied.

Shopper_column	shopper_op	shopper_value
Is_member	=	1

Table 4-6. *Alphabetical list of optional columns of DBOrderPromo component.*

Column	Description
active	The Boolean value in this column specifies whether the promotion is currently in effect. A value of one (1) indicates that the promotion is in effect; a value of zero (0) indicates that the promotion is not in effect.
date_end (optional)	The value in this optional column specifies the date the promotion ends, ending at 12:00:01 A.M. If you want the last day of a sale to be 3/31, you would specify a date_end of 4/1.
date_start (optional)	The value in this optional column specifies the date the promotion begins, starting at 12:00:01 A.M.
promo_description (optional)	The value in this optional column gives a brief description of the promotion. This description is displayed on the Promotions pages of the Adventure Works Manager application.
promo_name (optional)	The value in this optional column specifies a short name for the promotion. This name is used on the Promotions pages of the Adventure Works Manager application to identify the promotion.
promo_rank (optional)	The value in this optional column specifies the order in which promotions are applied. The lower the value, the sooner the promotion is applied. For more information on the order of promotions, see the following section, "The DBOrderPromo Component."

The shopper is first tested against the shopper criterion; if there is no match, the promotion is not applied. If the shopper does match the shopper criterion, then the other two criteria are applied to all the items in the order, producing two sets: the condition set (those matching the condition criterion), and the award set (those matching the award criterion). See Table 4-7.

The *shopper_** columns determine whether the promotion is available to the current shopper. Note that the *shopper_** columns correspond to the Shopper fields in the Price Promo pages of the Adventure Works Manager application. When the DBOrderPromo component saves the values in the *shopper_** columns to the Order Form, it adds _shopper_ to the value (for example, *is_member* becomes _shopper_is_member on the Order Form).

Table 4-7. *ShopperCriteria values of Adventure Works promotion manager.*

Value	Description
shopper_all (optional)	The Boolean value in this optional column indicates whether this promotion is available to all shoppers or to only a subset. If the value in this column is 1, the promotion is available to all shoppers. If the value in this column is 0 (FALSE), the promotion is available only to shoppers who meet the criterion specified by the combination of the values in the *shopper_column*, *shopper_op*, and *shopper_value* columns. This column is optional because the All Shoppers criterion can be indicated by using an at sign ("@") in each of the following three *shopper_* columns.
shopper_column	The value in this column is the name of a column in the shopper table that specifies whether a shopper is eligible for the promotion. An at sign ("@") in this column means "none." For example, for the Adventure Works membership promotion, the value in this column is *is_member*, which is the name of a column in the AW_shopper table.
shopper_op	The value in this column is an operator (<, <=, =, >=, >, or <>) that is used to compare the value in the column whose name is specified in the *shopper_column* column with the value in the *shopper_value* column. An at sign ("@)" in this column means "none."
shopper_value	The value in this column is compared with the value in the column whose name is specified in *shopper_column*. An at sign ("@") in this column means "none."

The *cond_** columns determine the condition criterion—if the shopper's order meets the condition specified, then the award discount is applied. Note that these columns correspond to the Buy fields in the Price Promo pages of the Adventure Works Manager application (see Table 4-8).

For the Adventure Works Hiking Boots Special promotion, the condition specified by the values in the *cond_value, cond_basis, cond_column, cond_op,* and *cond_min* columns is that the shopper must purchase a quantity of two items in department 8 (Boots) to receive the award discount.

The *award_** columns specify the award criterion—if the shopper's order meets the condition specified by the *cond_** columns, then the award discount is applied. Note that the *award_** columns correspond to the Get and At fields in the Price Promo pages of the Adventure Works Manager application (see Table 4-9).

Table 4-8. *Condition criterion values of Adventure Works promotion manager.*

Value	*Description*
cond_all (optional)	The Boolean value in this optional column indicates whether a condition is to be applied. If the value in this column is 1 (TRUE), the shopper can buy any product and then receive the award discount. If the value in this column is 0 (FALSE), the award discount is available only if the shopper's order meets the criterion specified by the combination of the values in the *cond_basis*, *cond_value*, *cond_column*, *cond_op*, and *cond_value* columns. This column is optional because the All Products criterion can be indicated by using an at sign ("@") in each of the following three *cond_* columns.
cond_basis	The value in this column—either P or Q—specifies whether the value in the *cond_min* column is a price (P) or a quantity (Q). For the Adventure Works Hiking Boots Special promotion, the value in this column is Q, specifying quantity.
cond_column	The value in this column is the name of a column in the product table that identifies the condition that must be met before the promotion is applied. For example, for the Adventure Works Hiking Boots Special promotion, the value in this column is *dept_id*, which is the name of a column in the AW_product_family table. An at sign ("@") in this column means "none."
cond_min	The value in this column specifies the minimum purchase necessary to be eligible for the promotion. This value is either a number of units of the product or a currency value. The interpretation of the value in the *cond_min* column depends on the value in the *cond_basis* column. For the Adventure Works Hiking Boots Special promotion, the value in the *cond_min* column is 2, indicating that the discount will be applied only if the shopper purchases two pair of boots. Note that the *cond_min* and *cond_basis* columns specify the minimum purchase for the order as a whole, not for individual items.
cond_op	The value in this column is an operator (<, <=, =, >=, >, or <>) that is used to compare the value in the column whose name is specified in the *cond_column* column with the value in the *cond_value* column. An at sign ("@") in this column means "none."
cond_value	This column identifies what product or products must be purchased before the promotion is applied. The value in this column is compared with the value in the column whose name is specified in *cond_column*. For example, for the Adventure Works Hiking Boots Special promotion, the value in this column is 8; this value is compared against the value in the *dept_id* column in the AW_product_family table (specified in *cond_column*). An at sign ("@") in this column means "none."

Table 4-9. *Alphabetical list of award criterion values of Adventure Works promotion manager.*

Value	Description
award_all (optional)	The Boolean value in this optional column indicates whether all products or only a subset are to be discounted if the shopper's order meets the condition specified in the *cond_** columns. If the value in this column is 1 (TRUE), then the award discount applies to any product as long as the order meets the condition. If the value in this column is 0 (FALSE), the award discount is applied only to the product(s) specified by the combination of the values in the *award_column, award_op,* and *award_value* columns. This column is optional because the All Products criterion can be indicated by using an at sign ("@") in each of the following three *award_* columns.
award_column	The value in this column is the name of a column in the product table that identifies a product or products. For example, for the Adventure Works Hiking Boots Special promotion, the value in this column is *dept_id*, which is the name of a column in the AW_product_family table. The value in the *dept_id* column will be compared against the value in the *award_value* column using the operator specified in the *award_op* column. An at sign ("@") in this column means "none."
award_max	The value in this column specifies the maximum number of items that can be purchased at the discounted price. A value of 0 means "no maximum," so the discount can be applied to as many of the award items as the shopper chooses. For example, for the Adventure Works Hiking Boots Special promotion, the value in this column is 1, which indicates that the shopper can purchase one pair of boots at the discounted price, no matter how many pair of boots are purchased to meet the condition criterion.
award_op	The value in this column is an operator (<, <=, =, >=, >, or <>) that specifies the relation between *award_column* and *award_value*. An at sign ("@") in this column means "none."
award_value	The value in this column specifies the value in the column specified by *award_column* that identifies the product or products that will be discounted. If this value is a number, it must be an integer value. For example, for the Adventure Works Hiking Boots Special promotion, the value in this column is 8, which is the value for the *dept_id* column in the AW_product_family table. The combination of the values in the *award_column, award_op,* and *award_value* columns specifies *dept_id = 8*, which indicates that the discount is to be applied to any one product in department 8 (Boots). An at sign ("@") in this column means "none."

(continued)

Table 4-9. *Alphabetical list of award criterion values of Adventure Works promotion manager. (continued)*

Value	Description
disc_type	The value in this column—either % or $—specifies whether the value in the *disc_value* column is to be interpreted as percentage ("%") or currency ("$"). For the Adventure Works Hiking Boots Special promotion, the value in this column is %, specifying percentage.
disc_value	The value in this column specifies the amount of the award discount. This value is either a percentage or a currency value. The interpretation of the value in the *disc_value* column depends on the value in the *disc_type* column. For the Adventure Works Hiking Boots Special promotion, the value in the *disc_value* column is 25, indicating that the discount is 25 percent. Note that the value entered for percentage is a floating-point number.

The DBOrderPromo component The Order Price Adjust stage of the store's Order Processing Pipeline must contain the DBOrderPromo component. In the Adventure Works store, this component runs the *price-promo-system query* to retrieve the data about the current promotions from the AW_promo_price table in the database. This query was added to the Content object by the following entry in the \SHOP\GLOBAL.ASA file:

```
Call MSCSContent.AddQuery("price-promo-system", "select↵
    promo_name, date_start, date_end, shopper_all,↵
    shopper_column, shopper_op, shopper_value, cond_all,↵
    cond_column, cond_op, cond_value, cond_basis, cond_min,↵
    award_all, award_column, award_op, award_value, award_max,↵
    disc_type, disc_value from AW_promo_price where active <> 0↵
    order by promo_rank", 0, adCmdText, 0, adOpenForwardOnly, 0)
```

The DBOrderPromo component checks the *date_start* and *date_end* fields to determine whether a given promotion is currently in effect. If it is, the component evaluates the *shopper_**, *cond_**, and *award_** fields to determine the rules of the promotion (that is, the shopper set, the condition set, and the award discount). If the conditions are met, the component adjusts the prices accordingly and sets the *_oadjust_adjustedprice* entry on the order form.

Note The Order Price Adjust stage of the pipeline can adjust the price of a given product only once per Order Form. For this reason, the order in which promotions are applied is important.

Ordering of promotions in the Adventure Works store is specified by the *promo_rank* column in the AW_promo_price table—the lower the value, the sooner the promotion is applied. Therefore, the Hiking Boots Special promotion (rank of 50) is applied before the Member Discount promotion (rank of 100). If the ranks were reversed, the Member Discount would be applied first, and the Hiking Boots Special promotion would never be applied, because the DBOrderPromo component would have already applied a 10 percent discount to all products, and the component cannot adjust the prices a second time.

Shop templates The Member Discount promotion is advertised on the Adventure Works Lobby page under the heading Membership. The Membership heading is a link that displays a membership information page (MEMBER_INFO.HTM). Clicking the Sign Up Now link displays a form (MEMBER_FORM.ASP) on which the shopper can register for membership. When the shopper has completed the form and clicks the Update button, the form fields are sent to the XT_SHOOPPER_UPDATE.ASP template, which updates the AW_shopper table in the database, setting the value in the *is_member* column to 1. This value is then used by the DBOrderPromo component to determine whether to apply the Member Discount promotion.

The Adventure Works Lobby page (LOBBY.ASP) advertises the Hiking Boots Special promotion under the heading Special Deal. The Special Deal heading is a link that displays the Boots page (SUBDEPT.ASP), from which the shopper can select the products that quality for the discount. The following code on the LOBBY.ASP template formats the link and passes the department ID for Boots (dept_id = 8) to the SUBDEPT.ASP template:

```
<A HREF="<% = Page.URL("subdept.asp", "dept_id", 8) %>">
<IMG SRC="/AW_assets/labels/special.gif" ALT="Special deal"↵
   HEIGHT=18 WIDTH=151 BORDER=0><BR>
</A>
<B><FONT SIZE=4>B</B></FONT>uy any Hiking Boot and get a 2nd↵
   pair for <b>25% off!</b>
```

On the Boots page, the shopper clicks a specific boot and the Product page for that boot is displayed. The shopper clicks the Add To Basket button, selecting a pair of boots for purchase, and the product's *sku_query*, *pf_id*, and size are sent to the XT_ORDERFORM_ADDITEM.ASP template as form fields.

The XT_ORDERFORM_ADDITEM.ASP template adds the product to the Order Form and then redirects the browser to the Shopping Cart page (ORDER_BASKET.ASP). Before the Shopping Cart page is displayed to the shopper, the RunPlan method runs the Order Form through the first twelve stages of the pipeline. During this processing, the DBOrderPromo component determines whether to apply a discount to the purchase. Because at this point the shopper has added only one pair of boots to the basket, no discount is applied.

Suppose that the shopper then edits the *Qty* field on the Shopping Cart page, increasing the quantity of the items to two. When the shopper clicks the Update button, the data is sent to the XT_ORDERFORM_UPDATE.ASP template. The XT_ORDERFORM_UPDATE.ASP template increases the quantity of boots on the order form to two pairs, and then redirects the browser to the Shopping Cart page (ORDER_BASKET.ASP). This time, when the RunPlan method passes the order form through the pipeline, the DBOrderPromo component determines that the shopper has met the condition specified in the *cond_** columns of the AW_promo_price table (buy two items from dept_id = 8) and applies the 25 percent discount to the second item, setting its *_oadjust_adjustedprice* entry on the Order Form to the discounted amount. This amount is then used in calculating the total amount of the order, and the updated Shopping Cart page is then displayed to the shopper.

Manager templates The Adventure Works Manager application provides an example of an easy-to-use interface for modifying the values in the AW_promo_price table. Clicking the Promos link on the Adventure Works Store Manager page displays the Promo Manager page. Clicking the Price Promotions link on the Promo Manager page displays the Price Promotions page, from which you can either edit the information for an existing promotion or add a new one. Clicking the name of an existing promotion displays the Edit Price Promo page (PROMO-PRICE_EDIT.ASP), on which you can modify or delete the existing promotion. Clicking the Add New Price Promotion link displays the New Price Promotion page (PROMO-PRICE_NEW.asp), on which you can add a new price promotion to the database.

Both the PROMO-PRICE_EDIT.ASP and the PROMO-PRICE_NEW.ASP templates display a form containing fields for specifying the promotion criteria. See these templates for the scripts used to edit an existing promotion or add a new one.

Querying Order Form Data

When the Order Form is saved to the database, it is serialized into an encoded binary format. When you initialize the instance of the DBStorage object that is to be used for storing the Order Form, you specify the name of the column in which the encoded Order Form is to be stored. For example, in the Clock Peddler \SHOP\GLOBAL.ASA file, the following statements create and initialize the DBStorage object for Order Forms:

```
REM --Create a storage object for the order forms (shopper's basket)
Set MSCSOrderFormStorage = Server.CreateObject("Commerce.DBStorage")
Call MSCSOrderFormStorage.InitStorage(MSCSDataSource, "ClockPed_basket", ↵
    "shopper_id", "Commerce.OrderForm", "marshalled_order", "date_changed")
```

The parameters to the InitStorage method specify the following (with the parameter used in the Clock Peddler example shown in parentheses):

■ The data source to be used for connecting to the database (MSCSData-Source)

■ The name of the table in which the data is to be stored (ClockPed_basket)

■ The name of the column that is the primary key that uniquely identifies rows in that table (shopper_id)

■ The type of object that the DBStorage object will be passing data to or retrieving data from (Commerce.OrderForm)

■ The name of the column in which the encoded order form data is to be stored (marshalled_order)

■ (Optional) The name of the column in which the date and time of each update are stored (date_changed)

Using the Clock Peddler example, when the DBStorage object saves the order form data to the database, it automatically inserts the date and time into the *date_changed* column, and saves the encoded order form into the *marshalled_order* column. The object uses these columns because they were specified when the object was initialized.

If you want to run queries against Order Form data, you can add additional columns to the database table in which the Order Form data is stored. If a column name exactly matches the name of an entry on the order form, the DBStorage object will automatically save the value for that entry into the column of the same name when the Order Form is saved. For example, if your database table contains a column named *cc_type*, the DBStorage object saves the value in the *cc_type* entry of the Order Form into that column.

If you want to use column names in your database table that do not match the names on the Order Form, you can specify a mapping between column names and the names of entries on the Order Form. This is done in the GLOBAL.ASA file any time after initializing the instance of the DBStorage object. For example, suppose that you added a column named *customer_name* to the ClockPed_basket table and you want to use it for storing the *ship-to-name* value from the Order Form. In the \SHOP\GLOBAL.ASA file of the Clock Peddler store, you would use the Mapping property of the DBStorage object to establish mapping between the column name and the Order Form entry name.

```
REM --Create a storage object for the order forms (shopper's basket)
Set MSCSOrderFormStorage = Server.CreateObject("Commerce.DBStorage")
```

```
Call MSCSOrderFormStorage.InitStorage(MSCSDataSource, "ClockPed_basket",↩
    "shopper_id", "Commerce.OrderForm", "marshalled_order", "date_changed")
MSCSOrderFormStorage.Mapping.Value("customer_name") = "ship-to-name"
```

When the CommitData or Insertdata method is used to save the Order Form data to the database, the DBStorage object automatically saves the value in the ship-to-name entry of the Order Form into the *customer_name* column. You can then run a query to retrieve the data in the column.

Figure 4-10 shows the entry names on an example Order Form:

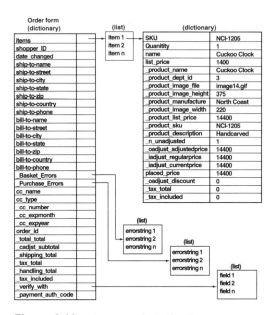

Figure 4-10. *An example Order Form.*

Using the Database in the Store

Commerce Server provides two means of implementing your site's interaction with the database that stores inventory, shopper, and receipt data.

The first of these involves using the DBStorage component to read and write data from Order Form or Dictionary components into the underlying database storage, or vice versa. Typically, you use the DBStorage component to insert, read, and update shopper and receipt data.

The second involves storing all your store's SQL queries in a central cache, where each query is associated with a string variable name, and then executing that query against the data source. This method is used generally to read and write inventory data.

The Content component provides a cache in which to store your queries. Using this component, you associate all the data source names (DSNs) and queries that your store uses with variable names, and then use the Datasource component's Execute method to execute the stored queries. Where the SQL statement that you execute is a *Select* query, the Execute method returns the query's results in a SimpleList of Dictionary components.

Creating a Content Component

To create a Content component, use the IIS 3.0 Server component's CreateObject method, identifying Commerce.Content as the component identifier:

```
Set Content = Server.CreateObject("Commerce.Content")
```

Although you can create a Content component anywhere in your store, you typically create this component in your store's *Application_OnStart* event, which you define in your GLOBAL.ASA file, and then set the Application component variable to MSCSContent.

Identifying the Database to Query

You identify the database you want to query by creating a data source name (DSN) and an associated DSN variable.

A data source name associates a name that you specify with a set of information about a data source, including the location of the data source, and the user information necessary to connect to it. The data source can be a Microsoft Access database, a Microsoft Excel spreadsheet, or any other application data for which an ODBC-compliant driver is installed on the system.

Before executing a query against an ODBC data source, you use the ODBC32 utility in the Windows NT Control Panel to configure a file or system DSN for that data source. The benefit of using a DSN is that applications querying the data source for which you configure a DSN do not need to know where the data is located; they need only to know the name that you've assigned the data source.

Next, you create a DSN variable based on the configured DSN by calling the Content component's AddDatasource method, as follows:

```
call Content.AddDatasource("clockped", "DSN=test;UID=sa;PWD=; ↵
    DATABASE=commerce")
```

The first part of AddDatasource is a string variable name that you use in your store to refer to this DSN. The second part is a connection string that identifies security information and the location or (in the case of SQL Server) the name of the database.

You can add any number of data source variables to a store, and can set the application-level MSCSDefaultDatasource to the DSN that you want to be the store's default. After you have added queries to the Content component to which you have added one or more data sources, you can use the Datasource or Content methods to retrieve a Datasource component for any DSN variable in the Content component cache:

```
Set Datasource = Content.Datasource("clockped")
' or Set Datasource = Content("clockped")

' Execute the query
Set simplelist = Datasource.Execute(…)
```

Adding Queries to the Content Component

Like DSNs, Content component queries can be identified within a store by the string variable names that you associate with them.

Use the AddQuery method to add queries to a Content component. These queries should be added to your store in the *Application_OnStart* event, which is defined in the store's GLOBAL.ASA file.

The following example from the Adventure Works starter store demonstrates how queries are added to the Content component:

```
REM Add all of the queries into Content component
Call MSCSContent.AddQuery("price-promo-system", "select promo_name, ↵
    date_start, date_end, shopper_all, shopper_column, shopper_op, ↵
    shopper_value, cond_all, cond_column, cond_op, cond_value, ↵
    cond_basis, cond_min, award_all, award_column, award_op, ↵
    award_value, award_max, disc_type, disc_value from AW_promo_price ↵
    where active <> 0 order by promo_rank")
Call MSCSContent.AddQuery("receipts-for-shopper", "select shopper_id, ↵
    order_id, date_entered, total, status, marshalled_receipt from↵
    AW_receipt where shopper_id = :1 order by date_entered")
' Rest of queries required for store operation…
```

The first part of AddQuery is a string resource identifier that you assign to the query, and the second part is the query's text. AddQuery also supports a number of optional parameters that significantly enhance database performance. For more information on these parameters, see the AddQuery component in Appendix F, "Commerce Server Component Reference Documentation."

Creating a Datasource Component

Use the Content component's Datasource method to create a Datasource component, based on a DSN variable that you have previously stored in the Content component's cache.

The following example from the Adventure Works sample store illustrates the creation of both a Content and a Datasource component. This code appears in the Adventure Works GLOBAL.ASA file, in the Shop folder:

```
REM Create a Content component for access to the database
Set MSCSContent = Server.CreateObject("Commerce.Content")
Call MSCSContent.AddDataSource("AW", MSCSDSN, 1, 0)
Set MSCSDatasource = MSCSContent.Datasource("AW")
```

Optionally, you can simply pass the name of the DSN variable to the Content component name, as follows:

```
Set MSCSDatasource = MSCSContent("AW")
```

Executing a Query

After using the Content component's Content or Datasource method to create a Datasource component, call the Datasource component's Execute or ExecuteADO method to execute a query that you have added to the Content component through a previous call to AddQuery.

```
<%
Set Content = Server.CreateObject("Commerce.Content")
' Add a single data source.
Call Content.AddDatasource("clockped", "DSN=test;UID=sa;PWD=;↵
    DATABASE=commerce", 1, 0)
' Add a query.
Call Content.AddQuery("get_products", "SELECT * FROM Products")
Set Datasource = Content.Datasource("clockped")
' Call execute
Set RS = Datasource.Execute("get_products")
%>
```

Although you can also pass the Execute method the text of an SQL statement, this method of query execution does not take advantage of the performance optimizations included in the Content component. For production stores, you should always pass Execute the name of a variable that represents a query that you have added to the Content component.

Using Parameterized Queries

In a *parameterized* query, the SQL query statement contains parameter markers that indicate search values that are supplied at run time to the Datasource component's Execute method. For parameterized queries added to the Content component, a colon, followed by a number that designates the parameter's place in the parameter list, serves as the parameter marker. Optionally, you can use the question mark ("?") as a parameter marker.

For example, where a parameterized query contains only one parameter marker, this number is 1:

```
Call MSCSContent.AddQuery("receipts-for-shopper", "select↵
    shopper_id, order_id, date_entered, total, status,↵
    marshalled_receipt from AW_receipt where shopper_id = :1↵
    order by date_entered")
```

In the following example, three parameter markers appear in the query, indicating that three values will be supplied at run time and bound to the SQL statement:

```
Call MSCSContent.AddQuery("variant-sku", "select sku from↵
    AW_product_variant where pf_id = :1 and (color_value = :2 or↵
    color_value is null or color_value='') and (size_value = :3↵
    or size_value is null or size_value='')")
```

The values to substitute for the parameter markers are supplied at run time as an optional parameter list to the Datasource component's Execute method. The following call to Execute runs the preceding query, and returns the first row in the query's results set:

```
Set productsku = DataSource.Execute("variant-sku",↵
    Cstr(Request("attr_1")), Cstr(Request("attr_2")),↵
    Cstr(Request("attr_3")))(0)
```

If the number of parameter values supplied to Execute does not match the number of parameter markers in the SQL query, Execute generates an error.

Navigating the Results of a Query

When the Execute method is used to execute an *SQL Select* query against a data source, Execute returns the results of the query in a SimpleList of Dictionary components. When you use the ExecuteADO method, the query's results are returned in an Active Server Pages (ASP) Recordset object. For information on how to navigate an ASP Recordset, see the *Active Server Pages Roadmap* at *http://www.microsoft.com/IIS.*

To navigate the results set returned by the Execute method, you can use the Visual Basic Scripting Edition (VBScript) For Each statement to iterate through the SimpleList, or you can use an index to reference the Dictionary members of the SimpleList.

The following example from the Adventure Works starter store illustrates the first method, using a For Each statement to read each member of the SimpleList into a Dictionary, and then using the Page component's Option method to display the sizes for an item.

```
<% set sizes = Datasource.Execute("sizes-for-family",↵
    Cstr(Request("pf_id"))) %>
<SELECT NAME="attr_3" size="1">
```

```
<% for each row_sizes in sizes %>
<% = Page.Option(row_sizes.size_value, "") %>
<% = Page.Encode(row_sizes.size_value) %>
<% next %>
</SELECT>
```

In the preceding group of statements, each iteration through the *sizes* Simple-List stores the current record in the *row_sizes* Dictionary. The value that appears to the right of the Dictionary's dot (.) operator references a column name in the queried table.

The following example performs the same operation as the previous one, but uses an index to iterate the SimpleList that contains the results set. In this example, the SimpleList acts as an array, and the SimpleList's Count property indicates the array's upper bound:

```
<% set sizes = Datasource.Execute("sizes-for-family",↵
    CStr(Request("pf_id")))%>
<SELECT NAME="attr_3" size="1">
<% for I = 0 to sizes.Count %>
<% = Page.Option(sizes(I).size_value, "")%>
<%=Page.Encode(sizes(I).size_value)%>
<% next %>
</SELECT>
```

If you are interested in retrieving only a single row in a result set, you can follow the call to Execute with a number value that indicates the SimpleList index that you want to retrieve, as follows:

```
<% set sizes = Datasource.Execute("sizes-for-family",↵
    CStr(Request("pf_id")))(0)%>
```

Note If the Dictionary element that stores a column value contains a Null value, that Dictionary entry is deleted. For this reason, a For Each iteration through a SimpleList of Dictionary components will move to the next non-Null value. When this occurs, the only way to retrieve the column name that contains the Null value is to index into the SimpleList and to reference the Dictionary key by name.

Using the Database to Store Shopper and Receipt Information

The DBStorage component, like the Content and Datasource components, is designed to simplify your store's interaction with the database, but serves a fundamentally different role in the store.

The Content component, as its name implies, is designed to provide a central cache for the queries that operate on the actual content—or inventory—for the store. The DBStorage component, on the other hand, is intended to provide for the fast and simple storage of shopper and receipt information.

Creating and Initializing a DBStorage Component

Use the IIS 3.0 Server object's CreateObject method to create a DBStorage component, as follows:

```
Set Storage = Server.CreateObject("Commerce.DBStorage")
```

This function call returns an uninitialized instance of a DBStorage component. Use the InitStorage method to initialize the returned component instance, as follows:

```
Storage.InitStorage(MMDatasource, "mx_receipt1", "order_id",↵
    "Commerce.Dictionary", "marshalled_receipt", "date_changed")
```

The parameters to InitStorage specify the following items of information:

- A Datasource. This must be a Datasource component that has been created using the Content component's AddDatasource method, and that you retrieve using the Content component's Datasource method.

- The name of the table in the referenced data source.

- A key into that table. This is the column name that the DBStorage component will use to key into the table to perform routine tasks such as data insertion and retrieval. This variable should identify the primary key into the underlying table.

- The program identifier of the component that you will use to pass data to and retrieve data from DBStorage methods. This component must be an OrderForm or Dictionary component.

- The name of a column for this DBStorage component instance to use for marshaling data. For more information on the marshaling column, see "InitStorage" in Appendix F, "Commerce Server Component Reference Documentation."

Attempting to call any other DBStorage method prior to calling InitStorage results in an error.

Using DBStorage to Locate a Record

How you use DBStorage to retrieve data from the database depends on how much data you want to retrieve. For example, if you want to retrieve a row where a group of columns contain a specified set of values, initialize two arrays to contain the column names and sought values, respectively, and use the LookupData method, as follows:

```
REM Attempt to determine if this shopper is already registered.
shopper_id = Page.GetShopperID

Dim keys(2)
Dim values(2)

keys(0) = "shopper_id"
keys(1) = "shopper_name"

values(0) = shopper_id
values(1) = Page.Request("shopper_name", Null, 1, 60)

exists = MSCSStorage.LookupData(Null, keys, values)

If IsNull(exists) Then
REM This shopper id and name do not exist in the specified↵
    columns.
```

The *keys* parameter in the example above designates the table columns in which to look for the *shopper_id* and *shopper_name*. If the LookupData method finds the row containing the column-value pair that you specify, then it returns a Dictionary component initialized with the contents of that row. Otherwise, it returns Null.

If LookupData finds more than one row containing the data that you specified, then it still returns Null. Consequently, unless you are searching for a column value that is sure to be unique for the column you are searching, you should use the LookupMultipleData method instead. This method returns a SimpleList of Dictionary components that contain the rows in which the specified column contains the specified data.

To retrieve a row based on the value stored in the column that you designated as the table's key in your initial call to InitStorage, you can use the GetData method to retrieve the column.

For example, given the following call to InitStorage:

```
REM Create a Storage object for the shopper information

Set MSCSShopperStorage = Server.CreateObject↵
    ("Commerce.DBStorage")
Call MSCSShopperStorage.InitStorage(MSCSDataSource,↵
    "AW_shopper", "shopper_id", "Commerce.Dictionary")
```

The following call to GetData returns the row that contains data on the current shopper:

```
shopper_id = Page.GetShopperID

If Not IsNull(shopper_id) Then
data = MSCSShopperStorage.GetData(Null, shopper_id)
End If
```

In this example, the GetData method searches the *shopper_id* column of the AW_shopper table for the specified shopper ID.

Using DBStorage to Modify a Record

Performing modifications to records using DBStorage is as simple as reading a record into a Dictionary or OrderForm component (using GetData, LookupData, or LookupMultipleData), modifying the contents of the component, and then passing the component to CommitData to update the row.

The following example from the AdventureWorks sample store adds an item to the Items collection in the OrderForm, and then commits the OrderForm to storage:

```
REM --add item to order form:
set productsku = mscsDataSource.Execute("variant-sku",↵
    Cstr(Request("pf_id")), Cstr(Request("product_color")),↵
    Cstr(Request("product_size")))(0)

sku = productsku.sku
set product = mscsDataSource.Execute("product-purchase",↵
    CStr(sku))(0)

set item = orderForm.AddItem(sku, product_qty,↵
    product.list_price)
item.pf_id = product.pf_id
item.pf_name = product.pf_name
item.list_price = product.list_price
item.quantity = product_qty
item.color_value = product.color_value
item.size_value = product.size_value

REM --commit order form back to storage:
call orderFormStorage.CommitData(Null, orderForm)
```

Using DBStorage to Delete a Row

You delete a row from a DBStorage component's underlying storage in one of the following ways.

First, you can initialize an OrderForm or Dictionary to describe the data you want to delete, and then pass the initialized component to the DBStorage component's DeleteData method. The following example deletes the contents of the shopper's Order Form storage by simply passing DeleteData an OrderForm that is initialized with the contents of the shopper's basket:

```
REM --clear out basket:
call orderFormStorage.DeleteData(Null, orderForm)
```

To delete an entire row based on the value stored in the column designated as the table's key, simply pass the value for that column to DeleteDataKey. For example, given that the following call to InitStorage has been called earlier:

```
Set MSCSShopperStorage = Server.CreateObject("Commerce.DBStorage")
Call MSCSShopperStorage.InitStorage(MSCSDataSource, "AW_shopper", ↵
    "shopper_id", "Commerce.Dictionary")
```

Then the following example deletes the information for a given shopper from the underlying AW_shopper table, provided that the specified shopper ID is found in the AW_shopper table's *shopper_id* column:

```
shopper_id = Page.GetShopperID
call MSCSShopperStorage.DeleteDataKey(Null, shopper_id)
```

Switching from Cookie to URL

If a store does not require shoppers to register, a shopper ID is generated the first time the shopper enters the store. If a store is configured to use cookies and the client browser supports cookies, the shopper ID is stored in a cookie on the shopper's computer. The Clock Peddler store, for example, stores the shopper ID in a cookie.

Alternatively, a store can be configured to pass the shopper ID in a URL.

To configure a store to pass the shopper ID in the URL,

1. Open your store's shop directory.

2. Open GLOBAL.ASA.

3. Locate the following line:

    ```
    Call MSCSShopperManager.InitManager("StoreName" , "cookie")
    ```

4. Change this line to

    ```
    Call MSCSShopperManager.InitManager("StoreName" , "url")
    ```

5. Add the following line to GLOBAL.ASA after the Application.Lock line:
    Application("MSCSSIDURLKey") = "mscssid".

This will cause the shopper ID to be appended to the URL across the store.

6. Save GLOBAL.ASA.

We have so far focused on scripting and the development tool for working with Commerce Server stores. Chapter 5 focuses on COM-based Commerce Server components.

Note There is an excellent tutorial on the Clock Peddler sample store that describes each and every page of the Clock Peddler store line-by-line, its purpose, and its programming. This tutorial is included on the companion product evaluation CD under the title "Building a Store" and under the heading "Basic Store Application: Tour of Clock Peddler."

Chapter 5

Commerce and Site Server Components

One distinguishing feature of this book is its deep coverage of Site Server's underlying technologies, such as COM. Chapter 3 discussed Active Server Pages, a scripting environment for Commerce Server. The chapter explored ASP's intrinsic object methods and properties, and provided examples of their usage. However, Chapter 3 did not address questions such as these: What are these components and objects? and How is a component developed?

Chapter 3 asserts that "Active server components support the Microsoft Component Object Model (COM) and can be written in virtually any programming language, including Visual Basic, C++, COBOL, and Java. COM objects are related to object linking and embedding (OLE) automation servers and can be called upon from a Web page (or other applications) to access and reuse prepackaged functionality.

This chapter covers these terms and technologies in depth, beginning with a history of COM to provide some background and context. It then covers the concepts and features of COM to help define the notion of components. Finally, this chapter shows you how to build components in a number of different languages. The beauty of this last section is that a developer can use the tools and techniques discussed with little understanding of the concepts. The wizards take care of all the overhead of writing COM interfaces, and they jump-start your development with a working skeleton of a component.

This chapter covers components in the context of ASP first, and then in the context of Commerce Server. You can use similar steps and techniques to develop components for all Site Server applications that are based on ASP. The only difference between ASP-based components, Commerce Server components, Site Server components, and others is that some components support additional interfaces. For example, Commerce Server's components implement the *IpipelineComponent*, *IpersistStreamInit*, and *ISpecifyPropertyPages* interfaces, in addition to the interfaces discussed in the "COM Interfaces" section below.

Prior to implementing a component, please look up the interfaces required in the specific product's documentation whose functionality you wish to extend with custom components of your own. For example, if you are building a component for the Visual InterDev development environment, a handful of unique interfaces for these components might exist.

While scripting is used for programming server pages, components are heavily used to implement server system functions. Site Server components are variations on components that implement Component Object Model (COM) interfaces. Having discussed scripting in the last two chapters, we now cover components in this chapter, beginning with an overview of COM.

COM[1] OVERVIEW

COM is a standard interface definition, not a language. It can be implemented in a number of languages. COM is the dialogue through which an application or object can query another application or object, execute methods of this application or object, and process results and errors returned from another application or object.

In addition to Microsoft and partners, other small, medium, and large software companies currently create COM Active controls, including companies such as Borland, Oracle, and Sybase/Powersoft. As a result of this work, more than 1,000 additional Active controls are available annually for Web producers to use.

Microsoft uses these controls heavily in its development tools, such as Front-Page, Visual InterDev (Visual Studio), Visual Basic, Visual C++, Visual Java++, and Active Control Pad. Microsoft's Internet Explorer supports Active, and Microsoft and third parties provide the Active plug-in for Netscape Navigator, enabling the broadest range of Internet users to view Active-enabled Web pages. In addition, a number of other third-party companies (14) that are designing and developing Web-related tools support these controls in their products.

---

1. In the context of this book, I use the terms COM, Active, ActiveX, Active controls, Active components, and Web controls interchangeably. They refer to the same set of technologies that extends the interactivity of World Wide Web content. Web sites come alive with this technology, using multimedia effects, interactive objects, and sophisticated applications that create an experience comparable to that of high-quality CD-ROM titles.

The Windows 32-bit operating systems currently support Active controls. Microsoft is working with Metrowerks to support Active on the Macintosh platform, and is also working with Bristol and Mainsoft to support COM on UNIX platforms. Developers who write Active controls and other Active objects will be able to reach the widest possible user audience with this cross-platform solution.

A Brief History of COM

Dynamic Data Exchange (DDE) was released in 1985 and was the primary mechanism for interfacing two applications of the Windows platform. Those who are familiar with DDE remember the Peek, Poke, and Execute methods. DDE was a good start but very limited in scope.

The next version was OLE 1, which was released in 1991 as a way to build compound documents on the platform. Compound documents were super documents that could be composed of a number of applications such as a Microsoft Excel worksheet added inside a Microsoft Word document.

In 1993 COM and OLE automation were added to OLE 1.0 to yield OLE 2.0. This simplified matters and extended OLE into what became the COM specification.

Finally, a very useful version of OLE called OLE Controls emerged in 1994, and a Network version of COM called Net OLE or Distributed COM (DCOM) also emerged.

The old OLE, based on DDE, was big, slow, and hard to code. These deficiencies are solved with COM and tool support. OLE was aimed at doing everything for everyone, whereas COM is focused, faster, smaller, and more robust.

COM Definition

A few months ago while attending Comdex, I had the opportunity to discuss Active components with a good fraction of about 250,000 people who were in attendance. Let's take a look at the Active component from a number of different perspectives.

COM is a standards-driven concept

While Microsoft originally developed COM for code reuse, it is a standards-driven concept now. A standards body outside of Microsoft called The Open Group COM governs the standard.

The Open Group formed in 1996 to act as the holding company for The Open Software Foundation (OSF) and X/Open Company Ltd. The Open Group provides a forum for collaborative development, standardization, and other open systems activities.

COM is related to OLE

If you remember, object linking and embedding (OLE) is the technology that makes it possible to show, change, and manipulate one document within another. For example, when you embed (Paste Special) a Microsoft Excel worksheet into Word, the technology that allows the Excel worksheet to be displayed and manipulated inside the Word document is OLE. Relative to COM, OLE is more powerful but more complex. While COM was optimized for code reuse, OLE also supports more complex operations such as in-place activation and drag-and-drop. To simplify matters, think of COM as a subset of OLE capabilities optimized to support third-party efforts.

COM is similar to the object paradigm

The COM paradigm is similar to objects at large, but at the application level. In most object-oriented programming languages, code is reused by creating (the *new* call) an instance of an existing class and sending it messages (asking it to do things). Why can't you create an instance of an application and send it messages? A programmer may want to know how to make an application reusable. This happens by wrapping the application in a COM interface support wrapper, allowing other applications to create instance(s) of the application, execute exposed methods, and access exposed properties.

COM is a code reuse technology

Suppose that AppA and AppB are applications written for a platform such as Win32. If each of these applications is COM-enabled, AppA can use AppB as an embedded component; there is no need for AppA to duplicate AppB's code internally. Once you design and debug a COM component, you can use the code again and again by simply calling the COM object's methods from your application. Refer to the "Building Components" section later in this chapter for more information.

COM is a versatile DLL

For those developers familiar with the concept of a dynamic link library (DLL), COM is a DLL with standard entry points added. So why use COM over the DLL technology? Because it makes the following problems easy to solve: locating the DLL, querying a DLL's name and capabilities, and keeping track of the DLL versions.

COM Requirements

In order to develop COM objects, you can use any one of the development environments this chapter discusses:

- VB-CCE (Control Creation Edition)

- C++ (VC++ 4.2 +ATL)

- C++ (VC++ 5.0)

- VB 4.0

- VB 5.0

To execute COM objects, you must use any one of the following server platforms:

- Windows 32 bit: IIS 2.0 or later

- UNIX (COM does not directly support UNIX platforms; however, review DCOM on UNIX for your specific needs.)

- Mac

- Mainframes

To execute COM objects, you must use any one of the following client platforms:

- Windows 32 bit

- UNIX

- Mac: IE 3.0 or later for Win95 and NT

- Browser that supports the <OBJECT> tag

Before attempting to run any samples, make sure IIS and the development environment are installed correctly. Follow the setup instruction for IIS and the development environment of your choice.

COM Interfaces

Let's peel the COM onion one more layer. Similar to OLE, COM interfaces are a standardized set of API specifications governing the interaction of a client application and a server application.

Suppose that every application on the platform responded to two basic questions uniformly: Who are you? and What do you do? COM interfaces present these two questions to an application and generate the response.

All COM objects implement at least one interface: *IUnknown* or an interface that is derived from *IUnknown* (see Figure 5-1). The Iunknown interface is a partner to a virtual function table containing pointers to three standard methods, QueryInterface(), AddRef(), and Release(), that implement the minimum interface.

In addition, the following rules apply to all interfaces implemented for a COM object:

- Interfaces must directly or indirectly inherit the methods of *IUnknown* (see Figure 5-2).

- Interfaces must have a unique interface identifier.

- Interfaces must be immutable: once they are created and published, no part of their definition may change.

- All interface methods should have a return type of remote procedure call (RPC) error handling.

- All string parameters in interface methods should be Unicode.

```
struct IUnknown
{
        virtual HRESULT Queryinterface (IID& iid, void  **ppvOBJ) = 0 ;
        virtual ULONG AddRef() = 0 ;
        virtual ULONG Release() = 0 ;
} ;
```

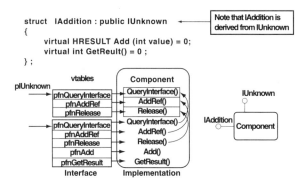

Figure 5-1. *Implementation of Iunknown interface.*

COM provides a standard set of interfaces and additional interfaces may also be supported (see Figure 5-2).

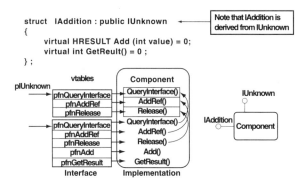

Figure 5-2. *A component supporting two interfaces.*

- *IUnknown*: The primary and required interface, the *IUnknown* interface includes the following methods:

  ❏ *QueryInterface()*: Returns a pointer to other supported interfaces (You can have other interfaces specified to you in addition to the *IUnknown* interface. This is how you access those custom interfaces at run time.)

  ❏ *AddReference()*: Used for counting the references of the object so you can free it when unused

❑ *Release()*: Used for counting the references of the object so you can free it when unused (The counterpart of *AddReference()*.)

■ *IDispatch*: The OLE automation interface

■ *IDataObject*: Used for storing and retrieving context data for the object

Interfaces are simply a binary standard. If you are familiar with C++ vtables, think of an interface as a vtable. The pointer to the vtable for the object of interest is returned from a *QueryInterface()* call. Once the interface is wrapped around the application, any other application can use it. Calls to methods in COM interfaces can cross process boundaries as long as both processes are running on the same machine. DCOM is the cross platform version of COM.

COM provides a standard set of interfaces, but these interfaces may not always be perfectly suited to your needs. Through custom interfaces, you can create new interfaces tailored to fulfill the specific needs of your application. Custom interfaces are extensions to the COM standard; they let you extend the standard behavior and still take advantage of the services the base interface provides. Like all COM interfaces, custom interfaces derive from the *IUnknown* interface and must contain the three methods of *IUnknown*. For additional details of COM standard and interfaces, please see "Understanding ActiveX and OLE," David Chappen, Microsoft Press, 1997).

BUILDING COMPONENTS

The beauty of COM is that you can build components for your unique purposes with little or no knowledge of the COM standard details. This section discusses a number of tools you can use for building COM objects and Web controls. Keep in mind that the result is the same control; however, it took me a day-and-a-half to build a control with Visual C++ using ATL version, and only five minutes to build one in VB. Conceivably, some hardware driver that you need as part of your objects' functionality might be written in C, C++, or MFC.

This section is heavily illustrated so you can quickly thumb through and glance at the simple steps below each figure to get a feel for how easily and quickly you can build a skeleton for a component. This section builds a skeleton ASP component in different languages to show COM's language-independence. Therefore, the illustrations and set of rudimentary steps are repeated for many flavors of languages and development environments. You may want to pick one as your favorite language, such as VB, VC++, or VJ++, and then select a development version such as VB 4.0 or VB 5.0. Then you can use one of the sections below to show you how easy and versatile developing a component can be. Here are all the different flavors from which to choose:

■ Developing Active Components in VB-CCE

■ Developing Active Components in C++ (VC++ 4.2 + ATL)

■ Developing Active Components in C++ (VC++ 5.0)

■ Developing Active Components in VB 4.0

■ Developing Active Components in VB 5.0

■ Developing Active Components in Visual J++

Additionally, Appendix I, "Using MFC to Create Order Processing Components," extends the topic of building components from the base Active Server Pages components, such as those discussed until now, and Commerce Server's Active components that implement the *IpipelineComponent*, *IpersistStreamInit*, and *ISpecifyPropertyPages* interfaces.

The next section builds the classic HelloWorld example in VB.

Developing Active Components in VB-CCE

The steps to develop an active component in VB Control Creation Edition (CCE) are the following:

1. Start VB-CCE or VB 5.0 or later. Click New and Project. As shown in Figure 5-3, the Visual Basic New Project screen appears.

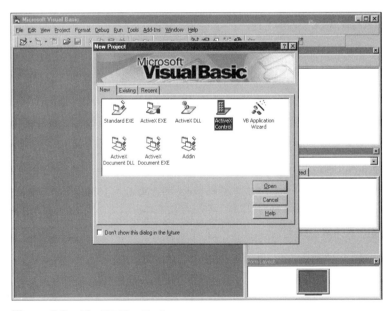

Figure 5-3. *The VB New Project screen.*

2. Create a new ActiveX control, as shown in Figure 5-4.

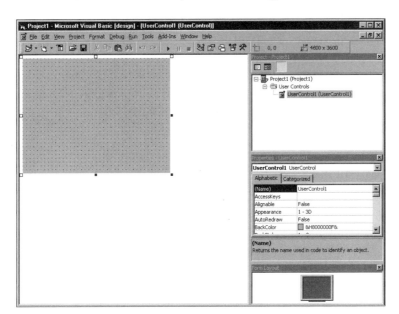

Figure 5-4. *Editors and property panes after creating an ActiveX control.*

3. In the middle left pane, rename *UserControl1* to *Hello* or your class name.

4. Add a method called Hello. Right click on Hello(Hello) in the upper right pane and select View Code.

5. Add code to the Hello method to print out your message.

6. Start up the ActiveX Control Interface Wizard, click Add-Ins from the menu bar, and select the ActiveX Control Interface Wizard, as shown in Figure 5-5.

7. You may select your interface members here. For this example, just follow through to finish by clicking Next (see Figure 5-6).

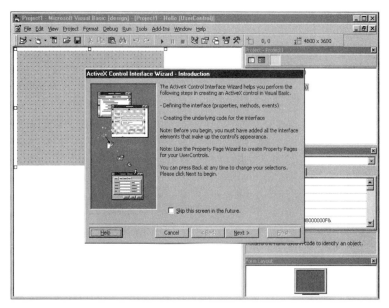

Figure 5-5. *Introduction page of the ActiveX Control Interface Wizard.*

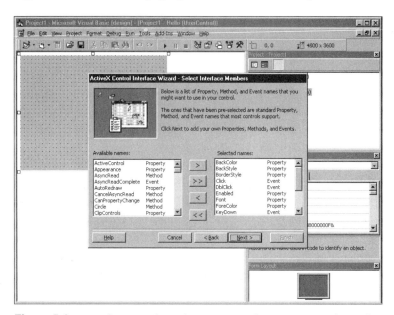

Figure 5-6. *Interface member selection page of ActiveX Control Interface Wizard.*

8. You may add your custom interface members here. Click Next (see Figure 5-7).

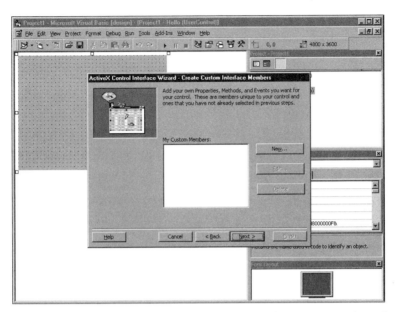

Figure 5-7. *Custom interface member entry page of ActiveX Control Interface Wizard.*

9. Click Next (see Figure 5-8).

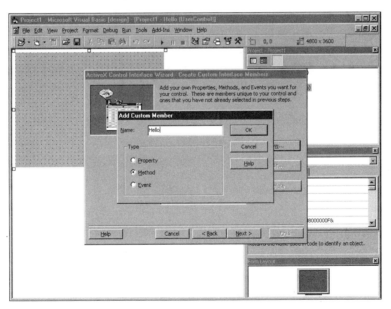

Figure 5-8. *Defining events and properties page of Control Interface Wizard.*

10. Click Next (see Figure 5-9).

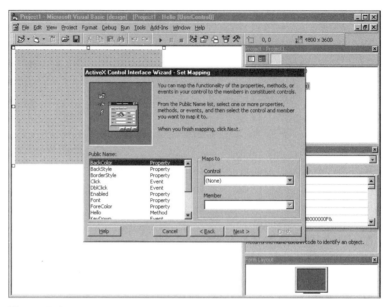

Figure 5-9. *Mapping events and properties.*

11. Click Next to move past the Set Attributes pane, taking the defaults.

12. Figure 5-10 provides instructions to test and debug your control. Follow the instructions that appear on your screen.

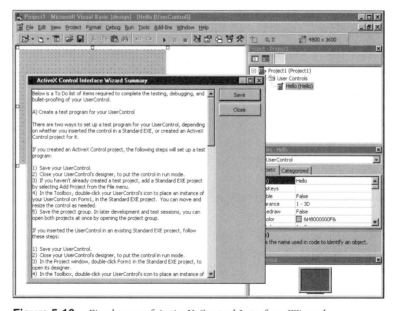

Figure 5-10. *Final page of ActiveX Control Interface Wizard.*

Now the skeleton for your component is ready. For additional details, please see the VBCCE product documentation. The next section outlines the steps to develop the same in C++.

Developing Active Components in C++ (VC++ 5.0)

To make an ATL COM object In VC++ 5.0,

1. Start VC++, click New, and under the Projects tab, select the ATL COM App Wizard (see Figure 5-11).

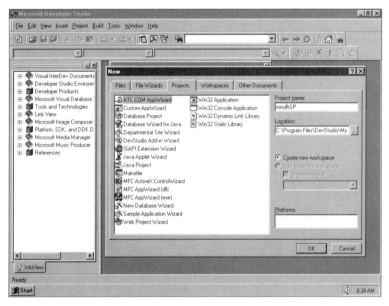

Figure 5-11. *The VC New Project screen.*

2. Click Finish to complete the skeleton of a COM object (see Figure 5-12 and Figure 5-13).

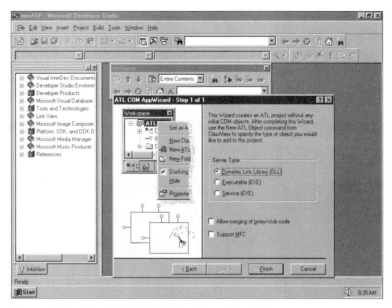

Figure 5-12. *The VC ATL COM AppWizard initial screen.*

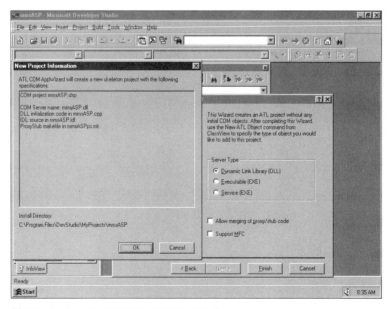

Figure 5-13. *The VC ATL COM AppWizard final screen.*

The project is created and *mmsASP.cpp* contains implementation of all the DLL Exports (see Figure 5-14).

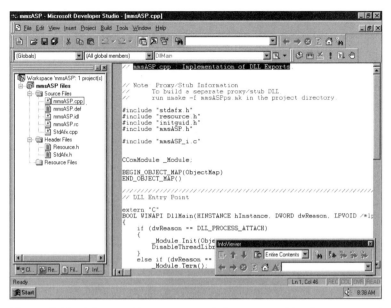

Figure 5-14. *The VC ATL component skeleton created by the AppWizard.*

The ATL component is now ready for additional development. For more details, please see VC++ version 5.0 product documentation.

Developing Active Components in VB 4.0

Components may also be developed in older versions of VB such as VB 4.0. To make a COM object In VB 4.0,

1. Select and open VB 4.0.

2. Click Tools.

3. Select Options.

4. Click the Project tab.

5. Type *myComp* in the Project Name text box.

6. Click OK.

You have now named the project *myComp*. VB uses the project name as the first part of the name that is referenced in order to use the server component in an ASP script. Reference a component from ASP as ProjectName.ClassName: myComp.myClass.methods.

The next section lays the groundwork for the *myComp.myClass* server component. Methods and properties provide the interface between Active Server components and VB scripts and other languages. Because browsers can request a script to run on the server, the server component must not bring up a dialog box on the server's screen because the screen will not be displayed on the client browser.

VB version 4.0 automatically creates a Visual Basic form. You will remove this default form from your project because it will not be used.

To remove the default form,

1. In the View menu, select Project.

2. Select Form1 within the *myComp* project window.

3. In the File menu, select Remove File.

To create a component in Visual Basic 4.0, you must first define a class. This class groups methods and properties of the object. In your project, it will be the place within which you specify your *myClass*'s methods.

To define a class,

1. From the Insert menu, choose Class Module.

2. Press the F4 key to display the Property Sheet for Class1.

3. Click the value 0 - Not Creatable for Instancing.

4. Click the arrow, then select 2 - Creatable MultiUse.

5. Triple-click Class1 to select the class name.

6. Type *myClass* to change the class name.

7. Click False for the property Public or type *t* to select True for the property Public.

8. Close the *myClass* property sheet.

The server component does require some programming code.
To add functions to *myClass*,

1. In the *myClass* class window of the editor, type the following lines:

```
.Public Function myFunction
.myFunction = some value   REM sets the return of the function.
Equivalent to return (some value) in C/C++.
End Function
```

2. Close the editor pane.

All server components require an entry (starting) point. This is the code that will be called when the object is first made available to a language. In VBScript,[2]

---

2. References are made to VBScript here. Could be JScript as well.

when *Server.CreateObject* is called, the *Sub Main* procedure of a server component (created with Visual Basic 4.0) is also called.

You may provide an empty (no statements) Sub Main procedure, if no initialization code is needed.

To add the *myClass* main entry point,

1. In the Insert menu, select Module.

2. In the Module 1 window, type *Sub Main*.

3. Press Enter.

   This automatically enters the following code:

   ```
   Sub Main()
   End Sub
   ```

   To save the project,

1. From the File menu, select Save Project.

2. In the File Name text box, type *c:\winnt\system32\inetsrv\asp\ cmpnts\myComp*.

3. Click the Save button to save.

4. Double-click the value *myComp* in the File Name text box to select it.

5. Type the name *myComp* for the Project file (.VBP).

6. Click the Save button to save the project.

Making the component an in-process component

VB allows you to create in-process Active components (OLE Automation Servers) and out-of-process Active components. An in-process Active component is a dynamic-link library (file name extension .DLL). An out-of-process Active component is an executable (file name extension .EXE) that runs as a separate process from the calling application. Because in-process components are in the same process space as the calling process, they provide better performance than out-of-process components.

To make the server component an in-process Active component,

1. Open the File menu.

2. Select Make OLE DLL File.

3. Click the Options button.

4. Select the Auto Increment check box.

5. Click OK.

6. Type *c:\winnt\system32\inetsrv\asp\cmpnts\ myComp.dl* in the File Name text box and click OK. (If you did not accept the default installation directory, substitute the name of your installation directory for \WINNT\SYSTEM32.)

7. Exit Visual Basic.

Registering the *myComp* server component

Next you will register the *myComp* server component. When a component is registered, it can be found and called easily and registry information about the component is recorded in the operating system.

To register the component,

1. Click the Start button on the taskbar.

2. Select Run.

3. Type *command*.

4. Press the Enter key.

5. Type *CD\winnt\system32\inetsrv\asp\cmpnts* at the command prompt. (If you did not accept the default installation directory, substitute the name of your installation directory for \WINNT\SYSTEM32.)

6. Press the Enter key.

7. Type *regsvr32 myComp.dll*.

8. Press Enter.

9. Click OK when a dialog box appears that says "DllRegisterServer in finance.dll succeeded."

10. Close the Command Prompt window.

Calling the *myComp* component from a script

To test the component, you can call the component from Active Server Pages, Visual Basic, Microsoft Office products that use VB for Applications, or any other OLE Automation controller.

To use the component,

1. Use the *Server.CreateObject* to create an instance of the *myComp* component named *myComp*.myClass.

2. Once you create an instance of a server component, make use of its methods and properties.

Developing Active Components in VB 5.0

Building a server component in VB 5.0 is similar to building it in version 4.0, but perhaps a bit more streamlined and easier.

To build a server component in VB 5.0,

1. Look first for a wizard (see Figure 5-15).

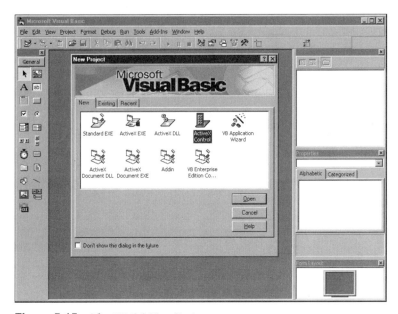

Figure 5-15. *The VB 5.0 New Project screen.*

2. If no wizard is present or you do not wish to use it, select New and select an ActiveX DLL project type.

Follow the steps above except:

The project is called Project1 by default. The server control is called UserControl1 (see Figure 5-16).

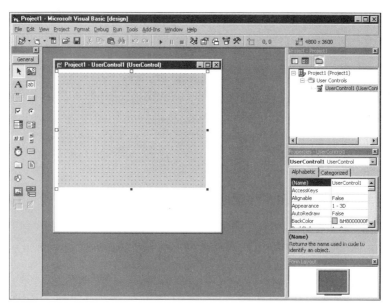

Figure 5-16. *Editors and property panes after creating an ActiveX control.*

Alternatively, use ActiveX DLL as the project type and you do not have to remove the form. *Project1* and *Class1* are the corresponding names (see Figure 5-17).

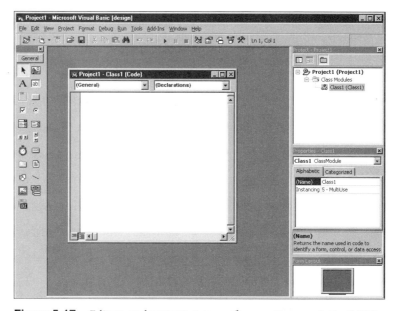

Figure 5-17. *Editors and property panes after creating an ActiveX DLL.*

VB 5.0 has tools for a number of related tasks. Please refer to the VB product documentation for details. We barely touched one task here. But that is another book in itself. The skeleton is now ready for additional development. For more details please see VB 5.0 product documentation.

Also note that depending on your version of C++ and VB, you can use properties to set the threading option for a class to make the task even simpler.

Developing Active Components in VJ++

Microsoft Visual J++ includes an ActiveX Component Wizard for Java. This wizard automates most of the process of turning a Java class into a COM object. You can develop your Java class and then run the wizard to generate a component (see Figure 5-18).

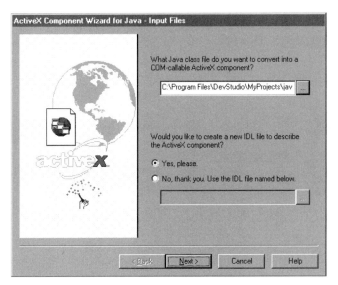

Figure 5-18. *The VJ++ ActiveX Component Wizard for Java's initial screen.*

To convert a Java class to a COM object using the ActiveX Component Wizard,

1. Start VJ++ and load the desired class or workspace.

2. Click Tools, then select ActiveX Component Wizard for Java.

3. In the Input Files dialog box, specify the Java source file containing the class you want to expose as a COM object. Also specify whether you want to create a new IDL file for the component or use an existing IDL file (see Figure 5-19).

4. Click Next to continue.

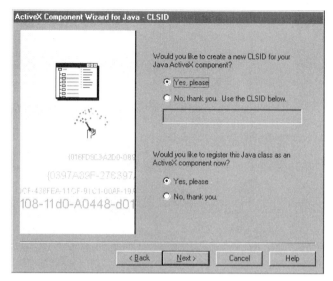

Figure 5-19. *The VJ++ ActiveX Component Wizard for Java's CLSID entry screen.*

5. In the CLSID dialog box, choose whether to generate a new CLSID or enter one manually. You can also optionally register the component now (see Figure 5-20).

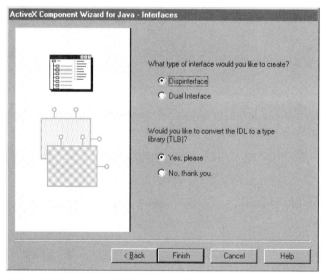

Figure 5-20. *ActiveX Component Wizard for Java Interfaces dialog box.*

6. Click Next to continue.

7. In the Interfaces dialog box, choose one of the following interface types: Disp Interface, an automation interface, or Dual Interface, an automation and a vtable-type interface.

8. Choose whether to create a type library (.TLB file) from the IDL file.

Now the Wizard will generate the files and IDs you specified and launch the MIDL Compiler. The MIDL Compiler is a replacement for the MkTypLib tool. It generates a type library (.TLB) and other supporting files.

9. In the Additional Steps dialog box, modify your class implementation and project build options so that the class is recognized as a COM component and the resultant .JAVA bytecode files are placed in the proper directory (see Figure 5-21).

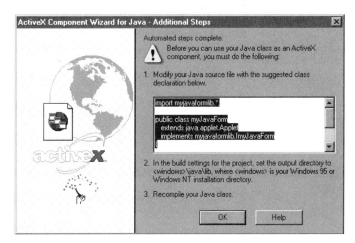

Figure 5-21. *Additional Steps dialog box of ActiveX Component Wizard for Java.*

10. Click Finish to continue.

11. Along with the files required to support COM—mainly the .IDL and .TLB files—the ActiveX Component Wizard also produces a class summary information file (SUMMARY.TXT), that describes the COM interface created for your class. Click OK.

For more information on the ActiveX Component Wizard for Java, run the Wizard and press the F1 key, or refer to VJ++ product documentation.

This concludes coverage of the Microsoft suite of tools supporting component development. The next section covers one last technical detail—threading in components.

MULTI-THREADED ISSUES

One issue remains that is worth further discussion here: threading. A component may run on the client side (browser) or the server side. Browser-side components usually don't involve threading issues, since only a single user uses them. However, server-side components are shared among many users and require attention to threading issues. For more information about standard techniques for coding threads, see *Advanced Windows* by Jeffrey Richter (Microsoft Press). The remainder of this chapter covers only an introduction to these concepts.

Starting with Microsoft Windows 95 and Microsoft Windows NT 3.51, OLE provides support for multi-threaded applications, allowing applications to make OLE calls from multiple threads. This multi-threaded support is called the apartment model. All components using multiple threads should follow this model. The apartment model requires that interface pointers are marshaled (using *CoMarshalInterface*, and *CoUnmarshalInterface*) when passed between threads.

Single-Threaded Objects

The single-threaded model is not recommended for server-side components such as those that will be called by Active Server Pages. Single-threaded objects run in exactly one thread, the one that called the *CoInitialize* method. Calls to these objects from other threads are marshaled to this thread. Only one thread at a time can enter a set of single-threaded objects, and it must be the same thread each time. The Web server creates a parked thread that calls *CoInitialize*, and then marshals object calls.

One disadvantage of single-threaded objects is that they cannot be stored in the Application object. The only way to create a single-threaded object with application scope is to declare it with an <OBJECT> tag. However, when you use this object, the Web server will lock the application down to a single thread, the one that created the object. This will reduce server performance significantly, so you should only consider it for Intranet applications. In addition, if you create a single-threaded object with session scope or store it in the Session object, the Web server will lock the session down to the single thread that created the object. Single-threaded objects are well suited for the client-side browsers such as IE 3.0 and 4.0.

Apartment-Threaded Objects

Use this threading model for components that will be called by Active Server Pages. Each apartment-model object can only be entered by one thread, the thread that called *CoCreateInstance*. However, an object server can support multiple objects each being entered simultaneously by different threads. Common data held by the object server must be protected against thread collisions.

The Web server creates an apartment-model object in the same thread that called *CoCreateInstance*. Calls to the object from the apartment thread are not marshaled. Requests that are in the same session as an apartment-model object are handled by the thread that created the apartment-model object.

There is one performance pitfall with this scheme. If you create an apartment-threaded object with session scope or store it in the Session object, the Web server will lock the session down to the single thread that created the object. Do not store these objects in the Session or Application objects. See Active Server built-in objects in Chapter 3. This locking notion also applies to free-threaded objects discussed below. Rather, mark objects as both, per the discussion later in this section.

Free-Threaded Objects

Free-threaded objects place no restrictions on which threads or how many threads can enter the object. The object cannot contain thread-specific data and must protect its data from simultaneous access by multiple threads.

The Web server creates free-threaded objects in a different thread than the one that called *CoCreateInstance*. All calls to the object are marshaled to a free-threading thread. One disadvantage of free-threaded objects is that they cannot be stored in the Application object.

Free-Threaded and Apartment-Threaded Objects

I highly recommend marking components that will be called by Active Server Pages as both free- and apartment-threaded. Active objects marked as both can be used in either apartment-threaded or free-threaded modes. You can enter them from multiple threads and protect their data from thread collisions. Also, they do not contain thread-specific data.

The Web server creates an object marked as both in a single thread, the one that serviced the request. The call to *CoCreateInstance* is not marshaled to another thread. However, if the object has session scope or is placed in the Session object, the Web server will not lock the session to that thread. Calls to the object from other requests in the same session are executed in the request thread.

Because objects marked as both guarantee to protect their data against multiple-thread access, you can use them for objects that have application scope. For additional details please see the threads and synchronization chapters of *Advanced Windows*, by Jeffrey Richter (Microsoft Press, 1997).

DISTRIBUTING ACTIVE SERVER COMPONENTS USING DCOM

Because Active components are COM objects, out-of-process server components can be seamlessly distributed over a server network using distributed COM (DCOM). This means that components requiring a heavy amount of processing can be distributed to application servers that work in conjunction with the Web server to efficiently process requests from users browsing the site. For example, a price look-up component that performs complex pricing calculations could be built as an Active Server component and distributed via DCOM to execute on a specialized application server.

The advantage of DCOM is that distributed computing is achieved with transparency to the developer. The Active Server scripting used to execute and manipulate the remote component is exactly the same as if the component were running directly on the Web server. Distributed solutions built with DCOM components offer more effective load balancing, higher performance applications, and greater fault tolerance for enterprise-class Web applications. For further reference, please see *Professional DCOM Programming* by Dr. Richard Grimes (Wrox Press Ltd., 1997).

Now that you understand the concept of components and have seen how to build COM in a few environments, you may review Appendix 5-1, "Using MFC to Create Order-Processing Components." This example is unique in two ways. First, it introduces MFC as an additional development environment for COM. Second, it illustrates the steps needed to build a Commerce Server pipeline component.

Chapter 6

Getting the Most from Your Site Server

Site Server Enterprise Edition can help add commerce capabilities to your Web site, deliver personalized experiences to customers, perform custom usage analysis across multiple Web servers, rapidly deploy your Web site, manage the quality and organization of your site, and help you make informed decisions about the future of your site.

Up till now we have concentrated on Commerce Server, a core component of Site Server Enterprise Edition, and we have been primarily concerned with planning, designing, and implementing a commercial storefront. In this chapter we cover a set of related servers, tools, and techniques to help you get the most from your Commerce Server site.

This chapter introduces the following enhancements:

- Sites that deliver audio/video content as their primary business or would like to enhance user experience with richer content

- Personalization systems to tailor the content to the individual user or groups

■ Content management tools including site analysis and reports that allow for ease of site content management

■ Content replication and distribution servers and tools that ease store content maintenance and dissemination in large environments

■ Community building servers such as chat, news, mail, and membership servers that further distinguish the site, differentiate the store, and help build and grow the store's business

■ Site Server performance simulator and capacity planning tool for ISPs and MIS administrators and managers to help with system planning

■ Search servers that implement the search functions of a store for local servers or Internet-wide

■ Usage analysis tool to pinpoint hot items and departments, identify trends, assess the market for new introductions, and to better understand the store traffic

A number of these servers, services, and tools are already included with the Site Server package, such as Commerce Server (Chapters 1 and 2), Visual InterDev (Chapter 4), Personalization System, Content Replication System, Usage Analyst, Enterprise Edition, Web Publishing Wizard, and Posting Acceptor. Site Server tools are introduced here and additional examples are provided in Chapter 7 where noted.

Other services and tools are packaged separately, such as Index Server, NetShow Server, Membership Server, News Server, Chat Server, Mail Server, Transaction Server, and Proxy Sever. Some services and tools (such as Index Server and NetShow Server) may be either included with the prerequisite software (NT, SQL, and IIS). Others may be stand-alone servers that help strengthen Site Server installations (such as Membership Server, News Server, Chat Server, Mail Server, Transaction Server, and Proxy Sever).

This chapter covers these other, complementary servers, services, and associated tools in two parts: Microsoft Commercial Internet Server's family members which include Membership Server, News Server, Chat Server, and Mail Server; and other Microsoft BackOffice servers such as Transaction Server and Proxy Server. Please visit *http://backoffice.microsoft.com* for more information on any of the servers covered in this chapter.[1]

The next section introduces Personalization Server, a component of Site Server.

---

1. Microsoft System Network Architecture (SNA) Server is not covered in this chapter. For information on SNA Server, please visit *http://backoffice.microsoft.com/sna.*

PERSONALIZATION SYSTEM

Personalization means matching the content to the user's personality or a group of users' preferences. For example, a user who has purchased an item from the store is likely to be interested in information about that item, such as promotions and new arrivals. Other groups might want certain content to be excluded from their viewing. The typical approach to personalization is to tag the content, profile the users, and match the profile to content when serving content.

One way people have addressed personalization in the past is with CGI scripts—programs written in C/C++ or Perl that dynamically generate content for a user—and cookies. Personalized Web sites take this evolution one step further by retaining information about each user and delivering the right content automatically to each user. The more the user visits the site, and the more the user describes himself or herself, the better the experience gets. This creates a feedback loop that continually increases customer satisfaction.

With the advent of Personalization System, implementing personalization became even simpler. Personalization System consists of add-on server components for Internet Information System (IIS) that provide sites with the ability to easily deliver unique, personalized dynamic content to each individual user of a Web site.

Personalization System's user property database, a versatile database repository of user information, stores and maintains information about users. This data is accessed and the information is mapped against the attributes of the content using the add-on server components. In this scheme a vocabulary of tags and some type of content tagging is implied. For example, you can insert Meta HTTP tags in the content that describe its attributes from among attributes that a provider may specify. Similarly, you can select and apply user property vocabulary to the user property database. In a simpler application, the vocabulary is the same for content tags and user properties. A simple example is provided in Chapter 7.

For technical details, a tutorial, and samples of using Personalization System's server component and user property database, please see Chapter 2 of the *Personalization System Web Page Author Guide*, "Using Personalization System ActiveX Component with Active Server Pages," under *Personalization System Documentation* after installation. Also in the same document, two additional components, "Sendmail" and "Voting," are discussed. These components are also available with Personalization System to help implement communications and community. For more information on Personalization System, please visit *http://backoffice.microsoft.com/products/features/Personalization/SiteServerE.asp*. The next section covers Usage Analyst, another component of Site Server.

USAGE ANALYST

If a store is configured to log user traffic, as is the Adventure Works sample store, some details of the user's visit are logged. The logs may get quite large for a busy store. Extremely large international malls and stores may generate logs as large as several hundred MB to 1 GB per day—if the visit is well detailed. The task of Usage Analyst is to read this data and generate reports that help in tuning the store and the content. You could use commercial database reporting tools, but Usage Analyst understands the format of the log files and is able to readily answer typical marketing questions about the target market and the store pages' ability to attract and retain customers. Site Analyst imports and analyzes usage data into twelve detail, thirteen summary, three audit, and four advertising reports suitable for advertising, auditing, and MIS departments. You may also define your own specialized reports.

The contents of one of Usage Analyst's audit reports is illustrated in Figure 6-1.

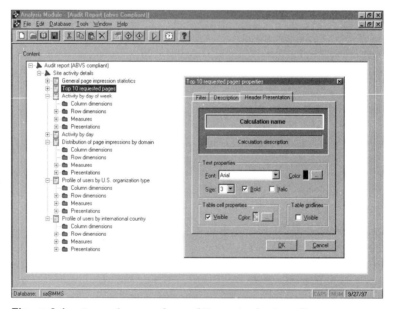

Figure 6-1. *A sample page of one of Usage Analyst's audit reports.*

Microsoft Usage Analyst supports standard and extended log files from the following servers on Windows NT and Unix operating systems:

- Apache
- O'Reilly Website
- CERN
- Process Software

- EMWACS

- Real Audio

- Microsoft Internet Server

- Spry

- Navisoft

- Webstar

- NCSA

- WU Archive Ftp

- Netscape

- Zeus

- Open Market

For technical details, a tutorial, and samples of Usage Analyst's import and analysis modules, please see *Usage Analyst's User's Guide* after installation. For more information on Usage Analyst, please visit *http://backoffice.microsoft.com/products/features/UsageAnalyst/SiteServerE.asp*.

The next section covers Site Analyst, a component of Site Server.

SITE ANALYST

Site Analyst can help you manage your store content. Typically, you cannot view content such as asset images, store pages, and links for the complete store, and include files all in one graph, and generating a printed report might take hours by hand. Site Analyst eases content management through the use of SiteMap, Analysis Log Report, and Quick Search.

SiteMap

SiteMap shows your entire Web site in an easy-to-understand, visual format. Site-Map includes graphical representations of the resources in your site, such as HTML pages and graphic images; audio, video, and program files; Java applets or Word files; Internet services such as Gopher and FTP; and others. The map is a powerful tool that helps you quickly identify your site's structure at a glance.

You can choose to see either the Tree view of the map or the Cyberbolic view, or both views at the same time. The Tree view provides a linear, hierarchical view of the map. The Cyberbolic view depicts the map items in a Web-like structure that emphasizes their interconnected nature. You'll discover which view you prefer as you work more with the program, and you can switch back and forth as you per-form different tasks or work with different maps.

Figure 6-2 illustrates Site Analyst's Tree and Cyberbolic views.

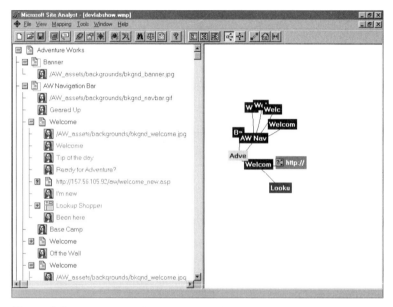

Figure 6-2. *Tree and Cyberbolic views of Site Analyst.*

Site Analyst can import usage data from a server's logs to combine static site information and dynamic user traffic information and generate a more complete view of the store and its traffic. This more complete view of the store supports more complex decision making.

Site Analyst helps you keep track of the various changes you make to your site. Depending on the remap options you choose, you can retain any annotations from the old map, review a new set of HTML site reports, and see which areas of the site are new, orphaned, or changed. Comparing different versions of your site can be especially useful if you want to track the various stages of your site's development: alpha, beta, and live.

Analysis Log Report

When you map a site, Site Analyst generates a set of linked HTML-formatted reports that you can use to evaluate your site and pinpoint problems. These reports help you analyze your site's resources, monitor content changes, find broken links and other errors, and more. In addition, because you view the reports in your browser, you may want to include some of them (such as the hierarchy or index reports) in your site as navigational aids. The reports are linked to each other, and are hyperlinked to the site resources. Once you've pinpointed a particular page or other map object that you want to examine, you can jump directly to it with a single mouse click.

Figure 6-3 illustrates the Adventure Works main page hierarchical report.

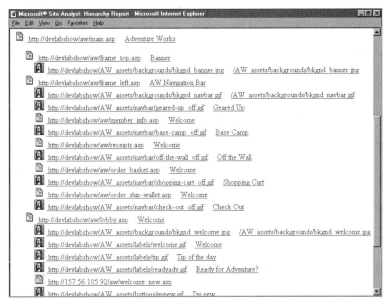

Figure 6-3. *Hierarchical report of Adventure Works main page.*

The Link Info window provides a wide range of information about the links in your site. For any object that you select on the map, you can see information about its links to other objects and about links (called InLinks) that point to the selected object. You can isolate the object's broken links, links to other sites (called Offsite links), links going in particular directions in the hierarchy, and more.

Quick Search

Searching is one of the most useful tools Site Analyst offers for analyzing your site. Use Site Analyst's Quick Search to find information fast or set up your own custom search. Searches can be narrow or broad, for a single object or for groups of objects. For example, you can search for a page that contains a particular text string, or you can search for all broken links in your site. You can search the entire map or confine your search to only a portion of it. You can perform AND/OR (Boolean) searches, and you can even search the results of a search to further refine the findings. You can search for specific object types (such as images or program files), or for any combination of properties (such as file sizes or modification dates).

Once you perform a search, the results appear in the Search Results window. From this window you can do any number of things: view properties for each object, view the selected object in your browser, even export the search results to HTML or to a database or spreadsheet. Searching in Site Analyst is versatile and powerful, and is a handy way to keep on top of site tasks you perform regularly.

Figure 6-4 illustrates the search results of the Adventure Works main page.

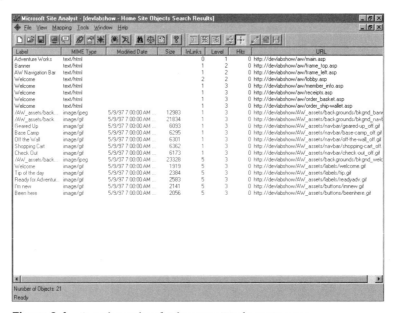

Figure 6-4. *Search results of Adventure Works main page.*

For more information on Site Analyst, please visit *http://backoffice.micro-soft.com/products/features/SiteAnalyst/SiteServerE.asp*.

The next section covers Content Replication System, a component of Site Server.

CONTENT REPLICATION SYSTEM

Content Replication System (CRS)[2] exists to help administrators move and update content to multiple servers at physically diverse locations. Once set up, CRS operates with little or no intervention from the system administrator. CRS allows content producers to publish to entire farms of content servers without directly connecting to the content farm.

---

2. CRS includes an SDK, which is available from Start-Programs-Content Replication System SDK after installation.

CRS replicates access control lists (ACLs), Web content, binary system files, scripts, and controls. CRS can be used in conjunction with Front Page, Visual Source Safe, or other document management systems. CRS is designed to operate on a global Internet scale, handling large volumes of content. CRS by itself has no theoretical limit as to the amount of data it can replicate. Replication time will be affected primarily by communications bandwidth and less so by disk I/O, server cache, processor capacity, and so forth. The largest single file that CRS can replicate is 2 GB.

CRS routinely replicates 200 thousand plus files representing many gigabytes of data as part of operating The Microsoft Network (MSN). CRS can run external commands during the replication as part of the defined project load script. You can schedule these commands to run before and after both sending and receiving a replication. CRS provides for full reporting of all of the activities in the Windows NT Event logs, Performance Monitor counters, and text-based diagnostic logs. Please see Appendix J for viewing Windows NT Event logs and NT Performance Monitor counters.

Why not just use FTP? In smaller shops, administrators may use their favorite copy or FTP program to duplicate or move content. For larger shops, however, Content Replication System (CRS) adds value in the following ways.

Stages to production servers Creating the content is only part of the picture. Once it's created, it has to be published to the production server. This might be as simple as copying the file to the production server in a nonprotected small Web shop. However, in a medium or large secure operations-based system, the server has security, accountability, and up-time requirements that must be met.

Mirrors servers for reliability Popular Web shops should mirror servers for the purposes of fault tolerance. As Web usage grows, the need for mirroring will emerge even with smaller sites.

Uses geographic distribution The primary Web site might be in Seattle, but a large portion of a company's customers might be in Europe; distributing large binaries over the Internet from a single location can bog network links, impacting the level of customer service. By building mirrors in remote locations, a company can distribute the network load and maintain service levels for customers.

Performs transaction-based replication The alternative to CRS is to wait for the files to be copied to the servers one at a time, and therefore have gaps of time when the content is "broken" due to pages linking to other pages that haven't been copied to the site yet. Content Replication replicates the entire set of changes to the server into a temporary directory. It then completes the entire update all at once using a Windows NT file renaming technique that decreases the time-gap for broken content to the absolute minimum. This technique also allows CRS to support rollback capabilities. By default, CRS retains the last two replications in the transaction directory.

Using the rollback command, you can bring back a given server to the previous state(s).

Performs incremental replication CRS replicates only the files that have changed since the last replication without checking the synchronization. CRS will chain a series of replications from machine to machine based on the project name and the route definition. This allows movement of content to machines in locations not directly connected to the source. SDK and examples for CRS are provided in Chapter 7.

For more information on Content Replication Server, please visit *http://back-office.microsoft.com/products/features/ContentReplication/SiteServerE.asp.*

The next section covers Posting Acceptor and Web Publishing Wizard, two components of Site Server.

POSTING ACCEPTOR AND WEB PUBLISHING WIZARD

In many environments you might want to have the server accept postings from users of or contributors to a site. A simple example is a news entity with disbursed contributors and sources. Posting Acceptor and Web Publishing Wizard are the server and client components that enable Web publishing.

Posting Acceptor

Microsoft Posting Acceptor (PA) is a server add-on tool that enables Web content providers to publish their content using HTTP Post RFC1867. After installing Posting Acceptor on your Web server, running NT Server, NT Workstation, or Windows 95, you will be able to provide a hosting service for users wanting to post Web content to your server.

Posting Acceptor allows Microsoft Internet Information Server (IIS) and Microsoft's Peer Web Services (PWS) to accept Web content from Microsoft Web Publishing Wizard/API and Netscape Navigator 2.02 or later through any standard HTTP connection. In conjunction with Microsoft Content Replication System (CRS), Posting Acceptor can also distribute content to more than one Web server simultaneously.

The mapping module for CRS is installed automatically when you install Posting Acceptor. If you have CRS installed on your system, you can use it to replicate content posted to your server or to other servers.

To use Posting Acceptor with the Content Replication System, set up an automatic project with a MapURL pointing to the content directory of your project. (For more information on setting up automatic projects, see the CRS Operations Guide available after installing the companion CD from Start-Programs-Content

Replication System. Two versions, HTML and Word, are available.) With the TargetURL and the MapURL being the same, posted content is saved in the content directory via the CRS mapping module.

If you have installed Microsoft Membership Server or any other authentication mechanisms supported by IIS/PWS, your publisher's client software can authenticate against your Web server to upload their files. If you have installed a security certificate on your Web server, your publishers will be able to upload their files securely via HTTPS (Hypertext Transfer Protocol Secure), assuming that their client supports SSL (Secure Socket Layer).

Web Publishing Wizard

On the client side, Microsoft Web Publishing Wizard automates the user submission tasks. By simply specifying a folder to send and a server to receive the folder, users are able to publish content files and folders to the Web server.

Figure 6-5 illustrates the Web Publishing Wizard's introductory page.

Figure 6-5. *Introductory page of Web Publishing Wizard.*

For more information on Posting Acceptor and Web Publishing Wizard, please visit *http://backoffice.microsoft.com/products/features/PostingAcceptor/SiteServerE.asp* and *http://backoffice.microsoft.com/products/features/WebPubWizard/SiteServerE.asp*.

The next section covers Index Server and Information Retrieval Server, two alternative servers for search and indexing content.

INDEX SERVER AND INFORMATION RETRIEVAL SERVER

You can implement content search and indexing for your site in at least two ways. With intranet sites you can use the Index Server, which is installed free of charge with installation of IIS. If you want to use an Internet site to index local as well as remote Internet sites, you can use the Information Retrieval Server, which is purchased separately. One major difference between the two schemes is the ability to "crawl" Web servers using HTTP protocol. Each scheme is briefly discussed below.

Searching and Indexing with Index Server

Think of the Index Server as the technology behind the search button on your Web site. Microsoft Index Server is a search engine integrated in IIS that provides users with access to documents on your Web site. Index Server is a free, downloadable component of Windows NT Server version 4.0 and IIS 3.0. Index Server performs full-text searches on HTML, text, and all Office documents in their original formats in seven languages.

Searching and Indexing with Information Retrieval Server

Index Server is well suited for local-host operations and LAN environments. Information Retrieval (IR) Server provides search and indexing capabilities across multiple servers and multiple Internet domains. The IR system separates the index and search services to allow you to run resource-intensive, full-text indexing routines on a server without reducing search throughput. This helps scalability.

IR supports distributed searching so that you can route queries to a single server or multiple servers with results collated transparently. Multiple copies (replicas) of a single index might exist. The system automatically load-balances queries across available servers. IR is not part of Site Server Enterprise Edition, but I always get the question when I talk of indexing, "Well, does it crawl HTTP?" The answer is yes, but this server package is part of the suite of complementary servers.

For more information on Index Server and Information retrieval Server, please visit *http://www.microsoft.com/ntserver/info/indexserver.htm*.

The next section covers NetShow Server, a component of Internet Information Server.

NETSHOW SERVER

NetShow enriches one-to-many communications using live and stored (on-demand) multimedia content. NetShow provides live multicasting of audio, on-demand streaming of stored audio, illustrated audio (audio synchronized with images), and full motion video.

NetShow can compensate for sub-optimal network conditions. Live and on-demand information has Forward Error Correction (FEC) information appended by the NetShow server prior to transmission. The system is able to automatically recover from typical Intranet transmission problems such as lost or out-of-sequence packets.

Microsoft NetShow exploits two key technologies to enhance a user's net-worked multimedia experience, while reducing the impact on the network's throughput: multicasting and streaming.

IP multicasting is an open, standards-based way to distribute identical information to many users simultaneously. This contrasts with regular TCP/IP (IP unicast) where you can send the same information to many clients, but you must transmit an individual copy to each user. To take full advantage of multicasting, the routers and other infrastructure components that make up Intranets and the Internet must be multicast-enabled. Microsoft, along with its NetShow partners, makes deploying this technology in a safe and controlled manner possible.

Normally when accessing networked multimedia content, you have to wait for the entire file to be transferred before you can use the information. Streaming allows you to see or hear the information as it arrives without having to wait. With Net-Show, Microsoft has developed an open streaming platform capable of high performance under demanding network conditions.

Live and On-Demand Video

NetShow server handles both live and on-demand video. Prerecorded (on-demand) content requires only the player and a prerecorded file formatted with an ASF extension, and can be served from any NT or non-NT server. The only requirement is the NetShow On-Demand player discussed below. Live content requires a NetShow Server in addition to the player. The server captures, compresses, and streams the live content. The same player is used for both live and on-demand content.

NetShow live content is handled by NetShow On-Demand on the server side and includes a corresponding NetShow On-Demand Player on the client side. Using a simple editor, ASF Editor described below, NetShow Player supports content at multiple-bit rates, ranging from audio at 14.4 to AVI at several MB per second.

NetShow Player enables the same functions as a regular VCR: the user can stop, pause, and start content. This enables a user to control the flow of content as appropriate for his or her needs.

Application developers can incorporate the ability to play illustrated audio and video content within a stand-alone client player or as an integrated part of a Web-based application. NetShow On-Demand provides a simple client SDK, which contains software and documentation that developers can use to add streaming support to Visual Basic and Visual C++ applications. The SDK includes an ActiveX control, reference documentation, and sample programs.

NetShow shines in the following areas.

Training Many organizations devote considerable resources to this critical area. By using NetShow to leverage the Intranet and extend the reach of professional instructors, an organization can maximize the value of this investment. NetShow makes it easy for the trainers to generate the content and easy for users to receive the training whenever and wherever they need it, live or on-demand.

Online events/virtual briefings With live streaming, everyone in an organization can listen live to important organizational briefings whether they are internal presentations or briefings or external groups such as press or analysts. Everyone on the network can follow the presentations as they are made regardless of their geographic location. With NetShow, if they miss the meeting they can see and hear a stored version later, on demand.

Guided tours You can attach an audio commentary to slides or Web pages and guide users through a demonstration of a product, process, or site. This portion only requires the on-demand components such as the editor and the player.

Online magazines and reference materials You can enhance the value of in-house publications such as human resource manuals by including audio or video content.

NetShow comes free with the installation of IIS. IIS also includes a base set of authoring tools for easily creating multimedia Web content. NetShow comes with simple starter tools to enable corporate content developers to prepare many popular content formats for streaming an illustrated audio. You can use files in WAV, AVI, QuickTime, PowerPoint, JPEG, GIF, and URL audio and video formats to generate illustrated audio.

Codec-independent architecture The NetShow software architecture is designed to be completely codec-independent. This means that the content provider can choose the compression scheme needed for a specific application and is not tied to a proprietary compression scheme.

ASF Editor With ASF Editor, a content author can create, test, and compile an ASF file to store illustrated audio content. The tool is designed to handle most of the issues of encoding and timing so that the author doesn't have to. It determines where to place objects—sounds, images, and URLs—so that they appear at the correct time during playback. It also has the ability to convert objects from one format or one level of quality to another. On networks with low bit rates, this ability becomes very useful in determining the tradeoffs between sound and image quality.

For more information on NetShow Server, please visit *http://www.micro-soft.com/netshow.*

Site Server is a member of selected Microsoft Commercial Internet Servers. Up to this section, all servers, services, and tools discussed, with the exception of IR server above, are part of Site Server Enterprise Edition or are available free of charge with the prerequisite NT/IIS server installation. More are available to enhance a Site Server installation, including Membership Server, News Server, Chat Server, Mail Server, Transaction Server, and Proxy Server.

Like Commerce Server, Membership Server, News Server, Chat Server, and Mail Server are also members of Microsoft Commercial Internet Servers. These servers are discussed in the next section. The last section of this chapter covers Transaction Server and Proxy Server, two servers from the back office family of servers.

MICROSOFT COMMERCIAL INTERNET SERVERS

Is an online store as good as a real mall store? What has happened to the touch of a personal visit in this land of wire? What is missing? Personalization is an excellent tool of the trade but it does not handle customer service, feedback forums, technical support, or a way to correspond. Many commercial grade mail, news, and chat servers are available. However, Microsoft Commercial Internet Server (MCIS) has a lot of advantages.

One advantage is that MCIS servers can be leveraged using existing technology and training. You can install Microsoft Commercial Internet Servers on the same hardware as Site Server or separately. You can manage MCIS servers such as News Server, Chat Server, and Mail Server using the same tools, design them using the same designers, develop them with the same technology talent, debug them using the same techniques, and ultimately scale and secure them using the same concepts as discussed throughout this book for Site Server.

Like Commerce Server, all members of the MCIS family of servers are built around ASP and COM/DCOM technologies; all are built upon NT/IIS technology; and all are candidates for complementing a Site Server installation to provide a fuller experience, closer relationship, better service, and to further develop the commercial online business.

Another advantage of MCIS servers is their ease of management. All MCIS servers enjoy the same management tools that Site Server provides. Based on LAN and Internet management tools, you can manage these servers on the Intranet and the Internet using the same graphical user and interfaces that Site Server offers.

MCIS also provides ease of scalability. One of the first questions that a potential Site Server evaluator asks is, "Now that I understand scalability of Commerce Server, how do the rest of the family members fare?" The short answer is, nicely. If you liked the scalability of Commerce Server, you'll love the family. The servers were designed to be industrial strength and support users in the order of tens of thousands to millions.

Finally, you can easily include these complementary servers and services into Site Server. In addition, the same tools such as Visual Studio development tools, database tools, and so on, apply to all Microsoft Commercial Internet Servers.

Commercial Internet Membership Server

While Membership Server is not a required component of Site Server, Membership Server is capable of managing the users of any and all of the MCIS servers from Commerce to Mail. Among other benefits, Membership Server provides single-signon for all Web applications. The following scenarios are examples of Internet businesses that can leverage the unique strengths of Membership Server.

An Internet Service Provider (ISP) wants to offer its users a dial-up network and application services such as e-mail and chat. Membership Server must scale to hundreds of thousands, or potentially millions, of users. Users should need only a single identity for all ISP applications and network services and only need to log on once to the ISP's services during an Internet session.

A large corporation wants to establish an Internet site to work more closely with its suppliers and distributors. Certain information is restricted to certain tiers of business partners and some information, such as order and account status, is private to individual partners.

An online service (OLS) has several third-party affiliates that must be able to remotely host their content and service offerings anywhere on the Internet. OLS members need to access third-party services that are bundled into their membership plan, and also want to transact for premium services offered to them by third parties. The remote third-party sites must be able to authenticate the members against the central OLS Membership Server and forward billing events to their OLS accounts. For security reasons, it is critical not to reveal a member's password to the third-party application site during authentication or consumption of services.

A large content-oriented Web site needs to build a closer relationship with its audience and begin to offer premium subscription services. The site creates several tiers of service including a free membership level and various paid tiers. The paid tiers of service are offered under several subscription plan options (annual, monthly, and so forth), as well as on an a la carte basis. Membership Server manages the various classes of members and their access rights, and also integrates with a separate billing system that can process transactions through a credit-card payment network.

For these and other scenarios, Membership Server provides a solution. Membership Server is a scalable, distributed authentication and access control system that enables service operators on the Internet to manage all of their customer relationships. Membership Server integrates with a wide range of Microsoft Internet application servers including Site Server, providing the foundation needed to build a commercial Internet service. The system includes facilities to authenticate users, authorize access to areas of an Internet site on a controlled basis, and generate billing events for processing by an external billing engine. The system is designed for use in the highly distributed Internet environment. Membership Server enables a service provider to deploy remote application servers anywhere on the Internet and tie them together into a central authentication, authorization, and billing system.

Among other things, Membership Server brings single signon out of the Intranet and into the Internet. Network operators and content providers need to control access to the network infrastructure and bill customers accordingly for use. The Internet creates new business opportunities for major service providers to affiliate with premium Internet content sites in providing users with access to third-party services on the Internet. In effect, a service provider can act as an aggregator of third-party premium content.

Membership Server is designed for high performance, scalability, and fault tolerance. The security database scales to over five trillion users. Billing events are generated that can be integrated with a third-party billing system.

For more information on Membership Server, please visit *http://backoffice.microsoft.com*.

Commercial Internet News Server

MCIS News is an Internet standards-based service for hosting electronic forums where individuals can share views and information in discussion groups. It delivers a commercial-grade implementation of Network News Transfer Protocol (NNTP) designed to meet the high traffic loads associated with mission-critical applications. It supports public, read-only, moderated, and authenticated newsgroups. An overview of News Server facilitates follows.

Public Internet newsgroups, such as Usenet, are popular because they provide an organized way for individuals to share views and information with other people interested in similar topics. Like chat services, newsgroups have proved to be effective tools for fostering community and attracting customers to Web sites and network operators. Services and sites that offer newsgroups develop customer loyalty, encourage customer visitation, and can reduce customer churn. Furthermore, network operators that rely upon time-usage–based pricing models benefit from the increased customer usage.

News services have proved to be an effective tool for online customer support. End users who don't require immediate responses to their support questions can post messages and return later. Other customers needing support benefit from this system, as they can view previous support posts and responses and find immediate answers to their questions. Another potential benefit is that end users will begin answering each other's support posts. Rather than relying on expensive telephone support, businesses can lower support costs and create an integrated online support solution using news and chat servers.

News Server enables ISPs and commercial Web sites to operate distributed bulletin board systems, public newsgroups, and private newsgroups on the Internet. News Server also publishes information among Intranet work groups. Internet Service Providers use News Server as the technology supporting collaborative, threaded discussion groups, which helps establish and maintain an active, loyal customer base.

News Server is a native NNTP server that supports open newsreader clients and interopcrates with other popular NNTP news servers. However, the standard NNTP authentication protocol sends passwords in clear text format over the network.

News Server supports the standard NNTP clear text format authentication protocol. News Server also supports an authentication extension that is based on the Windows NT Challenge/Response authentication[3] protocol that does not require sending passwords in clear text over the Internet. News Server supports Secure Socket Layer (SSL) encryption.

News Server may be configured to replicate newsgroups across other NNTP news servers. This distributed configuration of News Server distributes the load and improves performance.

Newsgroups may be local, remote, or moderator-approved. News Server supports built-in control messages to automatically create, check, or delete newsgroups for both private and public newsgroups. News Server supports popular NNTP extensions such as XOVER and XREPLIC.

For more information on MCIS News Server, please visit *http://backof-fice.microsoft.com.*

Commercial Internet Chat Server

Hosting chats can be beneficial. One benefit is that it helps build community. Chat is one of the most popular services offered on both the Internet and online services. It's an effective tool for attracting customers to Web sites and for reducing customer turnover. Sites that offer chat services enrich their content, encourage customer visits, and develop customer loyalty by fostering community. Services that rely upon usage-based pricing models benefit from increased customer usage that chat generates.

---

3. Server security is discussed in Chapter 7.

Chat is also an effective tool for administrating online customer support. Vendors can offer weekly product chats during which end users get real-time support for their questions. Rather than solely relying on the more expensive telephone support option, businesses can create an integrated online support solution utilizing chat and news technologies. These services can reduce operational costs. Telephone support organizations can also benefit from using chat technology internally. Chat technology allows support representatives to get real-time help from their peers while still communicating with customers. Microsoft Product Support Services currently uses Chat for this purpose.

Microsoft Internet Chat (MIC) is a system of client-server application components that provides real-time messaging between clients using the standard TCP/IP or UDP/IP protocols. MIC provides access controls on a per-channel basis and provides server-monitoring controls to enhance manageability of chat networks.

MIC extensions are designed to optimize secure data traffic over the network and provide for conferencing, virtual worlds, and multiplayer games. MIC can scale to at least double the size of today's largest IRC chat networks, or from the average 20 thousand chat room limit to an expected 20 million chat rooms.

MIC fully supports today's IRC protocol as well as extends it by providing a binary chat protocol that includes chat searches, a range of chat channel types and modes, and Unicode support. MIC supports all standard IRC clients as well as Microsoft chat clients. An SDK is also available for MIC, which contains API for extensibility and a family of controls for enabling chat on a Web page.

MIC supports multiple types of chats, including auditorium-style chats for large audiences, and public, private, and authenticated chats. MIC ships with a sample Active control that allows end users to chat within the boundaries of a page. The control may be surrounded by advertising, scrolling banners, Java applets, or static content. MIC also supports graphical chat clients such as Microsoft's Comic Chat client.

MIC provides a Chatsock API: a chat protocol-independent API. Developers can write text chat clients, 3-D chat clients, online game applications, virtual worlds, multiuser games, browser-based pagers, and real-time data feed tickers. Clients written to the Chatsock API can communicate with other IRC servers as well as MIC servers. Included in the server's SDK is a Chat client, Visual Basic wrappers, a checkers game, and sample data feeds to facilitate the development process.

For more information on MIC, please visit *http://backoffice.microsoft.com/product/chat*.

Commercial Internet Mail Server

MCIS Mail is a commercial grade, Internet standards-based mail system that scales up to millions of users. MCIS Mail provides a robust, native, and scalable implementation of standard Internet protocols. MCIS Mail provides full support for the

Internet standard Simple Mail Transfer Protocol (SMTP) and Post Office Protocol, version 3.0 (POP3).

MCIS Mail can utilize Membership Server to guarantee that a mail user is who they state they are. Mail also supports the Multipurpose Internet Main Extensions (MIME) standard for embedding objects into e-mail.

MCIS Mail is designed as a distributed service that can support tens of millions of mailboxes distributed over multiple sites. MCIS Mail supports efficient routing of mail to other sites. MCIS Mail's native implementation of Internet mail standards provides for high performance, reliability, and security. For more information on MCIS Mail, please visit *http://backoffice.microsoft.com/product/mail.*

This concludes a brief discussion of selected Microsoft Commercial Internet Servers. The last two sections cover two BackOffice servers, Microsoft Transaction Server and Microsoft Proxy Server.

MICROSOFT TRANSACTION SERVER

Microsoft Transaction Server (MTS) automatically provides applications with transaction support so that companies can rapidly build and easily modify server applications without sacrificing mission-critical reliability and scalability. MTS is designed to work with Internet and industry standards so that businesses can preserve investments in existing mainframe and UNIX systems while deploying modern applications using component software.

Microsoft Transaction Server combines the best features of transaction processing monitors, reliability, and scalability with the best features from object request brokers, distributed services, and components. Transaction Server provides the vital application infrastructure developers need and do not want to develop themselves. Independent software vendors that develop server solutions estimate that building this "plumbing" into their products consumes 30 to 40 percent of their development costs. Active Server Page applications will be able to plug right in to Transaction Server.

MTS addresses two main issues: lower-cost server development, and mainframe-class reliability.

Lower-Cost Server Development

Microsoft Transaction Server delivers a series of plumbing features to drive down the complexity and cost of building applications on the server. These features enable developers to focus on building business logic without having to build application infrastructure. The result is shorter development time, less complex programming, and easier deployment and integration. Lower-cost server development offers several features.

Accessible three-tiered application model Three-tiered applications—a design where presentation, business logic, and data are separated from each other—provide more deployment flexibility than two-tiered client/server programming, where application code is location-dependent. To date, businesses have had to purchase costly, high-end application platforms to enjoy the benefits of a three-tiered approach. Transaction Server provides an accessible three-tiered model on a commodity platform, delivering high-end distributed features.

Active language support Developers build Transaction Server applications as software components using tools that support Active components, including Microsoft Visual Basic, Visual C++, and Visual J++. This leverages existing investments in training, people, and the quarter billion dollar market for pre-built Active components.

Simple interfaces Server environments like transaction processing monitors and object request brokers require mastering hundreds of APIs before developers become productive. Transaction Server has only two main APIs, lowering training costs while improving developer productivity.

Automatic thread and process management Transaction Server manages low-level system resources, enabling components to automatically operate in a multiuser environment without forcing developers to build this complexity into their applications. Transaction Server provides just-in-time instantiation, making it easier to use components to deliver high-performance applications on servers.

Component packaging Transaction Server includes a component packaging service, so developers do not have to wrestle with the complicated logistics of integrating, installing, and deploying many components as a single application.

Database connection pool Transaction Server manages a pool of ODBC connections to a database, providing high-performance database access without forcing the developer to manage complex database synchronization issues.

Shared data Transaction Server provides a mechanism that makes it easy to share data among multiple concurrently executing objects without forcing the developer to program complex state-sharing and synchronization logic.

Sample applications as learning tools Transaction Server includes two sample applications to help developers come up to speed quickly on the product.

Mainframe-Class Reliability

Easier development only solves part of the problem that businesses will face with online server applications. Applications also need to run reliably and recover from failures accurately. Otherwise, records can be corrupted and business disrupted. The type of reliability and transaction processing features that have been running on mainframe applications for 25 years are essential for the new generation of online application servers. Transaction Server provides mainframe class recovery and reliability for NT/IIS-based systems by supporting transactions and isolating processes.

Support for transactions Transaction Server automatically provides transaction support to applications running on the server, providing a reliable failure isolation and recovery mechanism. Transaction support is transparent to the application programmer, making mainframe-class reliability available to a mass market of solution developers. This transparent support for transactions is a technology breakthrough compared to previous generations of transaction processing systems, where developers had to explicitly program low-level transaction control primitives into their applications.

Process isolation Using Transaction Server packages, developers and administrators can easily isolate components so they operate in their own system process, providing an additional level of failure isolation and data protection.

For more information on Transaction Server, visit *http://www.microsoft.com/transaction*.

The last section covers Microsoft Proxy Server.

MICROSOFT PROXY SERVER

Microsoft Proxy Server offers unprecedented control. You can designate who can access the Internet and which services they can use. Administrators can also establish additional credentials for logging on, set specific dialing hours or days of the week, and restrict access to certain sites altogether. You can also track use to ensure that workers are using their Internet access appropriately.

Microsoft Proxy Server helps ensure that Intranet users have quick access to the data they need. Its intelligent caching capabilities store frequently accessed Internet data on Intranet LANs where Intranet users access it as quickly as information on the local network. This helps to improve users' efficiency and keep costs down by reducing network traffic and congestion to and from the Internet.

Microsoft Proxy Server supports both TCP/IP and IPX/SPX protocols so you can use it with your existing network without modification. Proxy Server requires no end-user training because it works with existing Web browsers, desktop operating systems, and hardware platforms. Proxy Server integrates tightly with the Windows NT Server networking, security, and administrative interface, so you can centrally administer Proxy Server using the same tools. It complies fully with the CERN-proxy standard, which supports the HTTP, FTP, and gopher protocols, providing access to the widest possible range of browsers and Internet applications. Proxy Server supports the Secure Sockets Layer (SSL) for secure data communication through data encryption and decryption. And finally, Proxy Server improves response times and minimizes network traffic by caching a local copy of frequently requested Internet or Intranet data on a local computer.

Microsoft Proxy Server dynamically analyzes Internet and Intranet use and automatically identifies the most frequently used data to be cached, ensuring that users can access the most popular information quickly. It also enables administrators to define a time-to-live for all objects in the cache, helping to keep the information fresh and ensure maximum efficiency.

Microsoft Proxy Server blocks access to restricted sites by IP address or domain so you can ensure that your users are using their Internet privileges appropriately. Finally, Microsoft Proxy Server prevents unauthorized Internet users from connecting to your private network, keeping your sensitive data secure.

For more information on Microsoft Proxy Server, please visit *http://www.microsoft.com/proxy*.

This chapter covered all remaining Site Server components as well as other server tools and techniques to help you get the most from your Site Server installation. Chapter 7 discusses Site Server operations, security, and scalability.

Operating, Securing, and Scaling Your Site Server

Chapters 1 through 5 of this book discuss the notion that Site Server is an NT-based set of server technologies and client components to facilitate electronic commerce on the Internet. Chapter 6 discusses Site Server tools such as Usage Analyst and Site Analyst and focuses on Site Server from the view of a full life cycle workbench for developing, managing, maintaining, and growing an Internet commercial presence.

This chapter covers issues such as security, scaling, and performance monitoring, and operational issues such as coexisting in heterogeneous platform environments. When talking to ISPs and ICPs about Site Server, I always get some questions about the security and scalability of Site Server. Many ISPs and ICPs who host their own sites are also interested in installing Site Server in preexisting, mixed-platform environments.

SITE SERVER SECURITY

Everyone is concerned about Internet security. This chapter is not a replacement for a formal Internet security program. Many books exist today that cover the general topic of Internet security. This chapter covers the security mechanisms of Site Server as an aid to understanding and implementing a secure commercial site.

Because Site Server security mechanisms are based on the foundation of NT, IIS, and SQL Server security, these mechanisms apply across all Site Server technologies running on NT, IIS, and SQL Servers, including Commerce Server. In the case of Commerce Server, a security white paper is available on the companion CD from "Commerce Server Roadmap." However, this paper covers Commerce Server security only, and it assumes familiarity with NT, IIS, and SQL tools and techniques to implement the recommended steps and measures discussed in Commerce Server Roadmap's security article.

This chapter covers the underlying NT, IIS, and SQL Server security issues. Appendix J covers the NT, IIS, and SQL tools for implementing and managing security, such as NT User Manager.

NT Server Security

This section covers the concepts of NT user account domains and NT file system Access Control Lists (ACLs). In some operating system platforms, if you want to access files (or devices) on other workstations, you must have a separate account on each machine. In practical terms, this means that if you change your password and want to keep the same one on each machine you access, you must update the password separately on each system. This type of system account maintenance is a nuisance for large business or corporate network installations. As the number of workstations increases, the task of administering them increases proportionally. NT supports domains and single-signon to simplify account maintenance and use a single username and password across all domains.

Using NT Server Domain Controllers

An NT server can be a Primary Domain Controller, a Secondary Domain Controller, or a stand-alone server. A domain includes several workstations and one or more server machines. Server machines can be stand-alone or can act as domain controllers. When you log on, you select whether to log on to an account defined at your own workstation or on to an account located in your primary domain, the domain to which your machine belongs.

Windows NT stores account names and passwords in a database called the Security Accounts Manager (SAM) database. When you attempt to log on to the workstation, Windows NT checks the SAM database associated with the workstation to authenticate username and password. If you log on to an account on your workstation, the local authentication software uses the information stored in the workstation's SAM database to authenticate your logon. In contrast, if you log on to the domain, the local authentication software sends the logon request to the Primary Domain Controller or the Backup Domain Controller(s) for authentication. Hence, user authentication management is centralized.

NT Server Primary, Backup, and Domain Controllers The Primary Domain Controller has a SAM database that applies to the entire domain, and the Secondary Domain Controller maintains replicated copies of the database. This convenience frees the user from acquiring accounts on each server and improves fault tolerance. If a particular domain controller goes down, the system can dynamically direct a logon request to a different server.

Information on user accounts among different domains is shared using trust relationships. Trust relationship is a security term meaning that the workstation "trusts" the domain to determine whether the user's logon is legitimate. A trust relationship allows Windows NT to set up a secure channel between the two systems and to access resources on the domain without duplicating the user login and password information on two or more machines and domains. This is distinct from the way many mainframe server installations operate, where the user must be added to each machine's local user base.

A side effect of establishing a domain is that the user can also log on to a domain from any other workstation (or server) in that domain and access his or her own workstation remotely. For example, if a group has established a development or testing lab of NT systems in a domain, a user who has an account on this domain can log on to his or her account from any system in the lab using the same user ID and password while the user's account information can be remotely located on his or her own server.

The ability to create a network domain is convenient for medium-sized network installations in which several servers are used by a large number of workstations. In larger installations, such as corporate-wide networks, domains become very valuable; they allow a company to divide its resources into several discrete business units (domains) and to manage those units in a flexible manner.

NT Server Groups and Access Control Lists Most Unix systems maintain an access mask for three groups of users: user, group, and public. NT Server also maintains an access list for the same purpose. All Windows NT machines come with a set of predefined groups set up in the user manager. These groups are based around a set of common roles users generally play when working with a computer. Each group has a level of privileges and rights set up for them based around these roles. For example, the Administrators group members have more rights and privileges than the Users group members.

NT translates a user's name and password to an access token. This access token is then matched against Access Control Lists (ACLs). When dealing with files that are hosted on a drive formatted with the NT File System (NTFS), you have the capability of assigning access privileges to files on a directory or file-by-file basis. See the NT tools section of Appendix J for associated tools. The NTFS allows ACLs to be placed on directories, files, executables, and all system resources. ACLs can be used to implicitly or explicitly grant or deny access to a particular file or directory for a user or group of users. With NTFS and ACLs, you can control who has access to specific files and programs within directories and subdirectories.

Having covered the concepts of NT domains and Access Control Lists in this section, you are now ready to move on to IIS security topics.

IIS Security

IIS security is built on the Windows NT security model and provides additional Web monitoring and security features. For example, you can set read-only or execute-only access on the Web virtual directories by using Internet Service Manager. IIS also provides a way to deny access to computers with particular IP addresses. IIS also supports the Secure Sockets Layer (SSL) protocol, which securely encrypts data transmissions between clients and servers. The following sections explain how to configure Windows NT and the IIS services to protect your system.

Controlling access by monitoring anonymous access

On many Web servers, almost all WWW, FTP, and gopher access is anonymous; that is, the client request does not contain a user name and password. This occurs in the following cases:

■ When an FTP client logs on with the user name *anonymous*

■ When using gopher requests

■ When a Web browser request does not contain a user name and password in the HTTP header (this is the default on new Web connections with most browsers)

Even though the user is not logged on with an individual user name and password, you can still control and monitor anonymous access. Each Internet service maintains a Windows NT user name and password that is used to process anonymous requests. When an anonymous request is received, the service "impersonates" the user configured as the anonymous logon user. The request succeeds if the anonymous logon user has permission to access the requested resource, as determined by the resource's Access Control List (ACL). If the anonymous logon user does not have permission, the request fails. You can configure the WWW service to respond to a failed anonymous request by requiring the user to provide a valid Windows NT user name and password, a process called authentication.

Configuring the anonymous user account You can view and monitor the anonymous logon user account on the Service property sheets of Internet Service Manager (for the WWW, FTP, and gopher services). Each service running on the same computer can use either the same or different anonymous logon user accounts. Including the anonymous logon user account in file or folder ACLs enables you to precisely control the resources available to anonymous clients.

The anonymous logon user account must be a valid Windows NT user account on the server providing the Web services, and the password must match the password for this user in that computer's user database. User accounts and passwords are configured in the Windows NT User Manager by setting User Rights in the Policies menu. The anonymous logon user account must have the Log On Locally user right.

The IUSR_*computername* account is automatically created (with a randomly generated password) during IIS setup. For example, if the computer name is marketing1, then the anonymous access account name is IUSR_*marketing1*.

By default, all Web client requests use this account. In other words, Web clients are logged on to the computer by using the IUSR_*computername* account. The IUSR_*computername* account is permitted only to log on locally on the server providing the Web services.[1]

For the WWW and FTP services, you can allow or prevent anonymous access (all gopher requests are anonymous). For each WWW, FTP, and gopher service, you can change the user account used for anonymous requests and change the password for that account.

To allow anonymous access,

1. In Internet Service Manager, double-click the WWW service or the FTP service to display its property sheets.

2. Click the Service tab.

3. For the WWW service, select the Allow Anonymous check box.

4. For the FTP service, select the Allow Anonymous Connections check box. (If you want to continue to allow authenticated users to connect, be sure the Allow Only Anonymous Connections check box is not checked.)

5. Click OK.

---

1. The IUSR_*computername* account is also added to the group Guests. If you have changed the settings for the Guests group, those changes also apply to the IUSR_*computername* account. You should review the settings for the Guests group to ensure that they are appropriate for the IUSR_*computername* account.

To change the account or password used for anonymous access,

1. In Internet Service Manager, double-click the service to display its property sheets.

2. Click the Service tab.

3. In the Anonymous Logon user name box, type the new user name. The default user account is IUSR_*computername*, where *computername* is the name of your server. This account is created automatically when you set up Internet Information Server.

4. In the Password box, type the new password. A randomly generated password is automatically created for the IUSR_*computername* account when you set up Internet Information Server.[2]

Using the anonymous account on domain controllers When IIS is installed on a Primary or Secondary Domain Controller, the anonymous logon user account is created in the user account database of the domain (PDC). When IIS is installed on a domain member-server or a stand-alone server, the account is created on the local computer.

If IIS is installed on multiple domain controllers of the same domain, a separate user account is created in the domain user database for each Internet server computer. This does not cause any conflicts because each user name is unique, containing the name of the associated computer. However, you may find it more convenient to create a single anonymous logon user account in the domain to use for all IIS domain controllers in the domain. This can simplify administration of ACLs. To do this, follow these steps.

1. In User Manager for Domains, create a new anonymous logon user account in the domain. Be sure that you make this account a member of appropriate groups, give it a secure password, and give it the User Right (in the Policies menu) to log on locally.

2. On the Service property sheet of Internet Service Manager, specify the new anonymous logon user name and password. You must do this for each IIS service running on all Primary and Secondary Domain Controllers in the domain.

When later installing IIS on other domain controllers in the domain, be sure to use Internet Service Manager to modify the anonymous logon user name and password to match those created with User Manager for Domains. Do this for each IIS service installed.

---

2. If you change the password for this account, you must also specify the new password for the account in User Manager.

If you allow remote access only by the IUSR_*computername* account, remote users do not provide a user name and password, and have only the permissions assigned to that account. This prevents hackers from attempting to gain access to sensitive information with fraudulent or illegally obtained passwords. For some situations this provides the best security.

Controlling access by user or group

You can control access to your Web site by using the Windows NT User Manager to specify what certain users or groups of users are allowed to do on your server. You can further control access by requiring Web client requests to provide a user name and password that IIS confirms before completing the request.

Windows NT security helps you protect your computer and its resources by requiring assigned user accounts. Every operation on a computer running Windows NT identifies who is doing the operation. For example, the user name and password that you use to log on to Windows NT identifies who you are and defines what you are authorized to do on that computer.

What a user is authorized to do on a computer is configured in User Manager by setting user rights in the Policies menu. User rights authorize a user to perform certain actions on the system, including the Log on Locally right, which is required for users to use Internet services if Basic authentication is being used.

If you are using Windows NT Challenge/Response authentication, then the Access this computer from network right is required for users to use Internet services. By default, everyone has this right.

To increase security, follow these guidelines:

- Do not give the IUSR_*computername* account, the Guests group, or the Everyone group any right other than the Log on Locally or the Access this computer from network right.

- Make sure that all user accounts on the system, especially those with administrative rights, have difficult-to-guess passwords. In particular, select a good administrator password (a long, mixed-case, alphanumeric password is best) and set the appropriate account policies. Passwords can be set by using User Manager, or by typing at the system logon prompt.

- Make sure that you specify how quickly account passwords expire (which forces users to regularly change passwords), and set other policies such as how many bad logon attempts will be tolerated before locking a user out. Use these policies to prevent exhaustive or random password attacks, especially on accounts with administrative access. You can set these policies by using User Manager.

- Limit the membership of the Administrator group to trusted individuals.

- If you use the predefined Windows NT user accounts Interactive and Network for access control, make sure files in your Web site are accessible to these user accounts. In order for a file to be accessed by anonymous client requests or client requests using Basic authentication, the requested file must be accessible by the Interactive user. In order for a file to be accessible by a client request that uses Windows NT Challenge/Response authentication protocol, the file must be accessible by the Network user.

Controlling access by requiring a user name and password

You can restrict Web site access to only authenticated clients; that is, Web clients that supply a valid Windows NT user name and password. When you use authentication, no access is permitted unless a valid user name and password are supplied. Password authentication is useful if you want only authorized individuals to access your Web site or specific portions controlled by NTFS. You can have both anonymous logon access and authenticated access enabled at the same time.

The WWW service provides two forms of authentication: basic and Windows NT Challenge/Response (sometimes referred to as NTLM). Basic authentication does not encrypt transmissions between the client and server. Because Basic authentication sends the client's Windows NT user name and password in unencrypted packets over the networks, sophisticated intruders could use line-monitoring devices to learn user names and passwords.

Windows NT Challenge/Response authentication, currently supported only by Microsoft Internet Explorer version 2.0 or later, protects the password, providing for secure logon over the network. In Windows NT Challenge/Response authentication, the client account is the account with which the user logs on to the client computer. Because this account, including its Windows NT domain, must be a valid account on the Windows NT-based server running Internet Information Server, Windows NT Challenge/Response authentication is very useful in an Intranet environment, where the client and server computers are in the same, or trusted, domains. Because of the increased security, Microsoft recommends using the Windows NT Challenge/Response method of password authentication whenever possible.

You have both Basic and Windows NT Challenge/Response authentication enabled by default. If the browser supports Windows NT Challenge/Response, it uses that authentication method. Otherwise, it uses Basic authentication. Windows NT Challenge/Response authentication is currently supported only by Internet Explorer 2.0 or later.

You can require client authentication for all FTP service requests or only for anonymous requests that fail. The FTP service supports only Basic authentication; therefore, your site is more secure if you allow anonymous connections. Your site is most secure if you allow only anonymous FTP connections.

To enable authentication for the WWW service,

1. In Internet Service Manager, double-click the WWW service to display its property sheets.

2. Click the Service tab.

3. Select Basic (Clear Text), Windows NT Challenge/Response, or both.

To enable authentication for the FTP service,

1. In Internet Service Manager, double-click the FTP service to display its property sheets.

2. Click the Service tab.

To enable authentication for failed anonymous connections,

1. Clear (delete) the Allow Only Anonymous Connections check box.

2. To require all client requests to be authenticated, clear the Allow Anonymous Connections check box.

WARNING Basic authentication sends passwords across the network in clear text (that is, unencrypted).

Anonymous logons and client authentication interaction You can enable both anonymous connections and client authentication for the WWW service and for the FTP service. This section explains how IIS responds to these access methods when both are enabled.

Note that if client authentication is disallowed and anonymous connections are allowed, a client request that contains a user name and password is processed as an anonymous connection, and the server ignores the user name and password.

WWW service When the WWW service receives a client request that contains credentials (a user name and password), the anonymous logon user account is not used in processing the request. Instead, the user name and password received by the client are used by the service. If the service is not granted permission to access the requested resource while using the specified user name and password, the request fails, and an error notification is returned to the client.

When an anonymous request fails because the anonymous logon user account does not have permission to access the desired resource, the response to the client indicates which authentication schemes the WWW service supports. If the response indicates to the client that the service is configured to support HTTP Basic authentication, most Web browsers will display a user name and password dialog box, and reissue the anonymous request as a request with credentials, including the user name and password entered by the user.

If a Web browser supports Windows NT Challenge/Response authentication protocol, and the WWW service is configured to support this protocol, an anonymous WWW request that fails due to inadequate permissions will result in automatic use of the Windows NT Challenge/Response authentication protocol. The browser will then send a user name and encrypted password from the client to the server. The client request is reprocessed, using the client's user information.

If the WWW service is configured to support both Basic and Windows NT Challenge/Response, the Web server returns both authentication methods in a header to the Web browser. The Web browser then chooses which authentication method to use. Because the Windows NT Challenge/Response protocol is listed first in the header, a browser that supports the Windows NT Challenge/Response protocol will use it. A browser that does not support the Windows NT Challenge/Response protocol will use Basic authentication. Currently, Windows NT Challenge/Response authentication is supported only by Internet Explorer 2.0 or later.

FTP service When the FTP service receives a client request that contains credentials (a user name and password), the anonymous logon user account is not used in processing the request. Instead, the user name and password received by the client are used by the service. If the service is not granted permission to access the requested resource while using the specified user name and password, the request fails, and an error notification is returned to the client.

When an anonymous request fails because the anonymous logon user account does not have permission to access the desired resource, the server responds with an error message. Most Web browsers will display a user name and password dialog box, and reissue the anonymous request as a request with credentials, including the user name and password entered by the user.

If you need a WWW request authentication scheme not supported by the service directly, obtain a copy of the Win32 Software Development Kit (SDK), and read the ISAPI Filters specification on how to develop user-written ISAPI Filter dynamic-link libraries (DLLs) that handle request authentication. The Win32 SDK is available through the Microsoft Developer Network. For more information, visit the Microsoft home page (*http://www.microsoft.com/*).

Controlling access by setting folder and file permissions

Every access to a resource, such as a file, an HTML page, or an Internet Server API (ISAPI) application, is done by the services on behalf of a Windows NT user. The service uses that user's user name and password in the attempt to read or execute the resource for the client. You can control access to files and folders in two ways.[3]

---

3. File Allocation Table (FAT) file system partitions do not support access control. However, a FAT partition may be converted to NTFS by using the convert utility. Refer to Windows NT documentation for more information on using this utility.

- By setting access permissions in the Windows NT File System (NTFS)

- By setting access permissions in the Internet Service Manager

Setting NTFS permissions You should place your data files on an NTFS partition. NTFS provides security and access control for your data files. You can limit access to portions of your file system for specific users and services by using NTFS. In particular, it is a good idea to apply Access Control Lists (ACLs) to your data files for any Internet publishing service.

File and folder ACLs are configured by using the Windows NT Explorer. The NTFS file system gives you fine control on files by specifying users and groups that are permitted access and what type of access they may have for specific files and directories. For example, some users may have Read-only access, while others may have Read, Change, and Write access. You should ensure that the IUSR_*computername* or authenticated accounts are granted or denied appropriate access to specific resources.

You should note that the group Everyone contains all users and groups, including the IUSR_*computername* account and the Guests group. By default the group Everyone has full control of all files created on an NTFS drive. If conflicts arise between your NTFS settings and Microsoft IIS settings, the strictest settings will be used.

You should review the security settings for all folders in your Web site and adjust them appropriately. Generally you should use the settings in the following table:

Directory Type	*Suggested NTFS Access*
Content	Read access
Databases	Read and Write access
Programs	Read and Execute access

To secure your files on an NTFS drive,

1. Put your files on your NTFS drive and add them to your Web site by using the Directories property sheet in Internet Service Manager.

2. In Windows NT Explorer, right-click the folder (directory) you wish to secure (select your site root directory to secure the entire directory structure including subdirectories), and choose Properties.

3. In the Properties dialog box, choose the Security tab.

4. In the Security dialog box, choose Permissions.

5. In the Directory Permissions dialog box, click Add to add users and groups.

6. In the Add Users and Groups dialog box, add the users that should have access. Click OK.

7. In the Directory Permissions dialog box, select the users and groups that should have permissions.

8. From the Type Of Access list box, choose the permission level you wish for the selected user or group. Click OK.

To determine whether anyone has gained unauthorized access to sensitive files, you can audit the access of NTFS files and folders. For example, you can check for attempts by members of a specific user group to read files. You should review the audit records periodically to check for unauthorized access. To set auditing on a file or folder, use User Manager for Domains to enable auditing of File and Object Access, and then use Windows NT Explorer to specify which files to audit and which types of file access events to audit. To review audit entries, use Event Viewer. For more information on setting the audit policy for files and folders, see the Windows NT documentation.

Setting Internet Service Manager permissions When creating a Web publishing directory (folder) in Internet Service Manager, you can set access permissions for the defined home directory or virtual directory, and all of the folders in it. These permissions are those provided by the WWW service and are in addition to any provided by the NTFS. The permissions are called Read and Execute.

Read permission enables clients to read or download files stored in a home directory or a virtual directory. If a client sends a request for a file that is in a directory without Read permission, the server returns an error. Generally, you should assign Read permission to directories containing information to publish (HTML files, for example). You should disable Read permission for directories containing Common Gateway Interface (CGI) applications and Internet Server Application Program Interface (ISAPI) DLLs to prevent clients from downloading the application files.

Execute permission enables a Web client to run programs and scripts stored in a home directory or a virtual directory. If a client sends a request to run a program or a script in a folder that does not have Execute permission, the Web server returns an error. For security purposes, do not give content folders Execute permission.

A client request can invoke a CGI application or an Internet Server Application Program Interface (ISAPI) application. An example URL would be the following:

```
http://inetsrvr.microsoft.com/scripts/httpodbc.dll?lname=Smith.
```

For this request to be valid, the file HTTPODBC.DLL must be stored somewhere in the Web "publishing tree" (the directory structure that contains your content files; in this example, in the Scripts folder), and the folder it is stored in must have the Execute permission selected. This way the administrator can permit applications (CGI or ISAPI) to be run from a small number of carefully monitored directories.

To set access permissions for a directory[4] in Internet Service Manager,

1. Double-click the WWW service to display its property sheets, then click the Directories tab.

2. Select the folder for which you wish to set permissions.

3. Click Edit Properties. To allow Web clients to read and download the contents of a folder, select the Read check box. To allow Web clients to run programs and scripts in a folder, select the Execute check box.

4. Click OK, then click OK again to complete the operation.

Controlling access by IP address

You can configure Microsoft IIS to grant or deny access to specific IP addresses. For example, you can exclude a harassing individual by denying access to your server from a particular IP address, or prevent entire networks from accessing your server. Conversely, you can choose to allow only specific sites to have access to your service. IP address security is probably most useful on the Internet to exclude everyone except known users.

The source IP address of every packet received is checked against the IIS settings in the Advanced property sheet. If IIS is configured to allow access by all computers except those listed as exceptions to that rule, access is denied to any computer with an IP address included in that list. Conversely, if IIS is configured to deny all IP addresses, access is denied to all remote users except those whose IP addresses have been specifically granted access.

To deny access to a specific computer,

1. In the Advanced property sheet of Internet Service Manager, choose the Granted Access button and click Add.

2. In the IP Address box, type the IP address of the computer to be denied access to your site or click the button next to the IP Address box to use a DNS name, such as *www.company.com*.

---

4. I recommend that you set either Execute access or Read access on a folder, but not both. Executable scripts and programs should be kept in a virtual directory whose physical target is outside of the Web document root directory tree.

To deny access to a group of computers,

1. Select Group of Computers.

2. In the IP Address and Subnet Mask boxes, type the IP address and the subnet mask for a group to be denied access. Access will be granted to all computers except the ones in the window with an Access status of Denied.

3. In the Advanced property sheet, click OK.

Running other network services You should review all of the network services that you are using on any computer connected to the Internet. Run only the services that you need. The fewer services you are running on your system, the less likely a mistake will be made in administration that could be exploited. Use the Services application in Control Panel to disable any services not absolutely necessary on your Internet server.

You should also unbind unnecessary services from your Internet adapter cards. Use the Bindings feature in the Network application in Control Panel to unbind any unnecessary services from any network adapter cards connected to the Internet. For example, you might use the Server service to copy new images and documents from computers in your internal network, but you might not want remote users to have direct access to the Server service from the Internet.

If you need to use the Server service on your private network, disable the Server service binding to any network adapter cards connected to the Internet. You can use the Windows NT Server service over the Internet; however, you should fully understand the security and licensing implications.

When you are using the Windows NT Server service, you are using Microsoft NT networking—the server message block (SMB) protocol rather than the HTTP protocol—and all Windows NT Server Licensing requirements still apply. HTTP connections do not apply to Windows NT Server licensing requirements.

If you are running the Server service on your Internet adapter cards, be sure to double-check the permissions set on the shares you have created on the system. You should also double-check the permissions set on the files contained in the shares' folders to ensure that you have set them correctly.

Unless it is part of your strategy, you should not enable directory browsing on the Directories property sheet. Directory browsing potentially exposes the entire Web publishing file structure; if it is not configured correctly, you run the risk of exposing program files or other files to unauthorized access. If a default page (DEFAULT.HTM) is not present and directory browsing is enabled, the WWW service will return a Web page containing a listing of files in the specified directory. It is always advisable to have a DEFAULT.HTM page in any directory that you do not wish to be browsed.

Securing data transmissions with Secure Sockets Layer (SSL)

Previous sections of this chapter have dealt with securing your server from unauthorized access. This section discusses protocols that use cryptography to secure data transmissions to and from your server.

Microsoft IIS offers a protocol for providing data security layered between its service protocols (HTTP) and TCP/IP. This security protocol, called Secure Sockets Layer (SSL), provides data encryption, server authentication, and message integrity for a TCP/IP connection.

SSL is an industry-standard security protocol for Web browsers and servers on the Internet. SSL provides a security "handshake" that is used to initiate the connection between the browser and the server. This handshake results in the client and server agreeing on the level of security that they will use and fulfills any authentication requirements for the connection. Thereafter, SSL's only role is to encrypt and decrypt the byte stream of the application protocol being used (for example, HTTP). This means that all the information in both the HTTP request and response are fully encrypted, including the URL the client is requesting, any submitted form contents (such as credit-card numbers), any HTTP access authorization information (user names and passwords), and all the data returned from the server to the client.

An SSL-enabled server can send and receive private communication across the Internet to SSL-enabled clients (browsers), such as Microsoft Internet Explorer version 2.0 or later. However, SSL-encrypted transmissions are slower than unencrypted transmissions. To avoid reducing performance for your entire site, consider using SSL only for virtual folders that deal with highly sensitive information such as a form submission containing credit-card information.

To enable SSL security on a Web server, you must complete the following tasks:

- Generate a key pair file and a request file
- Request a certificate from a certification authority
- Install the certificate on your server
- Configure a directory to require SSL security

Keep in mind the following points when enabling SSL security: You can enable SSL security on the root of your Web site (\INETPUB\WWWROOT by default) or on one or more virtual folders; once enabled and properly configured, only SSL-enabled clients will be able to communicate with the SSL-enabled WWW folders; and URLs that point to documents on an SSL-enabled WWW folder must use *https://* instead of *HTTP://* in the URL. Any links using *HTTP://* in the URL will not work on a secure folder.

Generating a key pair As part of the process of enabling Secure Sockets Layer (SSL) security on your Web server, you need to generate a key pair and then acquire an SSL certificate. The new Key Manager application (installed with the product and located in the Internet Server program group) simplifies this procedure.

To generate a key pair,

1. In the Microsoft Internet Server submenu, click Key Manager, or click the Key Manager icon on the Internet Service Manager toolbar.

2. From the Key menu, click Create New Key.

3. In the Create New Key and Certificate Request dialog box, fill in the requested information, as follows:

NOTE Do not use commas in any field. Commas are interpreted as the end of that field and will generate an invalid request without warning.

Key Name	Assign a name to the key you are creating.
Password	Specify a password to encrypt the private key.
Bits	By default, Key Manager generates a key pair 1024 bits long. To specify a key that is 512 or 768 bits long, make the proper selection in this box. The more bits you specify, the greater your security. In international versions, the size of each key you create is 512 bits
Organization	Preferably International Organization for Standardization-(ISO) registered, top-level organization or company name.
Organizational Unit	Your department within your company, such as Marketing.
Common Name	The domain name of the server, for example, *www. mycompany.com*.
Country	Two-letter ISO country designation, for example, US, FR, AU, UK, and so on.
State/Province	For example, Washington, Alberta, California, and so on.
Locality	The city where your company is located, such as Redmond or Toronto.
Request File	Type the name of the file that will be created.

4. After filling out the form, click OK.

5. When prompted, retype the password you typed in the form and click OK. A busy cursor appears as the key is being created. When the key has been created, a screen appears giving you information about new keys and how to obtain a certificate.

6. After reading the New Key Information screen, click OK.

7. To save the new key, from the Servers menu, choose Commit Changes Now.

8. When asked if you wish to commit all changes now, click OK.

Your key will appear in the Key Manager window under the name of the computer for which you created the key. By default, a key is generated on your local computer. You can also set up a key pair on another server. From the Servers menu, click Connect To Server, and follow the previous procedure.

Moving a key pair to another server After creating a key pair, you can use Key Manager to move the key pair to another server.

To move a key pair to another server,

1. From the Servers menu, click Connect to Server, type the name of the server you want to move the key pair to, and click OK. The server name appears in the list of servers (the left column).

2. Select the key you want to move.

3. From the Edit menu, click Cut.

4. Select the server you want to move the key pair to.

5. From the Edit menu, click Paste.

You can copy a key pair to another server with the same procedure by substituting the Copy command for Cut.

Backing up keys With Key Manager you download key information from the registry into a file on your hard disk and then copy this file or move it to a floppy disk or tape for safekeeping. You can back up a private key pair file or a key with an installed certificate.

To back up a key or a private key pair file,

1. From the Key menu in Key Manager, choose Export Key and then Backup File.

2. After reading the warning about downloading sensitive information to your hard disk, click OK.

3. Type the key name in the File Name box and click Save.

The file is given a .REQ filename extension and is saved to your hard disk drive. You can then copy it or move it to a floppy disk or magnetic tape.

Loading backed up keys You can load backed up keys or private key pair files into Key Manager with the Import command.

To load a backed-up key,

1. From the Key menu in Key Manager, choose Import Key and then Backup File.

2. Select the file name from the list and click Open.

Loading a key created with KEYGEN.EXE and SETKEY.EXE If you have generated a key pair from the command line with the KEYGEN.EXE command and installed a certificate with SETKEY.EXE, you can load them into Key Manager with the Import command.

To load a key,

1. From the Key menu in Key Manager, choose Import Key and then KeySet.

2. In the Private Key Pair File box, type the file name for the key pair or click Browse and select the file.

3. In the Certificate File box, type the file name for the certificate or click Browse and select the file. Click OK.

4. Type the password for the private key in the Private Key Password box and click OK.

Acquiring and installing a certificate Once you have generated a key pair, you must get a certificate and then install that certificate with the key pair. The key generated by Key Manager is not valid for use on the Internet until you obtain a valid certificate for it from a certification authority, such as VeriSign. Send the certificate request file to the certification authority to obtain a valid certificate. Until you do so, the key will exist on its host computer but cannot be used. For instructions on acquiring a VeriSign certificate, refer to VeriSign's Web site at *http://www.ver-isign.com/microsoft/*.

After you complete your certificate request, you will receive a signed certificate from the certification authority (consult your certification authority for complete details). The Key Manager program will create a certificate file.

To install a certificate,

1. In the Internet Server program group, click Key Manager.

2. In the Key Manager window, select the key pair that matches your signed certificate. If you had backed up the key pair file, you have to load it first. For instructions, see the discussion on loading a key pair file earlier in this chapter.

3. From the Key menu, choose Install Key Certificate.

4. Select the Certificate file from the list (CERTIF.TXT, for example), and click Open.

5. When prompted, type the password that you used in creating the key pair. The key and certificate are combined and stored in the registry of the server.

6. From the Servers menu, choose Commit Changes Now.

7. When asked if you wish to commit all changes now, click OK.

You can back up a key and certificate combination by following the procedure about backing up keys described earlier in this chapter.

Configuring a directory to require SSL Once you have applied the certificate, you must enable the SSL feature from Internet Service Manager. SSL can be required on any virtual folder available in your Web site and is configured on the Directories property sheet.

To require SSL,

1. In Internet Service Manager, double-click the WWW service to display its property sheets, then click the Directories tab.

2. Select the folder that requires SSL security, then click Edit Properties.

3. Select the Require Secure SSL Channel option, and then click OK.

Several suggestions will help you with SSL configuration and operation. First, Microsoft recommends that you use separate content directories for secure and public content (for example, C:\INETPUB\WWWROOT\SECURE-Content and C:\INETPUB\WWWROOT\PUBLIC-Content).

Second, save your key file in a safe place in case you need it in the future. And store your key file on a floppy disk and remove it from the local system after completing all setup steps. Finally, don't forget the password you assigned to the key file.

SQL Server Security

Microsoft SQL Server supports three different security models. These models allow either complete integration with the NT domain model, no integration with the domain model, or a mix. These are configured by running Start menu, Programs, Microsoft SQL Server 6.5, SQL Setup.

Standard security

Standard security is the default option installed with SQL Server. It provides the simplest security model because security exists completely independent of the NT domain model. The level of access a user has to the database and its objects is determined by security settings within SQL Server itself. Authentication consists of comparing the provided user name and password against similar information maintained in the SQL Server database. This is the easiest security model to integrate with IIS.

Integrated security

Integrated security is the opposite end of the scale from standard. It is completely dependent upon NT security as far as who is granted access to the SQL Server database. In other words, when a user attempts a connection to the SQL Server, the connection will be made as the logged on user. Integrated security requires that SQL Server be configured to use Named Pipes as its protocol for network communication. Authentication is processed in the same manner as described earlier. Integrated security is not recommended for use with IIS on the NT platform.

Mixed security

Mixed security offers a combination of both of these security models. How a user attempts to establish connection to the SQL Server determines how the user is authenticated. Basically, if the user makes the connection of a trusted ODBC connection, authentication will be via NT's authentication process. If he or she does not, standard security is used, and the provided user name and password are simply compared to the SQL Server user database.

Commerce Server Security

The NT, IIS, and SQL server security topics provide some background and context for understanding the Commerce Server security document provided on the companion CD. You can access this security document from the directory *drive-name*:\Docs\Word\Security.Doc, and it is also available in the *Managing Security* section of the Commerce Server Roadmap (available from the Start menu in Programs\Commerce Server 2.0\Commerce Server Roadmap). Figure 7-1 shows the Commerce Server Roadmap's initial screen.

The "Managing Security" section of the Commerce Server Roadmap describes features and considerations related to the security of Commerce Server–based systems. Topics covered include browser security, database security, operating system server security, store file system security, store manager application security, transaction security, shopper security and privacy, and Web server security. Because Site Server security mechanisms are based on the foundation of NT, IIS, and SQL Server security, Commerce Server Roadmap assumes familiarity with NT, IIS, and SQL tools and techniques to implement the recommended steps and measures discussed in Commerce Server Roadmap's security article. For further details on security, please consult this article.

Figure 7-1. *Commerce Server Roadmap initial screen.*

Commerce Server includes the VeriFone vPOS Payment Component for online, real-time credit-card processing. The vPOS payment component is a Commerce Server pipeline component, which is registered as a Payment Stage component. It requires the value store name to be set for it to be operational.

The vPOS payment component reads the credit-card and billing information from the order form and performs the transaction using Secure Electronic Transaction (SET), a protocol supported by VISA and MasterCard for secure online credit card processing. VeriFone vPOS ships with a sample store called The Furniture Shoppe. This store demonstrates the capability of the VeriFone vPOS software. The store's Order Pipeline is preconfigured with the vPOS payment component and you can try out the store to evaluate the payment functionality provided by VeriFone vPOS. The store executes the vPOS payment component when a user makes a purchase. It also displays the appropriate receipt.

To enable vPOS for new stores,

1. Create the store in the Microsoft Commerce Server 2.0 system.

2. Launch the Control Panel, and double-click on the vPOS Admin applet.

3. Enable vPOS for the store by clicking Add Store.

4. Fill in the information in the Store Configuration dialog box. The store abbreviation should be the same as you use in Microsoft Commerce Server 2.0.

5. Open the pipeline configuration file for the store.

6. Drag and drop a Scriptor component in the payment stage and add the following code in the parameter area:

```
Sub mmsopen(config)
End Sub
Sub mmsexecute(config, orderform, context, flags)
    orderform.value("_store_name") = "[store_name]"
End Sub
Sub mmsclose()
End Sub
```

7. Drag and drop the vPOS payment component into the payment stage of the pipeline.

8. Customize the CONFIRMED.ASP file for your store so that it can display the receipt information that is placed on the order form by the VeriFone program vPOS. The VeriFone Furniture Shoppe's file XT_ORDERFORM_PURCHASE.ASP is a good example to use.

The next section covers scalability issues of Site Server.

SITE SERVER SCALABILITY

This section covers answers two common questions about Site Server scalability:

- What are the typical configurations of Site Server?

- How do I scale Site Server as user demand grows?

The next two sections address these questions beginning with Site Server's typical configurations.

Site Server Typical Configurations

This section explains some typical Site Server configurations. This is not an exhaustive set of all possible configuration options. However, they are actual configurations I use, or that third-party ISPs and ICPs have used, and are included to illustrate the basic concepts.

MSCS laptop demo configuration

The simplest configuration of Site Server is a laptop configuration used for demos and marketing activities. In this configuration I have often used a laptop Pentium 75 MHz CPU, with 500 MB of disk and 32 MB of memory. This system includes an Ethernet card and has access to a CD reader via the network or the docking station. For demos and planning sessions, I installed the following software on the laptop:

- NT Server 4.0 build 1381 (release) or higher plus Service Pack 2

- SQL 6.5 Server plus SQL Server SP2

- Microsoft Site Server Enterprise Edition 2.0 from the companion CD

- IE 3.0 or higher from the companion CD or *http://www.microsoft.com/ie*

This machine has served well for demos and talks. The system is capable of handling small loads of a few concurrent connections and provides response time in the order of 1–3 seconds when configured properly. Please see Site Server installation in Appendix A for installation details.

Site Server development configuration

The next configuration of Site Server is a development-type configuration used for Commerce Server development and staging. In this configuration I used a Pentium 133 MHz CPU with 1 GB of disk and 64 MB of memory. The machine includes an Ethernet card and a CD player. Software is the same as that described for the laptop configuration above, plus the following:

- Site Analyst site analysis tool (Site Server Enterprise Edition)

- WCAT load-generator and performance monitor (NT Resource Kit or Site Server Enterprise)

- Visual InterDev development environment (In practice, the Visual Studio suite of tools including VC++, VJ++, VB, and VI could be installed. The three alternative tools provide server-side component creation wizards to facilitate Site Server component creation. Please see Chapter 5 of this book.)

- Personal editors and tools including FrontPage

This machine served well during pilot development. The system is capable of handling medium loads of a thousand shoppers per hour and provides response time in the order of a fraction of second to a second when configured properly.

Site Server production prototype configuration

The next configuration of Site Server is a prototype for a production machine used for introductory operations and load testing. In this configuration a dual-Pentium 200 MHz CPU with 20 GB of disk and 128–256 MB of memory was used. The machine includes an Ethernet card, a CD player, and a fast RAID disk array. The software is the same as that described for the laptop configuration above.

This configuration is currently deployed at a number of existing retail commercial sites and serves single-store commercial sites quite well. The system is capable of handling medium loads of thousands of concurrent connections per hour and provides response time in the order of a fraction of a second.

The next section addresses the question "How do I scale Site Server as user demand grows?"

Web farms and very large-scale configurations

As demand grows, the load may be distributed using Web farms and large-scale database architectures. Web farms are discussed in this section and database scaling is covered in Appendix M, "SQL Server Scaling."

First, a word about planning for performance. A number of tools are available to simulate the performance of your specific configuration. One such tool is Web Capacity Analysis Tool (WCAT). WCAT runs simulated workloads on client-server configurations. Using WCAT, you can test how your IIS Server and network configuration respond to a variety of different client requests for content, data, or Hypertext Markup Language (HTML) pages. The results of these tests can be used to determine the optimal server and network configuration for your site. The Web Capacity Analysis Tool provides the following:

- Prepared, ready-to-run workload simulations to test the most common aspects of server performance (These simulations provide World Wide Web content files of varying sizes to test your server's response to different workloads.)

- Prepared workload simulations to test the response of your server to Internet Server Application Programming Interface (ISAPI) extensions and Common Gateway Interface (CGI) applications (You can run these simulations even if your server does not currently run any ISAPI extensions or CGI applications.)

- Prepared workload simulations to test the response of your server to Secure Sockets Layer (SSL) version 2.0 encryption

- Prepared workload simulations to test the response of your Hypertext Transport Protocol (HTTP) service to HTTP keep-alives (HTTP keep-alives are an optimizing feature of servers and browsers; an HTTP keep-alive maintains a client connection after the initial request is satisfied. HTTP keep-alives are part of the HTTP version 1.1 specification.)

- The ability to create and run your own client-server workload simulations

- The ability to use cookies, a technology supported by some Web sites (Cookies are a means by which, under HTTP, a server or script can maintain state information on the client workstation. Cookies are usually used to provide Web site customization features.)

■ The ability to test servers connected to more than one network

While WCAT is instrumental in simulating loads based on planned capacity, there are times when demand grows faster than planned. To handle larger than expected demand and based on additional analysis, you can deploy on a different hardware platform to boost single-server performance to the levels desired. NT and IIS run on a number of hardware platforms at different price/performance points. Consult your hardware manufacturer for a list of available configurations. If scalability of the hardware is an issue, use Requests For Proposals (RFPs) to select and establish an early relationship with your hardware vendor.

Site server is designed to support scalability across Web farms. To distribute the additional load of incoming requests across multiple servers, the DNS round-robin technique can be used to route connection requests to many servers in a Web farm. Figure 7-2 depicts Site Server Web farms.

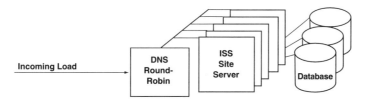

Figure 7-2. *Site Server Web farms using DNS round-robin technique.*

IIS includes a set of counters for the Windows NT Performance Monitor for tracking of performance factors specific to Site Server, such as the number of shoppers in the Order Processing Pipeline per second or the number of new shoppers per second. For more information, see "Monitoring Performance and Capacity Planning" in the DOCS directory of the companion CD, or "*Commerce Server Performance*" in the *Commerce Server Operations Guide*, both available from the Commerce Server Roadmap. NT Performance Monitor is described in Appendix J.

As demand grows further, separate the Web server (IIS) from the database (SQL) server. Ultimately, each of these servers can be scaled independently.

To set up Content Replication Server to easily deploy your content on IIS farms,

1. Click Start, Programs, Content Replication Server, CRS Web Administrator after installing CRS.

2. For additional details on CRS, see the CRS Start Page. Click Start, Programs, Content Replication Server, CRS Start Page for product documentation. This page also includes a link to the CRS Web Administrator page.

3. Read the documentation, and then click CRS Web Administration.

4. Click the Servers link to change the name of the local or remote server to be administered. Click OK when finished.

5. Click the Add Project link on this page. Enter a project name such as "Dailybatch1." Leave the Push Replication box checked. Click OK.

6. Enter the directory you want to replicate in the Project Directory box. Leave Include Subdirectories checked.

7. Click the Add target link in the lower pane. Figure 7-3 illustrates this step. Enter the name of the machine to replicate to. Click Save.

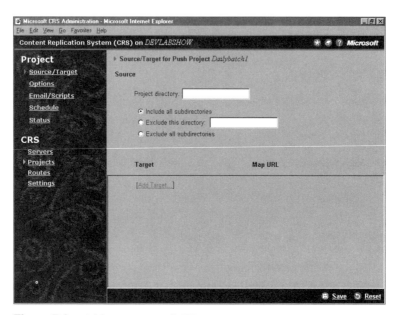

Figure 7-3. *Add target page of CRS.*

8. You can also set CRS up to send mail on success or failure of the replication project created. Click Settings and enter mail server and Sent by fields. You can set up different recipients for success, failure, or completion notification in the lower pane.

9. Test the project created.

Please also review the *Commerce Server Scalability* document included with the companion CD. This document focuses on getting the best performance from your Commerce Server. For SQL Server scaling please see Appendix M. The next section covers cases where Site Server is deployed in existing environments of heterogeneous nature.

HETEROGENEOUS PLATFORM ENVIRONMENTS

Today, corporate computer environments are often heterogeneous, that is, they have at least two different network operating systems on their standards list that must interoperate with both newer, Intranet client/server environments, and legacy computers and applications.

As network administrators attempt to make these systems work together, they find that the different network operating systems do not "speak" the same standard protocols and that there may be nonstandard or proprietary protocols in use in various parts of their networks. They need to discover ways to connect these networks together, enabling them to interoperate and complement each other.

This section discusses options for integrating NT into existing environments including Macintosh, Unix, and IBM mainframes.

Coexisting with Macintosh

Mac compatibility is accomplished through the Services for Macintosh package of Windows NT. Most Mac clients are Ethernet-capable with AppleTalk residing at the protocol level.[5] Services for Macintosh provides the following services:

File server for Mac An NT service that allows Macs to access NT server disk shares as a Hierarchical File System (HFS). A Mac file driver sits on top of the NTFS driver and implements HFS-style volumes and folders, so you can share only NTFS partitions in this way.

Print server for Mac Allows for Mac clients to share a printer on NT and vice versa. Mac Print translates PostScript Mac files into DIB format for non-PostScript printers.

For more information on the Services for Macintosh package of Windows NT, refer to the Windows NT Administration Guide.

To install the Services for Macintosh package,

1. Click Start, Control Panel and double-click on the Network application icon.

2. Select the Services tab and click Add.

3. Select Services for Macintosh from the list of additional NT Network Services list. Figure 7-4 depicts the Select Network Services dialog box of NT's Network Application.

---

5. If you have LocalTalk network interfaces, install a LocalTalk Network Interface Card (NIC) on the NT server and connect all such Macs to this NIC.

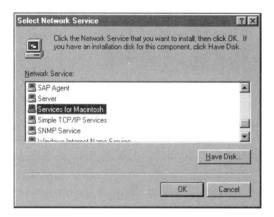

Figure 7-4. *Select Network Services dialog box of NT's Network Application.*

Coexisting with Unix

Most Unix clients are Ethernet-capable with TCP/IP residing at the protocol level. This section discussed connectivity options at the network, platform and tools, and database levels.

Network level Install an Ethernet card before setting up NT on the system. During setup, NT installs TCP/IP by default. At this point in the installation, either select DHCP as the protocol if DHCP is implemented on your net (perhaps on another NT or Unix system), or specify an address and disable DHCP.

Platform and tools level A number of third-party vendors provide Unix-like tools including *Cshell/Kshell*, *awk*, *grep*, *ls*, and so forth. MKS is an example of such a company from Canada that I have used. Others include Softway Systems and the GNU family of Win32 applications. These and other tools make NT look and feel more like a Unix system and for Unix shops, this is a way to jump-start development on NT.

Database level To access a Unix database from NT, install and configure an ODBC driver for the database on your NT server. Note the version of the driver from the documentation. Also ask for a driver that can run from a service (background task with no access to the desktop) and one that is running in the context of the system or an NT user system account (specifically created for the process to login as or NT administrator account). The trickiest part is getting the correct version and installing it. See Appendix J under "ODBC Tools" to create an ODBC data source name and for testing. For access to SQL Server from Unix, use your favorite library such as DBLib.

Coexisting with IBM Mainframes

Four mainframe programs and data access solutions exist from Microsoft. Two such solutions, Microsoft System Network Architecture (SNA Server) and DB2 Replicator, are discussed below.

Microsoft SNA Server In coexisting with IBM mainframes, one option is to use SNA Server for access to IBM mainframes data and applications, including AS/400 and 3090 series. For additional details on SNA Server, please visit *http://backoffice.microsoft.com/sna*. A number of third parties including Attachmate Corporation market similar SNA-related technologies including 3270 /50xx terminal emulation, High Level Language Application Programming Interface (HLLAPI), printer emulation and Logical Unit (LU, LU0, LU2, LU6.2, etc.), and Physical Unit (PU) emulation.

Replication mechanism Another option is to use a replication mechanism to copy a set of inventory or product tables between NT and IBM systems. A replication mechanism between DB2/CICS and SQL is available in later versions of SQL Server, and others are available from third parties.

MIGRATING TO THE WINDOWS NT PLATFORM

Here comes the tougher part of coexisting: What if you have to migrate an application from one platform to another? NT porting issues are discussed in this section.

Migrating from Unix to Win32

When migrating server applications from Unix to Windows NT, a few options are available:

- Running Unix apps on NT with a POSIX subsystem
- Using Unix libraries to port apps from Unix to Win32
- Porting apps from Unix to Win32 natively

Running Unix apps on NT via POSIX subsystem

At first, Unix programmers look at the NT POSIX subsystem as an option. However, it supports POSIX 1003.1, which was the only POSIX "dot" standardized when NT was first created. Since then, there has been little demand for extending this subsystem since most ISVs have converted their applications to Win32. The 1003.1 system is not too interesting for supporting full-featured apps since it does not support a number of required capabilities. However, many third parties support this option. OpenNT from Softway Systems, Microsoft's POSIX development partner, adds full POSIX 1 and 2 compliance to NT. For additional details, please visit *http://www.softway.com/OpenNT/home.htm*.

Applications such as VI, LS, and GREP are the main targets for the NT POSIX subsystem. Basic Unix applications, such as CGI applications, will find NT a very familiar environment. API calls like *open()*, *fopen()*, *read()*, and *write()* are available in the C run-time library of most Win32 C compilers. In addition, there is a one-to-one mapping of these Unix APIs to Win32 APIs: *open()* to *CreateFile()*; *read()* to

ReadFile(); *write()* to *WriteFile()*; *Ioctl()* to *DeviceIOControl()*; *close()* to *CloseFile()*, and so on.

Using Unix Libraries to Port Apps from Unix to Win32

The next option is using third-party Unix-like libraries to let their Unix application code compile as a Win32 executable. Few commercial (and at least one public domain) libraries are available.

Libraries ease the initial porting effort. For a graphical application, this may be the best alternative. Unix has a GUI based on the X Window System; Windows has Graphical Device Interface. While similar in concept, there is no direct mapping of X API to GDI API; however, a number of third parties offer porting solutions that do cover user interface porting, including a product by the name of NutCracker.

In addition, OpenGL library support is available for migrating Unix OpenGL-based applications. There are X clients and X servers for Windows including the porting libraries.

The potential disadvantage of this option is that a native Win32 port of an application will generally be faster and will inevitably have more functionality since it may be difficult for the application to step outside of its Unix "shell" inheritance, for example, to make direct Win32 calls to gain power from NT operating system.

Porting apps from Unix to Win32 natively

Using ANSI C/C++ libraries and commercial C compiler libraries, many of the traditional system calls Unix applications rely on are available to Win32 applications.

The output model of Stdio-based applications does not need to be changed, as the Win32 Console APIs mimic the Stdio model, and versions exist that use the Win32 Console APIs.

Berkeley socket-based applications need very few changes to work as Win32 applications. The Windows Sockets interface was designed for portability with BSD sockets, with minimal changes (which are clearly noted in the introductory sections of the WinSock specification). Many third parties are available to port your applications. Consider the following general guidelines.

NT supports DCE-compliant RPC, so RPC-based applications will be easily usable.

One of the largest areas of difference is in the process model of the two systems. Unix has fork(), Win32 does not. Depending on the use of fork() and the codebase, Win32 has two options that could be used: CreateProcess(), or Create-Thread().

Basically, a Unix app that forks multiple copies of itself can be ported to Win32 to either spawn multiple processes or run as a single process with multiple threads. If the Multiple Processes option is chosen, there are a number of IPC methods that can be used in Win32 to allow for communication between the processes and to update the code and data of the process to be exactly like the parent. Please see *Advanced Windows* by Jeffrey Richter from Microsoft Press.

Daemons are a class of processes running periodically in the background task queue. The equivalent in NT is the concept of an NT Service. A good description of how to set up an EXE to run as a service is discussed in the NT Resource Kit in detail. This includes setting up timer parameters and registry settings to enable the process to run as an NT service.

Migrating from Mac to Win32

When migrating server applications from Mac to Windows NT, there is really only the option of porting Mac applications directly to Win32 for native runs. MacApp is mostly used for development on the Mac and this environment is similar to the VC++ MFC environment. If you are also a MacApp programmer, take a look at MFC for porting. There is little mention of MFC in this book. However, MFC has been ported to Unix and Mac providing a backward compatibility route through the VC++ compiler. See *Cross-Platform Development Using Visual C++* by Chane Cullens and Ken Blackwell (M&T Books).

Chapter 8

Preview of Site Server 3.0

What is the future of Site Server 2.0? What directions will the product take? How does the release of Site Server 3.0 change any sites developed using the current 2.0 version? (Site Server version 3.0 is scheduled for release by the end of 1997.) This chapter previews Site Server Enterprise Edition 3.0 and contrasts it to the current 2.0 version to answer these and other related questions.

One major feature of Site Server 3.0 is that stores built in version 2.0 are fully compatible with 3.0 and run without any modifications. This means that Commerce Server 2.0 objects and the pipeline architecture of 2.0 are completely preserved in 3.0. A simple and powerful concept, 100 percent compatibility effectively protects all existing investments in version 2.0. However, Site Server 3.0 has evolved in a number of other areas.

MAJOR AREAS OF EVOLUTIONARY CHANGE

While Site Server 3.0 is based on and is upwardly compatible with Site Server 2.0, in version 3.0 Site Server components have evolved individually to offer richer functionality as well as work tightly and seamlessly with other components. For example, Personalization System as a component of Site Server 3.0 has been enhanced and extended in function, power, and ease of use. Additionally, Personalization System is fully integrated with Membership System. Data from both systems is unified and maintained in a single repository. This combined repository adds a layer of additional function, power, and ease of use.

In addition to compatibility with Site Server Enterprise Edition 2.0, the major areas of evolution are as follows:

■ Compatibility with Internet Information Server 4.0

■ Unification of content, usage, user, and commerce data into a single repository

■ Enhancements to Usage Analyst and Site Analyst

■ Enhancements and changes to sample sites that reflect product enhancements

■ Addition of Business Object Foundation

■ Seamless integration into Visual InterDev project model

Compatibility with Internet Information Server 4.0

Site Server 2.0 was announced in early summer of 1997. By the end of 1997, Internet Information Server (IIS) 4.0 will be available. IIS is a required component of Site Server. As a technology building block of Site Server, enhancements made to the IIS base products also reflect in the functionality and power of Site Server.

Site Server 2.0 was built upon IIS 3.0. While IIS 3.0 was a major force in the Web server market, IIS 4.0 more easily supports very large-scale Web implementations. Some of the features that help IIS 4.0 excel in these very large-scale Web implementations are described next.

One feature is built-in support for multiple virtual Web servers in the same box. IIS 4.0 also has built-in support for multiple virtual Web roots in the same box.

Another IIS 4.0 feature is superior process isolation and robustness. IIS 4.0 processes, such as ISAPI applications, may run both in a (IIS) parent's space or in their own isolated space. The latter case is far more robust and more resilient in the face of potential failures in these processes. In a complex site, many IIS processes and applications can be running at a given time. Some of these processes and application might be custom made; others might have been purchased from third parties. Process isolation protects the whole system from failures in its subsystems.

Another IIS 4.0 feature is its seamless support for transactions through tight integration with Microsoft Transaction Server (MTS). In addition to process isolation, IIS 4.0 is more tightly integrated with MTS. Chapter 6 introduced MTS and briefly discussed its features. Transaction Server automatically provides transaction support to applications running on the server, providing a reliable failure isolation and recovery mechanism. Transaction support is transparent to the application programmer, making mainframe-class reliability available to a mass market of solution developers. Transaction Server manages low-level system resources, enabling components to automatically operate in a multi-user environment without forcing developers to build this complexity into their applications. Transaction Server manages a pool of ODBC connections to a database, providing high-performance database access without forcing the developer to manage complex database synchronization issues manually.

In addition to IIS, some Site Server components have evolved individually and through tighter integration with other Site Server components. Examples include Site and Usage Analyst.

Unification of Content, Usage, User, and Commerce Data into a Single Repository

The Site Server 3.0 tool set has also evolved, most notably in the areas of site, content, and user analysis and reporting. In Site Server 2.0, Site Analyst, Usage Analyst, and Personalization System had their distinct data schema and repository. In Site Server 3.0, all content, usage, user, and commercial data is stored in a unified repository (see Figure 8-1).

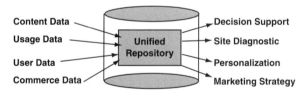

Figure 8-1. *Site Server 3.0 unified data repository.*

The major benefit of a single repository is superior quality of decision-making support data generated by the tools. For example, using Site Analyst in Site Server 2.0, you could view the structure and connectivity of store pages and links. In Site Server 3.0 you can cross-reference and view this data, along with other usage and user data, to not only show the structure and connectivity of a store, but also to highlight the paths that users are most likely to take through a store and conduct what-if analysis more readily.

Enhancements to Usage Analyst and Site Analyst

Usage Analyst and Site Analyst have evolved to support this unified view of the site data for ease of analysis and reporting. Usage Analyst now supports nearly 50 canned reports and visits spanning two or more servers. You can also import external data into Usage Analyst to augment existing user, usage, and site data.

Addition of Business Object Foundation

Commerce Server is no exception. In version 2.0, a single programmable Commerce Server store pipeline is supported. In 3.0, a number of pipeline categories exist. One such category of pipelines is the Business Object Foundation: the technology that supports business-to-business commerce. Today's businesses often out-source all or part of their fulfillment business to specialized external sources. Business Object Foundation technology supports a number of standard protocols such as Electronic Data Interchange (EDI), Internet HTTP-based format, XML, SMIME, and SMTP. Business Object Foundation is business-logic independent, to integrate seamlessly into existing business models and contractual arrangements. This technology that required additional development in 2.0 is now built into the Commerce Server component of Site Server 3.0.

Seamless Integration into Visual InterDev Project Model

Similarly, the development environment has been extended and enhanced. This evolutionary enhancement allows Visual InterDev to more easily manage the development of Site Server–based Web sites. Two notable enhancement are mentioned here.

Design-Time Components

COM was discussed in Chapter 5. Design-Time Components are COM objects that support additional "design-time" interfaces. Design-time interfaces make customizations to Site Server application objects and Commerce Server store objects easier. For example, in Commerce Server 2.0, once you generated or copied a store, the task of enhancing the store began. Having completed this enhancement to the store, you could now copy it as a base store. If you were to build a new store from foundation and enhance it to the same level, you would have to apply these enhancements manually and track them separately. The concept of a Design-Time Component is that of remembering the customizations made to a machine-generated store page. A Design-Time Component shows customization settings when viewed with VI, and you can easily view, track, modify, or apply the settings to other stores. As the name implies, a Design-Time Component interacts with the VI development environment during the page design cycle and stores all changes and customizations internally. Henceforth, you can ask the object about the specifics of the enhancements or recall the enhancements previously made for additional development. In Site Server 3.0, the process of customizing and tracking store enhancements is made easy.

Store directory structure enhancement

In Site Server 3.0, Commerce Server store directory structure is more closely integrated with VI. The manual steps in creating and copying this directory for customization, as described in Chapter 4, are now automated. Commerce Server pages can be edited and enhanced in their native install directory, and logistics of staging to production are made easier.

MAJOR AREAS OF REVOLUTIONARY CHANGE

While some of the differences between Site Server 2.0 and 3.0 are evolutionary, others are revolutionary—revolutionary through inclusion of previously stand-alone servers into the base Site Server 3.0 product. Chief among these servers are Microsoft Membership Server and Microsoft Transaction Server. The major areas of revolutionary change are as follows:

- Inclusion of Microsoft Transaction Server (MTS) and transaction-aware components

- Inclusion of Microsoft Membership Server and components into the base product

Inclusion of Microsoft Transaction Server (MTS)

What happens in Site Server 2.0 if you are in the middle of the last three stages of the pipeline and something goes wrong? The last three stages of the pipeline execute the completed order and store the information in the database. Executing the order may require adjusting the inventory, entering a General-Ledger (G/L) Entry, and issuing a fulfillment request. If lightning should strike in that moment after the inventory is decremented, but before the G/L entry and fulfillment request steps have been executed, you might have an incorrect G/L entry, lose the inventory, or never fulfill the order. Microsoft Transaction Server (MTS) addresses this type of risk. MTS allows for Site Server operations to be wrapped in a transaction layer to guarantee all-or-none execution of one or more steps or pages. Think of it as the cure for the common crash, or the online transaction processor of Windows NT. Inclusion of MTS with IIS 4.0 has had at least two major benefits for Site Server 3.0: transaction-aware pages, components, and pipelines; and component pooling for performance.

Transaction-aware pages, components, and pipelines

All ASP pages may now be transacted, meaning that the page is either executed free of error in whole, or completely rolled back. Any and all Site Server components and objects can now be transaction-aware and be registered with MTS for performance pooling and guarantee of execution. Site Server 3.0 includes a transaction-aware pipeline as well as the traditional nontransacted pipeline.

Components pooling for performance

Among other functions, MTS also manages thread pooling for MTS-compliant components. However, Site Server version 2.0 stores will not benefit from MTS component pooling, since in version 3.0 components are created on the fly and destroyed immediately after use. This concept should be very familiar to database and transaction programmers. Site Server 2.0 stores have certain long-lived objects, such as the database connection component, that are created once and stored throughout the sales cycle of a store to reduce the overhead of creation and deletion of these components on every page. In Site Server 3.0, you create the component just when it is needed, use it, and immediately release it. In this sense, introduction of MTS has been a revolutionary change not in terms of coding syntax, but rather in terms of the approach to developing a store page.

Inclusion of Membership System

Another stand-alone, optional server is Membership System, which was discussed in Chapter 6. Membership System is fully incorporated into the base Site Server 3.0 system. A by-product of this inclusion is unification of Membership System, Personalization System, and Directory Server. The concept of unifying the data repository was discussed above, and the same benefits are obtained from unification of the Membership and Personalization systems. A single uniform approach allows for access to all membership and user personalization data.

RECOMMENDATIONS FOR USE OF SITE SERVER 3.0 VERSUS 2.0

Site Server 3.0 is aimed more at managing large-scale sites with bulletproof transactions, unified repository, enhanced reporting capabilities, and full life cycle support (see Figure 8-2).

Figure 8-2. *Site Server development cycle.*

I recommend Site Server 2.0 for sites that are close to development or in the process of building a store, and for smaller and startup installations. Version 2.0 is a mature and reliable version.

I recommend Site Server 3.0 for sites with longer deployment cycles that are scheduled for development later in the first or second quarter of 1998, and for larger installations and more complex environments. Site Server version 3.0 better supports larger sites.

Appendix A

Installing Commerce Server 2.0[1]

This appendix describes how to run Commerce Server 2.0 Setup. In addition, it provides information about testing a new installation, adding or removing Commerce Server components for a custom configuration, and removing previously installed components.

For information about changes to Setup or other aspects of the Commerce Server release that occurred after production of this document, see the Commerce Server README, the README.TXT file in the \Docs\Commerce Server directory of the Commerce Server companion disc.

NOTE If you have stores that you built using Microsoft® Merchant Server 1.0, before installing Commerce Server 2.0, please see the *Commerce Server Conversion Guide*, available as the CONVER.DOC file in the \Docs\Commerce Server directory of the Commerce Server installation compact disc. The Commerce Server 2.0 stores supersede the Microsoft Merchant Server 1.0 stores.

---

1. Material in this appendix, available under \docs\Building a store.doc after installation of the companion CD for this book, is extracted from material provided by the Microsoft Site Server documentation group.

COMMERCE SERVER INSTALLATION CHECKLIST

This section provides a checklist of items to help you install correctly. Where appropriate, this appendix provides references to detailed instructions or additional information.

Software Requirements

Table A-1 lists software requirements for Commerce Server 2.0. Some of this software comes with Commerce Server and can be installed from links on the Commerce Server Setup main screen.

Table A-1. *Commerce Server 2.0 software requirements.*

Required Software	*Comments*
Microsoft Windows NT Server version 4.0 or later with Windows NT Service Pack 3	Commerce Server supports both FAT file systems and NTFS. Windows NT Service Pack 3 install can be started using links from the Commerce Server Setup main screen. Windows NT Service Pack 3 is also available from the *http://www.microsoft.com/ntserver/* site.
Transmission Control Protocol/Internet Protocol (TCP/IP)	Included with Windows NT. Use the Network utility in Control Panel to install and configure TCP/IP and related components.
Microsoft Internet Information Server (IIS) version 3.0	IIS 3.0 is included as a link from Windows NT Service Pack 3. Commerce Server requires only the World Wide Web Publishing service of IIS; therefore, if you do not need the FTP and Gopher services that are loaded with IIS, you can improve Commerce Server performance by turning off these services on the Commerce Server computer.
An ODBC-compliant database system	SQL Server 6.5 is the recommended database for Commerce Server. Information about SQL Server 6.5 is available from the *http://www.microsoft.com/SQL/* site.
SQL Server Service Pack 3 Note that SQL Server 6.5 must already be installed before installing Service Pack 3	SQL Server Service Pack 3 install can be started using links from the Commerce Server Setup main screen. SQL Server Service Pack 3 is also available from the *http://www.microsoft.com/ntserver/* site. Note that SQL Server 6.5 must already be installed before installing the Service Pack 3 update.

Required Software	Comments
A Web browser that supports tables For the Adventure Works store, a browser with frame support, such as Internet Explorer 3.0 or later or Netscape Navigator 3.0 or later	Internet Explorer 3.02 is included as an installation option from Windows NT Service Pack 3. You can also find recent versions of Internet Explorer on *http://www.micro-soft.com/ie/download/*. The Web browser does not need to be installed on the Commerce Server computer.

NOTE Netscape Navigator is fully supported for Commerce Server shopping operations. However, the Commerce Server HTML Help pages and ASP-based management tools, including the ASP-based Pipeline Editor, Host Administrator, and the Commerce Server Store Manager applications, are not supported in Netscape Navigator. Attempting to use these applications or view the HTML Help pages produces unexpected display effects. You must use Internet Explorer 3.02 or later for accurate viewing of Commerce Server HTML Help.

Internet Explorer 3.02 or later is required to manage Commerce Server stores using Host Administrator and the Store Manager applications.

Hardware Requirements

Before attempting to install Commerce Server, do the following:

- Decide on the file system to use for your configuration. For security reasons, I strongly recommend that you use NTFS.

- Decide on your machine configuration. You can install all components on the same computer or on different computers.

- Make sure your Commerce Server computer meets space and memory requirements.

- If SQL Server and Commerce Server are located on different machines, make sure the Windows NT logon account for the computer running Commerce Server is valid on the SQL Server computer.

The suggested system configuration for a single, dedicated Commerce Server installation is as follows:

- A system based on the Intel Pentium or Alpha processor

- A pointing device such as a mouse

- 64 MB random access memory (RAM)
- 55 MB free hard disk space for Commerce Server
- CD-ROM drive

SQL Server 6.5 requires approximately 85 MB of free disk space plus space for any store databases you create. SQL Server can be on the same computer as Commerce Server or on a different computer.

Other database systems may have different hardware requirements. For information, check the documentation for the product.

Database configuration

If you are using a database management system other than SQL Server, see "Using Oracle7 Database Management Systems" and "Using Other Database Management Systems" later in this appendix or for advice on configuring your database. If you are using SQL Server, continue using this section of the checklist.

To configure an SQL Server database,

1. Start SQL Server Enterprise Manager and register your SQL Server.

2. Configure SQL Server to start automatically at boot time.

3. Make sure there are enough user connections allotted for Commerce Server store processing. Use number of concurrent shoppers from requirements or enter 50 as a starting point.

4. Restart SQL Server.

5. Create two new database devices, one for the starter store database and one for a log file. Create a new database (16 MB is recommended) and a log (4 MB is recommended) and note the names you use for each.

6. If your TEMPDB database is not 4 MB or larger, enlarge it to 4 MB.

7. Truncate the database logs before installing.

File system requirements

Commerce Server supports both the FAT file system and the Windows NT File System (NTFS). Regardless of which file system you choose, Commerce Server provides security for site connections and transactions. If you are ready to set up a production store, however, I recommend that you build it on an NTFS partition. NTFS provides for stronger, more robust security and maximum file protection by enabling you to specify the types of access users have to each file and directory.

> **NOTE** The FAT file system does not provide secure hosting of multiple stores on a single computer. If you plan to host multiple sites that require security, you should use NTFS.

If you originally installed Commerce Server on a FAT-formatted system and want to move to NTFS, you can do so. However, changing from FAT to NTFS requires that you adjust discretionary access control lists (DACLs) for the stronger security provided in NTFS. Reinstalling Commerce Server resets the configurations of the installed starter stores but not the stores you built. For the stores you built yourself, you will need to set DACLs for each existing store.

COMMERCE SERVER PREINSTALLATION

Much planning and preparation is required before you can install Commerce Server. Here is a summary of these preinstallation activities:

■ Create a starter store database if you want to install Commerce Server starter stores. The database will be used for executing scripts that create database tables and load starter store data, as described in "Setting Up a Commerce Server Database."

In addition, be sure to complete the steps listed in the "Changing SQL Server Configuration," "Creating and Modifying Databases for SQL Server," and "Enabling IIS on Remote SQL Server Installations" sections of this appendix. You must complete the required steps described in these sections before continuing with Commerce Server Setup. When you have completed these activities, you can install Commerce Server from the Commerce Server Setup installation compact disc.

Commerce Server Database Setup

Prior to running Commerce Server Setup, you need to configure certain settings for your database management system. Topics in this section describe preparing Microsoft SQL Server and other database management systems for use with Commerce Server. In addition, this section covers creating the Commerce Server database that will contain data about products, departments, shoppers, and orders for the starter stores.

This section covers only a portion of SQL Server configuration and maintenance procedures; if you need more detailed information, see "SQL Server Books Online" or SQL Server online Help, both available after installation of the product from the Microsoft SQL Server folder in the Programs folder.

> **NOTE** Before attempting the procedures in the "Changing SQL Server Configuration," "Creating and Modifying Databases for SQL Server," and "Enabling IIS on Remote SQL Server Installations" sections in this appendix, make sure that SQL Server is connected. If it is not, start the server by right-clicking the name and clicking Start on the shortcut menu.

Using Microsoft SQL Server

Microsoft SQL Server version 6.5 or later is the recommended database management system for use with Commerce Server. Running Commerce Server Setup on an SQL Server database is the most automatic method of installing Commerce Server starter store data. Installing starter store data on other database management systems requires users to make some modifications, as described in "Using Oracle7 Database Management Systems" and "Using Other Database Management Systems" in this appendix.

> **NOTE** SQL Server (or any other database management system you use) does not have to reside on the same computer as other Commerce Server components.

Changing SQL Server configuration Prior to running Commerce Server Setup, you need to configure certain settings for SQL Server to ensure Commerce Server Setup works correctly.

To configure SQL Server settings,

1. Create a data device and a log device, and databases for each.

2. Set the number of user connections as required for Commerce Server–based stores to access the database.

3. Set the Auto Start At Boot Time option so SQL Server is always running when needed by Commerce Server.

4. Double the size of the TEMPDB database.

5. Truncate log on checkpoint.

6. On remote installations, make sure the SQL Server is accessible from the Commerce Server.

To configure SQL Server for Commerce Server after SQL Server Setup,

1. Register your Commerce Server machine by right-clicking the SQL 6.5 icon.

2. Click Register Server on the shortcut menu, enter the server name and a login ID and password, and then click Register.

NOTE You may get a message indicating that no connection can be made because the server is unavailable or does not exist. Click Yes to register the server anyway.

When registering your SQL Server, you will enter a login ID and password. By default, SQL Server Setup establishes an *sa* account with no password. You can use that account to load the tables needed by the Commerce Server starter stores. For security reasons, however, you should consider another account for your actual production environment.

---

3. Right-click the name of the SQL Server computer in the Server Manager window, and then click Configure on the shortcut menu.

4. In the Server Options tab, select Auto Start Server At Boot Time, or set this option using the Services dialog box in Control Panel.

5. In the Configuration tab, find the row containing values for user connections.

6. In the Current column, type the number of connections required. This number should support all connections required for Commerce Server plus connections required for other applications using SQL Server. The default setting is 15. Depending on your expected load, you must determine the appropriate setting for your configuration.

7. Stop and restart SQL Server to make these changes effective prior to running Commerce Server Setup.

Creating and modifying databases for SQL Server This section contains procedures for modifying the TEMPDB database installed by SQL Server plus procedures for creating a new data device, database, and log for use by the starter stores installed by Commerce Server Setup. Before attempting these procedures, make sure that SQL Server is running.

NOTE The following procedure describes creating a new device for expanding TEMPDB. You can also use an existing device with at least 4 MB of available space.

To create database devices, a database, and a log for the starter stores,

1. In SQL Enterprise Manager, click the plus sign ("+") beside the name of the SQL Server computer.

2. Right-click Database Devices.

3. On the shortcut menu, click New Device.

4. In the New Database Device dialog box, type the name and size of your new device (16 MB is recommended). Click Create Now. This will be the database device for your database.

5. Repeat steps 2 through 4 to create a new device for your log. Make the log database device 4 MB, and then close the dialog box.

6. Right-click Databases.

7. On the shortcut menu that appears, click New Database.

8. In the Data Device list box in the New Database dialog box, select the data device you just created. Type the name and size to use for your new database. You can use all of the device space for your database, or you can create several databases to manage your information. It is suggested, however, that you allow 16 MB for the starter store database.

9. In the Log Device list box, select the new device you created for the log, and then click Create Now.

NOTE Write down the names you use for the databases you create. You will need them during Commerce Server Setup.

10. Right-click the new database, and on the shortcut menu that appears, click Edit.

11. Click the Options tab and select the Truncate Log On Checkpoint check box.

12. Click OK.

To reconfigure TEMPDB,

1. Click the plus sign ("+") beside the server name to view the server contents.

2. Right-click Database Devices.

3. On the shortcut menu, click New Device to create a new device for TEMPDB.

4. In the New Device dialog box, type the name of the device you will use and type the size of the device in megabytes (at least 4 MB is required). Click Create Now.

5. In SQL Enterprise Manager, click the plus sign ("+") beside Databases.

6. Right-click TEMPDB.

7. On the shortcut menu, click Edit to expand TEMPDB to use the new device you created.

8. In the Edit Database dialog box, click Expand.

9. In the Data Device list box, select the name of the device you created (or an existing device you are using) and type 2 in the Size text box. Click Expand Now.

10. Click the Options tab and select the Truncate Log On Checkpoint check box.

11. Click OK.

NOTE This procedure is recommended to avoid problems with loading starter store data during Setup. However, some companies may not want to truncate the log in this manner. If your database administrator is managing the transaction logs, consult your administrator regarding this procedure.

Enabling IIS on remote SQL Server installations By default, the IIS World Wide Web Publishing Service runs under the Windows NT account IUSR_*computername*. If SQL Server resides on the same machine as IIS, the IUSR_*computername* account is used to establish connections to the SQL Server. However, if SQL Server resides on a separate machine from IIS, then the Windows NT IUSR_*computername* account needs to be given permissions on the SQL Server.

You can provide account permissions by enabling the Windows NT Guest account on the SQL Server. You can also provide access by adding the IUSR_*computername* Windows NT user account on the SQL Server computer

To enable the Windows NT Guest account on the remote SQL Server,

1. Log on to the Windows NT SQL Server computer as an administrator.

2. Click the Start button, point to Administrative Tools, then point to User Manager for Domains. Select the domain where your SQL Server resides.

3. Double-click the Guest user account.

4. Clear the Account Disabled check box.

   To add the IIS account as a user on your remote SQL Server machine,

1. Log on to the Windows NT SQL Server computer as an administrator.

2. Click the Start button, point to Administrative Tools, then point to User Manager for Domains.

3. On the User menu, click Select Domain and enter the your computer's domain name.

4. On the User menu, click New User.

5. Add IUSR_*computername* (or the IIS account you created on the remote computer) as a user.

6. Assign *Pwd* as the password.

7. Select the Password Never Expires check box (it should be the only selected check box).

For more information on configuring IIS to work with SQL Server, see the Microsoft Knowledge Base article number Q152828. Knowledge Base articles are available at *http://www.microsoft.com/kb/*.

SQL Server and ODBC system data source names In order to connect to the starter store database, Commerce Server requires at least one system data source name (DSN) for the starter stores. You can assign the same DSN to all stores running under Commerce Server or assign a different DSN to each store. For purposes of installing the starter stores, you can configure a single DSN for all stores. However, if your production stores' databases are distributed over different computers, you need to set up a different DSN for each store. In addition, if you are running a mall operation, you may also want to set up separate DSNs to restrict database access.

You are prompted to configure a system data source name for ODBC during Commerce Server Setup. For more information, see "Configuring the Database" in this appendix.

Using Oracle7 database management systems

Commerce Server supports Oracle7 database management systems, and Commerce Server Setup installs scripts to load starter store data for the Clock Peddler and Adventure Works stores. Commerce Server does not provide Oracle7 support for the Volcano Coffee and Microsoft Press starter stores.

To prepare Oracle7 systems for Commerce Server Setup, you must create a database for the starter stores. For information on creating databases on your Oracle7 systems, see your Oracle7 documentation.

During Commerce Server Setup, you are prompted to configure a system DSN for the store databases. To prevent startup errors, make sure to enter a password as you configure the DSN and complete the ODBC Oracle driver setup dialog box to specify your database connection information.

After you have configured the system DSN, Commerce Server Setup proceeds to install starter store database scripts for the Oracle system; however, it does not update those scripts. You need to update the scripts using SQL*Plus on your Oracle7 system. For instructions, see your Oracle documentation. Oracle scripts reside in the path *Commerce_Server_root*\Stores\Store_name\Sql\Oracle on your system after installation of Commerce Server, where *Commerce_Server_root* is the root you specified for the installation.

Using other database management systems

Commerce Server supports ODBC-compliant, ANSI-standard SQL–based database management systems; however, Commerce Server Setup does not install the starter store data for databases other than Microsoft SQL Server. When you run Commerce Server Setup, a dialog box appears indicating that database configuration cannot be done by Setup. You can click the Ignore button to complete other Setup operations.

You must create and configure databases before running Commerce Server Setup. In the case of SQL Server, this means creating database devices and databases. Commerce Server setup will load data into SQL Server databases. For other database systems, you must create database tables and load their data according to the instructions provided for your database management system.

Using the product documentation accompanying your database management system, create a database for the starter store data. You must also configure an ODBC system DSN using the ODBC utility in Control Panel. The Commerce Server Setup program gives you the opportunity to load software required for Commerce Server, as well as an option to install Commerce Server 2.0 files. Setup automatically detects the hardware platform in use. The following procedures are identical regardless of whether your equipment is based on the Intel Pentium or Alpha platform.

If you have not already installed an ODBC-compliant database, you must do so before installing Commerce Server. Information on SQL Server 6.5 is available from the *http://www.microsoft.com/SQL/* site.

COMMERCE SERVER INSTALLATION

This section covers the steps involved in installing Commerce Server. Be sure you have followed all the instructions in the "Commerce Server Preinstallation" section of this appendix before you proceed. You will need to run Commerce Server Setup to install Commerce Server. During setup, you will add a data source name (DSN) for the Commerce Server stores. For simplicity, select the same DSN for all stores.

Installing Commerce Server

To install Commerce Server,

1. Insert the Commerce Server installation compact disc in a CD-ROM drive.

2. In the Registration dialog box, type your name and organization and the CD Key number that appears on the back of your compact disc case and click Next.

3. View the Software License Agreement, and then click Yes to continue.

4. Click the Commerce option on the installation screen.

From the Commerce Server Setup main screen, you can choose from several options, depending on the software you want to install:

- To install Windows NT Service Pack 3, click the Windows NT Service Pack 3 option on the Commerce Server Setup main screen.

- To install the Active Server Pages and the ODBC 3.0 drivers included as a separate Setup option in Windows NT Service Pack 3, click the Active Server Pages option on the Commerce Server Setup main screen.

- To install SQL Server Service Pack 3, click the SQL Server 6.5 Service Pack 3 option on the Commerce Server Setup main screen.

Each of these options launches a separate setup program for the software being installed. In most cases, the setup program presents a license agreement and dialog boxes containing descriptive text or progress information. In addition, you may be required to restart your computer for the setup to complete.

NOTE SQL Server Service Pack 3 only needs to be installed on the computers running SQL Server.

Installing on multiple computers

For performance reasons, all Commerce Server components, including any stores that you create, must reside on the same computer as IIS. However, you can install Commerce Server and IIS, effectively cloning the installation, on as many computers as you have software licenses to cover.

Your database and database management system may reside on a separate machine. However, if your production stores' databases are distributed over different computers, you must set up a different data source name (DSN) for each database. For information about configuring a DSN, see "SQL Server and ODBC System Data Source Names" earlier in this appendix.

Setting Up on Alpha Computers

Setup automatically detects the Alpha platform and loads the appropriate Commerce Server files. Perform the procedures described in "Installing Commerce Server" for installing Commerce Server on an Alpha computer.

For information on the functionality of any third-party components you are using on the Alpha system, consult the software provider.

USING CUSTOM SETUP

If you prefer not to install the complete set of Commerce Server components, you can select the Custom option of Commerce Server Setup. Typically, you will use this option to install Commerce Server on multiple computers. You can also use Custom setup to include or exclude certain components (such as a third-party component or a specific starter store) from a single-computer installation.

In the Custom Installation Options dialog box, select additional components as appropriate for your chosen installation. For example, if you are installing a single-computer configuration, you can choose to exclude the Commerce Server SDK, a third-party component, or specific starter stores by clearing the check box next to the option.

The Required Components check box should be selected for all installations. When selected, Commerce Server Setup installs the Setup program files so that you can rerun Commerce Server Setup or make installation changes.

When you have selected the components you want, click Continue. From this point on, the steps are identical to the steps for the Complete Setup option described in the next section.

Running Commerce Server Setup

The Setup program detects the presence of Windows NT Server 4.0 and IIS 3.0. If these components are not present, Setup will prompt you to exit and install missing software. Setup also checks for file system type (FAT or NTFS) and configures Commerce Server accordingly.

Before Running Commerce Server:

- Make sure your logon account is a member of the Windows NT Administrators group.

- Configure your database management system as described in "Commerce Server Database Setup" earlier in this appendix.

- For online help, click Installation Instructions on the Commerce Server Setup main screen.

Setup automatically detects the hardware platform in use. The following procedures are identical regardless of whether your equipment is based on the *x*86 or Alpha platform.

To start Commerce Server Setup,

1. Click Commerce Server on the Component section of the Commerce Server Setup main screen.

2. When the Welcome dialog box appears, click the Continue button to proceed.

3. In the Name and Organization Information dialog box, complete the text boxes as appropriate and click OK to continue.

4. Click OK to confirm the name and organization information you typed; otherwise, click the Change button.

5. Click OK to confirm the Product ID number generated from the ID number that appears on the back of your compact disc case and click OK.

6. In the Destination Directory dialog box, click OK to install files in the default directory, C:\MICROSOFT COMMERCE SERVER. To install Commerce Server in a different location, click Change Folder, select a new directory, and then click OK.

7. In the Installation Choice dialog box, click Complete to install all the Commerce Server components on one computer, or click Custom to select specific components to install.

8. If prompted to stop the World Wide Web Publishing service, click Yes.

The Setup program begins copying the Commerce Server files to the computer.

Configuring the database

This section describes configuring a system DSN and connecting to the store database during Commerce Server Setup. These procedures apply to configuring a SQL Server or Oracle database. For information about other databases, see "Using Other Database Management Systems."

As Setup progresses, a dialog box appears for each starter store. To configure the database,

1. In the System Data Sources dialog box for Adventure Works, a driver is shown in the Installed ODBC Drivers list box, and existing data source names (DSNs) appear in the System Data Sources list box. Choose the

correct driver, and then click Add to create a new system DSN for use when connecting to the Commerce Server database.

2. Or, if you are using an Oracle database, select Oracle in the Installed ODBC Drivers list box and click Add to create a system DSN for your database. Thereafter, the ODBC Oracle driver setup dialog box appears. Complete this dialog box as appropriate.

NOTE When completing the ODBC driver setup dialog box for Oracle, make sure to include complete connection information for access to the database. Errors will occur during Commerce Server Setup if you do not provide a password for connecting to the Oracle database.

---

3. In the ODBC SQL Server Setup dialog box, type a data source name for your database in the Data Source Name box.

4. In the Server list box, select the name for the server on which your database is located.

5. Make sure the Use Trusted Connection check box is cleared.

6. Click the Options button.

7. When you click the Options button, additional areas appear in the ODBC SQL Server Setup dialog box. Type the name of the database you created for the Commerce Server starter stores in the Database Name text box. The database name must be valid or an error will occur.

8. After completing and verifying the values in the ODBC SQL Server Setup dialog box, click OK.

9. When the System Data Sources dialog box appears again, select the new system DSN from the System Data Sources list, and then click Select.

10. When the SQL Server Login dialog box appears, type your SQL Server login ID and password to connect to the database, click Options, select the database you want to use, and then click OK.

11. Create or select a system DSN and supply logon IDs and passwords for the remaining starter stores.

NOTE If you want to configure a separate system DSN for each starter store, repeat steps 2 through 7. If you want to use the same system DSN for all stores, repeat steps 6 and 7.

---

12. In the dialog box that prompts you to stop the World Wide Web Publishing service, click Yes. The Setup program continues copying the Commerce Server files to the computer.

13. After Setup is complete, a dialog box is posted to indicate status. Click OK.

Directories and Program Groups Installed by Setup

When Setup is complete, Commerce Server components and related files reside in a root directory named "Microsoft Commerce Server" (or in the directory you specified during Setup).

The following is a list of the contents of the default directory structure installed by Commerce Server Setup when you select the Complete option:

- The Docs folder contains product documentation in HTML and Microsoft Word format.

- The SDK folder contains the sample code and documentation for Commerce Server components and Wallet APIs.

- The Server folder contains the executable files for the store wizards and administration components and a folder for shared images.

- The Setup folder contains the files for rerunning Setup or for removing your Commerce Server installation.

- The Stores folder contains folders for each starter store listed below.

  - *Assets*. Contains the images or other multimedia files used in the store.

  - *Config*. Contains the configuration file (PIPELINE.PCF) for the store's order processing pipeline.

  - *Manager*. Contains all the files that make up the store's Manager application.

  - *Shop*. Contains all the files that make up the Shop application (the store itself).

  - *Sql*. Contains the SQL scripts that create the database schema and populate the database with data.

A new program group named Commerce Server 2.0 also appears on the Start menu. This program group contains icons or shortcuts for the following:

- Commerce Server Roadmap: A Web page designed to help you find information about Commerce Server

- Commerce Server SDK: A link to the Commerce Server SDK Roadmap, a Web page designed to help you find information about the Commerce Server SDK

- Commerce Server Setup: An option that launches Commerce Server Setup so that installation and uninstallation operations can be performed

- Host Administrator: A tool for creating and administering new stores

- Pipeline Editor: A tool for configuring the Order Processing Pipeline

- Read Me First: A link to the Commerce Server README file that contains information about Commerce Server that became available after release of this installation documentation

- Receipt Conversion Utility: A tool to help with converting Microsoft Merchant Server 1.0 data for use with Commerce Server 2.0

- Template Conversion Utility: A tool to help with converting Microsoft Merchant Server 1.0 store templates for use with Commerce Server 2.0

Other Setup Operations

In addition to installing the directories and program groups, Setup performs the following operations:

- For NTFS-formatted systems, sets DACLs to give full access to starter store directories, the starter stores' Manager directories, and the GLOBAL.ASA page, to the currently logged on user, *server_name*\ *user_name*, or, for domain controllers, *domain_name**user_name*

- For FAT-formatted systems, writes the *domain_name**user_name* of the currently logged on user into *store_name*\Manager\Include\ Auth_include.asp. This process establishes *domain_name**user_name* as having access to the Host Administrator and each of the stores' Manager pages

- Creates a local user's group called StoreManagers with full control access to the Store Builder Wizard and the pipeline configuration directories

- If the starter stores are installed, Setup performs the following steps:

  ❑ Adds the currently logged on user to the StoreManagers group

  ❑ Establishes the currently logged on user as the store owner for each store the user installs

---

NOTE For details about Commerce Server permission settings, see the topic in "Building a Store from the Foundation Up" in Chapter 1.

■ Installs the following Windows NT registry key: HKEY_ LOCAL_MACHINE\SOFTWARE\Microsoft\CommerceServer2.0\ Root=*installation_path*

■ If Internet Information Server is running during Commerce Server Setup, Setup stops IIS in order to copy files and reset registry settings

■ Creates IIS virtual directories used by Commerce Server (If you want to view your virtual directory settings in Internet Information Server, start Internet Service Manager, double-click the name of your Web server, and click the Directories tab.)

■ Updates the IIS BROWSCAP.INI file

The Browser Capability component provides your Active Server Pages scripts with a description of the capabilities of the client's Web browser. The BROWS-CAP.INI file is used by the Browser Capability component and contains information about many popular browsers.

When potential shoppers connect to your Commerce Server starter sites or to stores based on the starter sites or created using the Store Builder Wizard, the list in the BROWSCAP.INI file is used to determine the capabilities of their browser. Known browsers are sent pages using HTML forms, ActiveX controls, or plug-ins, depending on their listed capabilities. Unrecognized browsers get the lowest common denominator HTML forms pages.

Because having a current file is so important, you should check the site *http://www.microsoft.com/iis/* frequently to update your BROWSCAP.INI file.

Setup Verification

Commerce Server Setup restarts the World Wide Web Publishing service, if that service was already running when Setup began, and restarts Microsoft SQL Server (which was required to be running during Setup).

Access to your Commerce Server site over the Internet or intranet from your local machine requires that these services be running. To verify that all necessary services are running, use the Services utility in Control Panel.

To verify that all necessary services are running,

1. Double-click the Services icon in the Control Panel window.

2. In the Services dialog box, view the Status column. It should say "Started" for the following services: MSSQLServer and World Wide Web Publishing Service.

3. If any service is not started, click the service to select it from the list, and then click Start.

To start a service from the command prompt,

1. From the command prompt, type *net start*.

2. Type the name of the service:

   ❑ w3svc for World Wide Web Publishing Service, or

   ❑ mssqlserver for Microsoft SQL Server

Installation Testing

This section lists the steps involved in testing your Commerce Server installation. To test installation,

1. Verify that the MSSQLServer and World Wide Web Publishing services are running.

2. Check that you can see a store by using your browser to view the following page: *http://your_host_name/clockped/default.asp*. Note that you must have chosen to install the Clock Peddler starter store to view this page.

Commerce Server provides four examples of online stores that demonstrate how to implement various features of the product. To test your installation using a browser application such as Microsoft Internet Explorer, connect to one of the stores on a computer running Commerce Server using the following style of uniform resource locator (URL): *http://host_name/store_name/default.asp*.

When accessing the starter stores, you will substitute your host name and the name of the store you want to access.

You can also connect to Commerce Server Host Administrator (an application for building and copying stores), by using the following URL: *http://host_name/ mscs_hostadmin/default.asp*.

Type the following for access to the starter stores:

To Access	Use the Following URL
Clock Peddler store	http://*host_name*/clockped/default.asp
Volcano Coffee store	http://*host_name*/vc/default.asp
Microsoft Press store	http://*host_name*/mspress/default.asp
Adventure Works store	http://*host_name*/aw/default.asp

If you can connect to the site and browse the content, Commerce Server is correctly installed on your computer.

Setup Rerun

You can repeat Commerce Server Setup, for example, if you want to add or remove any of the components installed on a computer.

To rerun Commerce Server Setup,

1. Click Start, point to Commerce Server, and then click Commerce Server Setup.

2. In the Commerce Server Setup dialog box, click the button for the option you want (see below).

Option	Description
Add/Remove	Used to indicate specific components you want to install that modify your existing installation. Using the dialog box provided, you can select or clear the check boxes as appropriate.
Reinstall	Used to repeat the Setup process.
Remove All	Removes all Commerce Server files.

NOTE Any files that were not part of the initial installation will not be removed. You can remove these files using Windows NT Explorer.

When rerunning Setup, you can select the same system DSN or configure a new one.

An SQL Server Login dialog box does not appear when you reinstall Commerce Server unless the registry values for user logon ID and password do not match those set for SQL Server.

COMMERCE SERVER REMOVAL

This section describes removing Commerce Server from a computer. When you remove Commerce Server, Setup removes only Commerce Server components. The remove functionality of Commerce Server Setup adheres to the following guidelines:

■ Files the user added are not removed. For example, if you created a new store in addition to the installed defaults, the directory tree for the store is not removed.

■ All database information for the starter stores is removed, including data and tables.

■ Some programs install special database items that are not removed by Commerce Server Setup. For example, Visual InterDev creates a database called DTPROPERTIES that is not removed during uninstall of Commerce Server.

■ Other programs installed using Commerce Server Setup are not removed.

To remove Commerce Server,

1. Click Start, point to Commerce Server, and then click Commerce Server Setup.

2. In the Commerce Server Setup dialog box, click the Remove All button. This option removes all files, directories, and registry keys previously installed by Commerce Server Setup. The following message appears: *Are you sure you want to remove Commerce Server?*

3. Click OK to proceed.

NOTE Be sure to use Commerce Server Setup to remove your Commerce Server installation. If you attempt to delete files manually instead, certain settings and files may not be deleted; these residual files and settings may cause problems if you try to reinstall Commerce Server at a later time.

Appendix B

Commerce Server Planning

The problem with case studies is that each and every case is different than the others. Each business is unique in some ways.

This appendix discusses planning issues intended primarily for the third parties engaged in developing and deploying Commerce Server for a client. However, the issues are also applicable to internal MIS personnel who want to guarantee the success of the overall Site Server deployment project.

This section also helps in fleshing out customizations and enhancements required to a basic installtion of Commerce Server. Sample stores included with Commerce Server installation help illustrate how to use Commerce Server to offer hard goods on the Internet. A basic store may be developed using these sample stores in a matter of hours. However, Site and Commerce Server are flexible platforms that may be customized, personalized, and extended to adapt the technology to the unique needs of a business.You can use Commerce Server to offer soft goods such as research articles, magazines, books, software, intellectual property, realtime data, subscriptions to other online services, access to applications, access to other webs and pages, etc. You may need to modify and enhance an existing sample store to offer your goods and services. The questions outlined in this section also provide answers to the customizations and enhancements that turn a simple sample store into your store.

Good planning is needed in order to translate good technology into solid solutions. Most ICPs and ISVs have their own in-house planning methodology. This may be informal practices or formal steps in a document that guides the overall project planning, design, development, testing, and rollout phases.

The intent of this appendix is not to rewrite your existing practices, as these are unique to each business, industry, business cycle, and other special needs of the business. Its intent is rather to ask some questions that may shed light on the size and complexity of the work ahead and to help adapt your existing methods.

You can prototype a Commerce Server site in as little as two to four weeks, and in some cases a sample site can be operational in a matter of hours. You will still need to carefully assess, plan, develop, and implement your site, and also perform final acceptance testing of the system. This helps ensure delivery of quality results to the customers.

Most consultants and project managers are familiar with one or more system development methodologies and perhaps with Rapid Application Development methods as well. The steps outlined in this appendix are intended to augment such methodologies and assist you in your own site development. Here is an overview of what this appendix covers:[1]

- Assessment
  - External assessment
  - Internal assessment
- Planning
  - Country, state, and local tax considerations
  - Shipping considerations
  - Payment planning
  - Returns and customer credit planning
  - Commerce Server security planning
  - Multiple stores and mall considerations
  - Operational planning
  - Legacy system interface planning
  - Scalability planning
  - Response-time planning

Some additional comments are provided where needed and cross references for some topics are provided.

---

1. The Assessment and Planning headings loosely resemble associated tasks and topics in existing methodologies.

ASSESSMENT

During the assessment phase, you will answer a number of questions designed to size your engagement or project and to guide the server's development and successful deployment. You will develop, document, and approve the system's business, functional, and technical requirements. This task may take from one day to a few weeks depending on the size and complexity of your engagement. This task has at least two subtasks: external and internal assessment.

Internal Assessment

In this task, consider the following business and technical questions of the engagement or project starting with the business issues and continuing the technical questions. The first 14 are more business related. The remainder are more technology related.

1. Which industry segment does the client belong to and what are some factors that you should consider?

2. What are the sizes and definitions of the targeted audiences? Consider the size and definition of the existing customer base and the potential new business generated online.

3. How will the online channel augment and merge into the existing business processes? What are the convergence points: credits, customer services, support, sales, contact management, marketing, and so on?

4. How will you execute rollout and training for internal personnel and external customers? What resources will you need to transfer the technology or maintain it in-house? In this consideration, include internal customers, existing external customers, and potential first-time buyers. This latter group may be a much larger group than the former due to the Web's global nature.

5. What are the site's unique content needs?

6. What are the update cycles for content? For example, audio, video, news, and financial institutions have differing update requirements.

7. What are the existing content's conversion needs? At times, the store has been built in days but the conversion of all the historical data and existing content has taken weeks.

8. What are the centralized and decentralized control requirements? These requirements will also drive the architecture and the development of

Commerce Server components and its databases. See IIS administration in Appendix J.

9. What is the size of the expected audience for the server? What load will you have to manage? As a rule of thumb, if the size of the customer base for a company is known, chances are that a thousand times that number will "hit" the site in a given period just by virtue of surfing the Net. Only about 10 percent of this group will browse the pages and are potential customers. Perhaps 1–3 percent will purchase from the server. However, rules of thumb are hardly ever sufficient. Your customer is probably not typical. Your store's distribution will be as unique as your store. Knowing the percentage of shoppers who actually purchase item(s) is useful in load management and choice of load distribution. Use the WCAT tool and NT performance monitoring tool for ongoing analysis after you build a prototype. (WCAT is available with the Windows NT Resource Kit from Microsoft Press. It is a load simulator for use in planning and development stages.) Ultimately, the key to ongoing success is return visits.

10. What changes are required to the infrastructure in order to support potentially higher business volumes?

11. What special needs do the customers and clients have that are not answered by the base Commerce Server? How much customization and interfacing do you need?

12. Do you need to augment the server with other system services such as chat for community building, customer support, etc.? Please refer to Chapter 6, "Getting the Most from Your Site Server," for an overview of the systems and services available to augment Commerce Server.

13. Will the store be selling services or soft goods? See Chapter 2 under the heading "Commerce Server Customization."

14. Is Commerce Server intended for exclusive use, or offered as a mall in which other businesses may participate?

15. What applications and customizations are required to allow all business participants to access, control, manage, and participate in the ongoing Internet channel operations?

16. What are the target response times, considering that no design has control over the Internet's turn-around times?

17. What are the existing technologies to which the server must interface? This includes the following:

❑ Platforms such as Unix and IBM (see "Heterogeneous Platform Environments" in Chapter 7)

❑ Databases such as existing Oracle and Informix databases (see ODBC and SQL sections in Appendix J)

❑ Applications such as accounting, reporting, and management software[2] (see Appendix I, "Using MFC to Create Order Processing Components")

18. How familiar are the internal MIS personnel with the NT Server technology? From an operational point of view and ongoing support, the degree of familiarity with the NT platform drives the training and maintenance needs of the system. Should you require training, consult your Microsoft authorized training provider.

With a firm understanding of the answers to these questions you are now ready to plan the deployment cycle.

External Assessment

In this task, consider the following business questions:

1. What is the expected growth rate of the industry in which the business operates, and what trends support online commerce? For a retailer, the industry as a whole is moving toward lower costs of goods sold and higher volumes in order to meet market needs and competitive pressures. Most retailers are also bound by geography. A virtual nationwide presence for a retailer might cost tens of thousands of dollars, while a real presence in a mall store in New Mexico alone might be hundreds of thousands of dollars. Typically, a real presence is an order of magnitude more expensive to establish and maintain. Other industries have unique forces of their own.

2. What are the competitive forces in the market for the given industry? Is this business a pioneer or a follower in online commerce, and what should the initial posture and technology scale be?

PLANNING

To flesh out business issues, crystallize the requirements, and assess technical architecture and initial design, you could use a conference room pilot during this planning stage. Commerce Server can run as a stand-alone system on a single 486 box,

---

2. Great Plains, Platinum, and SAP have systems that run on NT.

see "Site Server Typical Configurations" in Chapter 7. This pilot can be scaled up to thousands of Web servers, accessing an additional thousands of database servers during production stages as the need arises, see "Scaling Site Server" in Chapter 7. In practice, however, there are limits to the number of servers that your DNS or MIS environment can support.

You will need to consider a number of issues to help plan for Commerce Server's deployment cycle. The following sections discuss each of these issues in more detail.

Country, State, and Local Tax Considerations

Commerce Server supports a number of domestic and international locales through its third-party tax components. Please refer to Appendix H, "Hexadecimal Codes for Countries," for a complete list of locales supported. If your target locale is not listed or tax and shipping modules are not installed by default for these locales, consult third-party providers or Microsoft sales, Microsoft consulting, or Microsoft marketing. In addition to the simple-tax component provided by Microsoft for tax calculations, TaxWare and TanData are two third parties that support tax calculation for a number of locales.

Shipping Considerations

Using components that plug in to the shipping stage of the order processing steps, you can easily program Commerce Server to handle any required shipping method. For an overview of the order processing components, please refer to the product documentation included on the companion CD in the Docs directory under the title "Order Processing Component System." A number of third-party components are also available or planned for handling your shipping requirements. If your needs are more complex, consult third-party providers or a Microsoft sales, consulting, or marketing contact. Alternatively, you can build these component using the techniques discussed in Chapter 5 and Appendix I, "Using MFC to Create Order Processing Components."

Payment Planning

You will need a relationship with a bank to clear Commerce Server transactions online in real time. A discussion of Commerce Server's real-time payment processing system in included in Appendix D, "VeriFone vPOS Software Included with Commerce Server 2.0."[3]

Some retailers prefer to simply develop an application that allows existing credit department personnel to also manage this part of the business. Chapter 4,

---

3. VeriFone is one third-party provider of online, real-time clearance third-party software. For an up-to-date list of other providers, consult your Microsoft sales, consulting, or marketing group.

under the section "Building a Site Server Customer Data Browser Application," shows an application developed for browsing the Commerce Server shopper table (or any table) for this purpose. You can develop the application in minutes using VI's Form Wizard.

Returns and Customer Credit Planning

You can handle customer returns and credits in one of the following ways:

- Using 800 service numbers, which may be advertised on the Final Purchase Page 1 of 1

- Using e-mail, which may be advertised on the Final Purchase page. Please see Chapter 6 under "Commercial Internet Mail Server"

- Using Commerce Server's complementary services, such as Chat Server. Please see Chapter 6 under "Commercial Internet Chat Server"

This is one area that promote return business and the issues and technologies required should be considered carefully.

Commerce Server Security Planning

While VeriFone vPos clearing engines employs Secure Electronics Transactions (SET) protocol, where credit card information is kept secret and only a reference to the transaction is transmitted over the Internet, you may require SSL configuration for your Commerce Server to protect transmission of other information and Web pages. This is especially true for soft goods, intellectual property, or financial data. Please see the Commerce Server security discussion in Appendix J for configuring SSL on your system.

Multiple Stores and Mall Considerations

Internet service (or solution) providers and merchants might want to offer their Commerce Server installation services to others. Commerce Server is capable of mall configuration out of the box. In this release, each virtual store owns its own Shopping Cart. In the physical world, this makes sense. For example, you cannot shop at one store in a mall and leave for another store with the cart, without checking out (paying for) the merchandise. Any number of stores may be housed in a single Commerce Server installation. However, this might affect your hardware requirements and Commerce Server architecture and configuration so that the additional volume can be supported without loss of response time.

Operational Planning

Once you have deployed the system, what are your ongoing staffing and operational needs? Commerce Server data and sale logs require periodic review and, in some cases, auditing per the requirements of your client or company. Beyond these requirements and based on the assessment stage described above, the following issues might require additional staffing:

■ Commerce Server reporting. Please see Chapter 6 under "Site Analyst" and "Usage Analyst."

■ Capacity monitoring and reporting. Please see Appendix L, "IIS Audit Logs and Performance Monitoring," and Chapter 7's discussion of the WCAT tool under "Web Farms and Very Large-Scale Configurations."

After the initial deployment and testing phase, Commerce Server hardware, database, or your network might require periodic review to keep the system tuned, back up system logs, and perform periodic upgrades and customization. These needs are typical of most hardware installations and can be handled through the existing operational staff of the MIS department or the Internet service provider.

Legacy System Interface Planning

Custom development is required to interface Commerce Server to existing accounting, reporting, and business management packages that reside on legacy systems. Commerce Server provides an API to accomplish this task. Use the Commerce Server API (discussed in the file titled OPPInterfaces.doc) and Site Server Order Processing Pipeline (discussed in the file titled Order Processing.doc) after installation, these files are located in the file *installdirectory*\SDK\Docs.

Database Scalability Planning

In addition to the single-machine installation, Commerce Server allows a distributed architecture over multiple machines. In the simplest form, Commerce Server, database server, and stores all run on a single machine.

The database server resides on an SQL-compliant server. Each store installed on Commerce Server requires its own database. While you can configure different application architectures for each store, all the schema and tables for a single store should reside on one database.[4] In other words, during setup, each of the sample stores can be pointed through an ODBC DSN to a different database server, or all can point to the same database server. Upon installation, all the tables of a single store will be accessed through its single ODBC DSN. However, the databases for other stores can reside on different servers. You can use any SQL database that is

---

4. This restriction does not apply to MTS-enabled servers.

ODBC-compliant, including Informix, Oracle, and SQL Server. The only requirement is that an ODBC driver is available for the NT from Microsoft or a third-party provider. For further details and a list of ODBC vendors, please refer to the "ODBC Tools and Techniques" and "SQL Server Tools and Techniques" sections in Appendix J.

Response Time Planning

If your site has strict response time requirements, you should incorporate these requirements into the scaling of the system. Having developed a first prototype for your site, you can use WCAT to profile response times under different load scenarios to yield the desired user acceptance level.

This section included some questions that are common to most Site/Commerce Server deployments. A firm understanding of these issues and other unique characteristics of the business will help guide successful deployment of your site, on-time and within budget.

These questions and issues are not exhaustive of all cases. However, they allow for a good start to the methodologies.

Building a BuyNow Store

Building a BuyNow store is a bit of a variation on the store building processes discussed in Chapter 1. You build a BuyNow store through a process similar to building a regular store, discussed in Chapter 1 in the "Build Process" section. However, a BuyNow store does not contain the product-browsing and information-gathering pages of a regular store. The number of pages for a BuyNow store is far fewer and limited only to processing a completed order cycle (the last cycle of a regular store). All the product, shopper, and credit-card information is sent to the server and processed in one step. On the browser (client) side, BuyNow is an object, as specified below.

To build a page using BuyNow control,

1. Follow the techniques discussed in Chapter 1, "Build Process."

2. Cut and paste the following code into the host page's HTML or as another frame in an existing frame set (replace *servername* with the name of your Web server host computer, and *storename* with the name of your store).

```
<OBJECT ID=buyNowObject
CLASSID="clsid:787F0090-729F-11D0-B7C6-00AA00A2013E"
     TYPE="application/x-oleobject"
CODEBASE="http://servername/storename/buynow.cab#Version=1,0,0,0005" >
     Remark Double check this version number for currency, before use.
     <PARAM Name="Url" Value="http://servername/storename/cybframe.asp" >
```

```
<PARAM Name="EndUrl" Value="http://servername/storename/cancel.asp" >
<PARAM Name="Resizable" Value="False" >
<PARAM Name="dlgHeight" Value="455" >
<PARAM Name="dlgWidth" Value="550" >
</OBJECT>
```

This code is directly embedded on any HTML page, Commerce Server or not, or it may be added via an HTML frame to the target page. No ASP is required; only browser support for the HTML <OBJECT> tag is needed. The examples included with the product release use the latter scheme and the frame holds the object as well as a rotating advertisement. The target page may be a Site Server page or any other server's page. Please see also the BuyNow topic under the \Docs\Word\Using Buy-Now on the companion CD.

VeriFone vPOS Software Included with Commerce Server 2.0[1]

The following excerpts from a README file come from the VeriFone vPOS software included with Commerce Server 2.0. These excerpts describe the capabilities and functions of VeriFone vPOS software. This README is also available, after installation of the product, from the installer.

---

1. Material in this appendix, available under \docs\Building a store.doc after installation of the companion CD for this book, is extracted from material provided by the Microsoft Site Server documentation group.

VERIFONE PART NUMBER
VPN S4700-01, VERSION 2.0

Thanks for reading this! It contains important information about the VeriFone vPOS software and how it integrates with the Microsoft Commerce Server version 2.0 software.

This version of the vPOS software is not capable of processing real credit-card transactions. It uses unvalidated merchant and bank test certificates, and is configured to only talk to test gateways. Real credit-card transactions require the services of an acquiring bank and a corresponding vPOS version.

For a list of the financial institutions supporting VeriFone vPOS software, please see the Financial Partners section of VeriFone's Web site.

We recommend that you do not enter valid credit-card numbers into the payment forms because payment information is saved in a database, appears in reports, and (depending on your system configuration) may be transmitted over public networks using unvalidated test certificates—or even in the clear. This version does not have full security in payment information handling.

Test Certificates

The Test Certificates are for testing purposes only. You agree to use the Test Certificates for this purpose only. No attempt has been made by VeriFone, Inc. or GTE to verify the accuracy and/or authenticity of the information included in the Test Certificates.

GTE AND VERIFONE, INC. SHALL NOT BE LIABLE IN ANY WAY FOR LOSS OR DAMAGE INCURRED BY ANY PARTY THAT MAY BE CAUSED BY THE USE OF, OR RELIANCE ON, THIS TEST CERTIFICATE OR AS A RESULT OF ANY COMPROMISE OR DISCLOSURE OF ANY OF THE TEST CERTIFICATE PRIVATE KEYS IN THE HIERARCHY. GTE AND VERIFONE, INC. MAKE NO WARRANTIES EXPRESS, IMPLIED, OR OTHERWISE, INCLUDING MERCHANTABILITY OR FITNESS FOR A PARTICULAR PURPOSE, RELATING TO THE TEST CERTIFICATE.

Overview

The vPOS software consists of four basic components:

- The vPOS Engine
- The vPOS Payment Component
- The vPOS Terminal Interface
- The vPOS Site Administration Application

The vPOS Engine runs as an NT service and provides the back-end payment protocol, configuration, and logging support for the other components.

The vPOS Payment Component is the COM-based payment component and is available to Microsoft Commerce Server 2.0 stores for the payment stage of the order pipeline.

The vPOS Terminal Interface provides an HTML forms-based user interface for operator-initiated payment transactions, administration, and terminal configuration.

The vPOS Site Administration Application is a control panel applet for adding vPOS functionality to new and existing stores.

Release Notes

Terminal Interface and IIS

The vPOS Terminal Interface has been tested with IIS 3.0. Future versions of IIS may have a different access control mechanism as compared to IIS 3.0. If the access control fails to work with future versions of IIS, you may need to manually apply access control to vPOS Terminal Interface. For more information please refer to the VeriFone vPOS Product Support Web site.

Sample store

This version of VeriFone vPOS comes preconfigured with a sample store called The Furniture Shoppe. This store is configured to demonstrate the capability of the VeriFone vPOS software. To enable vPOS for other sample stores in the Microsoft Commerce Server 2.0 distribution, please refer to the accompanying document on the vPOS Payment Component.

Test gateway

The vPOS in this version is configured to run in a Development mode, i.e., transactions are sent to a test gateway running on the same machine as the vPOS software. This "local" test is useful for determining that the vPOS is correctly installed and for experimenting with it before actually resolving network connections and running transactions with a bank's gateway. Naturally, this slows down transaction processing times because the vPOS installation is simulating a bank on the same machine.

Web server port number

The VeriFone vPOS software comes configured with port 80 for the test gateway. In case you are running your Web server on a port other than 80, you will need to modify the port setting for the test gateway. You need to change the Port value in the registry key HKEY_LOCAL_MACHINE\SOFTWARE\VeriFone\vPOS\Stores*storename*\API\ADT\LocalTest\PDT\0 (replace *storename* with the name of the directory containing the store's files). You need to restart the vPOS Engine service after making this change.

The URLs in this readme for the vPOS Terminal Interface and the sample store mentioned above may not work because they are configured for localhost:80. You may need to manually enter the URLs with the correct port number.

Uninstalling vPOS

You may uninstall the VeriFone vPOS software by choosing Uninstall vPOS Merchant Software from the VeriFone vPOS Merchant Software program group. Note that after uninstalling several files will be left yet marked for deletion. These files will be removed after the next reboot. Also, the following files may not have been automatically removed during uninstall from the *system_root*\system32 directory and should be removed: vPOSAdmin.cpl, storemgmt.dll, PCL.dll, sds.dll.

CGI Program Permissions

Some of vPOS's components run as CGI programs. These programs need the ability to read from and write to the registry and potentially the ability to access a remote database. These programs will likely run in the appropriate system context unless you have configured your Web server otherwise.

Case-Sensitivity

In this release, the vPOS does not work properly on a case-sensitive database. Please make sure you use it on a case-insensitive database management system. Also, store names as entered during install (and set in the registry) are case-sensitive and they must exactly match when referenced in the vPOS URLs.

vPOS and Database Information in the Registry

The DSN as well as the username/password for the DSN are stored in the registry. Users are responsible for ensuring adequate security for their NT registry.

Example Cards

When testing, you may wish to use card number 4200 0000 0000 0000 as an example of a valid number but unacceptable card, and 4242 4242 4242 4242 as a valid and acceptable card (as defined by the local test gateway). The vPOS is configured to accept card numbers in the specific ranges for Visa, MasterCard, American Express, and Discover. An example of a number outside any of these specific ranges is 8282 8282 8282 8282.

Handling Card Numbers

An important vPOS security issue is the protection of customer card numbers on your system. Several security measures are in place, including encryption of card numbers in the vPOS data tables and access control on the Terminal Interface. Effective operation of these measures requires some diligence on your part; please consult the vPOS User's Guide for detailed recommendations.

The security measures limit the exposure of card numbers in the vPOS user interface. One place they do appear is when performing a Capture as a follow-on to an Authorize from the Review Transactions results. The card number appears there to facilitate a "manual" Capture in the unlikely circumstance where an online Capture is not possible.

OLE Permissions

The vPOS Payment Component and the vPOS Engine use OLE to communicate, and this places some restrictions on the security contexts in which these components run. The installation configures these components to both run as NT LocalSystem; if you change either to login as a user, be sure to change both to the same user.

Oracle Support

The vPOS software has basic support for Oracle 7 databases as well as the default Microsoft SQL Server.

Terminal Interface Access Control

Here are a few subtle aspects of Terminal Interface access control.

- When using Microsoft Internet Explorer 3.0 (or later) to access the Terminal Interface, it may use NT challenge/response to automatically authenticate you without a username/password dialog. Other browsers will ask for a username/password.

- When the database software is running on a different machine than the vPOS, the Admin User's domain name must also be valid on the database machine. Therefore, you may need to specify a domain name as part of your username when authenticating.

Differences Between JavaScript 1.0 and JavaScript 1.1

Microsoft JScript is based on JavaScript as it was available for Netscape Navigator 2.0 and later, generally called JavaScript 1.0. Navigator 3.0 implements a different version of JavaScript, generally called JavaScript 1.1. Differences between JavaScript 1.0 and 1.1 will produce incompatibilities between JScript and JavaScript 1.1. The differences are enumerated below, in no specific order.

- JavaScript 1.1 provides a new object called *image*. This object allows you to change the images of a document without reloading the document. Not currently supported in JScript.

- JavaScript 1.1 adds a new event handler, *onMouseOut*. Not currently supported in JScript.

- JavaScript 1.1 adds the Area object, which is an array of links for an image map. Not currently supported in JScript.

- JavaScript 1.1 supports the Option object, which is an array of the options implemented for *selection* and that allows you to change the text of the option at run time. Not currently supported in JScript.

- JavaScript 1.1 supports the opener property of the Window object. This provides a way of calling functions in a still open but not active window. Not currently supported in JScript.

- The *setfocus()* property has been added to JavaScript 1.1, but is not supported in either JavaScript 1.0 or JScript.

- JavaScript 1.1 allows a limited form of error trapping with the onError event handler. This is not available in JavaScript 1.0 or JScript.

- JavaScript 1.1 has a *javaEnabled* method that permits detection of whether or not a browser has Java enabled. JScript doesn't support this, and it is unclear whether JScript even can support this since Java functionality is achieved within Internet Explorer through a different mechanism (ActiveX) than in Navigator.

- JavaScript 1.1 adds the reload method to force the reloading of a page; JScript has no equivalent method.

- JavaScript 1.1 adds the reset method, which simulates the click event of a reset button; JScript has no equivalent method.

The *location.replace* and *location.reload* form elements are currently absent from JScript. JScript form elements don't have type fields: you cannot reference, for instance, *myButton.type*.

Commerce Server Component Reference[1]

Commerce Server components are a group of active server components, such as those discussed in Chapter 5 and Appendix I, that provide the run-time environment for the presentation of online stores. These components are regpistered on your system as ActiveX server components when you install Commerce Server. Like the components included with Active Server Pages (ASP), Commerce Server components support methods and properties that you call and set from within the Visual Basic Scripting Edition (VBScript) or JScript server-side code that runs your Commerce Server store.

Commerce Server components, however, provide an extensive set of services that Active Server Pages do not provide, services that simplify and automate many of the tasks that you would have to perform manually to build a working store with ASP components alone. Such tasks include reliably maintaining state data across multiple sessions, accessing and modifying content stored in a database, logging

---

1. Material in this appendix, available under \docs\Building a store.doc after installation of the companion CD for this book, is extracted from material provided by the Microsoft Site Server documentation group.

store traffic for marketing and diagnostic purposes, and automatically processing order data through the Order Processing Pipeline (OPP).

This appendix describes Commerce Server components and includes definitions of the methods and properties that they support. For a tour of the online stores that use these components, see Appendix G.

Commerce Server defines the following server components:

Component	Description
Content	Provides a cache in which to store string variables that you associate with data source names (DSNs) and SQL queries.
DataFunctions	Supports a collection of functions that validate the format of data for database storage or for processing by the OPP.
Datasource	Executes queries that you specify. These can be SQL queries that you construct at run time, or that you have associated with string variables and stored in a Content component cache.
DBStorage	Supports flexible interaction with the database, primarily for the storage of receipt and order information.
Dictionary	Provides in-memory storage of name-value pairs.
MessageManager	Provides a cache in which to store shopper messages that the OPP uses to describe error conditions.
OrderForm	Supports the in-memory storage of shopper and purchase information for the current shopping session.
OrderPipeline	Loads the pipeline configuration (.PCF) file that contains the pipeline configuration information for your store.
Page	Simplifies the layout of HTML pages, and the interaction between these pages and the data sources used by your store.
StandardSManager	Supports the creation, deletion, and retrieval of unique shopper identifiers.
SimpleList	A list of variants.
TrafficLogfile	Supports logging store events to a text file.
TrafficTable	Supports logging store events to database tables.

GETTING STARTED

This appendix provides information on the Commerce Server components that you use to build online stores. The components explained in this document do not include the Order Processing Pipeline (OPP) components.

This appendix assumes that you are familier with Visual Basic Scripting Edition (VBScript) or with JScript, and with the use of one of these languages within Active Server Pages (ASP). For a tutorial on VBScript, see the VBScript tutorial included with the Active Server Pages Roadmap. For information on Active Server Pages, see the Active Server Pages Roadmap.

As you use the information provided here to script online stores, you should be particularly aware of two VBScript features that figure prominently in the use of Commerce Server component methods.

First, as with other ActiveX Server components, all variables passed to Commerce Server components are of a single data type: **Variant**. A **Variant** is a special kind of data type that can contain different kinds of information, depending on how it's used. Because **Variant** is the only data type in VBScript, it's also the data type returned by all functions in VBScript.

Second, many of the methods implemented in Commerce Server components take optional parameters. This means that if you do not supply a value for these parameters, a default value is assumed. How you reference optional parameters in your call to Commerce Server component methods depends upon a parameter's position in the parameter list.

The following, for example, uses the **DataFunctions** component's **ValidateNumber** method to illustrate the various ways in which you use optional parameters. This method, which determines if a value that you supply falls within a given numerical range, has the following syntax:

*DataFunctions.***ValidateNumber(***Value, MinimumValue, MaximumValue***)**

The *Value* parameter references the number that you want to test against a set of range values. *MinimumValue* and *MaximumValue* designate the low and high ends of that range. If *Value* falls between *MinimumValue* and *MaximumValue*, **ValidateNumber** returns TRUE; otherwise, FALSE.

However, because the *MinimumValue* and *MaximumValue* parameters are optional, you can call this method in several ways. For example, if you are interested only in determining whether the value that you have supplied exceeds a certain minimum, call **ValidateNumber** as follows:

```
bValid = Page.ValidateNumber(Value, MinimumValue)
```

In this example, you do not reference *MaximumValue*, because you do not want to compare *Value* to a maximum number, because the parameter is optional, and because it appears at the end of a parameter list. However, because *MaximumValue* is not specified, its *default value* is assumed. In the case of **ValidateNumber**, *MaximumValue* defaults to Null, which means simply that the parameter is ignored in the range evaluation.

If, however, you wanted to test a value against a maximum value, but not against a minimum value, you would call **ValidateNumber** as follows:

```
bValid = Page.ValidateNumber(Value, Null, MaximumValue)
```

Note that you cannot simply eliminate the Null placeholder for *Minimum-Value* in this case, because *MinimumValue* appears to the left, in the parameter list, of a value that you specify. This parameter's default value is Null, which means that the parameter is ignored in the range valuation, and *Value* is tested only against *MaximumValue*.

Finally, although there is never a reason to leave out both the optional arguments to **ValidateNumber**, you could call **ValidateNumber** as follows:

```
bValid = ValidateNumber(Value)
```

In this case you do not have to specify Null for either optional argument, because this call uses no optional argument that appears to the left of another specified optional argument. Since both *MinimumValue* and *MaximumValue* appear at the end of the argument list and are not referenced, both default to Null, which means that both values are ignored in the valuation. In such a call, **ValidateNumber** returns TRUE.

APPLICATION-LEVEL COMMERCE SERVER COMPONENTS

Commerce Server components are created on a per-application or per-page basis. Where a component has application scope, it is initialized as an ASP **Application** object variable, and can be accessed from within any page in your store.

Application object variables are declared, and should be initialized, in your store's GLOBAL.ASA file. The GLOBAL.ASA file resides in each directory of a Commerce Server store. This global configuration file defines the **Application_OnStart** event handlers, as well as **Session** and **Application** variables.

Commerce Server stores generally avoid the use of **Session** variables, primarily because the use of **Application** variables is more efficient in terms of memory overhead, and because **Session** variables are not designed for use in a multimachine configuration.

However, all Commerce Server stores use **Application** variables to store references to component instances that need to be created and used on a per-application basis. Here is an example in which a store's **StandardSManager** component is created within the GLOBAL.ASA file, and is initialized to an **Application** variable:

```
Set ShopperManager = Server.CreateObject(
"Commerce.StandardSManager" )

Set Application( "MSCSShopperManager" ) = ShopperManager
```

In this example, because the **MSCSShopperManager** variable references a component instance, the VBScript **Set** keyword is required. Once the **Application** variable **MSCSShopperManager** is set to the created **StandardSManager** component, you can use that **Application** variable to call **StandardSManager** methods, as follows:

```
ShopperID = Application( "MSCSShopperManager"
).CreateShopperID()
```

Although the name that you assign **Application** variables is usually arbitrary, the names that you assign **Application** variables that reference Commerce Server components require naming conventions. This requirement arises from the facts that Commerce Server components occasionally need to retrieve information stored by other Commerce Server components, that they must use the ASP scripting context to retrieve the **Application** component that stores this information, and that the **Application** component requires that components querying its internally stored variables identify these variables specifically by their string variable names.

Thus, in the example above, the name you assign to the **StandardSManager** component instance is arbitrary, but the **Application** component variable referencing this instance must be **MSCSShopperManager**.

The following table lists the mandatory **Application** variable names that you use to store per-application component instances:

Variable	Purpose
MSCSContent	Stores the instance of the **Content** component.
MSCSDataFunctions	Stores the instance of the **DataFunctions** component.
MSCSDefaultDatasource	Stores the variable name of the default data source for the store.
MSCSMessageManager	Stores the instance of the **MessageManager** component.
MSCSOrderFormStorage	Stores the instance of the **DBStorage** component that you are using to store **OrderForm** data.
MSCSOrderPipeline	Stores the application instance of the **OrderPipeline** component.
MSCSReceiptStorage	Optional. Stores the instance of the **DBStorage** component that the Order Processing Pipeline uses to store purchase data.
MSCSShopperManager	Stores the instance of the **StandardSManager** component.
MSCSShopperStorage	Stores the application instance of the **DBStorage** component in which you store shopper data.
MSCSTraffic	Stores the application instance of the **TrafficTable** or **TrafficLogfile** component that you use to log store traffic.

The following **Application**-level variables are not required. However, for component methods that require values that these variables reference, you must specify the value in the call to the component method, or you must initialize these variables.

Variable	Purpose
MSCSDisableHTTPS	A Boolean value that indicates whether secure HTTP is enabled.
MSCSIDUrlKey	Indicates the name to be used in the name part of a name-value pair when the shopper's shopper ID is appended to a URL.
MSCSInsecureHostName	The name of the insecure host. This name is used by the **URL** method to generate an insecure URL to a store page.
MSCSSecureHostName	The name of the secure host. This name is used by the **SURL** method to generate a secure URL to a store page.

THE SIMPLELIST AND DICTIONARY COMPONENTS

The **SimpleList** and **Dictionary** components are general purpose collection components that Commerce Server components use to store lists and name-value pairs in memory.

A **SimpleList** component is simply a list of **Variant**s that supports enumeration. In Commerce Server, the **SimpleList** component is used to store the results of executed SELECT queries, and can be used for any task that requires a list data structure.

The **SimpleList** component supports the following methods:

Method	Description
Add	Adds the specified item to the list.
Delete	Deletes an item based upon a specified index value.

The **SimpleList** component supports the following property:

Property	Description
Count	A read-only number that identifies the number of elements in the **SimpleList**.

To create a **SimpleList** component, use the Active Server Pages (ASP) **Server** object's **CreateObject** method, specifying **Commerce.SimpleList** as the component's program identifier. After creating a **SimpleList** component, you can use the **SimpleList**'s **Add** and **Delete** methods to add and remove items from the underlying list. To retrieve elements, you can index into the list, as you would index into an array, or you can use the Visual Basic Scripting Edition For Each statement to iterate through the **SimpleList**'s contents.

To create a **SimpleList** component, use the Active Server Pages (ASP) **Server.CreateObject** method, specifying **Commerce.SimpleList** as the component's program identifier.

```
<%
    Set SimpleList = Server.CreateObject("Commerce.SimpleList")

    ' Add an item

    Call SimpleList.Add("Hello")
%>
```

The **Dictionary** component consists of name-value pairs. The **Dictionary** component defines no methods, but supports the following properties:

Property	Description
Count	A read-only number that identifies the number of elements in the **Dictionary**.
Value	A variable that identifies the value of a given **Dictionary** key.

For example, in the following statement, **Dictionary** identifies the **Dictionary** variable, shopper_id is the key to the dictionary, and this key is initialized to the value of the current shopper's shopper ID:

```
Dictionary.shopper_id = Page.GetShopperID(Null)
```

To create a **Dictionary** component, specify the **Commerce.Dictionary** program identifier:

```
<%

Set Dictionary = Server.CreateObject("Commerce.Dictionary")
Set SimpleList = Server.CreateObject("Commerce.SimpleList")

Dictionary.shopper_id = Page.GetShopperID

SimpleList.Add(Dictionary)

REM Later, to retrieve the added dictionary.

Set SrcDict = SimpleList(0)

%>
```

You can use the VBScript **For Each** statement to iterate through the values stored in a **Dictionary** component. Assuming a **Dictionary** variable named *Dict*, the following statements, for example, output the values of a **Dictionary**'s keys to the page:

```
<% For Each Element In Dict %>
<% Response.Write(Dict.Value(Element)) %>
<% Next %>
```

The following example enumerates the names of the keys themselves (as opposed to their values) and outputs the key names to the page:

```
<% For Each Name In Dict %>
<% Response.Write(Name) %>
<% Next %>
```

When a **SimpleList** consists of **Dictionary** components, you use the dot (.) operator between the **SimpleList** element and the **Dictionary** key to reference the **Dictionary** element. For example, the following statement references the shopper_id **Dictionary** key in the third element of a **SimpleList**:

```
shopper_id = SimpleList(2).shopper_id
```

Because both the **SimpleList** and the **Dictionary** are collection objects, you can use the **For Each** statement to iterate through the contents of either object. For example, the following example outputs the value for the shopper_id key for every **Dictionary** in the **SimpleList**:

```
<% For Each Element in SimpleList %>
<% = Element.shopper_id %>
<% Next %>
```

THE CONTENT COMPONENT

The **Content** component provides a straightforward way for stores to create and maintain a group of variables that identify the queries and data source names (DSNs) needed to interact with a store's inventory. You can use **Content** component methods to associate string variables with configured system and file DSNs, to associate SQL query strings with application-wide variables, and to create the **Datasource** components through which these queries are executed.

The **Content** component supports the following methods:

Method	Description
AddDatasource	Associates a string variable with a configured system or file DSN and stores this variable in the **Content** component cache.
AddQuery	Associates a string variable with an SQL statement and stores this variable in the **Content** component cache.
Datasource	Returns a **Datasource** component based on the variable name associated with a DSN variable. The **Datasource** method is the default method for the **Content** component.

Overview

Use of the **Content** component begins with the creation of a DSN variable, a string variable that you associate with a DSN that you have created using the ODBC32 Control Panel utility. You use the Content component's **AddDatasource** method to add a DSN variable to the **Content** component. Because the **Content** component will contain all the DSNs and queries used by your store to retrieve store content, this component should be created to have application scope. This means that it should be created in the **Application_OnStart** subroutine in your store's GLOBAL.ASA file:

```
REM -- Create a content object and data source for connection⤴
   to the database

Set  MSCSContent = Server.CreateObject("Commerce.Content")
Call MSCSContent.AddDatasource("ClockPed", MSCSDSN)
```

This example call to **AddDatasource** assigns the string name ClockPed to the data source identified by *MSCSDSN*. *MSCSDSN* is simply a string variable that contains the connection string necessary to access the database, and is defined in The Clock Peddler's DSNINCLUDE.ASP file as follows:

```
MSCSDSN = "DSN=Stores;UID=sa;PWD=;APP=;DATABASE=Commerce"
```

In this string, *Stores* identifies the DSN that you assigned this data source when you configured it using the ODBC32 Control Panel utility, and *Commerce* identifies an SQL Server database that you specified when you created the DSN. Note that the string above is a sample connection string, and that the actual connection string varies from one data source to another.

After adding a DSN variable—ClockPed, in this example—to the **Content** component, you use the **AddQuery** method to add your store's queries to the component:

```
REM -- Add queries to the content object for use in our pages

call MSCSContent.AddQuery("departments", "select * from ⤴
   ClockPed_dept")
Call MSCSContent.AddQuery("products-by-dept", "select sku, ⤴
   name, dept_id, manufacturer, list_price, image_file,⤴
   image_width, image_height, description from ClockPed_product⤴
   where dept_id = convert(numeric,:1)")
Call MSCSContent.AddQuery("department", "select * from ⤴
   ClockPed_dept where dept_id = convert(numeric,:1)")
Call MSCSContent.AddQuery("product", "select sku, name, ⤴
   dept_id, manufacturer, list_price, image_file, image_width, ⤴
   image_height, description from ClockPed_product where ⤴
   sku = :1")
```

The first parameter to **AddQuery** identifies the name by which you will reference this query when you execute it, and the second parameter contains the query's SQL text. The values that follow the text of the query consists of parameters you can use to enhance significantly the speed and efficiency with which queries are executed.

To execute one of the queries added above, you need to use the **Content** component's **Datasource** method to create a **Datasource** component, and then call its **Execute** method, referencing the string name that you have associated with the query. Here is the call that creates this component in the Clock Peddler store:

```
Set MSCSDataSource = MSCSContent.Datasource("ClockPed")
```

Once you have created a **Datasource** component, it has access to all the queries in the **Content** component cache. Consequently, you use the **Datasource** component's **Execute** method to execute a query stored in the **Content** cache without directly referencing the **Content** component through which the **Datasource** component was originally created. For example, the following call, which appears in the Clock Peddler's DEFAULT.ASP file, calls the **Execute** method on the *departments* query that was added to the **Content** component earlier in this section, and iterates through the **SimpleList** of the query's results to display the Clock Peddler's departments on the page:

```
<UL>
    <% set depts = MSCSDataSource.Execute("departments") %>
    <% for each dept in depts %>
        <LI><A HREF="<% = mscsPage.URL("dept.asp", "dept_id", ⤶
        dept.dept_id) %>"><% = mscsPage.Encode(dept.dept_name)
%>></A>
    <% next %>
</UL>
```

Because the pages in your store need to access a central collection of queries and DSNs, you should create the **Content** component to have **Application** scope. This means that this component must be created in the **Application_OnStart** event, which you define in your **shop** directory's GLOBAL.ASA file, and initialize the **Application** object variable **MSCSContent** variable to reference these components. Additionally, if your store uses more than one DSN, you should identify one of the **Datasource** names that you create as the store's default data source. To do this, initialize the Application-level **MSCSDefaultDatasource** variable to reference the string variable name of the data source. The following example, which contains a subset of the statements that appear in the Clock Peddler's GLOBAL.ASA file, illustrates this initialization:

```
<SCRIPT LANGUAGE=VBScript RUNAT=Server>
Sub Application_OnStart

REM -- Create a content object and data source for connection ⤶
to the database

Set  MSCSContent = Server.CreateObject("Commerce.Content")
Call MSCSContent.AddDatasource("ClockPed", MSCSDSN, 1, 0)
```

```
REM -- Set up the Application intrinsic object

Application.Lock

Set Application("MSCSContent")        = MSCSContent
Application("MSCSDefaultDatasource") = "ClockPed"

Application.Unlock
End Sub

</SCRIPT>
```

Note that the **Datasource**, unlike the **Content** component, is created on a per-page basis. For example, in the Clock Peddler store, the SHOP.ASA file is included in every file that needs to retrieve a data source from the **Content** component, and includes the following statement:

```
Set MSCSDatasource = Application("MSCSContent")("ClockPed")
```

SQL Server and Oracle Database Considerations

As you configure your database to take maximum advantage of the optimizations that the **Content** component offers, you should be aware of the following issues that arise with SQL Server and Oracle databases.

First, SQL Server allows *block fetches* of binary data only when all timestamps, image, text, and other long data is specified after all non-long data. This can be accomplished without modifying a database schema by simply specifying the column names in the correct order in the SQL query instead of using *. Oracle does not allow block fetching at all, and requires row retrieval in all cases.

Second, Active Data Objects (ADO) can be run in different threading models, depending on the underlying database drivers. If the underlying driver for a database does not support multiple threads, then ADO must be marked as using apartment-model threading, which can drastically reduce performance of all database operations when the database is being accessed by many users simultaneously.

However, for database drivers that provide for multiple threading, you can achieve impressive performance gains by specifying ADO as free-threaded. You must specify this explicitly because ADO is marked as apartment-model by default. To run ADO with a different threading model, run either the MAKEFREE.BAT or the MAKEAPT.BAT batch files. These files are located in the ADO installation directory, which is usually C:\PROGRAM FILES\SYSTEM\ADO. SQL Server drivers available from Microsoft support multiple threads.

Parameterized Queries and Parameter Binding

In a parameterized query, the SQL query statement contains parameter markers that indicate search values that are supplied at run time to the **Datasource** component's **Execute** method. For parameterized queries added to the **Content** component, a colon, followed by a number that designates the parameter's place in the parameter list, serves as the parameter marker. Optionally, you can use the question mark ("?") as a parameter marker.

Because the **Content** component provides optimized query execution, it handles parameters differently than do Active Data Objects (ADO). When you pass parameters to the **Execute** or **ExecuteADO** methods, these parameters are bound in the order in which they are passed in. Moreover, because the **Content** component has no way of knowing the underlying database schema, it relies solely on the **Variant** type of the value passed in as a parameter to determine how to store it. Thus, if a parameter is to be bound to a character column, it must be a string value.

Despite this consideration, the **Content** component can bind two types of Null values to database columns: Null string values and Null integers. A Null string value can be inserted into columns that are marked as **char, varchar, long varchar**, **datetime**, or **binary** by specifying an empty string ("") for the parameter value. You can insert a Null value into an integer column by specifying the Null keyword as the parameter value.

The following parameter binding issues arise specifically in connection to Oracle databases:

All integers are bound as double-precision variables. This means that to insert a parameter value into an integer column in an Oracle database, you must use the **TO_NUMBER** macro to reference the parameter value in your query statement, and you must cast the parameter value to **CDbl** when you execute the command. Attempting to pass the parameter value as an Integer Variant results in a type mismatch error.

```
Set Content = Server.CreateObject("Commerce.Content")

call Content.AddDatasource("MSPress", ConnectionString)

call Content.AddQuery("put_author_ids", "INSERT INTO⤴
    MSPRESS_AUTHOR(AUTHOR_ID) VALUES(TO_NUMBER(:1)")

set Rs = Datasource.Execute("put_author_ids", CDbl(125))
```

To insert date values into an Oracle date column, you must enclose the date value in the TO_DATE macro, as follows:

```
call Content.AddQuery("insert_date", "INSERT INTO MSPRESS_BASKET ⤴
    VALUES('Joe Smith', TO_DATE(:1, 'MM/DD/YY HH:MI:SS PM'), NULL))
```

```
Set Connection = Datasource.CreateADOConnection

Set adoRs = Datasource.ExecuteADO(Connection, "InsertDate",↵
    CStr(Now))
```

Thread Pooling

Thread pooling is turned off in ADO by default. Commerce Server relies heavily on database connection pooling, and it is crucial to database performance that this feature is properly set. To enable database connection pooling, set the following registry value to 1:

```
HKEY_LOCAL_MACHINE\System\CurrentControlSet\W3SVC\Asp\↵
    Parameters\StartConnectionPool.
```

When using Connection Pooling, to increase database performance, be sure to select the Generate Store Procedure option in the DSN SQL Server Driver Startup menu. To uncheck this option, double-click on the system DSN for your SQL Server database in the ODBC32 Control Panel utility.

AddDatasource

The **AddDatasource** method associates a configured file or system data source name (DSN) with a string alias.

Syntax
Content.**AddDatasource(** *Alias, ConnectionString*)

Parameters

Alias   A string that identifies the name by which you will reference the DSN in your store.

ConnectionString   A string that contains connection and login information.

Remarks
If you use more than one DSN in a store, you should specify one of them as the default DSN for the store. To do this, set the **Application** object variable **MSCSDefaultDatasource** to reference the string variable name that you have associated with a DSN that you have added to the **Content** component query collection.

Example
The following example, from the AdventureWorks sample store, creates a **Content** component, adds a DSN variable to the component, and makes that DSN the default DSN for the store:

```
REM Create a Content component for access to the database
Set  MSCSContent = Server.CreateObject( "Commerce.Content" )
Call MSCSContent.AddDataSource("AW", MSCSDSN)
```

```
Set  MSCSDatasource = MSCSContent.Datasource("AW")

' Later, in Application_OnStart
Application("MSCSDefaultDatasource") = "AW"
```

Applies to
Content

See also
AddQuery

AddQuery

The **AddQuery** method adds a query variable to the **Content** component.

Syntax
*Content.***AddQuery** *QueryName, QueryText, Timeout, CommandType, Maximum-Rows, CursorType, CursorSize, RetrievalMethod*

Parameters

QueryName	A string variable that identifies the query. This name must be a non-Null string, but can contain spaces, numbers, and other non-Null characters.
QueryText	The SQL text of the query.
Timeout	An optional number that specifies the period of time, in seconds, to wait for the database to respond after an operation has been executed. A value of 0 indicates that the defaults for the database driver. This value should be increased for database operations that are slow, or during operations that are known to take more time than is allowed by the default.
CommandType	An integer constant that specifies the kind of command that *QueryText* represents. Specifying the precise type of the command (as opposed to **adCommandUnknown**) results in faster execution time. The following table lists the possible constant values:

Constant	Value	Description
AdCmdText	1	Evaluates *SQLText* as a textual definition of a command.
AdCmdTable	2	Evaluates *SQLText* as a table name.
AdCmdStoredProc	4	Evaluates *SQLText* as a stored procedure.
AdCmdUnknown	8	The type of command for the *SQLText* value is not known. This is the default value.

MaximumRows   The maximum number of rows to return. The default value is 0. Specifying a value greater than 0 for queries that always return a small number of rows can substantially reduce the speed of query execution.

CursorType   An optional integer constant that references the ADO cursor type. The *CursorType* is used most often in conjunction with the *CursorSize* parameter. This parameter can contain one of the following values:

Constant	*Value*	*Description*
AdOpen-ForwardReadOnly	0	Forward-only cursor. Identical to a static cursor except that you can only scroll forward through records. This improves performance in situations when you only need to make a single pass through a recordset. (Default.)
AdOpenKeyset	1	Keyset cursor. Like a dynamic cursor, except that you can't see records that other users add, although records that other users delete are inaccessible from your recordset. Data changes by other users are still visible
AdOpenDynamic	2	Dynamic cursor. Additions, changes, and deletions by other users are visible, and all types of movement through the recordset are allowed, except for bookmarks if the provider doesn't support them.
AdOpenStatic	3	Static cursor. A static copy of a set of records that you can use to find data or generate reports. Additions, changes, or deletions by other users are not visible.

CursorSize   A number that specifies the number of rows to gather at one time. Specifying a default of 1 optimizes the server-side cursor by ensuring that the server never has to retrieve more than a single row in server memory at a time. The default value is 0.

RetrievalMethod   An optional parameter that specifies the method to use to retrieve data from the results set. The default value is 2 (Unknown). If you are using an Oracle database, the block retrieval method is unavailable; you must use the row retrieval option. The following values can be used for this parameter:

Value	Description
0	Block retrieval. This method indicates that the result set contains no long text or binary data, or that the database fully supports block retrieval of long data.
1	Row retrieval. Indicates that the database supports the retrieval of long data, but only on a row-by-row basis.
2	Unknown. When you use this value, you effectively ask the system to determine for itself which method to call by searching for columns that contain binary data.

Remarks

When you execute a query using the **Datasource** component's **Execute** method, you can simply pass **Execute** the name you have associated with the query through a call to **AddQuery**.

Although you can also pass the **Execute** method the SQL text of a query that you have not added to the **Content** component, this results in a degradation in performance. For optimal efficiency, you should always pass **Execute** query variables stored by **AddQuery** in the **Content** component's query list.

Additionally, if you pass **Execute** the text of your query, the **Datasource** component internally uses a set of default values for the *Timeout, CommandType, MaximumRows, CursorType*, and *CursorSize* values described above, and you cannot override these defaults.

Applies to
Content

See also
AddDatasource

Datasource

The **Datasource** method returns a **Datasource** component for the specified data source name (DSN) variable. *DSN* references a DSN variable added to the **Content** component cache through a previous call to **AddDatasource**.

Syntax
Content.**Datasource (***DSN***)**

Parameters
DSN: A string that identifies the variable name associated with a DSN through a previous call to **AddDatasource**.

Example

The following example from the Clock Peddler sample store creates a **Content** component, adds a DSN variable to the component, and then uses the **Datasource** method to create a **Datasource** component instance for that DSN:

```
REM -- Create a content component and data source for connection ↵
    to the database
Set  MSCSContent = Server.CreateObject( "Commerce.Content" )
Call MSCSContent.AddDatasource("ClockPed", MSCSDSN)
Set  MSCSDatasource = MSCSContent.Datasource("ClockPed")
```

Note that you can also use the variable name of the **Content** component to retrieve a **Datasource** component, as follows.

```
Set MSCSDatasource = MSCSContent("ClockPed")
```

THE DATAFUNCTIONS COMPONENT

The **DataFunctions** component supports a group of methods that perform locale-based data type handling and value range checking on values that you submit to the database or that you pass in an **OrderForm** component to the Order Processing Pipeline.

The **DataFunctions** component supports the following property:

Property	Description
Locale	A number that specifies the default locale value to be used to format date, time, money, and number values.

The **DataFunctions** component supports the following methods:

Method	Description
CleanString	Processes a string. This processing can include stripping out white spaces, modifying the case of the string, and validating that the length of the string falls within a given range.
ConvertDateString	Converts a string representation of the Date to a **Date Variant**, based on the specified locale.
ConvertDateTimeString	Converts a string representation of the **Date** and **Time** to a **Date Variant**.
ConvertFloatString	Converts a string representation of a floating point number to a **Double Variant**.
ConvertMoneyString-ToNumber	Converts a string representation of a monetary value to a number.
ConvertNumberString	Converts a string representation of a number to an **Integer Variant**.
ConvertTimeString	Converts a string expression of a time value to a **Date Variant**.

Date	Returns a string representation of the specified **Date Variant**.
DateTime	Returns a string representation of the specified **Date Variant**.
Float	Returns a string representation of a floating-point number.
Money	Returns a formatted currency string, based on the specified locale.
Time	Returns a string representation of the specified Date Variant, based on the specified locale.
ValidateDateTime	Checks the value of a date and/or time against a specified range.
ValidateFloat	Checks the value of a floating-point number against a given range.
ValidateNumber	Checks the value of a number against a given range.

Overview

The **DataFunctions** component supports methods that make it possible to perform locale-based data type conversions and value-range validation on values submitted to your store, or submitted by your store to the Order Processing Pipeline or the store's database.

The **DataFunctions** component's methods fall into two categories:

■ The conversion methods. These methods convert string expressions of dates, currency, or number values to **Variant** expressions of those values, or vice versa. Thus, a string expression of a date value is converted to a **Date Variant** that contains that value, and this conversion is performed based on the locale that you specify. Conversely, you can use **DataFunctions** methods to convert a Date value to a string expression of that value.

■ The range-checking methods. These methods ensure that the data that you submit for storage in the database falls within the validation rules that you have prescribed for given fields. For example, if you create a field in an SQL Server database table that is of data type **varchar** and that can store a maximum of 50 characters, you can use the **DataFunctions** component's **CleanString** method to ensure that the string is sized appropriately for storage in that field.

■ The Order Processing Pipeline (OPP) methods. These include the **RunProduct**, **RunPlan**, and **RunPurchase** methods, which run an initialized **OrderForm** through various stages of the OPP.

The **Page** component supports a group of **Request** methods that combine the capabilities of the **DataFunctions** component's conversion and validation methods and that apply these capabilities to URL arguments. Because the **Page** component relies on the **DataFunctions** component for its implementation of these methods, you must create the **DataFunctions** component for your store to have application scope. This means that you create an instance of this component in your shop directory's GLOBAL.ASA file and initialize the created component instance to the **Application** object **MSCSDataFunctions** variable.

Locale

The **Locale** property stores a number value that indicates the locale to be used by default by **DataFunctions** methods to format date, time, money, and number information. Where **DataFunctions** methods or **Page Request** methods take a locale value for a parameter, if that value is not supplied, the value to which you initialize this property is used. For a list of the numbers that you can store in this property, see Appendix H, "Hexadecimal Codes for Countries."

The following initializes the **Locale** property to the locale identifier for the United States:

```
DataFunctions.Locale = &H0409
```

Applies to
DataFunctions

CleanString

The **CleanString** method processes a string, based on the specified locale. This string processing can include stripping out white spaces, modifying the case of the string, and validating that the length of the string falls within a given range. If successful, **CleanString** returns the processed string; otherwise, Null.

Syntax
DataFunctions.**CleanString**(*String, MinLength, MaxLength, StripWhite, StripReturn, Case, Locale*)

Parameters

String	The text of the string to process.
MinLength	Optional. This parameter indicates the minimum length against which the length of *String* must be validated. The default value for this parameter is 0.
MaxLength	Optional. This parameter indicates the maximum number against which the length of *String* must be validated. The default value for this parameter is 65,535.
StripWhite	Optional. This parameter is a Boolean value that indicates whether the white spaces should be stripped from *String*. The default value is TRUE.

StripReturn	Optional. This parameter is a Boolean value that indicates whether the carriage returns should be stripped from *String*. The default value is TRUE.
Case	Optional. This parameter indicates the case to which the string should be converted. The default value for this parameter is 0, which results in no modification to the case of the string. If *Case* is 1, the string is converted to uppercase. If *Case* is 2, the string is converted to lowercase.
Locale	Optional. This number specifies the locale to use to process the string. If this value is not specified, the value of the **DataFunctions** component's **Locale** property is used.

Example

The following represents a sample call to **CleanString**:

```
Dim Result
Result = MSCSDataFunctions.CleanString(strData, 1, 10, TRUE, TRUE, 1)
```

The values passed to **CleanString** in this example indicate that the value in *strData* should be range-tested to ensure that it is longer than one character, shorter than ten, that any white spaces or carriage returns in the string should be removed, and that the string should be converted to uppercase. Because the **Locale** parameter is not specified in this example, the call defaults to the value specified in the **DataFunctions** component's **Locale** property.

Applies to

DataFunctions

See also

RequestString

ConvertDateString

The **ConvertDateString** method converts the specified string to a **Date Variant**, based on the specified locale. If successful, **ConvertDateString** returns the **Date Variant** containing the converted value; otherwise, Null.

Syntax

Page.**ConvertDateString(***String, Locale***)**

Parameters

String	A string representation of the date to convert.
Locale	Optional. This number specifies the locale to use to process the string. For a list of valid locale values, see Appendix H, "Hexadecimal Codes for Countries." If this value is not specified, the value of the **DataFunctions** component's **Locale** parameter is used.

Applies to

DataFunctions

See also

ConvertTimeString, ConvertDateTimeStringDate

ConvertDateTimeString

The **ConvertDateTimeString** converts the specified **DateTime** value to a **DateTime Variant**, based on the specified locale. If successful, **Convert-DateTimeString** returns a **DateTime Variant**; otherwise, Null.

Syntax

*DataFunctions.***ConvertDateTimeString(***DateTime, DateLocale, TimeLocale***)**

Parameters

DateTime	A string that specifies the date/time value to format.
DateLocale	Optional. This number specifies the locale to use to convert the date. For a list of valid locale values, see Appendix H, "Hexadecimal Codes for Countries." If this value is not specified, the value of the **DataFunctions** component's **Locale** parameter is used.
TimeLocale	Optional. This number specifies the locale to use to convert the time. For a list of valid locale values, see Appendix H, "Hexadecimal Codes for Countries." If this value is not specified, the value of the **DataFunctions** component's **Locale** parameter is used.

Applies to

DataFunctions

See also

ConvertDateString, ConvertTimeStringDateTime

ConvertFloatString

The **ConvertFloatString** method converts a string expression of a floating-point number to a **Double Variant**, based on the specified locale. If successful, **Convert-FloatString** returns the **Double Variant**; otherwise, Null.

Syntax

*DataFunctions.***ConvertFloatString(***Float, Locale***)**

Parameters

Float	A string expression of the number to convert.

Locale   Optional. This number specifies the locale to use to convert the string. For a list of valid locale values, see Appendix H, "Hexadecimal Codes for Countries." If this value is not specified, the value of the **DataFunctions** component's **Locale** parameter is used.

Applies to
DataFunctions

See also
Float, ValidateFloat

ConvertMoneyStringToNumber

The **ConvertMoneyStringToNumber** converts the specified string as money, based on the specified locale. If successful, **ConvertMoneyStringToNumber** returns a number that represents the value of the specified string in the base monetary unit of the specified locale; otherwise, Null.

Syntax
DataFunctions.**ConvertMoneyStringToNumber(***Money, Locale***)**

Parameters
Money   A string representation of the money to convert.

Locale   Optional. This number specifies the locale to use to convert the string. For a list of valid locale values, see Appendix H, "Hexadecimal Codes for Countries." If this value is not specified, the value of the **DataFunctions** component's **Locale** parameter is used.

Remarks
The **ConvertMoneyStringToNumber** method returns the monetary value in the base monetary unit for a given locale. Thus, given a value in dollars, **ConvertMoneyStringToNumber** returns the number of cents in the dollar value.

Additionally, **ConvertMoneyStringToNumber** does not round values up. For example, if you pass this method 123.009, the method returns 12300, not 12301.

Applies to
DataFunctions

See also
ConvertFloatString, ConvertNumberString

ConvertNumberString

The **ConvertNumberString** method converts a string expression of a number to an **Integer Variant**, based on the specified locale. If successful, **ConvertNumberString** returns an **Integer Variant** containing the converted value; otherwise, Null.

Syntax

*DataFunctions.***ConvertNumberString(***Number, Locale***)**

Parameters

Number   A string representation of the number to convert.

Locale   Optional. This number specifies the locale to use to convert the string. For a list of valid locale values, see Appendix H, "Hexadecimal Codes for Countries." If this value is not specified, the value of the **DataFunctions** component's **Locale** parameter is used.

Remarks

The **ConvertNumberString** method is designed to accept only integers. Passing a floating-point number as the *Number* parameter results in an error. To convert floating-point numbers, use **ConvertFloatString**.

Example

The following example uses **ConvertNumberString** to convert 123,000 from a string to a number:

```
StrNum = "123,000"
NNum = DataFunctions.ConvertNumberString(StrNum)
```

In this example, the call to **ConvertNumberString** returns the following value:

```
123000
```

Applies to

DataFunctions

See also

Number, ValidateNumber

ConvertTimeString

The **ConvertTimeString** method converts a string expression of a time value to a **Date Variant**, based on the specified locale. If successful, **ConvertTimeString** returns a **Date Variant** that contains the time; otherwise, Null. Additionally, if the string expression contains a date, **ConvertTimeString** returns Null.

Syntax

*DataFunctions.***ConvertTimeString(***Time, Locale***)**

Parameters

Time   A string that specifies the time to convert.

Locale   Optional. This number specifies the locale to use to convert the string. For a list of valid locale values, see Appendix H, "Hexadecimal Codes for Countries." If this value is not specified, the value of the **DataFunctions** component's **Locale** parameter is used.

Example

The following example converts the provided time value, and outputs the value to the page:

```
<% Time = DataFunctions.ConvertTimeString("3:30PM") %>
<% =Hour(Time)%>
<%=Minute(Time)%>
<%=Second(Time)%>
```

The *Time* variable that is returned by **ConvertTimeString** in this example is actually a **Date Variant** in which the date part has been set to Null. Therefore, you would not use the VBScript **Date** function to attempt to extract the date from this value.

Applies to

DataFunctions

See also

Time, ValidateDateTime

Date

The **Date** method converts a **Date Variant** to a string expression of the specified date, based on the specified locale. If successful, **Date** returns the specified value as a string; otherwise, Null.

Syntax

DataFunctions.**Date(***Date, Locale***)**

Parameters

Date   The date to format.

Locale   Optional. This number specifies the locale to use to convert the date to a string. For a list of valid locale values, see Appendix H, "Hexadecimal Codes for Countries." If this value is not specified, the value of the **DataFunctions** component's **Locale** parameter is used.

Applies to

DataFunctions

See also

ConvertDateString

DateTime

The **DateTime** method converts a **Date Variant** to a string expression of the **Date** value, based on the specified locale. If successful, **DateTime** returns a string expression of the value; otherwise, Null.

Syntax

DataFunctions.**DateTime(***DateTime, Locale***)**

Parameters

DateTime	The date/time value to convert.
Locale	Optional. This number specifies the locale to use to convert the **Date Variant** to a string. For a list of valid locale values, see Appendix H, "Hexadecimal Codes for Countries." If this value is not specified, the value of the **DataFunctions** component's **Locale** parameter is used.

Applies to

DataFunctions

See also

Date, Time, ConvertDateTimeString

Float

The **Float** method converts the floating-point number that you specify to a string expression of that number, based on the specified locale. If successful, **Float** returns a string expression of the specified number; otherwise, Null.

Syntax

DataFunctions.**Float(***Float, Locale***)**

Parameters

Float	The floating-point number to convert.
Locale	Optional. This number specifies the locale to use to convert the floating-point number to a string. For a list of valid locale values, see Appendix H, "Hexadecimal Codes for Countries." If this value is not specified, the value of the **DataFunctions** component's **Locale** parameter is used.

Applies to

DataFunctions

See also

ConvertFloatString

Money

The **Money** method converts the specified money value to a string, based on the specified locale. If successful, **Money** returns a string expression of the monetary value; otherwise, Null.

Syntax
*DataFunctions.***Money**(*Money, Locale*)

Parameters

Money — The money value to convert to a string, specified in the base monetary unit of the locale used to perform the conversion.

Locale — Optional. This number specifies the locale to use to convert the **Money Variant** to a string. For a list of valid locale values, see Appendix H, "Hexadecimal Codes for Countries." If this value is not specified, the value of the **DataFunctions** component's **Locale** parameter is used.

Applies to
DataFunctions

See also
ConvertMoneyStringToNumber

Number

The **Number** method converts an **Integer Variant** to a string, based on the default or specified locale. If successful, **Number** returns the string expression of the supplied number value; otherwise, Null.

Syntax
*Page.***Number**(*Number, Locale*)

Parameters

Number — The number to convert to a string.

Locale — Optional. This number specifies the locale to convert the number to a string. For a list of valid locale values, see Appendix H, "Hexadecimal Codes for Countries." If this value is not specified, the value of the **DataFunctions** component's **Locale** parameter is used.

Example
Given the number 123, the following call to **Number** returns a string expression of that number:

```
strNumber = Page.Number(123)
```

Applies to
DataFunctions

See also
ConvertNumberString

Time

The **Time** method converts the specified time value to a string expression of the time. If successful, **Time** returns the string expression of the time value that you supply; otherwise, Null.

Syntax
*DataFunctions.***Time(***Time, Locale***)**

Parameters

Time	The time value to convert.
Locale	Optional. This number specifies the locale to convert the time to a string. For a list of valid locale values, see Appendix H, "Hexadecimal Codes for Countries." If this value is not specified, the value of the **DataFunctions** component's **Locale** parameter is used.

Applies to
DataFunctions

See also
ConvertTimeString

ValidateDateTime

The **ValidateDateTime** method tests a date, time, or date/time value against a specified range. If the value falls within the given range, **ValidateDateTime** returns TRUE; otherwise, FALSE.

Syntax
*DataFunctions.***ValidateDateTime(***DateTime, LowDateTime, HighDateTime***)**

Parameters

DateTime	The date to test against the provided range. This value can be a date, a time, or both.
LowDateTime	Optional. This value designates the low end of the range. The default value for this parameter is Null, which means that *LowDateTime* is ignored in the valuation.
HighDateTime	Optional. This value designates the high end of the range. The default value for this parameter is Null, which means that *HighDateTime* is ignored in the range valuation.

Applies to
DataFunctions

See also
ValidateNumber

ValidateFloat

The **ValidateFloat** method tests a floating-point number against a specified numerical range. If the specified number does not fall within the given range, **ValidateFloat** returns FALSE; otherwise, TRUE.

Syntax
DataFunctions.**ValidateFloat(***Value, Minimum Value, Maximum Value***)**

Parameters

Value	The floating-point number to validate.
MinimumValue	Optional. This value, if specified, is a number that represents the low end of the range. The default value for this parameter is Null, which means that *MinimumValue* is ignored in the range valuation.
MaximumValue	Optional. This value, if specified, designates the high end of the range. The default value for this parameter is Null, which means that *MaximumValue* is ignored in the range valuation.

Applies to
DataFunctions

See also
ValidateNumber

ValidateNumber

The **ValidateNumber** method tests the value of a number against a specified numerical range. If the specified number does not fall within the range, **ValidateNumber** returns FALSE; otherwise, TRUE.

Syntax
DataFunctions.**ValidateNumber(***Value, Minimum Value, Maximum Value***)**

Parameters

Value	The value to compare with the low and high ends of the specified range.

MinimumValue — An optional value that specifies the low end of the range. The default value for this parameter is Null, which means that *MinimumValue* is ignored in the range valuation.

MaximumValue — An optional value that specifies the high end of the range. The default value for this parameter is Null, which means that *MaximumValue* is ignored in the range valuation.

Applies to
DataFunctions

See also
ValidateDateTime

THE DATASOURCE COMPONENT

The **Datasource** component executes queries against a system or file DSN, and where appropriate, returns query results in a **SimpleList** of **Dictionary** components, or in an Active Data Objects (ADO) **Recordset** object. The queries that you execute can be SQL statements declared as string variables in the page in which you execute the query, or query variables cached in a **Content** component.

You do not use the Active Server Pages (ASP) **Server** object's **CreateObject** method to create a **Datasource** component. Instead, you use the **Content** component's **Datasource** method, which creates the component based on the DSN variable that is cached by the **Content** component. Once you have created a **Datasource** component, the **Datasource** has access to the **Content** component's cache of queries.

For more information on the **Content** component, see "The Content Component" section of this appendix.

The **Content** component supports the following methods:

Method	Description
CreateADOConnection	Returns a read-only **Connection** object. You can pass this object as a parameter to **ExecuteADO**.
Execute	Executes the specified query against a data source, and where appropriate, returns the results in a **SimpleList** of **Dictionary** components.
ExecuteADO	Executes the specified query on an open Active Data Objects (ADO) **Connection**, and where appropriate, returns the results in an ADO **Recordset** object.

Overview

Although you can use the **Datasource** component to perform any operation that you need to perform on your store database, Commerce Server stores generally use this component in two contexts:

- To execute queries that retrieve product information for display on a page.

- To retrieve product information for storage in an **OrderForm**.

CreateADOConnection

The **CreateADOConnection** method returns a **Connection** object that represents an open, read-only connection. If you want, you can have results sets returned in the ADO **Recordset** object (as opposed to being returned as a **SimpleList** of **Dictionaries**).

Syntax
Datasource.**CreateADOConnection()**

Parameters
None

Applies to
Datasource

See also
ExecuteADO

Execute

The **Execute** method executes the specified query and returns the results of the query, if any, in a **SimpleList** of **Dictionary** components.

Syntax
Datasource.**Execute(***SQL, Parameters***)**

Parameters

SQL	The string resource identifier of a query added to a **Content** component through a previous call to **AddQuery**, or the SQL text of the query.
Parameters	Optional. One or more parameters to bind to the parameter markers in *SQL*.

Remarks

You can also pass the **Execute** method the text of a query, but this method does not take advantage of the speed optimizations built into the **Content** component, and is not advised. If the SQL parameter to **Execute** is the text of a query, the following values, which you cannot override, are used to specify the query's timeout, command type, maximum rows fetched, cursor type, and cursor size. For more information on these values, see **AddQuery**.

Applies to

Datasource

See also

Datasource, AddQuery

ExecuteADO

The **ExecuteADO** method executes the specified query on an open Active Data Objects (ADO) connection and returns the results of the query, if any, in an ADO **Resultset** object.

Syntax

*Datasource.***ExecuteADO(***Connection, SQL, Parameters***)**

Parameters

Connection	An open ADO connection. The caller creates this connection by using the **Server** object's **CreateObject** method, specifying ADO.Connection as the program identifier, and then by using the **Connection's Open** method to open a data source name (DSN).
SQL	The string resource identifier of a query added to a **Content** component through a previous call to **AddQuery**, or the SQL text of the query.
Parameters	One or more parameters to bind to the parameter markers in *SQL*.

Applies to

Datasource

See also

Execute

THE DBSTORAGE COMPONENT

The **DBStorage** component provides for the easy management of routine store tasks, such as the retrieval, storage, and updating of order and shopper data.

Although the **DBStorage** component, like the **Datasource** component, interacts with the store's database management system (DBMS), it fills a fundamentally different role within a store. The **Datasource** component is typically used for the general management of data that is retrieved from the database for display to the shopper. For example, in the Commerce Server sample stores, product pages are populated by using the **Datasource** component to execute queries kept in the store's **Content** component. The **Content** component, as its name indicates, associates string variables with queries designed to manage store content.

The **DBStorage** component, on the other hand, is generally used to manage purchase and receipt data, reading such data out of **OrderForm** and **Dictionary** components that are initialized at run time, and writing the data to the underlying database storage.

The **DBStorage** component supports the following property:

Property	Description
Mapping	Maps a database column to an entry in the **OrderForm** or **Dictionary** that **DBStorage** uses to insert and retrieve data.

The **DBStorage** component supports the following methods:

Method	Description
CommitData	Updates a record in the data source to new values.
DeleteData	Deletes specified data from the data source.
DeleteDataKey	Deletes one or more elements based upon the specified key value.
GetData	Returns the data that you specify.
InitStorage	Initializes the **DBStorage** component.
InsertData	Inserts the data that you specify.
LookupData	Returns a single record based on keys and values that you specify.

Overview

The **DBStorage** component supports the management of shopper, **OrderForm**, and basket data for Commerce Server stores.

The following example, from the Microsoft Press sample store, illustrates how Commerce Server stores use the **DBStorage** component. First, in the store's GLOBAL.ASA file, the store creates an application-wide **DBStorage** component instance for its order, purchase, and shopper data. The **DBStorage** component that is created to temporarily store order data is the store's order form storage. The component created for shopper data represents the store's shopper storage, and the receipt component represents the store's receipt storage.

Because these components are created on a per-application basis, and are stored as IIS 3.0 **Application** object variables, they are created in the store's GLOBAL.ASA file, and the **Application** variables **MSCSOrderFormStorage**, **MSCSShopperStorage**, and **MSCSReceiptStorage** are set to reference these component instances, as follows:

```
REM  Create a Storage component for the shopper information
Set  MSCSShopperStorage = Server.CreateObject( "Commerce.DBStorage" )
Call MSCSShopperStorage.InitStorage(MSCSDatasource, "MSPress_shopper",↩
   "shopper_id", "Commerce.Dictionary")

REM  Create a storage component for the order forms
Set  MSCSOrderFormStorage = Server.CreateObject( "Commerce.DBStorage" )
Call MSCSOrderFormStorage.InitStorage(MSCSDatasource, "MSPress_basket",↩
   "shopper_id","Commerce.OrderForm","marshalled_order", "date_changed")

REM Create a storage component for receipts
Set MSCSReceiptStorage = Server.CreateObject( "Commerce.DBStorage" )
Call MSCSReceiptStorage.InitStorage(MSCSDatasource, "MSPress_receipt",↩
   "order_id","Commerce.OrderForm", "marshalled_receipt",↩
   "date_entered")
MSCSReceiptStorage.Mapping.Value("_total_total") = "total"


' Later in global.asa
' Set up the Application intrinsic object
Application.Lock
     Set Application("MSCSOrderFormStorage") = MSCSOrderFormStorage
     Set Application("MSCSShopperStorage")   = MSCSShopperStorage
     Set Application("MSCSReceiptStorage")   = MSCSReceiptStorage
Application.Unlock
```

When a shopper visits the Microsoft Press store, the store attempts to retrieve the shopper's shopper ID. This is a globally unique identifier that was assigned to this shopper on a previous visit to the store. If unable to retrieve this ID, the **StandardSManager** for Microsoft Press creates an ID for the shopper, and that ID is ultimately committed to shopper storage.

If the shopper elects to add one or more of the books featured by Microsoft Press to his or her shopping basket, the shopper's shopper ID, as well as purchase item information, is added to an **OrderForm**, and the contents of that **OrderForm** are committed to the order form storage. At any time during the session, should the shopper wish to view the contents of the shopping basket, the contents of the shopper's order form storage are read into an **OrderForm** and the **OrderForm** contents are output to the page.

At the conclusion of a shopping session, if the shopper chooses to finalize the purchase of the selected items, the contents of the shopper's order form storage are read into an **OrderForm** component and this component is passed to the OPP. After processing the purchase, the OPP writes the order information read from the **OrderForm** into the store's receipt storage, and the store deletes the information for this session from the order form storage.

CommitData

The **CommitData** method updates one or more records in the database storage.

Syntax
*DBStorage.***CommitData**(*Null, Data*)

Parameters

Null	This parameter is not used.
Data	A component initialized with the updated data. This component can be either an **OrderForm** or a **Dictionary**, but must correspond to the component type specified as the program identifier in the initial call to **InitStorage**.

Example
The following example from the AdventureWorks store uses the **Datasource** component's **Execute** method to retrieve information from a database table, initializes an **OrderForm** to contain that information, and uses **CommitData** to write that **OrderForm** to storage:

```
REM -- add item to order form:
set productsku = DataSource.Execute("variant-sku",
Cstr(Request("attr_1")), Cstr(Request("attr_2")),
Cstr(Request("attr_3")))(0)

sku = productsku.sku
set product = DataSource.Execute("product-purchase", ⤶
    CStr(sku))(0)
set item = orderForm.AddItem(CStr(sku), product_qty, ⤶
    product.list_price)
item.pf_name = product.pf_name
item.placed_price = product.placed_price
item.quantity = product_qty
item.color_value = product.color_value
item.size_value = product.size_value

REM -- commit order form back to storage:
call orderFormStorage.CommitData(Null, orderForm)
```

Applies to
DBStorage

See also
InitStorage, InsertData

DeleteData

The **DeleteData** method deletes data from a **DBStorage** component.

Syntax
DBStorage.**DeleteData(***Null, Data***)**

Parameters

Null	This parameter is not used.
Data	A component initialized with the data to delete. This component can be either an **OrderForm** or a **Dictionary**, but must correspond in type to the component type specified as the program identifier in the initial call to **InitStorage**.

Example
The following example from the AdventureWorks store appears in the **OrderForm-Purchase** utility function in XT_ORDERFORM_PURCHASE.ASP. This user-defined routine, which is called after a purchase has been written by the OPP to receipt storage, uses **DeleteData** to delete the purchase data from order form storage. The result is that should the user return to BASKET.ASP, which reads from order form storage to display the contents of the shopper's basket, the basket would be empty:

```
REM -- retrieve order form from storage:
on error resume next
set orderForm = orderFormStorage.GetData(Null, shopperID)
on error goto 0
if IsEmpty(orderForm) then
  OrderFormPurchase = null
  exit function
end if

REM -- retrieve args from form:
success = OrderFormPurchaseArgs(orderForm)
if not success then
  OrderFormPurchase = null
  exit function
end if

REM -- commit:
call orderFormStorage.CommitData(Null, orderForm)
```

```
REM -- purchase:
call page.RunPurchase(orderForm)

if orderForm.[_Basket_Errors].Count > 0 then
   REM show basket errors
   Response.redirect Page.URL("basket_errors.asp")
end if

if orderForm.[_Purchase_Errors].Count > 0 then
   for each item in orderForm.[_Purchase_Errors]
      errorStr = errorStr & "<LI>" & item
   next
Response.redirect page.URL("error.asp", "error", errorStr)
end if

order_id = orderForm.order_id

REM -- clear out basket:
call orderFormStorage.DeleteData(Null, orderForm)
```

Applies to
DBStorage

See also
InsertData

DeleteDataKey

The **DeleteDataKey** method deletes the data corresponding to the specified key.

Syntax
*DBStorage.***DeleteDataKey(** *Null, Value***)**

Parameters

Null	This parameter is not used.
Value	The key value for the row to be deleted.

Remarks
The **DeleteDataKey** method differs from the **DeleteData** method in that the former requires only the value stored in the underlying table's key column. This is the column specified as the key to the underlying table through a previous call to **InitStorage**.

Thus, if you specify an IDENTITY field in an SQL table as the key into the data source, you could delete all the columns for a specified row by simply providing the appropriate counter value. Alternatively, you could initialize a **Dictionary** component to the values stored in one or more columns, and pass this initialized component to **DeleteData**.

Applies to
DBStorage

See also
DeleteData

GetData

The **GetData** method retrieves the specified data from a **DBStorage** component and returns the data in an **OrderForm** or **Dictionary** component.

Syntax
DBStorage.**GetData**(*Null, Key, Value*)

Parameters

Null	This parameter is not used.
Data	The key value for which to get data.

Applies to
DBStorage

See also
InitStorage, LookupData

InitStorage

The **InitStorage** method initializes a **DBStorage** component. You must call this method immediately after component creation, and before calling any other **DBStorage** component methods.

Syntax
DBStorage.**InitStorage**(*Datasource, Table, Key, ProgID, MarshalColumn, DateChanged*)

Parameters

Datasource	A data source retrieved through a previous call to the **Content** component's **AddDatasource** method.
Table	The table within the data source to maintain the data.
Key	The column name that the **DBStorage** object uses as a key into the database table. This column should be marked to contain unique values.

ProgID	The component in which data passed to or retrieved by **DBStorage** methods will be stored. This parameter can be "**Commerce.Dictionary**" for storing **Dictionary** components or "**Commerce.OrderForm**" for storing **OrderForm** components.
MarshalColumn	Optional. A column that stores data for which no appropriate column exists in the data source table. For more information on the *MarshalColumn* parameter, see the "Remarks" section below.
DateChanged	The date on which the change was made.

Applies to
DBStorage

Remarks
The **InitStorage** method initializes a data source for use by a Commerce Server component. The data source that you specify in **InitStorage**'s *Datasource* parameter must be one that you have added to a **Content** component using **AddDatasource**, and that you have retrieved using the **Content** component's **Datasource** method.

The *ProgID* parameter references the component that will be used to store the data that you pass to the **DBStorage** component's **GetData**, **InsertData** and **CommitData** methods.

The *Key* parameter references a column in the table referenced by *Table* that the **DBStorage** component uses to key into the data source table. It is recommended that this column be configured at table creation to store only unique values.

The *MarshalColumn* parameter is used to store data that does not appropriately belong in any other column in the data source table. For example, should you specify *my_column* as the column in which you want to store data, and no such column exists, then the value that you specify for that column will be stored in the column that you specify as your marshalling column.

Example
The following example illustrates how to create and initialize a **DBStorage** component:

```
REM Create a Content component for access to the database

Set MSCSContent = Server.CreateObject("Commerce.Content")
Call MSCSContent.AddDataSource("AW", MSCSDSN)

REM Use the Datasource method to retrieve the Datasource
component.

Set MSCSDatasource = MSCSContent.Datasource("AW")

REM Create a Storage component for the order form information
```

```
Set MSCSOrderFormStorage =
Server.CreateObject("Commerce.DBStorage")

Call MSCSOrderFormStorage InitStorage(MSCSDatasource,
"AW_basket", "shopper_id", "Commerce.OrderForm",
"marshalled_order", "date_changed")
```

See also
"The Content Component," "The Datasource Component"

InsertData

The **InsertData** method inserts data into the database storage.

Syntax
*DBStorage.***InsertData(***Null, Data***)**

Parameters

Null	This parameter is not used.
Data	A component that contains the data to insert. The type of this component corresponds to the component type specified as the program identifier in the initial call to **InitStorage**.

Example
The following example creates and initializes a **Dictionary** component with a set of values, and then inserts the component's data into a database table:

```
<% Set Dictionary = Server.CreateObject("Commerce.Dictionary")
Dictionary.order_id = orderID
Dictionary.shopper_id = shopperID
Dictionary.status = 5
call MSCSReceiptStorage.InsertData(Null, Dictionary)
%>
```

Applies to
DBStorage

See also
InitStorage, CommitData

LookupData

The **LookupData** method retrieves a single row from the data source based on column names and values that you specify, and returns the results of the operation in a **Dictionary** component.

Syntax

DBStorage.**LookupData**(*Null, Column, Value*)

Parameters

Null	This parameter is not used.
Column	An array containing the column names that you want to query.
Value	An array containing the values that you want to query.

Remarks

The *Column* and *Value* arrays that you pass to **LookupData** share an index-to-index relationship. This relationship means that they must contain an identical number of members and that the value stored in Value(*N*) will be searched for in the column specified by Column(*N*).

Because the **LookupData** method returns only a single row of data, specifying column and value information that would result in the retrieval of more than one row results in an error.

Example

The following example uses two arrays to store column names and values, and passes these arrays to **LookupData**:

```
Column(0) = "shopper_id"
Value(0) = "23234"

Set Obj = Storage.LookupData(Null, Column, Value)
```

Applies to

DBStorage

See also

LookupMultipleData

LookupMultipleData

The **LookupMultipleData** method retrieves multiple results from the database table and returns these results in a **SimpleList** of **Dictionary** components.

Syntax

DBStorage.**LookupMultipleData**(*Null, Column, Values*)

Parameters

Null	This parameter is not used.
Column	An array containing the columns to query for the specified values.
Values	An array containing the values that correspond to the column names to use as the basis for the lookup.

Remarks

The *Column* and *Value* arrays that you pass to **LookupMultipleData** share an index-to-index relationship. This means that they must contain an identical number of members and that the value stored in *Value(N)* will be searched for in the column specified by *Column(N)*. If the number of elements in *Column* does not equal the number of values in *Value*, **LookupMultipleData** returns Null.

Applies to

DBStorage

See also

LookupData

THE MESSAGEMANAGER COMPONENT

The **MessageManager** component provides for the storage and retrieval of language-specific messages that are used by the Order Processing Pipeline (OPP) to return errors generated during **OrderForm** processing.

Because the **MessageManager** stores messages used by the OPP to generate error information, the **MessageManager** should be initialized to have application scope. This means that you should create this component in your **\SHOP** directory's GLOBAL.ASA file, and should initialize the **Application MSCSMessageManager** variable to reference the created component instance.

The **MessageManager** component supports the following property:

Property	*Description*
DefaultLanguage	Specifies the default language for the **MessageManager**.

The **MessageManager** component supports the following methods:

Method	*Description*
AddLanguage	Adds a new language to the **Message Manager**.
AddMessage	Adds a new message to the **Message Manager**.
GetLocale	Returns the locale for the specified language.
GetMessage	Returns the message associated with the specified string identifier.

Overview

Error handling in Commerce Server stores involves the interaction of the **Page**, **OrderForm,** and **MessageManager** components with the OPP. An overview of the purchase process clarifies how this interaction occurs in the context of store operation.

The running of the OPP originates when the **Page** component calls one of the **Run*** methods, such as **RunPlan** or **RunPurchase**, to pass the OPP an initialized **OrderForm**. How the OPP processes this **OrderForm** depends, to some degree, on the contents of the pipeline configuration file (.PCF) for a given store. Generally, however, where an OPP component encounters errors in the **OrderForm**, the component stores the error in the **OrderForm**'s **_Basket_Errors** or **_Purchase_Errors** members.

For every error condition that the OPP encounters in an **OrderForm**, there will be an associated error variable. For example, if an item referenced in the **OrderForm** does not reference an item in a store's inventory, the OPP stores the error string associated with the **pur_badsku** error in the **OrderForm**'s **_Basket_Errors** member. When the **Run*** method returns, you can examine the contents of the **_Basket_Errors** member and notify your shoppers of the error.

The variable names of the error messages that the OPP generates are hardcoded; the variable **pur_badsku** in the preceding example cannot be named anything else. However, the text associated with error conditions is flexible, and will usually depend on the store's locale and the cultural context that the store represents.

The work of associating text strings with error variables is the work of the **MessageManager**. You create a **MessageManager** component in your store's GLOBAL.ASA file, and once you have created this component, you use the **MessageManager**'s **AddLanguage** method to add *languages* (or dialects) to the component, and then use the **AddMessage** method to associate messages with error variables.

The addition of a language to the **MessageManager** simply associates a locale identifier with a string variable name that identifies the dialect to the **MessageManager**. Each group of messages for a given language is called a message set. When determining which message set to use to raise an error in the **OrderForm**, the OPP uses the language that you specify as the default language when you initialize the **MessageManager**, or uses the **Messages** property on the **Page** component.

The addition of messages to the **MessageManager** associates a message both with a string name that identifies the error condition and with a language previously added to the **MessageManager**. Thus, you might have four different text strings associated with the **pur_badsku** error, one for each dialect that you want to support. Remember that you must associate a message with each error that can be raised by the OPP for your store. If the OPP encounters an error condition, but finds no associated message in your **MessageManager** cache, the error is ignored.

The following statements from the GLOBAL.ASA file for the Microsoft Press sample store illustrate the creation and initialization of a **MessageManager**:

```
REM  Create a message manager and initialize for rest of system

Set  MSCSMessageManager = Server.CreateObject("Commerce.MessageManager")

Call MSCSMessageManager.AddLanguage("usa", &H0409)
MSCSMessageManager.defaultLanguage = "usa"

Call MSCSMessageManager.AddMessage("pur_out_of_stock", "At least one ⏎
    item is out of stock.")

Call MSCSMessageManager.AddMessage("pur_badsku", "Products in your ⏎
    basket were deleted because they don't exist in this store.")

Call MSCSMessageManager.AddMessage("pur_badplacedprice", "Prices of ⏎
    products in your basket have been updated.")

Call MSCSMessageManager.AddMessage("pur_noitems", "An order must have ⏎
    at least one item.")

Call MSCSMessageManager.AddMessage("pur_badshopper", "Unknown shopper.")

Call MSCSMessageManager.AddMessage("pur_badshipping", "Unable to ⏎
    complete order. Cannot compute shipping cost.")

Call MSCSMessageManager.AddMessage("pur_badtax", "Unable to complete⏎
    order. Cannot compute tax.")

Call MSCSMessageManager.AddMessage("pur_badhandling", "Unable to ⏎
    complete order. Cannot compute handling cost.")

Call MSCSMessageManager.AddMessage("pur_badverify", "Changes to the ⏎
    data require your review. Please review and resubmit.")

Call MSCSMessageManager.AddMessage("pur_badpayment", "There was a ⏎
    problem authorizing your credit.  Please verify your payment ⏎
    information or use a different card.")
```

Note If you create a custom OPP component, you can define any message that the component is programmed to retrieve from the **MessageManager**. For example, you can add a message called *wipeout* to your **MessageManager**, provided that your OPP component knows that a message called *wipeout* exists.

The MessageManager and the Order Processing Pipeline (OPP)

The following table lists the **MessageManager** messages that are used by the default implementation of the OPP and identifies the components that use these messages.

Message	Used by component	Under this condition
pur_badhandling	RequiredHandling	Added to the **OrderForm**'s **_Purchase_Errors** collection when the handling cost for an order cannot be computed.
pur_badpayment	RequiredPayment	Added to the **OrderForm**'s **_Purchase_Errors** collection when credit card information cannot be authorized.
pur_badplacedprice	RequiredItemAdjust	Added to the **OrderForm**'s **_Basket_Errors** collection when the price of an item does not correspond to the price contained in the **OrderForm**.
pur_badshipping	RequiredShipping	Added to the **OrderForm**'s **_Purchase_Errors** collection when the shipping for an order cannot be computed.
pur_badsku	RequiredProdInfo	Added to the **OrderForm**'s **_Basket_Errors** collection when a SKU in the **OrderForm** references an item that is not contained in the store's inventory.
pur_badtax	RequiredTax	Added to the **OrderForm**'s **_Purchase_Errors** collection when the tax on a purchase cannot be computed.
pur_badverify	RequiredTotal	Added to the **OrderForm**'s **_Purchase_Errors** collection when the data in an **OrderForm** has been changed, requiring review by the shopper.
pur_noitems	RequiredOrderCheck	Added to the **OrderForm**'s **_Purchase_Errors** collection when the OPP is passed an empty **OrderForm**.
pur_out_of_stock	FlagInventory, LocalInventory	Added to the **OrderForm's _Purchase_Errors** collection when an item referenced in the **OrderForm** is out of stock.

DefaultLanguage

Use the **DefaultLanguage** property to specify the default language for the **MessageManager**. When you use **AddMessage** to add messages to the **MessageManager** and do not specify a language for those messages, they are associated with the language specified in this property.

The **DefaultLanguage** property is initialized in the GLOBAL.ASA file as follows, where *usa* references a language that has been added to the **MessageManager** using the **AddLanguage** method:

```
MessageManager.DefaultLanguage = "usa"
```

AddLanguage

The **AddLanguage** method adds a new language/message set to the **MessageManager**.

Syntax
MessageManager.**AddLanguage(**_Language_, _Locale_**)**

Parameters

Language	A string identifier for the language/message set to add to the **MessageManager**.
Locale	An optional number that uniquely identifies the locale to associate with the added language. For a list of possible values for this parameter, see Appendix H, "Hexadecimal Codes for Countries."

Remarks

The **AddLanguage** method adds a user-identified language to the **MessageManager** and associates that language with a system-defined locale. In subsequent calls to **MessageManager** component methods, the caller needs to identify the language, but does not need to identify the locale.

Because the language name that you pass to **AddLanguage** is a string identifier that you choose, any number of languages can be associated with a single locale.

Example

The following example from the AdventureWorks store adds a language called *usa* to the **MessageManager** and uses the **MessageManager**'s **DefaultLanguage** property to make the added language the default language for the store:

```
Call MSCSMessageManager.AddLanguage("usa", &H0409)
MessageManager.defaultLanguage = "usa"
```

Applies to
MessageManager

See also
AddMessage, DefaultLanguage, GetMessage

AddMessage

The **AddMessage** method adds a message to the **MessageManager**.

Syntax
*MessageManager.***AddMessage**(*Name, Value, Language***)**

Parameters

Name	A string that identifies the message to add. This name must be known to an OPP component that will use the message to identify an error condition.
Value	The text of the message to add.
Language	An optional parameter that designates the string resource identifier of the language with which to associate the message. This value, if specified, should designate a language added through a previous call to **AddLanguage**. If this value is not supplied, the language specified in the **MessageManager**'s **DefaultLanguage** property is used.

Remarks
The *Language* part of the **AddMessage** method identifies a language identifier added to this **MessageManager** through a previous call to **AddLanguage**.

Example
The following example from the AdventureWorks sample store adds the **pur_bad-payment** message to the **MessageManager**. The message associated with **pur_badpayment** is inserted into the **_Purchase_Errors_** collection in the **Order-Form** if a customer has provided invalid credit card information:

```
Call MSCSMessageManager.AddMessage("pur_badpayment", "There was↵
   a problem authorizing your credit.  Please verify your↵
   payment information or use a different card.", "usa")
```

Applies to
MessageManager

See also
GetMessage

GetLocale

The **GetLocale** method returns a number that identifies the locale for the specified language.

Syntax

MessageManager.**GetLocale(***Language***)**

Parameters

Language The string identifier of the language for which you want to retrieve the locale. This identifier references a language that you have added to the **MessageManager** through a previous call to **AddLanguage**.

The *Language* parameter is optional. If this value is not specified, **GetLocale** returns the locale for the language to which you have initialized the **MessageManager**'s **DefaultLanguage** property.

Remarks

Like **GetMessage**, **GetLocale** is typically not called from within a store. Instead, it is used by the OPP to retrieve the locale for a message that describes an error that the OPP has encountered during a purchase.

Applies to

MessageManager

See also

AddLanguage, DefaultLanguage, GetMessage

GetMessage

The **GetMessage** method returns the value of the specified message.

Syntax

MessageManager.**GetMessage(***Name, Language***)**

Parameters

Name The name of the message to return. This is the name associated with this message when it was added to the **MessageManager** through a call to **AddMessage**.

Language An optional string value that identifies the language with which to associate the message. This string specifies a language that was added to the **MessageManager** through a previous call to **AddLanguage**. If this value is not specified, the message is associated with the language identified by the **MessageManager**'s **DefaultLanguage** property.

Remarks
The **GetMessage** method is seldom called from within a store. Instead, it is used by OPP components to retrieve the messages that describe errors that occur in the purchase process.

Applies to
MessageManager

See also
GetLocale

THE ORDERFORM COMPONENT

The **OrderForm** component provides for the in-memory storage of shopper and purchase information. Commerce Server stores use the **OrderForm** component to store the items that a shopper has chosen to purchase and to store receipt information that reflects a given shopper's purchase history.

The **OrderForm** component supports the following methods:

Method	Description
AddItem	Adds an item to the **OrderForm**.
ClearItems	Clears the *Items* collection from the **OrderForm**.
ClearOrderForm	Empties the **OrderForm**.

Overview

The **OrderForm** component is defined internally as a structured group of **SimpleList** and **Dictionary** components, and includes the methods required to add items, clear items, and clear the entire **OrderForm** itself. The following represents the structure of this component.

The base of the **OrderForm** component is a **Dictionary** component that contains information that describes the entire order. This includes shopper information, such as the shopper's shopper ID, name, and address, as well as order cost information, such as purchase subtotal, tax, shipping, and total.

A number of the elements of the **OrderForm**'s base **Dictionary** component include underscore characters. The appearance of an underscore character in an element name indicates that these items are not saved to the store's order form storage. These elements are saved instead to the store's receipt storage when the purchase is finalized.

The OrderForm and DBStorage

Typically, an **OrderForm** component is created on a per-page basis and reflects the contents of the order form storage. This is a **DBStorage** component that you create in a store's GLOBAL.ASA file and that you assign to the **Application** object's **MSCSOrderFormStorage** variable. As shoppers add or remove items to and from their shopping baskets, these items are written to the order form storage. When a shopper wishes to view basket items, these items are read from the order form storage into an **OrderForm** component, and from the **OrderForm** component onto a page that displays basket contents to the shopper.

The Clock Peddler sample store illustrates one way of implementing this interaction between the **OrderForm** and DBStorage components. When a Clock Peddler customer places an item into the shopping basket, the Clock Peddler calls **OrderFormAddItem**, a utility function defined by the Clock Peddler in XT_ORDERFORM_ADDITEM.ASP. This routine retrieves from storage the basket items associated with the current shopper's shopper ID. The additional items that the shopper wishes to purchase are also added to the **OrderForm** component, and this component is committed to the order form storage.

The shopper is then directed to BASKET.ASP, which reads the order form storage information for this shopper into an **OrderForm** component, and then writes the contents of that **OrderForm** to the page to display the current contents of the shopper's basket.

The OrderForm and the Order Processing Pipeline

Throughout the course of a shopping session, the **OrderForm** component is presented by the **Page** component to the OPP for preliminary processing. When a shopper finalizes a purchase, the **Page** component's **RunPurchase** method is used to finalize the purchase. The **RunPurchase** method invokes the OPP on the **Order-Form**. The OPP writes the purchased items to receipt storage, if receipt storage is in use, after which you can delete them from order form storage.

The Clock Peddler store illustrates this process. In the Clock Peddler, each time a shopper adds items the shopping basket, the additions are written to order form storage. The shopper is then redirected to the BASKET.ASP file, which loads the current shopper's basket from order form storage into an **OrderForm** component, and passes the initialized component to the **Page** component's **RunPlan** method.

The **RunPlan** method runs the **OrderForm** through the first twelve stages of the OPP and amends the **OrderForm** to contain the purchase subtotal, total, shipping cost, and tax. Additionally, where a discrepancy exists between the **Order-Form**'s price for an item and the actual price of an item, the **OrderForm** is adjusted to reflect the actual price, and an error string is written to the **_Basket_Errors_** list, which is included in the **OrderForm** component. The text of that error depends on the string that you have associated with a given variable in the **MessageManager** for this store. For more information on the relationship between the OPP and the **MessageManager**, see "The MessageManager Component" section.

At the conclusion of a shopping session, if the shopper opts to finalize the purchase, a store loads the order form storage data into an **OrderForm** component a second time and uses the **Page** component's **RunPurchase** method on the **Order-Form**. The OPP writes the contents of the **OrderForm** to receipt storage, if receipt storage is used by the store. Receipt storage designates a **DBStorage** component that is created for the storage of store receipts, and that is assigned to the **Application** object's **MSCSReceiptStorage** variable.

Once a purchase has been successfully run through the OPP, the store can delete the order from order form storage. For more information on the relationship between the **OrderForm** and **Page** components, see "The Page Component" section.

AddItem

The **AddItem** method adds an item to the *items* element of an **OrderForm** component. For a list of the elements included in an *items* member, see the beginning of "The OrderForm Component" section.

Syntax
OrderForm.**AddItem**(*SKU, Quantity, Price*)

Parameters

SKU	The SKU of the item to add.
Quantity	A number indicating the quantity of the item to add.
Price	The placed price of the item.

Remarks
Typically, one or more of the values that you pass to **AddItems** represents information that you retrieve from inventory using the **Datasource** component's **Execute** method to run a query cached in the **Content** component for the store. The Clock Peddler store, for example, defines an **OrderFormAddItem** utility function that uses the Active Server Pages (ASP) **Request** component to retrieve the SKU and the quantity from the calling page, and then uses the **Datasource** component to execute a query with the product SKU to locate the product's list price.

Applies to
OrderForm

See also
ClearOrderForm, ClearItems

ClearItems

Empties the **items** collection on the **OrderForm**.

Syntax
OrderForm.**ClearItems**()

Parameters
None

Remarks
A store uses the **ClearItems** method to respond to a shopper's having opted to cancel a purchase. This method affects only the information in the items collection. Other **OrderForm** information, such as **_oadjust_subtotal** and **_total_total**, is modified only if you run the OPP on this **OrderForm** by calling the **Page** component's **RunPlan** or **RunPurchase** method.

To empty the entire contents of the **OrderForm**, call the **ClearOrderForm** method.

Applies to
OrderForm

See also
ClearOrderForm

ClearOrderForm

The **ClearOrderForm** method empties the entire **OrderForm** component.

Syntax
OrderForm.**ClearOrderForm**()

Parameters
None

Applies to
OrderForm

See also
ClearItems

THE ORDERPIPELINE COMPONENT

The **OrderPipeline** component is a file-based component that you use to identify the configuration of the Order Processing Pipeline (OPP) for your store, and to identify the file to which the OPP should log errors that occur during the purchase process.

The **OrderPipeline** component supports the following methods:

Method	Description
LoadPipe	Loads the OPP configuration settings for your store from a pipeline configuration (.PCF) file located in your store's CONFIG directory.
SetLogFile	Identifies the file to which to log OPP errors.

LoadPipe

The **LoadPipe** method loads the OPP configuration settings for your store from a pipeline configuration file located in your store's CONFIG directory.

Syntax
OrderPipeline.**LoadPipe(***Filename***)**

Parameters
Filename   The path to the configuration file.

Applies to
OrderPipeline

See also
SetLogFile

SetLogFile

The **SetLogFile** method identifies the file to which the OPP logs errors that occur when the OPP is run on an **OrderForm**.

Syntax
OrderPipeline.SetLogFile(*Filename***)**

Parameters
Filename   The name of the file to which to log transactions.

Applies to
OrderPipeline

See also
LoadPipe

THE PAGE COMPONENT

The **Page** component supports methods that simplify the creation and layout of Active Server Pages (ASP) HTML pages.

Page component methods fall into the following categories:

■ *The Formatting methods*: These methods include **Justify**, **Option**, and **Check**, and are intended to make it possible for you to easily format HTML page items, and where applicable, to determine HTML item values based on a run-time evaluation of other variables used in your page.

■ *The Validation methods*: These include the **Request*** methods, which retrieve values from a URL argument, convert the values to given data types based on a locale value, and validate these values against a specified range.

The **Page** component supports the following properties:

Property	Description
Context	A read-only value that contains the IIS 3.0 scripting context.
Messages	A number that identifies the language to use to return basket and purchase errors.

The **Page** component supports the following methods:

Method	Description
Check	Generates the word CHECKED based upon a supplied value.
Encode	Encodes an argument in HTML.
GetShopperID	Returns the unique shopper ID for the current shopper.
IncrShopperPerfCtrs	Increments the value of the **Total New Shoppers** Performance Monitor counter.
Option	Generates an option button on a page.
ProcessVerifyWith	Reads the contents of hidden fields created using the **VerifyWith** method into an **OrderForm**'s **_verify_with** dictionary.
RequestDate	Retrieves a named date value from the query string, checks that value against a specified range, and performs locale-based validation on the value.

RequestDateTime	Retrieves a named date/time value from the query string, checks the value against a specified range, and performs locale-based validation on the value.
RequestDefault	Attempts to retrieve a named value from the query string and returns a default value if the there is no value with the specified name.
RequestFloat	Retrieves a named floating-point value from the query string, checks the value against a specified range, and then validates the value, based on the specified locale.
RequestMoneyAs-Number	Retrieves a named monetary value from the query string, checks the value against a specified range, and validates the value, based on the specified locale.
RequestNumber	Retrieves a named number value from the query string, checks the value against a specified range, and validates the value, based on the specified locale.
RequestString	Retrieves a named string value from the query string and performs extensive processing on a string, based on the specified locale.
RequestTime	Retrieves a named time value from the query string, checks the value against a specified range, and validates the value, based on the specified locale.
RunPlan	Invokes the Order Processing Pipeline (OPP) to perform preliminary processing on an **OrderForm**.
RunProduct	Runs an **OrderForm** through the **Product Information**, **Merchant Information**, **Shopper Information**, and **Item Price Adjust** stages of the OPP.
RunPurchase	Runs the OPP on an **OrderForm** component that contains the contents of order form storage for the current shopper.
SURL	Generates a secure URL based on the local path to a file. This URL includes the shopper ID, where applicable.
URL	Generates a full URL based on the local path to a file. This URL includes the shopper ID, where applicable.
VerifyWith	Outputs to the page hidden fields that contain verification values.

The Page Component and the StandardSManager

If you initialize the **StandardSManager** for your store in **url** mode, the shopper ID for the current shopper is passed from page to page in the URL when you invoke the **Page** component's **SURL** or **URL** method. To pass the shopper ID from page to page in this fashion, however, you must do the following:

Initialize an **Application**-level **MSCSIDURLKey** variable to identify the key that will appear in the name-value pair that is appended to URLs. For example, if you initialize this variable as follows:

```
Application.Lock
    Application("MSCSIDUrlKey") = "shopper_id"
Application.Unlock
```

a call to the **Page** component's **SURL** or **URL** methods resolve to the following **URL**:

```
http://server/store/page.asp?shopper_id=Q4JPXNCDN3S12H30GM00LX9HFKUC0XU
```

When you create the shopper ID, you must use the **Page** component's **Put-ShopperID** method, rather than the **StandardSManager**'s implementation of this method.

The Page Component's Request Methods

The **Page** component supports a group of methods that begin with **Request*** that apply locale-based data type conversion and value range-checking to values retrieved from a URL argument. Performing these operations on user input ensures that values retrieved through a page can be inserted without error into the store's database storage or passed to the OPP in an **OrderForm** component without generating pipeline or page syntax errors.

The following example illustrates how to use one of these methods—**RequestDate**—to perform locale-based data type conversion and range validation on a URL argument.

This example assumes that the date value is entered via the following form:

```
<FORM METHOD ="POST" ACTION="PROCESS.ASP">
<INPUT TYPE="Text" NAME="Date">
<INPUT TYPE="SUBMIT" NAME="ACTION" VALUE="Send Info">
</FORM>
```

If the user enters the date into the text box in this form and clicks on the Send Info button, the value of this form field can be retrieved by the **RequestDate** method as follows:

```
StrDate = Page.RequestDate("Date", "2/28/97", "1/1/97",
"12/31/97")
If IsNull(StrDate)
    REM  RequestDate failed.
```

The first parameter to **RequestDate** specifies, in this case, the name of the form field from which the data was submitted. If this textbox is empty, the second parameter to **RequestDate**, "2/28/97," becomes the date that **RequestDate** processes. First, the string expression of the date is converted to a date value based on a specified locale, and then the value is checked against the date range specified by the third and fourth parameters. In the example above the locale is not specified, so **RequestDate** uses the value of the **DataFunctions** component's **Locale** property as the basis of the conversion.

Context

The **Context** property is a read-only property on the **Page** component that contains the Active Server Pages (ASP) scripting context. A store builder never needs to retrieve the contents of the **Context** property, and uses it only as a parameter to other Commerce Server methods that need access to the ASP context.

Messages

The **Messages** property identifies the language to use to return basket and purchase errors in the **OrderForm**. This value must identify one of the languages added to the **MessageManager** through a call to that component's **AddLanguage** method.

Check

Generates into a page the word CHECKED if the value specified in the *Value* parameter is a nonzero value. This is useful for setting the default values of radio buttons and checkboxes in forms.

Syntax
Page.**Check**(*Value*)

Parameters

Value   An integer that is evaluated to determine whether the word CHECKED should be inserted at the place in a page where the call to **Check** appears.

Example
The following example from the AdventureWorks management pages checks the radio button if the recordset column *award_all* evaluates to TRUE:

```
<INPUT NAME="award_all"  VALUE=0  TYPE="radio"
<% = Page.Check(Cbool(promo("award_all") = 0)) %>>
```

Applies to
Page

See also
Option

Encode

The **Encode** method applies HTML encoding to the specified expression, using character entities in place of accented characters and to escape special characters such as & and <.

Syntax

Page.**Encode**(*Expression*)

Parameters

Expression   The expression to encode.

Applies to

Page

GetShopperID (Page)

The **GetShopperID** method returns the unique shopper ID for the current shopper.

Syntax

Page.**GetShopperID**()

Parameters

None

Remarks

If the current shopper does not have a shopper ID, **GetShopperID** returns Null.

See also

PutShopperID (Page)

IncrShopperPerfCtrs

The **IncrShopperPerfCtrs** method increments the value of the **Total New Shoppers** Performance Monitor counter.

Syntax

Page.**IncrShopperPerfCtrs**()

Parameters

None

Applies to

Page

Option

The **Option** method generates a list option on a page and assigns it the value and selection state that you specify.

Syntax

Page.**Option**(*Value, State*)

Parameters

Value	A variable containing the option's value.
State	A number that indicates whether the list option is selected. If this value is equal to *Value*, then the HTML keyword SELECTED is inserted in the definition of the option list.

Applies to
Page

See also
Check

ProcessVerifyWith

The **ProcessVerifyWith** method reads the contents of hidden fields created using the **VerifyWith** method into an **OrderForm**'s **_verify_with** dictionary. When the **RunPlan** or **RunPurchase** method runs the **OrderForm** through the OPP, the contents of this **Dictionary** are compared to the contents of the appropriate fields on the **OrderForm** to ensure that a page has not been altered between presentation and final purchase.

Syntax
*Page.***ProcessVerifyWith(***OrderForm***)**

Parameters

OrderForm	An **OrderForm** component that contains the basket for the current shopper.

Applies to
Page

See also
VerifyWith

PutShopperID (Page)

The **PutShopperID** method writes the specified shopper ID to a cookie, and/or stores it for use in a URL or SURL, depending on the initialization mode of the **StandardSManager** for the store.

Syntax
*Page.***PutShopperID(***ShopperID***)**

Parameters

ShopperID	An ID that uniquely identifies this shopper.

Remarks

Where the **PutShopperID** method stores the specified shopper ID depends on the **StandardSManager** initialization mode. In **URL** mode, this method writes the shopper ID to the request so that the **URL** and **SURL** methods add the shopper ID to the URL from this page.

If you initialize the **StandardSManager** in **url** mode, you cannot use the **StandardSManager**'s implementation of **PutShopperID** to store the shopper ID on the client system. Instead, you must use the **Page** component implementation.

Applies to

Page

See also

GetShopperID (Page), SURL, URL

RequestDate

The **RequestDate** method retrieves a named value from the query string and converts it to a **Date Variant** based on the specified or default locale.

Optionally, **RequestDate** also checks the date against a specified date range. If the requested name has no value in the query string, **RequestDate** uses the default value that you specify as the basis for conversion and validation. If **RequestDate** succeeds, it returns the validated value as a **Date Variant**; otherwise, Null.

Syntax

Page.**RequestDate(***Name, Default, LowDate, HighDate, Locale***)**

Parameters

Name	The name of the value to retrieve from the query string.
Default	A default value to use as the basis of the conversion and validation, in the event that the specified name has no value. The default value for this parameter is Null, which means that the parameter is ignored.
LowDate	An optional date value that specifies the low end of the range against which to validate *Date*. The default value is Null, which means that this parameter is ignored.
HighDate	An optional date value that specifies the high end of the range against which to validate *Date*. The default value is Null, which means that this parameter is ignored.
Locale	A number that specifies the locale to use to convert the date. If this value is not specified, the **DataFunctions** component's **Locale** property is used to validate the date.

Applies to

Page

See also
RequestDateTime, ConvertDateString

RequestDateTime

The **RequestDateTime** method retrieves a named value from the query string and converts the value to a **Date Variant**, based on the specified or default locale. Optionally, **RequestDateTime** validates the date/time value against a minimum and maximum value that you specify. If **RequestDateTime** succeeds, it returns the **Date Variant** containing the converted, validated value; otherwise, Null.

Syntax
*Page.***RequestDateTime(** *Name, Default, LowDateTime, HighDateTime, Locale***)**

Parameters

Name	The name of the value to retrieve from the query string.
Default	A string that contains the value to process if the requested name does not exist or contains no value.
LowDateTime	An optional value that specifies the low end of the range. The default value for this parameter is Null, which means that this parameter is ignored.
HighDateTime	An optional value that specifies the high end of the range. The default value for this parameter is 0, which means that this parameter is ignored.
Locale	A number that identifies the locale to be used to convert the date/time string. If this parameter is not specified, **Request-DateTime** uses the value of the **DataFunctions** component's **Locale** property.

Example
See "The Page Component's Request Methods."

Applies to
Page

See also
RequestDate, RequestTime

RequestDefault

The **RequestDefault** method retrieves a named value from the query string as a **String Variant** and substitutes a default value if there is no query string value for the specified name. If successful, **RequestDefault** returns the value; otherwise, Null.

Syntax
*Page.***RequestDefault(***Name, Default***)**

Parameters

Name	The name of the value to retrieve from the query string.
Default	The value to supply if the requested name contains no value.

Example

The following example attempts to retrieve the value for the query string value named shopper_phone. If there is no query string value named shopper_phone, the call to **RequestDefault** returns "Not Supplied":

```
shopper_phone = Page.RequestDefault("shopper_phone", "Not
Supplied")
```

Applies to

Page

RequestFloat

The **RequestFloat** method retrieves a named value from the query string and converts it to a **Double Variant**, based on the specified or default locale. Optionally, **RequestFloat** also checks that number against the specified range and validates the number based on the specified locale. If there is no query string value with the specified name, or if the name has no value, **RequestFloat** uses a specified default value as the basis for the conversion, range-checking, and validation. If **Request-Float** succeeds, it returns the converted, validated value; otherwise, Null.

Syntax

*Page.***RequestFloat(** *Name, Default, LowFloat, HighFloat, Locale***)**

Parameters

Name	The name of the value to retrieve from the query string.
Default	A string expression of the value on which to base validation if the specified query string name does not exist or contains no value.
LowFloat	An optional number that specifies the low end of the range of values against which to validate the converted value. The default value for this parameter is 0, which means that this parameter is ignored.
HighFloat	An optional number that specifies the high end of the range of values against which to validate the converted value. The default value for this parameter is 0, which means that this parameter is ignored.

Locale | An optional number that identifies the locale to use to convert the value. If this value is not specified, the value of the **DataFunctions** component's **Locale** property is used.

Example
See "The Page Component's Request Methods."

Applies to
Page

See also
RequestNumber

RequestMoneyAsNumber

The **RequestMoneyAsNumber** method retrieves a named value from the query string and converts it to a **Long Variant** containing the value of the element in the base monetary units of the locale that you specify, or of the default locale.

If the requested name does not exist, or does not contain a value, **RequestMoneyAsNumber** uses a specified default value as the basis for the conversion, range-checking, and validation. If **RequestMoneyAsNumber** succeeds, it returns the converted, validated value in the base monetary unit of the appropriate locale; otherwise, Null.

Syntax
*Page.***RequestMoneyAsNumber(***Name, Default, LowMoney, HighMoney, Locale***)**

Parameters

Name | The name of the value to retrieve from the query string.

Default | A string expression of the value on which to base validation if the specified query string name does not exist or contains no value.

LowMoney | An optional monetary value that specifies the low end of the range against which to validate the converted value. The default value for this parameter is 0, which means that this parameter is ignored.

HighMoney | An optional monetary value that specifies the high end of the range against which to validate the converted value. The default value for this parameter is 0, which means that this parameter is ignored.

Locale | An optional number that specifies the locale to use to convert *Value*. If this parameter is not used, then the **DataFunctions** component's **Locale** property is used to convert *String*.

Example
See "The Page Component's Request Methods."

Applies to
Page

See also
RequestFloat, RequestNumber

RequestNumber

The **RequestNumber** method retrieves a named value from the query string and converts it to a **Long Variant**, based on the specified locale.

Optionally, **RequestNumber** checks the converted number against a range and validates it based on the specified locale. If the requested name does not exist, or does not contain a value, **RequestNumber** uses a specified default value as the basis for the conversion, range-checking, and validation. If **RequestNumber** succeeds, it returns the converted, validated value in an **Integer Variant**; otherwise, Null.

Syntax
Page.**RequestNumber(***Name, Default, LowNumber, HighNumber, Locale***)**

Parameters

Name	The name of the value to retrieve from the query string.
Default	A string expression of the value on which to base conversion and validation if the specified query string name does not exist or contains no value.
LowNumber	An optional number value that specifies the low end of the range against which to validate the converted value. The default value for this parameter is 0, which means that this parameter is ignored.
HighNumber	An optional number value that specifies the low end of the range against which to validate the converted value. The default value for this parameter is 0, which means that this parameter is ignored.
Locale	An optional number that specifies the locale to use to convert *Value*. If this parameter is not used, then the **DataFunctions** component's **Locale** property is used to convert *String*.

Example
See "The Page Component's Request Methods."

Applies to
Page

See also
RequestFloat

RequestString

The **RequestString** method retrieves a named value from the query string and performs string processing on it. This processing may involve stripping out leading and trailing white spaces, blanking out carriage returns, checking the string's length against a specified range, and validating the string based on the specified locale. If the requested **URL** argument does not exist, or does not contain a value, **Request-String** bases processing on the default string that you specify. If **RequestString** succeeds, it returns the processed string; otherwise, Null.

Syntax

Page.**RequestString**(*Name, Default, MinStrLen, MaxStrLen, StripWhite, StripReturn, Case, Locale*)

Parameters

Name	The name of the value to retrieve from the query string.
Default	The string to return if the specified query string name does not exist or contains no value.
MinStrLen	An optional parameter that indicates the minimum length against which the length of *String* must be validated. The default value for this parameter is 0, which means that this parameter is ignored.
MaxStrLen	An optional parameter that indicates the maximum length against which the length of **String** must be validated. The default value is 65,535.
StripWhite	An optional Boolean value that indicates whether the leading and trailing white spaces should be stripped from the string. The default value for this parameter is FALSE.
StripReturn	An optional Boolean value that indicates whether the carriage returns should be stripped from the string. The default value for this parameter is FALSE.
Case	An optional value that indicates the case to which the string should be converted. The default value for this parameter is 0, which results in no modification to the case of the string. If *Case* is 1, the string is converted to uppercase. If *Case* is 2, the string is converted to lowercase.
Locale	An optional number that specifies the locale to be used as the basis of the conversion. If this value is not specified, **Request-String** uses the value of the **DataFunction** component's **Locale** property.

Example

See "The Page Component's Request Methods."

Applies to
Page

RequestTime

The **RequestTime** method retrieves a named value from the query string and converts the value to a **Date Variant**, based on the specified or default locale. Optionally, **RequestTime** also checks the time against a specified range. If **RequestTime** succeeds, it returns the converted, validated value as a **Date Variant** in which the time element has been zeroed out; otherwise, Null.

Syntax
*Page.***RequestTime(** *Name, Default, LowTime, HighTime, Locale***)**

Parameters

Name	The name of the value to retrieve from the query string.
Default	A string expression of the value on which to base the conversion if the specified query string name does not exist or contains no value.
LowTime	An optional parameter that specifies the low end of the range. The default value is Null, which means that this parameter is ignored.
HighTime	An optional parameter that specifies the high end of the range. The default value is Null, which means that this parameter is ignored.
Locale	A number that specifies the locale to use to convert the date/time value. If this value is not specified, the **DataFunctions** component's **Locale** property is used to convert the date/time value.

Applies to
Page

See also
RequestDate

RunPlan

The **RunPlan** method invokes the OPP to perform preliminary processing on an **OrderForm** component that contains the contents of the current shopper's order form storage. For more information on order form storage, see the beginning of "The DBStorage Component" section.

Syntax
*Page.***RunPlan(***OrderForm***)**

Parameters

OrderForm   An **OrderForm** component that contains the contents of the order form storage for the current shopper.

Remarks

The **RunPlan** method does not result in the purchase of the items referenced in the specified **OrderForm**'s **items** collection. Instead, **RunPlan** runs the **OrderForm** through all but the last two stages (the Payment and Accept stages) of the OPP.

Typically, **RunPlan** is used to set nonsensitive information such as shipping, billing address data, and adjusted price information in the **OrderForm**, and then compute the total. If the OPP encounters errors, it stores these errors in the **Order-Form**'s **_Basket_Errors_** collection.

Once **RunPlan** has been run on an **OrderForm**, and the shopper has confirmed the purchase, the store calls **RunPurchase** on the modified **OrderForm** to write the **OrderForm**'s contents to receipt storage.

Applies to

Page

See also

RunProduct, RunPurchase

RunProduct

The **RunProduct** method runs an **OrderForm** through the **Product Information**, **Merchant Information**, **Shopper Information**, and **Item Price Adjust** stages of the OPP. The **Item Price Adjust** stage writes the adjusted price for a given item to the **OrderForm** Item's **_iadjust_currentprice** member. By comparing the value of this member with the Item's **list_price** member, you can determine if an item is on sale.

Syntax

Page.**RunProduct(***OrderForm***)**

Parameters

OrderForm   An **OrderForm** component initialized with the items on which to check the current price.

Applies to

Page

See also

RunPlan, RunPurchase

RunPurchase

The **RunPurchase** method runs the OPP on an **OrderForm** component that contains the contents of order form storage for the current shopper.

Syntax
Page.**RunPurchase(***OrderForm***)**

Parameters

OrderForm   An **OrderForm** component that contains the contents of order form storage for the current shopper.

Remarks
RunPurchase runs the entire OPP on the **OrderForm**. If no errors are encountered in the **OrderForm**, the OPP writes the **OrderForm**'s contents to receipt storage. For more information on receipt and order form storage, see the beginning of "The DBStorage Component" section.

Applies to
Page

SURL

The **SURL** method generates a properly formatted, secure HTTP URL based on the provided filename and an optional list of name-value arguments. This URL includes the server name, the virtual directory in which the file is stored, and the name of the file itself.

Additionally, if the **StandardSManager** for the application is initialized in url mode, the **SURL** method uses the value stored in the **MSCSIDUrlKey Application** object variable as the name in a name-value pair, the value of which is the current shopper's shopper ID. For more information on how the **Page** component coordinates with the **StandardSManager** component, see the description of the **URL** method.

Syntax
Page.**SURL(***Filename, Arguments***)**

Parameters

Filename   The name of the file for the **SURL** to reference.

Arguments   An optional list of arguments that identify the name-value pairs to be appended to the **SURL**.

Note The **SURL** and **URL** methods assume that your store is one directory level deep, and that the store name is the same as the virtual root. Where either of these assumptions is untrue, you should not use these methods to construct a URL to a page.

Applies to
Page

See also
URL

URL

The **URL** method generates a URL based on the specified filename and an optional list of name-value arguments. This URL includes the server name, the virtual directory in which the file is stored, and the name of the file itself.

In addition, if the **StandardSManager** for the application is initialized in **url** mode, the SURL method uses the value stored in the **MSCSIDUrlKey Application** object variable as the name in a name-value pair, the value that is the current shopper's shopper ID.

Syntax
*Page.***URL**(*Filename, Arguments***)**

Parameters

Filename   The name of the file to reference in the URL.

Arguments   An optional list of name-value pairs.

Remarks
The **URL** method serves several purposes within the context of a Commerce Server store. First, **URL** is a useful HTML utility function that spares the store builder the need to map a file to the HTTP path to that file, or to manually build name-value pairs into the query string appended to the URL. For example, the following call to **URL**,

```
<%= Page.URL("filename.asp", "sku", sku) %>
```

resolves to the correct HTTP path to filename.ASP, and appends the *sku* name and *sku* value to that URL as follows:

```
Http://servername/virtual_directory/filename.asp?sku=13428
```

More importantly, where the **StandardSManager** is initialized in **url** mode, a call to **URL** appends the value stored in the **Application** object's **MSCSIDUrlKey** variable, along with the current shopper's shopper ID, to the resulting HTTP path.

Thus, where the **Application** object's **MSCSIDUrlKey** variable is initialized as follows,

```
Application("MMSURLKey") = "current_shopper")
```

and where the **StandardSManager** is running in **url** mode, the sample call to **URL** included earlier in this section resolves to the following:

```
Http://servername/virtual_directory/filename.asp?sku=13428&↵
    current_shopper=12345
```

For more information on **StandardSManager** initialization modes, see **Init-Manager** in "The StandardSManager Component" section.

Note The **SURL** and **URL** methods assume that your store is one directory level deep, and that the store name is the same as the virtual root. Where either of these assumptions is untrue, you should not use these methods to construct a URL to a page.

Applies to
Page

See also
SURL

VerifyWith

The **VerifyWith** method outputs a group of hidden fields that identify the **OrderForm** fields to be used to verify that an order has not been altered between presentation of the **OrderForm** and final purchase. When the form is submitted, the **ProcessVerifyWith** method on the target page stores these fields in a dictionary in the **OrderForm**, which then passes that **OrderForm** to the OPP. In the OPP, the **RequiredTotal** component compares the values in these fields with the _verify_with dictionary on the order form and generates an error if there is a mismatch.

Syntax
page.**VerifyWith**(*OrderForm, Arguments*)

Parameters
OrderForm	Component that contains the values to verify.
Arguments	One or more arguments that identify the **OrderForm** fields to use for verification.

Remarks
The **VerifyWith** method verifies **String**, **Number**, or **Double Variant**s. This method cannot be used to verify a **Date Variant**.

Example

The following example generates hidden fields containing the values stored in the **_total_total**, **ship_to_zip**, and **_tax_total** fields of the supplied **OrderForm** component:

```
<% = Page.VerifyWith(order, "_total_total", "ship_to_zip",↵
    "_tax_total") %>
```

When the page containing this call is loaded in the client browser, the document source for the page would contain the following HTML script (assuming a total of 123.00, a zip code of 98029, and a tax of 8.75):

```
<INPUT TYPE="HIDDEN" NAME="_VERIFY_WITH_" VALUE="123.00">
<INPUT TYPE="HIDDEN" NAME="_VERIFY_WITH_" VALUE="98029">
<INPUT TYPE="HIDDEN" NAME="_VERIFY_WITH_" VALUE="8.75">
```

Applies to

Page

See also

ProcessVerifyWith

THE STANDARDSMANAGER COMPONENT

The **StandardSManager** component supports methods that facilitate the run-time creation, deletion, and retrieval of shopper IDs.

The **StandardSManager** component supports the following methods:

Method	Description
CreateShopperID	Creates and returns a unique shopper ID.
DeleteShopperID	Deletes a shopper ID.
GetShopperID	Retrieves the shopper ID from the cookie, if available. Otherwise, returns an empty string.
InitManager	Initializes the **StandardSManager** with information that determines how shopper IDs will be stored and retrieved.
PutShopperID	Stores the shopper ID in a cookie on the client system.

StandardSManager Initialization Modes

After creating a **StandardSManager** component, but before calling its **GetShopperID** or **PutShopperID** methods, you must initialize the **StandardSManager**. To do this, you call the **StandardSManager**'s **InitManager** method, specifying the store name and the *initialization mode*. The **StandardSManager**'s initialization mode determines how the Page component's **GetShopperID** and **PutShopperID** methods retrieve and store shopper IDs.

The following modes are available:

Mode	Behavior
cookie	**PutShopperID** stores the shopper ID in a cookie on the client system. **GetShopperID** retrieves this cookie.
cookieurl	**PutShopperID** stores the shopper ID in a cookie on the client system and in the URL. **GetShopperID** attempts to retrieve the shopper ID first from the cookie, and then from the URL.
url	**PutShopperID** appends the shopper ID to the URL, using the **MCSIDUrlKey** as the name part of the URL argument. **GetShopperID** retrieves the shopper ID from the URL.
urlcookie	**PutShopperID** stores the shopper ID in a URL, and stores it as a cookie on the client system. **GetShopperID** attempts to retrieve the shopper ID first from the URL, then from the cookie.

Shopper Identifiers and Active Server Pages (ASP) Session Identifiers

The **StandardSManager** component, like the IIS 3.0 **Session** object, can issue per-user identifiers that facilitate the maintenance of state data across a session. However, significant differences exist in how the **StandardSManager** and the **Session** object function, both internally and within the context of a store. Because of these differences, you should never use IIS 3.0 session identifiers in a Commerce Server store to identify a store user.

First, the IIS 3.0 session ID is unique only across a single user session. Once that session concludes, a server running IIS may assign that session ID to another user. Consequently, it is not advisable to use a IIS-issued session ID as a unique key. Shopper IDs, on the other hand, are designed to persist across multiple sessions, so these identifiers can be used as a reliable key into the database tables in which you maintain shopper information.

Additionally, in a multiple-server environment, the IIS 3.0 session ID carries no guarantee of uniqueness. Two IIS 3.0 server **Session** objects are likely to issue the same session ID to different users. Shopper IDs, on the other hand, are designed to be unique even across multiple servers, so that where the same store is running across multiple servers, the shopper ID remains a reliable means of tracking shopper information, both for state-maintenance and for persistently stored purchase operations.

Creating a StandardSManager Component

Use the IIS 3.0 **Server** object's **CreateObject** method to create a **StandardSManager** component, specifying the "Commerce.StandardSManager" program identifier:

```
Set StandardSManager =
Server.CreateObject("Commerce.StandardSManager")
```

The **StandardSManager** component is created on a per-application basis, and in the store's GLOBAL.ASA file, it should be assigned to the **Application** object's **MSCSShopperManager** variable.

CreateShopperID

The **CreateShopperID** method creates and returns a new shopper ID.

Syntax
*StandardSManager.***CreateShopperID**()

Remarks
The **CreateShopperID** method has no parameters, and returns the newly created shopper ID. For more information on **StandardSManager** modes, see the section "**InitManager**."

Applies to
StandardSManager

See also
InitManager

GetShopperID (StandardSManager)

The **GetShopperID** method returns the shopper ID from a cookie stored on the client system.

Syntax
*StandardSManager.***GetShopperID**(*Null*)

Parameters
Null This parameter is not supported.

Remarks
If no shopper ID is stored on the client system, **GetShopperID** returns an empty string.

Applies to
StandardSManager

See also
PutShopperID (StandardSManager)

InitManager

The **InitManager** method initializes the **StandardSManager** component to the specified store key and mode.

Syntax

StandardSManager.**InitManager(***StoreKey, Mode***)**

Parameters

StoreKey   The name of the store.

Mode   A string that indicates how shopper information is to be stored. See the "Remarks" section below.

Remarks

The mode that you specify indicates whether the **StandardSManager** will run in **cookie** or **url** mode. The mode in which the **StandardSManager** runs determines how shopper IDs will be stored and retrieved. The following table lists the possible values of this parameter:

Mode	Description
cookie	Indicates that the **StandardSManager** should store the shopper ID in a cookie.
cookieurl	Indicates that the **StandardSManager** should first attempt to write the shopper ID to a cookie, and if this fails, to a URL.
url	Indicates that the **StandardSManager** should store the shopper ID in a URL.
urlcookie	Indicates that the **StandardSManager** should first attempt to write the shopper ID to a URL, and if this fails, to a cookie.

Applies to

StandardSManager

See also

PutShopperID (StandardSManager)

PutShopperID (StandardSManager)

The **PutShopperID** method stores a shopper ID in the cookie or a URL/SURL, depending on the mode in which the **StandardSManager** is running.

Syntax

StandardSManager.**PutShopperID(***Null, ShopperID***)**

Parameters

Null   This parameter is no longer supported.

ShopperID   The shopper ID to store.

Remarks

If the shopper ID is put to a URL, you can retrieve it by passing the value you set for the application-level **MSCSSIDUrlKey** to the IIS 3.0 **Request** object.

Applies to

StandardSManager component

THE TRAFFICLOGFILE COMPONENT

The **TrafficLogfile** component provides Commerce Server stores with the ability to log user information and store events to a plain text file.

The **TrafficLogfile** component supports the following properties:

Property	Description
BlankSubstitution	Specifies the character to substitute for blank spaces.
ColumnDelimiter	A string that specifies the ASCII characters to use to separate columns in the log file.
ColumnSubstitution	Specifies the character to be used as the column delimiter if the data itself contains the character previously specified as the **ColumnDelimiter**.
LocaleDate	Specifies the locale to use to format dates in the log file. The default is American (&H0409).
LogTime	Specifies the locale to use to format time in the log file. The default is American (&H0409).
RowDelimiter	Specifies the character to use to delimit rows. The default is a carriage return followed by a linefeed (Chr(10)).
RowSubstitution	Specifies the character to be used as the row delimiter if the data itself contains the character previously specified as the **RowDelimiter**.

The **TrafficLogfile** component supports the following methods:

Method	Description
InitTraffic	Initializes the **TrafficLogfile** component with the filename to which to log traffic and (where applicable) a store key.
LogTraffic	Logs traffic data to a data source or file.

Overview

To create a **TrafficLogfile** component, use the **Server.CreateObject** method, specifying "Commerce.TrafficLogfile as the component's program identifier:

```
Set Traffic = Server.CreateObject("Commerce.TrafficLogfile")
```

After creating the component, and before calling its **LogTraffic** method, use the **InitManager** method to initialize the component, specifying the types of information you want to log. The following table lists the items of information that you can log:

Field	Description
args_*argname*	Logs a page or form argument.
event	Used to store the event description.
event_time	The time at which the event was logged.
http_*argname*	Logs environment variables, such as REFER and USER_AGENT (for example, http_REFER). Note that, in names containing hyphens, an underscore is used instead of a hyphen because database column names cannot contain hyphens.
item_requested	The SKU of the requested item.
remote_addr	Logs the IP address of the client machine.
remote_host	Logs the host name of the client machine (in some cases, this value may be an IP address).
shopper_id	The unique identifier of the current shopper.
store_name	Used to store the store name.

If you create a **TrafficLogfile** component in your store's GLOBAL.ASA file, you should initialze the **Application** object variable **MSCSTraffic** to reference the component instance.

InitTraffic (TrafficLogfile)

The **InitTraffic** method initializes the **TrafficLogfile** component by identifying the kinds of store events to log.

Syntax
TrafficLogfile.**InitTraffic(***StoreName, FileName, Arguments***)**

Parameters

StoreName	The name of the store. This value is written to the log file to identify the store that logged the event.
FileName	The local path to the file to which events and data are logged.
Arguments	A list of arguments that identify the events you want to log. These include the events defined by Commerce Server, as well as events that you define.

Applies to
TrafficLogfile

LogTraffic (TrafficLogfile)

The **LogTraffic** method logs event or shopper information to the log file for this **TrafficLogfile** component.

Syntax

*TrafficLogfile.***LogTraffic(***ShopperID, Event, ItemRequested, Context***)**

Parameters

ShopperID	The shopper ID of the shopper that loaded the page that triggered the event.
Event	A string that identifies the event to log.
ItemRequested	The filename of the requested item.
Context	The **Page** component's **Context** property. This read-only property is initialized when the **Page** component is created, and references the Active Server Pages (ASP) scripting context.

Remarks

If you have initialized the **Application** object variable **MSCSTraffic,** then this method is called for you automatically.

Applies to

TrafficLogfile

THE TRAFFICTABLE COMPONENT

The **TrafficTable** component provides Commerce Server stores with the ability to log user information and store events to a database table.

The **TrafficTable** component supports the following methods:

Method	Description
InitTraffic	Initializes the **Traffic** component with the data source or filename to which to log traffic and (where applicable) a store key.
LogTraffic	Logs traffic data to a data source or file.

Overview

To create a **TrafficTable** component, use the **Server.CreateObject** method, specifying "Commerce.TrafficTable" as the component's program identifier:

```
Set Traffic = Server.CreateObject("Commerce.TrafficTable")
```

After creating the component, and before calling its **LogTraffic (Traffic-Table)** method, use the **InitManager** method to initialize the component, specifying the table to which you want to log. The following table lists the items of information that you can log:

Field	Description
args_*argname*	Logs a page or form argument.
event	Used to store the event description.

event_time	The time at which the event was logged.
http_*argname*	Logs environment variables, such as REFER and USER_AGENT (for example, http_REFER). Note that, in names containing hyphens, an underscore is used instead of a hyphen because database column names cannot contain hyphens.
item_requested	The SKU of the requested item.
remote_addr	Logs the IP address of the client machine.
remote_host	Logs the host name of the client machine (in some cases, this value may be an IP address).
shopper_id	The unique identifier of the current shopper.
store_name	Used to store the store name.

InitTraffic (TrafficTable)

The **InitManager** method initializes the **TrafficTable** component with information such as the data source or file to which store events will be logged, the store key, and where applicable, the table name.

Syntax
Traffic.**InitTraffic**(*Datasource, StoreKey, TableName*)

Parameters

Datasource	A variable that identifies the **Datasource** component for the table to which you want to log.
StoreKey	The name of the store. The value specified in this parameter is used by **TrafficTable** to identify the store that logged the event.
TableName	The name of the table in the referenced data source. This parameter is used only if you are logging to a database table.

Applies to
TrafficTable

See also
LogTraffic (TrafficTable)

LogTraffic (TrafficTable)

The **LogTraffic** method logs event information to a database table.

Syntax
Traffic.**LogTraffic**(*ShopperID, Event, ItemRequested, Context*)

Parameters

ShopperID	The ID of the current shopper.
Event	The event to log.

ItemRequested   The SKU of the item requested.

Context   The **Page** component's **Context** property.

Applies to
TrafficTable

See also
InitTraffic (TrafficTable)

Tour of Clock Peddler Starter Store[1]

The Clock Peddler starter store is an example of a simple, basic Commerce Server store. By examining the logic of the store's structure, templates, queries, GLOBAL.ASA entries, and database schema, you will gain an understanding of the closely coupled interrelationships among its fundamental elements. The Clock Peddler starter store has the following characteristics:

- The store is designed for all Web browsers that support tables and cookies. No advanced browser features are used.

- The store works with any screen resolution.

- The store has a two-level hierarchy: department and product.

- The store sells only one type of product; therefore, every product shares the same attributes (price, description).

---

1. Material in this appendix, available under \docs\Building a store.doc after installation of the companion CD for this book, is extracted from material provided by the Microsoft Site Server documentation group.

■ The store doesn't use searching because there is only a small number of individual products.

■ The store's customers are not asked to register before entering the online store, which means that the shopper must enter a shipping address for each order.

Note that the Clock Peddler Store is a completely separate application from the Clock Peddler Manager application. For a description of the .ASP templates that make up the Manager application, see "Basic Manager Application: Tour of Clock Peddler" in "Building a Store.Doc" available from the \Commerce Server\Docs directory after installation of Commerce Server from the companion CD.

SHOPPER IDS

The Commerce Server **StandardSManager** object generates a shopper ID (a random 32-character string based on a Windows NT Global Unique ID) to keep track of the shopper's shopping basket, whether the store requires the shopper to register before shopping or not. If the store requires a shopper to register, the shopper ID, as well as information that the shopper enters, is saved in a database table. On each new visit to the store, the shopper signs in and the previously assigned shopper ID is used for the session.

If the store does not require shoppers to register, a shopper ID is generated the first time the shopper enters the store. If the store is configured to use cookies and the client browser supports cookies, the shopper ID is then stored in a cookie on the shopper's computer. Alternatively, the store can be configured to pass the shopper ID in the URL. In this case, a new shopper ID is generated each time the shopper visits the store; shoppers must enter their address and payment information each time they make a purchase, and receipts are not retained from session to session. The Clock Peddler store does not ask shoppers to register, and it stores the shopper ID in a cookie.

The **StandardSManager** object handles creation of shopper IDs. In the Clock Peddler store, the **StandardSManager** object is instantiated by the following statements in the \SHOP\GLOBAL.ASA file:

```
REM -- Create a Shopper Manager to deal with managing shopperId values
Set  MSCSShopperManager = Server.CreateObject("Commerce.StandardSManager")
Call MSCSShopperManager.InitManager("ClockPed", "cookie")
```

Also in the \SHOP\GLOBAL.ASA file, the object reference is stored as a variable in the **Application** object by the following statement:

```
Set Application("MSCSShopperManager") = MSCSShopperManager
```

Note that this **Application** variable must have the name **MSCSShopperManager**, because other Commerce Server objects expect this string.

The shopper ID itself is generated on the page. The \SHOP\INCLUDE\ SHOP.ASP file (which is included on every page template) first gets the **Application** variable by the following statement:

```
Set MSCSShopperManager = Application("MSCSShopperManager")
```

The shopper ID is generated by the following statements in the SHOP.ASP file:

```
REM -- manually create shopper id
ShopperID = mscsPage.GetShopperId
if IsNull(ShopperID) then
    ShopperID = MSCSShopperManager.CreateShopperID()
    Call mscsPage.PutShopperId(ShopperID)
end if
```

When the shopper's browser requests a page in the Clock Peddler store application, the **GetShopperID** method of the **MSCSShopperManager** checks for the existence of a shopper ID. If no shopper ID exists, the **CreateShopperID** method generates one. The **PutShopperID** method is then used to put the shopper ID into the MSCSPage object to make it available to other **MSCSPage** methods.

A store can pass the shopper ID from page to page either in a cookie or in the URL or both. This is determined when the instance of the **StandardSManager** object is initialized in the GLOBAL.ASA file. If the shopper ID is passed in the cookie, the **MSCSShopperManager** puts the shopper ID into the cookie.

The shopper ID must be stored in the **Page** object in order for you to use any **Page** object methods that require the shopper ID. This includes the **URL** method, which passes the shopper ID in the URL. The **PutShopperID** method is used to store the shopper ID in the **Page** object. The shopper ID is then accessible to the **URL** method, which appends it to any generated URL using the **MSCSSIDURLKey** string specified in the GLOBAL.ASA file.

About Cookies

The Clock Peddler store uses a cookie to store the shopper ID. A cookie is a small file (approximately 1 KB) generated by the server and stored locally on the client computer. When a shopper connects to a page using a browser that supports cookies, Commerce Server generates a cookie and sends it to the browser, which saves it on the shopper's computer.

When the shopper adds an item to the basket, the data is stored in the Clock-Ped_basket table along with the shopper ID. If the shopper exits from the store without completing the purchase and then returns later, the shopper ID stored in the cookie is used to retrieve that shopper's basket.

Some browsers do not support cookies, and other browsers provide a way to turn off the cookie functionality. If the shopper is using a browser that does not support cookies, the purchasing process in the Clock Peddler store cannot be completed. If the cookie has been deleted from the shopper's computer, a new shopper ID is generated the next time the shopper visits the store.

THE CLOCK PEDDLER DATABASE SCHEMA

The database schema for the Clock Peddler store reflects the fact that the products all have the same attributes and that there are only two levels of hierarchy: departments and products. The Setup program creates the Clock Peddler schema by executing the schema.sql script, which is located in the \clockped\Sql\Sqlsvr folder.

Basket Table: ClockPed_basket

This table stores the shopper's order along with the shopper ID. This table is required if the store uses an instance of the **DBStorage** object for Order Form storage (which Clock Peddler does). The instance of the **DBStorage** object is initialized in the \SHOP\GLOBAL.ASA file with the name of the table, the key, the type of object that the table will be storing, and the columns in which the data is to be stored. The following entry in the Clock Peddler \SHOP\GLOBAL.ASA file creates and initializes the object:

```
REM -- Create a storage object for the Order Forms (shopper's basket)
   Set  MSCSOrderFormStorage = Server.CreateObject("Commerce.DBStorage")
   Call MSCSOrderFormStorage.InitStorage(MSCSDataSource,↵
      "ClockPed_basket", "shopper_id", "Commerce.OrderForm",↵
      "marshalled_order", "date_changed")
```

Shopper basket has the following parameters:

Column	Datatype	Description
date_changed	datetime Null	The date the order was changed.
marshalled_order	image Null	All order information in encoded form.
shopper_id	varchar(32) primary key	Unique identifier for this shopper.

Product Table: ClockPed_product

This table stores information about each individual product that can be ordered from the Clock Peddler store. The Setup program populates the table by executing the data_product.sql script, which is located in the \ClockPed\Sql\SQLSvr folder. In the Clock Peddler store, each product description is stored in the database as HTML markup so it is formatted correctly on generated pages.

Column	Datatype	Description
dept_id	int Null	Identifier of the department this product belongs to.
description	text Null	Description of this product, used on product page.
image_file	varchar (20) Null	File name of the product image.
image_width	int Null	Width of the image displayed on the generated page.
image_height	int Null	Height of the image displayed on the generated page.
list_price (This column is required by the default pipeline.)	int NOT Null	Manufacturer's list price for this product. Price is stored as an integer. For example, a price of $19.95 would be stored as 1995. When a page is generated, the integer is formatted correctly according to the MSCSDataFunctions.Locale = &H0409 entry in the \SHOP\GLOBAL.ASA file.
manufacturer	varchar (50) Null	Name of manufacturer.
name	varchar (50) Null	Name of this product.
sku (This column is required by the default pipeline.)	varchar (30) primary key	Unique SKU number for this product.

Department Table: ClockPed_dept

This table stores information about each department in the store. The Setup program populates the table by executing the data_dept.sql script, which is located in the \ClockPed\Sql\SQLSvr folder.

Column	Datatype	Description
dept_description	varchar (200) Null	Description of this department
dept_id	int primary key	Unique identifier for this department
dept_name	varchar (50) Null	Name of this department

THE CLOCK PEDDLER QUERIES

Most of the database queries used in the Clock Peddler store are stored in the instance of the **Content** object (**MSCSContent**) by its **AddQuery** method. The GLOBAL.ASA file contains the entries that create an instance of the **Content** object and add the queries to it. (For more information, see "Clock Peddler Store Initialization and Configuration" later in this appendix.) For example, the following statement in the \SHOP\GLOBAL.ASA file stores the full text of the query named "product" in **MSCSContent**:

```
Call MSCSContent.AddQuery("product", "select sku, name, dept_id,↵
    manufacturer, list_price, image_file, image_width, image_height,↵
    description from ClockPed_product where sku = :1",0,adCmdText,0,↵
    adOpenForwardOnly,0)
```

In the following example (from the PRODUCT.ASP template), the **Request** object retrieves the value of the *sku* argument from the URL, and the **Cstr** function expresses the value as a string. (Note: *Request("sku")* is abbreviated syntax; the statement could also be written *Request.QUERYSTRING("sku").*) The **Execute** method runs the specified query (**product**), passing it the *sku*. The result set is assigned the variable name *product*:

```
set product = MSCSDataSource.Execute("product", Cstr(Request("sku")))(0)
```

If it becomes necessary to change a query, you can change it once in the GLOBAL.ASA file rather than having to change it on every page where the query is used.

Query name	SQL text	Result
department	"Select * from ClockPed_ dept where dept_id = :1", 0, adCmdText, 0, adOpenForwardOnly, 0	Returns all columns from the ClockPed_dept table where the dept_id = (the argument value passed in from the page that called this query).
departments	"select * from Clock-Ped_dept", 0, adCmdText, 0, adOpenForwardOnly,0	Returns all columns from the ClockPed_dept table.
product	"select sku, name, dept_id, manufacturer, list_price, image_file, image_width, image_height, description from ClockPed_product where sku = :1", 0, ad-CmdText, 0, adOpenForwardOnly, 0	Returns the specified columns from the Clock-Ped_product table where the sku = (the argument value passed in from the page that called this query).

Query name	SQL text	Result
products-by-dept	"select sku, name, dept_id, manufacturer, list_price, image_file, image_width, image_height, description from ClockPed_product where dept_id = :1", 0, adCmdText, 0, adOpenForwardOnly, 0	Returns the specified columns from the ClockPed_product table where the dept_id = (the argument value passed in from the page that called this query).

CLOCK PEDDLER STORE INITIALIZATION AND CONFIGURATION

Two files support the initialization and configuration of the Clock Peddler store application:

- The \SHOP\GLOBAL.ASA file creates the application-level objects and stores them in the IIS **Application** object so their properties and methods are available throughout the application.

- The \SHOP\INCLUDE\SHOP.ASP file sets up page variables that are common across all pages. This file is included on every page template.

The four starter stores have one additional configuration file that is not needed in stores generated by the Store Builder Wizard. This file—\SHOP\INCLUDE\ DSN_INCLUDE.ASP—specifies the DSN, the database, the user ID, and the password for connecting to the database. It is included in the GLOBAL.ASA file. (When the Store Builder Wizard generates a new store, the connect string is written directly into that store's \SHOP\GLOBAL.ASA file. The connect string for the new store's Manager application, however, is written into the \MANAGER\INCLUDE\ DSN_INCLUDE.ASP file.)

Setting Up Global Store Variables

Each of the starter stores has a DSN_INCLUDE.ASP file located in the \storename\Shop\Include folder. The Commerce Server Setup program writes data into the DSN_INCLUDE.ASP files for each of the starter stores and their Manager applications. The DSN_INCLUDE.ASP file is saved in the \storename\Shop\Include and \storename\Manager\Include folders, and it is included in the GLOBAL.ASA file.

In stores generated by the Store Builder Wizard, the information is written directly into the \SHOP\GLOBAL.ASA file rather than being stored in a separate DSN_INCLUDE.ASP file. (However, the Manager application generated by the Store Builder Wizard does have a separate DSN_INCLUDE.ASP file, located in the \storename\Manager\Include folder.)

This section explains the statements that appear in this file. Please use Visual Interdev, available on the companion CD, or another text editor to refer to the *storename*\SHOP\INCLUDE\ DSN_INCLUDE.ASP file while reading this section.

```
<SCRIPT LANGUAGE=VBScript RUNAT=Server>
```

The <SCRIPT> tag specifies the language used to write the event script. (**Sub** and **Function** statements can appear only inside a <SCRIPT> tag.) The **Vbscript** parameter defines the language as Visual Basic Scripting Edition. The **Server** parameter specifies that the event script is to be processed on the server instead of being sent to the browser.

```
Function MSCSDSN
    MSCSDSN = "DSN=DSNname;UID=sa;PWD=;DATABASE=databaseName"
End Function
```

This function initializes a variable called *MSCSDSN* with the DSN, the user ID, the password, and the name of the database used for the store.

The GLOBAL.ASA file

The GLOBAL.ASA file initializes and configures the store by creating the instances of the Commerce Server objects and storing pointers to them in the **Application** object. (The GLOBAL.ASA entries take the place of the Windows registry entries used in Merchant Server version 1.0.) Because the GLOBAL.ASA file initializes the entire application, its file name extension is .ASA, which stands for Active Server Application (as opposed to .ASP for Active Server Pages, used for page templates).

Each store has two versions of the GLOBAL.ASA file—one is used when the store is open for business, and the other is used when the store is closed. This section explains the statements that appear in the GLOBAL.ASA file that are used when the store is open. While reading this section, please use Windows Notepad or another text editor to refer to the GLOBAL.ASA file located in the \Stores\Clock-Ped\Shop folder.

```
<!-- REM include DSN and DB connect string info from setup -->
<!--#INCLUDE FILE="include/dsn_include.asp" -->
```

This statement includes the DSN_INCLUDE.ASP file, which provides the connect string used for connecting to the database.

Note   In stores generated by the Store Builder Wizard, the information in DSN_INCLUDE.ASP is written directly into the GLOBAL.ASA file rather than being included.

```
<SCRIPT LANGUAGE=VBScript RUNAT=Server>
```

The <SCRIPT> tag specifies the language used to write the event script. (**Sub** and **Function** statements can appear only inside a <SCRIPT> tag.) The VBScript parameter defines the language as Visual Basic Scripting Edition. The Server parameter specifies that the event script is to be processed on the server instead of being sent to the browser.

```
Sub Application_OnStart
```

This statement initializes the IIS **Application** object with the series of statements between here and the **End Sub** statement (at the end of the file). The application starts the first time the server receives a request for any of the pages in the /CLOCKPED virtual directory (which maps to the C:\MICROSOFT COMMERCE SERVER\STORES\CLOCKPED directory tree). The application remains running until you make a change to the \SHOP\GLOBAL.ASA file. As soon as the server receives the next request for a page in that virtual directory, the GLOBAL.ASA file is recompiled and the application restarts.

```
REM -- ADO command types
    adCmdText       = 1
    adCmdTable      = 2
    adCmdStoredProc = 4
    adCmdUnknown    = 8
```

These statements create a page variable to represent each of the ADO **Command Type** properties. This is for convenience, because the variable name is easier to remember than the number representing the property. Only the **adCmdText** property is used in the Clock Peddler Store application, but the others are included to demonstrate their use for merchants who may want to modify the application. The **adCmdText** property indicates that **CommandText** is to be evaluated as a textual definition of a command.

```
REM -- ADO cursor types
    adOpenForwardOnly = 0 '# (Default)
    adOpenKeyset      = 1
    adOpenDynamic     = 2
    adOpenStatic      = 3
```

These statements create a page variable to represent each of the ADO **Cursor Type** properties. This is for convenience, because the variable name is easier to remember than the number representing the property. The **adOpenForwardOnly** property specifies a cursor that can scroll forward through records (this improves performance in a single pass through a recordset). The **adOpenKeyset** property specifies a keyset cursor (you cannot see records that other users add, but data changes are visible). The **adOpenDynamic** property specifies a dynamic cursor (additions, changes, and deletions by other users are visible; all types of movement through the recordset are allowed except bookmarks). The **adOpenStatic** property specifies a static cursor (static copy of a recordset that you can use to find data; additions, changes, or deletions by other users are not visible).

```
REM -- Create a content object and datasource for connection ↵
    to the database
Set MSCSContent = Server.CreateObject("Commerce.Content")
```

The **CreateObject** method creates an instance of the **Content** object. The **Set** statement assigns it to the variable name *MSCSContent*. This object interacts with the Commerce Server database and stores database queries used to populate the store pages.

```
Call MSCSContent.AddDatasource("ClockPed", MSCSDSN, 1, 0)
Set MSCSDataSource = MSCSContent.Datasource("ClockPed")
```

The **AddDatasource** method adds a connect string (used for connecting to the database) to the **MSCSContent** object. The *ClockPed* parameter specifies a string variable name that will be used throughout the store templates to refer to the datasource being added. The MSCSDSN parameter specifies the connect string, which comes from the DSN_INCLUDE.ASP file included at the start of GLOBAL.ASA. The 1 parameter specifies that the connection should return a block cursor, and the 0 specifies that there is no limit on the number of rows returned. The **Set** statement assigns the *MSCSDatasource* variable name to the *ClockPed* datasource that was added in the previous statement.

```
REM -- Add queries to the content object for use in our pages
call MSCSContent.AddQuery("departments", "select * from ↵
    ClockPed_dept",0,adCmdText,0,adOpenForwardOnly,0)
```

The **AddQuery** method adds a query to the **MSCSContent** object so the query can be used for retrieving data from the database. The first parameter (in this case, *departments*) specifies the name of the query, and the second parameter gives the exact SQL text of the query. Each of the subsequent **AddQuery** statements adds another query to the object.

```
REM -- Create the Order Processing Pipeline
   Set  MSCSOrderPipeline = Server.CreateObject("Commerce.OrderPipeline")
   pathPipeConfig = server.mappath("/ClockPed") & ↵
     "\..\config\pipeline.pcf"
```

The **CreateObject** method creates an instance of the **OrderPipeline** object. The **Set** statement assigns it to the variable name *MSCSOrderPipeline*. The **mappath** method maps the /CLOCKPED virtual directory to the corresponding actual path on the server. The **&** operator concatenates the specified path and file name (\..\CONFIG\PIPELINE.PCF) to the /CLOCKPED virtual directory, and the resulting path and file name are assigned to the variable name *pathPipeConfig*.

```
Call MSCSOrderPipeline.LoadPipe(pathPipeConfig)
```

This statement initializes the instance of the **OrderPipeline** object by loading the pipeline configuration file (PIPELINE.PCF) from the specified location (the value of *pathPipeConfig*).

```
REM -- uncommenting the following line will create a log file ⏎
    when the pipeline is run
REM Call MSCSOrderPipeline.SetLogFile("c:\temp\pipeline.log")
```

This statement sets up a log file, which is useful for debugging the Order Processing Pipeline.

```
REM -- Create a message manager for use by the pipeline
    Set MSCSMessageManager = ⏎
        Server.CreateObject("Commerce.MessageManager")
```

The **CreateObject** method creates an instance of the **MessageManager** object, which stores error strings used by the components of the Order Processing Pipeline. The **Set** statement assigns the object to the variable name *MSCSMessageManager*.

```
Call MSCSMessageManager.AddLanguage("usa", &H0409)
    MSCSMessageManager.defaultLanguage = "usa"
```

The **AddLanguage** method adds a language to the **MSCSMessageManager** object by specifying a name-value pair to represent that language. Each set of messages is represented by a name-value pair to allow for easy localization of a store. The *usa* parameter specifies the string variable used for this language, and the *&H0409* parameter specifies the language ID code (in this case, for U.S. English) used by Microsoft Windows. The **&H** convention indicates that the *0409* value is hexadecimal. The **defaultLanguage** method specifies the language that is to be used for displaying messages. Several different language sets may be added to the **MessageManager** object, but the one that is actually used for message display is the language specified by the **defaultLanguage** method. This mechanism enables you to easily switch to a message set for a different language to facilitate store localization.

```
Call MSCSMessageManager.AddMessage("pur_out_of_stock", ⏎
    "At least one item is out of stock.")
```

The **AddMessage** method adds a message to the message set. The first parameter (**pur_out_of_stock**, in this case) is the name of the message; this name is called by components in the Order Processing Pipeline that generate errors, and therefore must exactly match the string expected by the component. For a list of message names used by the Commerce Server components, see the **MessageManager** component in the Commerce Server Component Reference Documentation in Appendix F. The second parameter is the actual text of the message as it will be displayed to the shopper; unlike the message name, this text can be changed. Note that the message text may contain variables as in the following example: *"The value for %(label)s must be greater than or equal to %(min)s."* Each of the subsequent **Add-Message** statements adds another message to the object.

```
REM -- Create a Shopper Manager to deal with managing shopperId values
Set MSCSShopperManager = Server.CreateObject("Commerce.StandardSManager")
Call MSCSShopperManager.InitManager("ClockPed", "cookie")
```

The **CreateObject** method creates an instance of the **BStandardSManager** object. The **Set** statement assigns it to the variable name *MSCSShopperManager*. The **Call** statement initializes the *MSCSShopperManager* object with a name-value pair. The *ClockPed* parameter specifies a string variable that represents the store's datasource; the **cookie** parameter specifies that the Clock Peddler store puts the generated shopper ID into the cookie (as opposed to the URL or both).

```
REM -- Example Storage object for the shopper information (Not needed ↵
    for ClockPed's guest model)
REM Set  MSCSShopperStorage = Server.CreateObject("Commerce.DBStorage")
REM Call MSCSShopperStorage.InitStorage(MSCSDataSource, ↵
    "ClockPed_shopper", "shopper_id", "Commerce.Dictionary")
```

These statements demonstrate how to create a storage object for storing shopper information in the database. (The Clock Peddler store does not retain shopper information; therefore, these statements are commented out.) The **CreateObject** method creates an instance of a **DBStorage** object. The **Set** statement assigns it to the variable name *MSCSShopperStorage*. The **Call** statement initializes the *MSCSShopperStorage* object. The *MSCSDatasource* parameter specifies the connect string (as defined in the **AddDatasource** method of the **Content** object, earlier in the GLOBAL.ASA file). The *ClockPed_shopper* parameter specifies the name of the database table that is to be used, and the *shopper_id* parameter specifies the primary key in that table. The **Commerce.Dictionary** parameter specifies that the data passed to or retrieved by the **DBStorage** object will be stored in a **Dictionary** object.

```
REM -- Create a storage object for the Order Forms (shopper's basket)
Set  MSCSOrderFormStorage = Server.CreateObject("Commerce.DBStorage")
Call MSCSOrderFormStorage.InitStorage(MSCSDataSource, ↵
    "ClockPed_basket", "shopper_id", "Commerce.OrderForm", ↵
    "marshalled_order", "date_changed")
```

These statements create a storage object for storing Order Forms in the database. The **CreateObject** method creates another instance of a **DBStorage** object. The **Set** statement assigns it to the variable name *MSCSOrderFormStorage*. This object will be used for storing the shopper's Order Form for use by the Order Processing Pipeline. The **Call** statement initializes the *MSCSOrderFormStorage* object. The *MSCSDatasource* parameter specifies the database connect string (as defined earlier in the GLOBAL.ASA file). The *ClockPed_basket* parameter specifies the name of the database table where the order data is to be stored, and the *shopper_id* parameter specifies the primary key in that table. The **Commerce.OrderForm** parameter specifies that the data passed to or retrieved by the **DBStorage** object will be stored in an **OrderForm** object. The *marshalled_order* and *date_changed* parameters specify the column names for the Order Form data. (The entire Order Form is stored in encoded form in the *marshalled_order* column, and the date of the **InsertData** or **CommitData** event is automatically stored in the *date_changed* column.)

```
REM -- Example storage object for receipts
REM Set  MSCSReceiptStorage = Server.CreateObject("Commerce.DBStorage")
REM call MSCSReceiptStorage.InitStorage(MSCSDataSource, ⏎
    "ClockPed_receipt", "order_id", "Commerce.OrderForm", ⏎
    "marshalled_receipt", "date_entered)
```

These statements demonstrate how to set up storage of shopper receipts in the database. The **CreateObject** method creates an instance of a **DBStorage** object, which is given the variable name *X!O!A!MSCSReceiptStorage*. The **InitStorage** method initializes the storage object with the datasource (specified by *MSCSDatasource*) and the name of the database table (*ClockPed_receipt*A*). The *order_id* parameter specifies the primary key in that table. The **Commerce.OrderForm** parameter specifies that the data passed to or retrieved by the **DBStorage** object will be stored in an **OrderForm** object. The *marshalled_receipt* and *date_entered* parameters specify the column names that determine what receipt data is saved. (The entire Order Form is stored in encoded form in the *marshalled_receipt* column, and the date of the **InsertData** or **CommitData** event is automatically stored in the *date_entered* column.)

```
REM -- Example database traffic server
REM Set  MSCSTraffic = Server.CreateObject("Commerce.TrafficTable")
REM call MSCSTraffic.InitTraffic(MSCSDataSource, "ClockPed", ⏎
    "ClockPed_traffic")
```

The statements in this section are an example showing how to set up storage of traffic data in the database. The **CreateObject** method creates an instance of a **TrafficTable** object, which is assigned the variable name *MSCSTraffic*. The **Init-Traffic** method initializes the object with the datasource (specified by **MSCSData-Source**), the name of the store (*ClockPed*), and the name of the database table (*ClockPed_traffic*) to be used for storing traffic data.

```
REM -- Example file traffic server
REM Set  MSCSTraffic = Server.CreateObject("Commerce.TrafficLogfile")
REM call MSCSTraffic.InitTraffic("ClockPed", "c:\ClockPed_traffic.log", ⏎
    "store_name", "shopper_id")
```

The statements in this section are an example showing how to set up storage of traffic data in a log file. The **CreateObject** method creates an instance of a **TrafficLogfile** object, which is assigned the variable name *MSCSTraffic*. The **InitTraffic** method initializes the object with the name of the store (*ClockPed*), and the full path name of the log file (c:\CLOCKPED_TRAFFIC.LOG) to be used for storing traffic data. The *store_name* and *shopper_id* parameters specify what traffic data is to be logged.

```
REM -- Create a data functions object for validation
Set  MSCSDataFunctions = ⤶
     Server.CreateObject("Commerce.DataFunctions")
MSCSDataFunctions.Locale = &H0409
```

The **CreateObject** method creates an instance of the **DataFunctions** object. The **Set** statement assigns it to the variable name *MSCSDataFunctions*. This object performs string conversion and validation. The **Locale** property specifies the Windows country code for the United States, which is used to determine the proper format for money, time, and dates.

```
REM -- Set up the Application intrinsic object
Application.Lock
```

The **Lock** method locks the **Application** object so no conflicts occur when setting its variables.

```
Set Application("MSCSContent")         = MSCSContent
Set Application("MSCSOrderPipeline")    = MSCSOrderPipeline
Set Application("MSCSOrderFormStorage") = MSCSOrderFormStorage
Set Application("MSCSShopperManager")   = MSCSShopperManager
Set Application("MSCSMessageManager")   = MSCSMessageManager
Set Application("MSCSDataFunctions")    = MSCSDataFunctions

REM Set Application("MSCSShopperStorage") = MSCSShopperStorage
REM Set Application("MSCSReceiptStorage") = MSCSReceiptStorage
REM Set Application("MSCSTraffic")        = MSCSTraffic
```

These statements store object references as variables in the **Application** object, thereby making the objects' methods and properties available on subsequent Web pages. The variables must have the exact names shown above in bold text because other objects expect these strings. The commented *MSCSShopperStorage*, *MSCSReceiptStorage*, and *MSCSTraffic* statements are examples that show the statements that would be necessary if the Clock Peddler store saved shopper information, receipts, and traffic data in the database.

```
Application("MSCSDefaultDatasource") = "ClockPed"
```

This statement creates and stores the **MSCSDefaultDatasource** variable in the **Application** object. The **MSCSDefaultDatasource** variable specifies the name of the datasource used for the Clock Peddler store (as defined earlier in the GLOBAL.ASA file using the **AddDatasource** method on the **Content** object). This **Application** variable must have the exact name **MSCSDefaultDatasource**.

```
REM -- uncomment the next line if you use "url" for ⅋
    ShopperManager above
REM Application("MSCSSIDURLKey") = "mscssid"
```

This statement is included as an example to demonstrate how to specify the string that is used to pass the shopper ID from page to page in the URL. The statement is not used in the Clock Peddler store because the shopper ID is stored in the cookie. (Whether the store puts the shopper ID into a cookie, the URL, or both is specified when initializing the **MSCSShopperManager** object, earlier in the GLOBAL.ASA file.) If you use the URL, you must set this variable; otherwise, the **MSCSShopperManager** object will be unable to get the shopper ID argument from the URL. The value of this variable (in this case, *mscssid*) is a string used as an argument in the URL. For example:

```
Http://hostname/aw/Default.asp?mscssid=8DMR9UGXF5SH2H1K0GM009BKFWWVADFQ
Application("MSCSDisableHTTPS") = 1
```

This statement creates and stores the **MSCSDisableHTTPS** variable in the **Application** object. Setting this variable to 1 turns off the use of secure HTTP. The **MSCSDisableHTTPS** variable is useful for debugging and testing a new store because page generation is faster; however the value should be set to 0 to enable secure HTTP when the store goes online. This **Application** variable must have the exact name **MSCSDisableHTTPS**.

```
Application("MSCSInsecureHostName") = ""    ' use this host
Application("MSCSSecureHostName")   = ""    ' use this host
```

This statement creates and stores the **MSCSInsecureHostName** and **MSCSSecureHostName** variables in the **Application** object. The two host name variables specify the names of the server(s) used for secure and insecure store ports. If no server is specified, the default is the current host machine (the *hostname* that appears in the URL: *http://hostname/ClockPed*). These **Application** variables must have the exact names **MSCSInsecureHostName** and **MSCSSecureHostName**.

```
REM --------------------------------------------
REM CONSTANTS
REM --------------------------------------------
Application("StoreName") = "The Clock Peddler"
```

This statement creates a constant called *StoreName* and assigns its value as *The Clock Peddler*.

```
Application.Unlock
```

The **Unlock** method unlocks the **Application** object so other clients can once again modify its variables.

```
End Sub
```

This statement ends the **Application_OnStart** event.

Setting Up Page Variables

The SHOP.ASP file is included in every Clock Peddler store template. Its purpose is to set page variables and to generate a shopper ID. This section explains the statements that appear in the SHOP.ASP file. Please use Windows Notepad or another text editor to refer to the \CLOCKPED\SHOP\IINCLUDE\SHOP.ASP file while reading this section.

```
REM -- set up page vars:
Set mscsPage = Server.CreateObject("Commerce.Page")
```

The **CreateObject** method generates an instance of the **Page** object. The **Page** object provides access to methods that facilitate the layout of the page and run various stages of the Order Processing Pipeline. The **Set** statement assigns the **Page** object to the variable name *mscsPage*.

```
REM -- get application vars:
Set MSCSDataSource = Application("MSCSContent")("ClockPed")
```

This statement assigns the *ClockPed* datasource stored in the **Content** object to the variable name *MSCSDataSource*. This property is accessible because the **Content** object is stored in the **Application** object.

```
Set MSCSShopperManager = Application("MSCSShopperManager")
```

This statement creates a page variable named *MSCSShopperManager* and assigns its value as the global **MSCSShopperManager** in the **Application** object. The **MSCSShopperManager** object generates shopper IDs.

```
Set MSCSOrderFormStorage = Application("MSCSOrderFormStorage")
```

This statement creates a local page variable named *MSCSOrderFormStorage* and assigns its value as the global **MSCSOrderFormStorage** variable in the **Application** object. The **MSCSOrderFormStorage** object is used for storing the shopper's Order Form for use by the Order Processing Pipeline.

```
Set MSCSDataFunctions = Application("MSCSDataFunctions")
```

This statement creates a local page variable named *MSCSDataFunctions* and assigns its value as the global **MSCSDataFunctions** variable in the **Application** object. The **MSCSDataFunctions** object performs string conversion and validation.

```
REM -- manually create shopper id
ShopperID = mscsPage.GetShopperId
```

The **GetShopperId** method gets the shopper ID from the cookie, and it is then assigned the variable name *ShopperID*.

```
if IsNull(ShopperID) then
```

If the shopper ID is null (that is, if no shopper ID was found in the cookie), then the following statements are executed.

```
ShopperID = MSCSShopperManager.CreateShopperID()
```

The **CreateShopperID** method generates a new shopper ID, and it is assigned the variable name *ShopperID*.

```
Call mscsPage.PutShopperId(ShopperID)
```

The **PutShopperId** method stores the newly created shopper ID in the cookie (because the Clock Peddler GLOBAL.ASA file specifies "cookie"). In addition, it stores the shopper ID in the **Page** object for the duration of the page.

```
end if
```

This statement ends the set of conditional statements.

```
REM -- page color constant:
color_clockpedbg = "#FFFFC0"
```

This statement defines a constant named *color_clockpedbg*. The value of the constant is the HTML color #FFFFC0.

THE CLOCK PEDDLER STORE TEMPLATES

The Clock Peddler store uses a simple two-level hierarchy: individual products are contained within departments. The store requires one template to display the departments and another template to display the products. A third template generates the lobby page:

- The lobby page is generated by the DEFAULT.ASP template.

- The department page is generated by the DEPT.ASP template.

- The product pages are generated by the PRODUCT.ASP template.

Several other Active Server Pages templates generate the pages used during the purchasing process. Some templates (whose file names begin with "XT_") perform behind-the-scenes processing, while others generate the pages displayed to the shopper:

- When the shopper clicks the Add To Basket button on a product page, the XT_ORDERFORM_ADDITEM.ASP template adds the item to the Order Form on the server.

- The Shopping Basket page, which shows the shopper the items currently in the Order Form, is generated by the BASKET.ASP template.

- When the shopper edits the quantity of an item, deletes an item, or clears all items, the XT_ORDERFORM_UPDATE.ASP template makes the changes to the Order Form on the server.

- The Address Form page, on which the shopper specifies the shipping and billing addresses, is generated by the ORDERFORM.ASP template.

- When the shopper clicks the Total button on the Address Form page, the XT_ORDERFORM_PREPARE.ASP template processes the address on the server.

- The Credit Card Information page, on which the shopper enters payment information, is generated by the PURCHASE.ASP template.

- When the shopper clicks the Purchase button on the Credit Card Information page, the XT_ORDERFORM_PURCHASE.ASP template processes the payment @BL = information on the server.

- The Purchase Confirmation page, which displays the order tracking number, is generated by the CONFIRMED.ASP template.

By examining in detail the structure of the .ASP templates, you can see how pages are generated dynamically. The statements on the template page run queries or perform other actions resulting in data being displayed on the generated Web page. As you build your own online store, it is crucial that you understand these interrelationships.

Use Windows Notepad or another text editor to examine the Active Server Pages template files in the \CLOCKPED directory. Launch the Clock Peddler store, visit each page, and use the View Source command on your browser to examine the HTML markup generated from the template. The statements used in each major template are explained in detail in the following sections.

The Clock Peddler Store Lobby

The lobby is the entrance to the store. It contains a dynamically generated list of the departments in which shoppers can shop.

The DEFAULT.ASP template

The DEFAULT.ASP template, located in the \Clockped\Shop folder, generates the lobby page. This section explains the statements that appear in this template. Please use Windows Notepad or another text editor to refer to the MAIN.ASP template file while reading this section.

```
<!--#INCLUDE FILE="include/shop.asp" -->
```

This statement includes the SHOP.ASP file, which sets page variables.

```
<!--#INCLUDE FILE="include/header.asp" -->
```

This statement includes the HEADER.ASP template, which generates the header at the top of the page.

```
<UL>
<% set depts = MSCSDataSource.Execute("departments") %>
```

The **Execute** method runs the query named *departments*. This query was stored in the **Content** object by a statement in the GLOBAL.ASA file. The **Set** statement assigns the variable name *depts** to the returned Data Set.

```
<% for each dept in depts %>
    <LI><A HREF="<% = mscsPage.URL("dept.asp", "dept_id", ⏎
        dept.dept_id) %>"><% = mscsPage.Encode(dept.dept_name) ⏎
        %></A>
    <% next %>
</UL>
```

The **For Each...Next** statement repeats the enclosed statements for each row of the *depts* data. The standard HTML <LI> tag is applied to format each row as a list item. The **URL** method on the **MSCSPage** object generates a URL to the DEPT.ASP template with the specified argument. The *dept_id* parameter specifies the argument that will be passed in the URL, and the *dept.dept_id* parameter specifies the value to be used for the *dept_id* argument (the number of the current row in the *depts* data). The **Encode** method on the **MSCSPage** object displays the result of the *dept.dept_name* expression, which is the name of the department in the current row of the *depts* data. Each row of the *depts* data is processed similarly. Note that this code automatically reflects the change if you add or remove a department from your store.

The **URL** method automatically retrieves the virtual directory for the application (either /STORENAME or /STORENAME_MGR, depending on the location of the GLOBAL.ASA file that initialized the current application), and adds the actual path to the URL (in this case, *http://hostname/ClockPed*). In stores in which the shopper ID is passed in the URL, the **URL** method also adds the shopper ID to the end of the resulting URL. The following illustration shows the HTML that is generated by the **For Each...Next** statement and its enclosed statements:

```
<!--#INCLUDE FILE="include/footer.asp" -->
```

This statement includes the FOOTER.ASP template, which generates the footer at the bottom of the page. Included files are stored in the \ClockPed\Shop\Include folder.

The Clock Peddler Department Page

When the shopper clicks a department link on the lobby page, the URL for that link passes the *dept_id* argument to the template processor. The *dept_id* argument is used to look up the appropriate department's data when generating the department page.

The DEPT.ASP template

The DEPT.ASP template generates the department page. This section explains the statements that appear in this template. Please use Windows Notepad or another text editor to refer to the DEPT.ASP template file while reading this section.

```
<!--#INCLUDE FILE="include/shop.asp" -->
```

This statement includes the SHOP.ASP file, which sets page variables.

```
<!--#INCLUDE FILE="include/header.asp" -->
```

This statement includes the HEADER.ASP template, which generates the header at the top of the page.

```
on error resume next
```

This statement turns off error handling to ensure that the next statement will not generate an error. This is necessary because in VBScript, the **set** statement expects an object, but the following **set** statement could return either an object or Null (which would ordinarily result in an error). Error handling is reinstated immediately following the next statement by the **On Error Goto 0** statement.

```
set deptinfo = MSCSDataSource.Execute("department", ↵
    CLng(Request("dept_id")))(0)
```

The IIS **Request** object retrieves the value of the *dept_id* argument from the URL or posted form field, and the **CLng** function expresses the value as an integer. The **Execute** method runs the specified query (*department*), passing it the *dept_id*, and returns a **SimpleList**. The 0 parameter specifies that only the first record in the list is used, and that record is assigned the variable name *deptinfo*. Note that for consistency, the **Execute** method always returns a list, even if the query selects only a single record. Therefore, it is necessary to explicitly specify the row, even though in this case, there is only one row.

```
on error goto 0
```

This statement reinstates error handling that was disabled earlier with the **On Error Resume Next** statement.

```
if Not IsEmpty(deptinfo) then %>
```

The **If** statement specifies that if the *deptinfo* variable has been initialized with a value (that is, if there are departments), then the following statement is run.

```
<H1><% = mscsPage.Encode(deptinfo.dept_name) %></H1>
```

The **Encode** method displays the department name on the page. The *dept_name* property returns the value in the *dept_name* field in the *deptinfo* query result set.

```
<% = mscsPage.Encode(deptinfo.dept_description) %>
```

The **Encode** method displays the description of the department on the page. The *dept_description* property returns the value in the *dept_description* field in the *deptinfo* query result set.

```
<% set deptproducts = MSCSDataSource.Execute("products-by-dept", ↵
   CLng(Request("dept_id"))) %>
```

The **Request** object retrieves the value of the *dept_id* argument from the URL, and the **CLng** function expresses the value as an integer. The **Execute** method runs the specified query (*products-by-dept*), passing it the *dept_id*. The result set is assigned the variable name *deptproducts*.

```
<UL>
<% for each product in deptproducts %>
   <LI><A HREF="<% = mscsPage.URL("product.asp", "sku", product.sku) ↵
      %>"><% = mscsPage.Encode(product.name) %></A>
   by <% = mscsPage.Encode(product.manufacturer) %>
   <% next %>
</UL>
```

The **For Each...Next** statement repeats the enclosed statements for each row of the *deptproducts* data. The standard HTML <LI> tag is applied to format each row as a list item. The **URL** method on the **MSCSPage** object generates a URL to the PRODUCT.ASP template. The *sku* parameter specifies the argument that will be passed in the URL, and the *product.sku* parameter specifies the value to be used for the *sku* argument (the sku for the current row in the *deptproducts* data). The **Encode** method on the **MSCSPage** object displays the result of the product.name expression, which is the name of the product in the current row of the *deptproducts* data.

The **URL** method automatically retrieves the virtual directory for the application (either /STORENAME or /STORENAME_MGR, depending on the location of the GLOBAL.ASA file that initialized the current application), and adds the actual path to the URL (in this case, *http://hostname/Clockped*). In stores in which the shopper ID is passed in the URL, the **URL** method also adds the shopper ID to the end of the resulting URL. The following illustration shows the HTML that is generated by the **For Each...Next** statement and its enclosed statements:

```
<% else %>
   <p>
   Department not available
```

If *dept_info* is Null (that is, if there is no department information), the words *Department not available* are displayed on the generated page.

```
<% end if %>
```

This ends the **If...Then...Else** construct that specifies the page elements to be displayed depending on whether there is department information in the result set.

```
<!--#INCLUDE FILE="include/footer.asp" -->
```

This statement includes the FOOTER.ASP template, which generates the footer at the bottom of the page. Included files are located in the \ClockPed\Shop\Include folder.

The Clock Peddler Product Pages

When the shopper clicks a product link on the department page, the URL for that link passes the sku argument to the template processor. The sku argument specifies which product's data is used in generating the product page.

The PRODUCT.ASP template

The PRODUCT.ASP template generates the product pages. This section explains the statements that appear in this template. Please use Windows Notepad or another text editor to refer to the PRODUCT.ASP template file while reading this section.

```
<!--#INCLUDE FILE="include/shop.asp" -->
```

This statement includes the SHOP.ASP file, which sets page variables.

```
<TITLE>Product '<% = Request("sku") %>'</TITLE>
```

This statement sets the <TITLE> tag for the page. The **Request** object returns the value of the *sku* argument in the HTTP request.

```
<!--#INCLUDE FILE="include/header.asp" -->
```

This statement includes the HEADER.ASP template, which generates the header at the top of the page.

```
on error resume next
```

This statement turns off error handling to ensure that the next statement will not generate an error. This is necessary because in VBScript, the **Set** statement expects an object, but the following **Set** statement could return either an object or Null (which would ordinarily result in an error). Error handling is reinstated immediately following the next statement by the **On Error Goto 0** statement.

```
set product = MSCSDataSource.Execute("product", ⤶
    Cstr(Request("sku")))(0)
```

The **Request** object returns the value of the *sku* argument from the HTTP Request, and the **Cstr** function expresses the value as a string. The **Execute** method runs the specified query (*product*), passing it the sku. The result set is assigned the variable name *product*. The 0 parameter specifies that only the first record in the list is used, and that record is assigned the variable name *product*. Note that for consistency, the **Execute** method always returns a list, even if the query selects only a single record. Therefore, it is necessary to explicitly specify the row, even though, in this case, there is only one row.

```
on error goto 0
```

This statement reinstates error handling that was disabled earlier with the **On Error Resume Next** statement.

```
if Not IsEmpty(product) then %>
```

The **If** statement specifies that if the *product* variable has been initialized with a value (that is, if there are products), then the following statement is run.

```
<H1><% = mscsPage.Encode(product.name) %> by ↵
    <% = mscsPage.Encode(product.manufacturer) %></H1>
```

This statement displays the name and manufacturer of the product on the page. The **name** property returns the value of the name field in the *product* data. The **Encode** method displays the value on the page. The **manufacturer** property returns the value of the manufacturer field in the *product* data. The **Encode** method displays the value on the page.

```
<% if Not IsNull(product.image_file) then %>
```

This **If...Then...Else** construct specifies the page elements to be displayed depending on whether there is an image file in the result set. The **image_file** property returns the value of the *image_file* field in the *product* data. If the value is not equal to Null (that is, if the file name of an image is stored there), the following statements are executed.

```
<IMG SRC="/ClockPed_assets/prodimg/<% ↵
    = mscsPage.Encode(product.image_file) %>"
WIDTH="<% = mscsPage.Encode(product.image_width) %>"
HEIGHT="<% = mscsPage.Encode(product.image_height) %>">
```

The *image_file* property returns the value of the *image_file* field (a file name) in the *product* data. The **Encode** method displays the file name in the <IMG SRC> tag. The **image_width** and **image_height** properties return the values of the corresponding fields in the product data, and the **Encode** methods display the values in the WIDTH= and HEIGHT= attributes of the <IMG SRC> tag.

```
<% else %>
Image not available
```

If the value of the *image_file* field in the product data is Null (that is, if there is no image file), the **Not IsNull** statement (located just inside the table tag) returns FALSE, and the words *Image not available* are displayed on the generated page.

```
<% end if %>
```

This ends the **If...Then...Else** construct that specifies the page elements to be displayed depending on whether there is an image file name in the result set.

```
<% = MSCSDataFunctions.Money(product.list_price) %>
```

The **list_price** property returns the value of the *list_price* field (an integer) in the *product* data. The **Money** method formats the value appropriately according to the following entry in the GLOBAL.ASA file: *MSCSDataFunctions.Locale = &H0409*, which specifies the locale code for the United States.

```
<A HREF="<% = mscsPage.URL("xt_orderform_additem.asp", "sku", ⤸
    product.sku) %>"><IMG SRC="/MSCS_images/buttons/btnaddbskt1.gif"⤸
    WIDTH="112" HEIGHT="24" BORDER="0" ALT="Add to Basket" ⤸
    ALIGN="MIDDLE"></A>
```

These statements call the template that adds the product to the shopper's basket. The **URL** method generates a URL to the specified template (XT_ORDER-FORM_ADDITEM.ASP) and passes it the argument *sku*, with its value equal to the value of the *sku* field in the *product* data. When the shopper clicks the **Add To Basket** button, the XT_ORDERFORM_ADDITEM.ASP template is invoked on the server. For more information about the processing that occurs in this template, see "Adding Items to the Shopping Basket" on the next page.

```
<% if Not IsNull(product.description) then %> ⤸
    <% = product.description %><% end if %>
```

If the *description* field in the *product* data is not empty (that is, if there is a description), then the description is displayed on the page.

```
<% else %>
<p>Product not available
```

If the *description* field in the *product* data is empty, then the words *Product not available* are displayed on the generated page.

```
<% end if %>
```

This ends the **If...Then...Else** construct that specifies the page elements to be displayed depending on the number of products in the result set.

```
<% REM   footer: %>
<!--#INCLUDE FILE="include/footer.asp" -->
```

This statement includes the FOOTER.ASP template, which generates the footer at the bottom of the page. Included files are located in the \ClockPed\Shop\Include folder.

The Header and Footer on Clock Peddler Pages

If the same item is used on a number of different pages, it is most efficient to create that item once, store it, then include it on every page where it is needed. The header and footer used on every Clock Peddler page are generated by .ASP templates that are included on the page template by the following statements:

```
<!--#INCLUDE FILE="include/header.asp" -->
<!--#INCLUDE FILE="include/footer.asp" -->
```

The header contains the Clock Peddler logo, the navigation bar, and a horizontal rule (line). The header is created by the HEADER.ASP template.

The footer contains a horizontal rule (line), the store slogan, and the copyright statement. The footer is created by the FOOTER.ASP template.

THE CLOCK PEDDLER SHOPPING PROCESS

The shopping process consists of the following steps:

1. Adding items to the Shopping Basket

2. Displaying the Shopping Basket

3. Modifying the Basket contents

4. Gathering the address information

5. Processing the address information

6. Gathering credit-card information

7. Placing the order

8. Displaying the purchase confirmation

   Each step is further discussed below.

Adding Items to the Shopping Basket

A shopper adds an item to the shopping basket by clicking the **Add to Basket** button on a Product page (PRODUCT ASP). A script on the PRODUCT.ASP template invokes the XT_ORDERFORM_ADDITEM.ASP template, which adds the item to the basket. For information about the PRODUCT.ASP template, see "The Clock Peddler Product Pages" later in this section.

The XT_ORDERFORM_ADDITEM.ASP template

The XT_ORDERFORM_ADDITEM.ASP template is called when the shopper clicks the **Add To Basket** button on a Product page. This template adds an item or items to the basket, and then displays the Shopping Basket page.

Note that the first part of the template consists of a function declaration. The processing does not actually begin until the **Call** statement near the end of the template.

This section explains the statements that appear in this template. Please use Windows Notepad or another text editor to refer to the XT_ORDERFORM_ADD-ITEM.ASP template file while reading this section.

```
function OrderFormAddItem(byVal orderFormStorage, byVal shopperID)
```

This section declares the **OrderFormAddItem** function and its arguments. The arguments pass the Order Form storage object and the shopper ID.

```
product_qty = 1
```

This statement creates the *product_qty* page variable and sets its value to 1.

```
REM -- retrieve sku:
set product_sku = Request("sku")
```

The **Request** object returns the value of the *sku* argument that the browser passed from the Product page. The **Set** statement assigns this value to the *product_sku* variable name.

```
REM -- retrieve Order Form from storage:
on error resume next
```

This statement turns off error handling to ensure that the next statement will not generate an error. This is necessary because in VBScript, the **Set** statement expects an object, but the following **set** statement could return either an object or Null (which would ordinarily result in an error). Error handling is reinstated immediately following the next statement by the **On Error Goto 0** statement.

```
set orderForm = orderFormStorage.GetData(null, shopperID)
```

The **GetData** method uses the **orderFormStorage** object to retrieve the Order Form data for the given shopper ID. The **Set** statement assigns the data to the *orderForm* variable name.

```
on error goto 0
```

This statement reinstates error handling that was disabled earlier with the **On Error Resume Next** statement.

```
if IsEmpty(orderForm) then
```

If an Order Form is not found, the following statements are run to create an Order Form.

```
REM -- create a new orderform:
    set orderForm = Server.CreateObject("Commerce.OrderForm")
    orderForm.shopper_id = shopperID
    orderForm.date_created = Now
```

The **CreateObject** method creates an instance of the **OrderForm** object, and gives it the variable name *orderForm*. The next statement takes the shopper ID and inserts it into the **shopper_id** property of the **orderForm** object. The **Now** function returns the current date and time according to the computer's system date and time, and the resulting value is stored in the *date_created* property of the **order-Form** object.

```
REM -- add item to orderform:
    set item = orderForm.AddItem(CStr(product_sku), product_qty, 0)
```

The **AddItem** method takes three parameters: *product_sku*, *product_qty*, and *placed_price*. The value of zero (0) for placed_price specifies that the value of the required **list_price** column in the ClockPed_product table should be used. The **AddItem** method adds an item dictionary to the items list on the Order Form, and then stores the values for *product_sku*, *product_qty*, and *placed_price* in the dictionary. This item is then assigned the variable name *item*.

```
REM -- insert orderform in storage:
call orderFormStorage.InsertData(null, orderForm)
```

The **InsertData** method saves the Order Form data to the database.

```
else
  REM -- add item to orderform:
  set item = orderForm.AddItem(CStr(product_sku), product_qty, 0)
```

If an Order Form does exist, the **AddItem** method adds an item dictionary to the items list on the Order Form, and then stores the values for *product_sku*, *product_qty*, and *placed_price* in the item dictionary. This item is then assigned the variable name *item*.

```
REM -- commit orderform back to storage:
    call orderFormStorage.CommitData(null, orderForm)
```

The **CommitData** method updates the existing Order Form data in the database with the new item data.

```
end function %>
```

This statement marks the end of the function declaration that began at the top of the page.

Note The execution of the function occurs in the following statements.

```
<!--#INCLUDE FILE="include/shop.asp" -->
```

This statement includes the SHOP.ASP file, which provides the Order Form storage object and the shopper ID, both of which are used as arguments to the function.

```
<%
Call OrderFormAddItem(MSCSOrderFormStorage, ShopperID)
```

This statement runs the **OrderFormAddItem** function defined in the top section of this template, passing it the Order Form storage object and the shopper ID as arguments.

```
REM -- go to basket page:
Response.Redirect mscsPage.URL("BASKET.ASP")
```

This statement displays the Basket page after the item has been added to the Order Form. The **URL** method generates the URL to the BASKET.ASP template, and the **Redirect** method causes the browser to attempt to connect to the resulting URL.

Displaying the Shopping Basket

The Shopping Basket page displays a list of the products the shopper has added to the basket, along with price information. On the Shopping Basket page, the shopper can modify the quantity of an item, delete any or all items from the basket, or proceed with the purchase. For information about editing the quantity or deleting items, see "Modifying the Basket Contents" later in this section.

The Shopping Basket must contain at least one item before the purchase process can begin. The shopper initiates the purchase by clicking either the **Pay** button on the navigation bar at the top of the page or the **Purchase** button on the Shopping Basket page, at which point the Address page is displayed so the shopper can enter a ship-to address. See "Gathering the Address Information" later in this section.

The BASKET.ASP template

The BASKET.ASP template generates the Shopping Basket page. This section explains the statements that appear in this template. Please use Windows Notepad or another text editor to refer to the BASKET.ASP template file while reading this section.

```
<%@ LANGUAGE = VBScript %>
```

This statement specifies that the scripts on the page are written in VBScript.

```
<% Response.Buffer = TRUE %>
```

The **Buffer** property indicates whether to buffer the page output (wait to send a response to the client until all the server scripts on the page have been processed or until a **Flush** or **End** statement). The property is set to TRUE in the Clock Peddler store, which indicates that no output is sent to the client until all scripts have been processed.

```
<% Response.Expires = 0 %>
```

The **Expires** property specifies the length of time before a cached page expires. If the shopper returns to this page before it expires, the cached page is displayed. In the Clock Peddler store, this property is set to 0, which specifies that the cached page expires immediately (essentially, the page is not cached). Therefore, the basket will be regenerated each time the shopper sees it.

```
<!--#INCLUDE FILE="include/shop.asp" -->
```

This statement includes the SHOP.ASP file, which sets page variables.

```
<%
on error resume next
```

This statement turns off error handling to ensure that the next statement will not generate an error. This is necessary because in VBScript, the **Set** statement expects an object, but the following **Set** statement could return either an object or Null (which would ordinarily result in an error). Error handling is reinstated immediately following the next statement by the **On Error Goto 0** statement.

```
set mscsOrderForm = MSCSOrderFormStorage.GetData(null, ShopperID)
```

The **GetData** method retrieves the Order Form from the database for the shopper identified by the shopper ID. The **set** statement assigns the data to the *mscsOrderForm* variable name.

```
on error goto 0
```

This statement reinstates error handling that was disabled earlier with the **On Error Resume Next** statement.

```
if IsNull(mscsOrderForm) or IsEmpty(mscsOrderForm) then
```

The **IsNull** function returns TRUE if the *mscsOrderForm* variable contains no valid data (which indicates that no items have yet been added to the basket). The **IsEmpty** function returns True if the *mscsOrderForm* variable is uninitialized (that is, if a basket has not yet been created). If either is True, the following statements are run to create an Order Form.

```
Set mscsOrderForm = Server.CreateObject("Commerce.OrderForm")
```

The **CreateObject** method creates an instance of the **OrderForm** object and assigns it the variable name *mscsOrderForm*.

```
orderFormItems = null
nOrderFormItems = 0
```

These statements set these page variables to Null and 0, indicating that there are no items on the Order Form.

```
else
```

If the **IsNull** function returns FALSE (which indicates that there are one or more items in the basket), the following statements are run.

```
mscsPage.RunPlan(mscsOrderForm)
```

The **RunPlan** method invokes the Order Processing Pipeline and processes the *mscsOrderForm* through all pipeline components except payment and acceptance. This ensures that the following two statements correctly set the number of items on the Order Form. (If a product no longer exists in the database but still exists on the shopper's Order Form, running the **RunPlan** method deletes that item from the Order Form.)

```
set orderFormItems = mscsOrderForm.Items
```

The **Items** property returns a list of dictionaries—one dictionary for each item in the *mscsOrderForm* data (each dictionary contains a set of name-value pairs specific to the item). The **Set** statement assigns this list to the *orderFormItems* variable name.

```
nOrderFormItems = orderFormItems.Count
```

The **Count** property returns the number of items in the *orderFormItems* list, then the value is assigned to the *nOrderFormItems* variable name.

```
end if
%>
```

This statement ends the conditional code that either creates an Order Form or sets Order Form variables appropriately depending on whether an Order Form exists.

```
<!--#INCLUDE FILE="include/header.asp" -->
```

This statement includes the HEADER.ASP template, which generates the header at the top of the page.

```
<% if Not IsNull(mscsOrderForm) then  %>
```

If the *mscsOrderForm* contains data, then the following error-handling statements are run.

```
<% if mscsOrderForm.[_Basket_Errors].Count > 0 then
```

The **_Basket_Errors** list on the Order Form contains any shopping basket errors generated in the Order Processing Pipeline when the **RunPlan** method was executed. The **Count** property returns the number of errors. This statement specifies that if the number of errors is greater than zero (that is, if there are errors), then the following statements are run.

```
call MSCSOrderFormStorage.CommitData(null, mscsOrderForm) %>
```

The **CommitData** method updates the existing Order Form data in the database.

```
<UL>
    <% for each errorStr in mscsOrderForm.[_Basket_Errors] %>
        <li><% = errorStr %></li>
    <% next %>
</UL>
```

The **For Each...Next** statement iterates through each error string in the **_Basket_Errors** list, displaying each string as a separate list item on the Shopping Basket page.

```
<% end if %>
```

This statement ends the conditional code that displays any errors on the Shopping Basket page.

```
<% end if %>
```

This statement ends the conditional code that invokes error handling if there are items on the Order Form.

```
<% if nOrderFormItems > 0 then %>
```

This **If...Then** statement runs the following statements if the number of items in the Order Form is greater than zero (that is, if there are items in the Order Form).

```
<% if nOrderFormItems > 1 then %>
<P>You have <% = nOrderFormItems %> items in your shopping basket:
```

This **If...Then** statement specifies the text to be displayed on the generated page if there is more than one item in the Order Form.

```
<% else %>
<P>You have <% = nOrderFormItems %> item in your shopping basket:
```

If there is only one item on the Order Form, this statement specifies the text to be displayed on the generated page.

```
<% end if %>
```

This statement marks the end of the conditional code that specifies the text to be displayed, depending on the number of items in the Order Form.

```
<FORM METHOD="POST"
  ACTION="<%= mscsPage.URL("XT_ORDERFORM_UPDATE.ASP", "opcode", ⏎
    "edit_qty") %>">
```

When the shopper clicks the **Update Order** button on the Shopping Basket page, the values of the form elements are sent to the XT_ORDERFORM_UPDATE.ASP template. The **URL** method generates a URL to the specified template (XT_ORDERFORM_UPDATE.ASP) and passes it the argument *opcode*, with its value equal to the string *edit_qty*. For more information, see "Modifying the Basket Contents" later in this section.

```
<% for iLineItem = 0 to nOrderFormItems - 1
```

This **For** statement indicates that the statements between here and the **next** statement should be repeated for each item in the order.

```
set lineItem = orderFormItems(iLineItem) %>
```

The first time through this loop, this **Set** statement sets the value of the variable *lineItem* to the first item in the *orderFormItems* data. The value of *iLineItem* is incremented each time through the loop.

```
<% = lineItem.[_product_sku] %>
```

This statement displays on the page the value of the **_product_sku** property (retrieved from the item dictionary on the Order Form).

```
<INPUT TYPE="TEXT"
    NAME="<% = "qty" & iLineItem %>"
    SIZE="3,1"
    VALUE="<% = mscsPage.Encode(lineItem.quantity) %>">
```

The NAME attribute provides a unique identifier used when the contents of the Qty input field (on the page) are transferred to the server. The **&** operator concatenates the string *qty* with the value of the *iLineItem* variable, and the resulting string is used as the value of NAME. The VALUE attribute specifies the initial value to be displayed in the Qty input field on the generated page. The **quantity** property returns the value of the **quantity** property in the *lineItem* data, and the **Encode** method displays the quantity as the initial value of the field.

```
<% = mscsPage.Encode(lineItem.[_product_name]) %>
```

This statement displays on the page the value of the **_product_name** property (retrieved from the item dictionary on the Order Form).

```
<% = MSCSDataFunctions.Money(lineItem.[_product_list_price]) %>
```

This statement displays on the page the value of the **_product_list_price** property (retrieved from the item dictionary on the Order Form). The **Money** method formats the expression as money and displays the value on the page in the **Unit Price** box. The **Money** method formats the value appropriately according to the following entry in the \SHOP\GLOBAL.ASA file: *MSCSDataFunctions.Locale = &H0409*, which specifies the locale code for the United States.

```
<% = MSCSDataFunctions.Money(lineItem.[_oadjust_adjustedprice]) %>
```

This statement displays on the page the value of the **_oadjust_adjustedprice** property (retrieved from the item dictionary on the Order Form). The **Money** method formats the expression as money and displays the value on the page in the **Total Price** box. The **Money** method formats the value appropriately according to the following entry in the \SHOP\GLOBAL.ASA file: *MSCSDataFunctions.Locale = &H0409,* which specifies the locale code for the United States.

```
<A HREF="<% = mscsPage.URL("XT_ORDERFORM_UPDATE.ASP", "opcode", ⤶
   "delete_item", "item", iLineItem) %>"> <IMG SRC= ⤶
   "/MSCS_Images/buttons/btnremove1.gif" BORDER="0" ALT="Delete item"></A>
```

When the shopper clicks the **Delete** button beside an item, the **URL** method generates a URL to the specified template (XT_ORDERFORM_UPDATE.ASP) and passes it two arguments: *opcode,* with the string *delete_item* as its value, and *item,* with its value equal to the value of *iLineItem.* For more information, see "Modifying the Basket Contents" later in this section.

```
<% next %>
```

This statement indicates the end of processing of the first item in *iLineItem.* The function returns to the for *iLineItem = 0 to nOrderFormItems - 1* statement and repeats until the end of the items.

```
<% = MSCSDataFunctions.Money(mscsOrderForm.[_oadjust_subtotal]) %>
```

This statement displays on the page the value of the **_oadjust_subtotal** property (retrieved from the Order Form). The **Money** method formats the expression as money and displays the value on the page in the **Subtotal** box. The **Money** method formats the value appropriately according to the following entry in the \SHOP\GLOBAL.ASA file: *MSCSDataFunctions.Locale = &H0409,* which specifies the locale code for the United States.

```
<FORM METHOD="POST"
   ACTION="<%= mscsPage.URL("XT_ORDERFORM_UPDATE.ASP", "opcode", ⤶
      "clear_items") %>">
```

When the shopper clicks the **Clear Order** button on the Shopping Basket page, the values of the form elements are sent to the XT_ORDERFORM_UP-DATE.ASP template. The **URL** method generates a URL to the template and passes it the argument *opcode,* with the string *clear_items* as its value.

```
<FORM METHOD="POST"
   ACTION="<% = mscsPage.URL("orderform.asp") %>">
```

When the shopper clicks the **Purchase** button on the Shopping Basket page, the values of the form elements are sent to the ORDERFORM.ASP template. The

URL method generates a URL to the template. For more information, see "Gathering the Address Information" later in this section.

```
<% end if %>
```

This statement marks the end of the conditional code that displays the basket contents on the page.

```
<% if nOrderFormItems = 0 then %>
    <BLOCKQUOTE>
        <STRONG>Your basket is empty.</STRONG>
    </BLOCKQUOTE>
<% end if %>
```

This code displays the words *Your basket is empty* if there are no items in the basket.

```
<% REM   footer: %>
<!--#INCLUDE FILE="include/footer.asp" -->
```

This statement includes the FOOTER.ASP template, which generates the footer at the bottom of the page. Included files are located in the \ClockPed\Shop\Include folder.

Modifying the Basket Contents

On the Shopping Basket page (BASKET.ASP), the shopper can edit the quantity of an item, delete one or more items, or clear all items from the basket. From the Shopping Basket page, the edit, delete, or clear request is sent to the XT_ORDERFORM_UPDATE.ASP template, where the requested action is processed. When the action has been processed, the Shopping Basket page is redisplayed.

The XT_ORDERFORM_UPDATE.ASP template

This template provides the functionality that updates the basket by modifying the quantity of an item, deleting an item, or clearing all items. Note that the first part of the template consists of two function declarations. The processing does not actually begin until the **Call** statement near the end of the template.

This section explains the statements that appear in this template. Please use Windows Notepad or another text editor to refer to the XT_ORDERFORM_UP-DATE.ASP template file while reading this section.

```
<%
function ItemUpdate(byRef orderForm, byVal opcode)
```

This section of the template declares the **ItemUpdate** function and its arguments. The arguments pass the Order Form and the *opcode* (which is passed from the BASKET.ASP template).

```
if Request("item").Count <> 1 then
   ItemUpdate = false
      exit function
end if
```

The **Count** property returns the number of *item* arguments in the HTTP request. If the number is anything other than 1 (an error condition), the *ItemUpdate* variable is set to FALSE and the function ends. The item argument is used to identify a specific item to be deleted when the shopper clicks that item's **Remove Item** button; therefore, only one *item* argument is passed from the Shopping Basket page at a time.

```
item_index = Request("item")
```

This statement creates an *item_index* variable and sets it equal to the value of the *item* argument that was passed from the Basket page.

```
set orderItems = orderForm.Items
```

The **Items** property returns a list of dictionaries—one dictionary for each item in the *orderForm* data (each dictionary contains a set of name-value pairs specific to the item). The **Set** statement assigns this list to the *orderItems* variable name.

```
set item = orderItems(item_index)
```

The **Set** statement creates a variable named *item* and sets its value to the value of the **item_index** property in the *orderItems* data.

```
select case opcode
```

The **Select Case** statement runs the following **Case** statement, depending on the value of the *opcode* argument (which is passed in from the preceding page in the URL).

```
case "delete_item"
```

If the value of the *opcode* argument passed from the preceding page is the string *delete_item*, the following **Call** statement is run.

```
call orderItems.Delete(item_index)
```

The **Delete** method deletes from the items list in the Order Form the item identified by the value of the *item_index* argument.

```
end select
```

This statement marks the end of the **select case** processing.

```
ItemUpdate = true
```

This statement sets the *ItemUpdate* variable to TRUE.

```
end function
```

This statement marks the end of the first function declaration.

```
function OrderFormUpdate(byVal orderFormStorage, byVal page,↵
   byVal shopperID)
```

This section of the template declares the **OrderFormUpdate** function and its arguments. The arguments pass the Order Form storage object, the **Page** object, and the shopper ID.

```
REM -- determine the opcode:
if Request("opcode").Count <> 1 then
   REM -- no opcode:
   OrderFormUpdate = false
   exit function
end if
```

The **Count** property returns the number of *opcode* arguments in the HTTP request. If the number is anything other than 1 (an error condition), the *OrderFormUpdate* variable is set to FALSE and the function ends.

```
opcode = Request("opcode")
```

This statement sets the *opcode* variable to the value of the *opcode* argument passed from the Shopping Basket page.

```
REM -- get the Order Form:
on error resume next
```

This statement turns off error handling to ensure that the next statement will not generate an error. This is necessary because in VBScript, the **Set** statement expects an object, but the following **Set** statement could return either an object or Null (which would ordinarily result in an error). Error handling is reinstated immediately following the next statement by the **On Error Goto 0** statement.

```
set orderForm = orderFormStorage.GetData(null, shopperID)
```

The **GetData** method retrieves the Order Form data for the given shopper ID from the database. The **Set** statement assigns the data to the *orderForm* variable name.

```
on error goto 0
```

This statement reinstates error handling that was disabled earlier with the **On Error Resume Next** statement.

```
if IsEmpty(orderForm) then
   OrderFormUpdate = false
   exit function
end if
```

If no Order Form is found, the *OrderFormUpdate* variable is set to FALSE and the function ends.

```
select case opcode
```

The **Select Case** statement runs one of the following two **Case** statements, depending on which one matches the value of the *opcode* argument (which is passed in from the preceding page in the URL).

```
case "delete_item"
```

If the value of the *opcode* argument passed from the preceding page is the string *delete_item*, the following statements are run.

```
if not ItemUpdate(orderForm, opcode) then
    OrderFormUpdate = false
    exit function
end if
```

If the **ItemUpdate** function returns FALSE (if there is no *item* argument in the URL from the Basket page), the *OrderFormUpdate* variable is set to FALSE and the function ends.

```
case "edit_qty"
```

If the value of the *opcode* argument passed from the preceding page is the string *edit_qty*, the following statements are run.

```
set orderItems = orderForm.Items
```

The **Set** statement creates a variable named *orderItems* and sets its value to the value of the **Items** property in the *orderForm* data.

```
for index = orderItems.Count - 1 to 0 step - 1
```

This **For...Next** statement indicates that the statements between here and the **Next** statement should be repeated for each item in the order. The **Count** property returns the number of items in the *orderItems* data. The **step** keyword specifies that the number should be decreased by one each time.

```
set item = orderItems(index)
```

Each time through this loop, this **Set** statement sets the value of the variable item to the item specified by *index* in the *orderItems* data. The value of *index* is decreased by one each time through (this is set by the preceding statement).

```
qty = page.RequestNumber("qty" & index, 0, 0, 999)
```

The current value of *index* is concatenated with the string qty, resulting in an argument key name such as qty1, qty2, and so on. The **RequestNumber** function retrieves the current value of the argument referred to by this constructed key name, converts it to a number datatype, and validates its value against the specified parameters. The first zero (0) parameter is the default value that is used for the argument if no value exists. The second zero parameter specifies the minimum value for the argument, and the **999** parameter specifies the maximum value. The function returns Null if the value is not a number between 0 and 99. No locale value is given; therefore the function uses the default locale specified in the GLOBAL.ASA file.

```
if Not IsNull(qty) then
```

If the *qty* variable has a value, then the following statements are run.

```
if qty = 0 then
    call orderItems.Delete(index)
```

If the value of *qty* for the current item is 0, the **Delete** method deletes the item from the Order Form. (Setting an item's quantity to 0 on the Shopping Basket page is an alternate method of deleting the item.)

```
else
    item.quantity = qty
```

If the *qty* is not 0 (that is, if there is a quantity specified), the value is stored in the **quantity** property of the *item* data.

```
end if
```

This statement ends the conditional processing that either deletes the item or sets its **quantity** property depending on the value of *qty* passed in from the Basket page.

```
else
    REM -- in case of error quantity remains the same
    end if
```

If the value of *qty* is empty, the existing **quantity** property is left unchanged rather than reporting an error.

```
case "clear_items"
    orderForm.ClearItems
```

If the value of the *opcode* argument passed from the Shopping Basket page is the string *clear_items*, then the **ClearItems** method removes all items from the items list on the Order Form.

```
case else
    REM -- invalid opcode:
    OrderFormUpdate = false
    exit function
```

If the value of the *opcode* argument passed from the Shopping Basket page is anything other than *clear_items*, *edit_qty*, or *delete_item*, the *OrderFormUpdate* variable is set to FALSE and the function ends.

```
end select
```

This statement marks the end of the **select case** processing.

```
REM -- write Order Form back to storage:
call orderFormStorage.CommitData(null, orderForm)
```

The **CommitData** method updates the existing Order Form data in the database.

```
OrderFormUpdate = true
```

This statement sets the *OrderFormUpdate* variable to TRUE.

```
end function
%>
```

This statement marks the end of the second function declaration.

NOTE The execution of the functions occurs in the following statements.

```
<!--#INCLUDE FILE="include/shop.asp" -->
```

This statement includes the SHOP.ASP file, which sets page variables.

```
<%
Call OrderFormUpdate(MSCSOrderFormStorage, mscsPage, ShopperID)
```

This statement runs the **OrderFormUpdate** function defined earlier in this template, passing it the Order Form storage object, the **Page** object, and the shopper ID as arguments.

```
REM -- go to basket page:
Response.Redirect MSCSPage.URL("BASKET.ASP")
%>
```

This statement displays the Basket page after the item has been added to the Order Form. The **URL** method generates the URL to the BASKET.ASP template, and the **Redirect** method causes the browser to attempt to connect to the resulting URL.

Gathering the Address Information

After reviewing and (if necessary) modifying the contents of the basket, the shopper begins the actual purchase by clicking either the **Purchase** button on the Shopping Basket page or the **Pay** button on the navigation bar at the top of the page. The Address Form page is then displayed, on which the shopper enters the address to which the merchandise is to be shipped.

Shoppers do not register when shopping at the Clock Peddler online store; therefore, the billing and shipping address must be entered for each order because no shopper address information is retained on the server. (Online stores that gather address information at the time a shopper registers can simply ask the shopper to confirm the existing address information.)

The ORDERFORM.ASP template

The ORDERFORM.ASP template generates the Address Form page. This section explains the statements that appear in this template. Please use Windows Notepad or another text editor to refer to the ORDERFORM.ASP template file while reading this section.

```
<!--#INCLUDE FILE="include/shop.asp" -->
```

This statement includes the SHOP.ASP file, which sets page variables.

```
<%
on error resume next
```

This statement turns off error handling to ensure that the next statement will not generate an error. This is necessary because in VBScript, the **Set** statement expects an object, but the following **Set** statement could return either an object or Null (which would ordinarily result in an error). Error handling is reinstated immediately following the next statement by the **On Error Goto 0** statement.

```
set mscsOrderForm = MSCSOrderFormStorage.GetData(null, ShopperID)
```

The **GetData** method retrieves the Order Form data from the database for the given shopper ID. The **Set** statement assigns the data to the *mscsOrderForm* variable name.

```
on error goto 0
```

This statement reinstates error handling that was disabled earlier with the **On Error Resume Next** statement.

```
if IsNull(mscsOrderForm) or IsEmpty(mscsOrderForm) then
```

The **IsNull** function returns TRUE if the *mscsOrderForm* variable contains no valid data (which indicates that no items have yet been added to the basket). The **IsEmpty** function returns TRUE if the *mscsOrderForm* variable is uninitialized (that is, if an Order Form has not yet been created). If either is TRUE, the following statements are run.

```
Set mscsOrderForm = Server.CreateObject("Commerce.OrderForm")
```

The **CreateObject** method creates an instance of the **OrderForm** object and assigns it the variable name *mscsOrderForm*.

```
mscsOrderItems = null
nOrderFormItems = 0
```

These statements set these page variables to Null and 0, indicating that there are no items in the Order Form.

```
else
```

If the **IsNull** function returns FALSE (which indicates that there are one or more items in the basket), the following statements are run.

```
set orderFormItems = mscsOrderForm.Items
```

The **Items** property returns a list of dictionaries—one dictionary for each item in the *mscsOrderForm* data (each dictionary contains a set of name-value pairs specific to the item). The **Set** statement assigns this list to the *orderFormItems* variable name.

```
nOrderFormItems = orderFormItems.Count
```

The **Count** property returns the number of items in the *orderFormItems* list, then the value is assigned to the *nOrderFormItems* variable name.

```
end if
%>
```

This statement ends the conditional code that either creates an Order Form or sets variables appropriately depending on whether an Order Form exists.

```
<!--#INCLUDE FILE="include/header.asp" -->
```

This statement includes the HEADER.ASP template, which generates the header at the top of the page.

```
<% if nOrderFormItems = 0 then %>
   <BLOCKQUOTE>
      <STRONG>Your basket is empty.</STRONG>
   </BLOCKQUOTE>
```

These statements display the words *Your basket is empty* if there are no items in the basket.

```
<% else %>
```

If there are items in the basket, the subsequent statements are run to generate the address input forms.

```
<TD>
If you need to change any items, please go to the <A HREF="<% ↵
   = mscsPage.URL("BASKET.ASP") %>">shopping basket</A> to ↵
   correct them.
```

The **URL** method generates the URL to the BASKET.ASP template.

```
<FORM METHOD="POST"
   ACTION="<% = mscsPage.URL("xt_orderform_prepare.asp") %>">
   <INPUT TYPE="HIDDEN" NAME="bill_to_country" VALUE="USA">
   <INPUT TYPE="HIDDEN" NAME="ship_to_country" VALUE="USA">
```

When the shopper clicks the **Total** button on the Address Form page, the values of the form fields are sent to the XT_ORDERFORM_PREPARE.ASP template. The **URL** method generates the URL to the XT_ORDERFORM_PREPARE.ASP template.

The **bill_to_country** and **ship_to_country** are posted as HIDDEN fields whose value is *USA*. The **ship_to_country** value is used in the pipeline by the tax component.

```
<INPUT TYPE="TEXT"
   NAME="ship_to_name" SIZE="54,1"
   VALUE="<% = mscsPage.Encode(mscsOrderForm.ship_to_name) %>">
```

The VALUE attribute specifies the initial value to be displayed in the **Name** input field. The **ship_to_name** property returns the value of the corresponding field in the *mscsOrderForm* data, and the **Encode** method displays the name as the initial value of the field. Each of the remaining fields in the address forms on this page is handled in the same way.

```
<% end if %>
```

This statement ends the conditional code that displays either the address forms or the words *Your basket is empty*.

```
<% REM   footer: %>
<!--#INCLUDE FILE="include/footer.asp" -->
```

This statement includes the FOOTER.ASP template, which generates the footer at the bottom of the page.

Processing the Address Information

When the shopper clicks the **Total** button on the Address Form page, the address information is sent to the XT_ORDERFORM_PREPARE.ASP template, where the address information is processed. If the action is successful, the Credit Card Information page is displayed. If an error occurs, the error page is displayed.

The XT_ORDERFORM_PREPARE.ASP template

This template provides the functionality that adds the shopper's address information to the *orderFormStorage* object. Note that the first part of the template consists of two function declarations. The processing does not actually begin until the **Success** statement near the end of the template.

This section explains the statements that appear in this template. Please use Windows Notepad or another text editor to refer to the XT_ORDERFORM_PRE-PARE.ASP template file while reading this section.

```
<% Response.Buffer = TRUE %>
```

The **Buffer** property indicates whether to buffer the page output (wait to send a response to the client until all the server scripts on the page have been processed or until a **Flush** or **End** statement). The property is set to TRUE in the Clock Peddler store, which indicates that no output is sent to the client until all scripts have been processed.

```
<% Response.Expires = 0 %>
```

The **Expires** property specifies the length of time before a cached page expires. If the shopper returns to this page before it expires, the cached page is displayed. In the Clock Peddler store, this property is set to 0, which specifies that the cached page expires immediately (essentially, the page is not cached). Therefore, the basket will be regenerated each time the shopper sees it.

```
<%
function OrderFormPrepareArgs(byRef orderForm, byVal page,⤸
    byRef errorFields)
```

This section of the template declares the **OrderFormPrepareArgs** function and its arguments. The arguments pass the Order Form, the **Page** object, and the *errorFields* object.

```
OrderFormPrepareArgs = true
```

This statement sets the *OrderFormPrepareArgs* variable to TRUE.

```
REM -- ship to:
ship_to_name = page.RequestString("ship_to_name", null, 1, 100)
```

The **RequestString** function retrieves the value of the *ship_to_name* form field passed from the ORDERFORM.ASP template, converts it to a string, and validates it against the specified parameters. The *null* parameter specifies that if no value is available for **ship_to_name**, the default value is Null, resulting in display of an error specified by the next group of statements. (The *null* parameter essentially makes this a required field, because an error is generated if no value has been entered.) The 1 and 100 parameters specify the minimum and maximum permissible number of characters in the string.

```
if IsNull(ship_to_name) then
    errorFields("ship_to_name") = "ship to name must be a string ⤸
        between 1 and 100 characters"
    OrderFormPrepareArgs = false
```

If the value of the **ship_to_name** field is Null, then the specified error string is inserted into the **ship_to_name** property of the *errorFields* object, and the value of the *OrderFormPrepareArgs* variable is set to FALSE. The *errorFields* object is created later in this template.

```
else
    orderForm.ship_to_name = ship_to_name
```

If there is a value for the **ship_to_name** field, the value is stored on the Order Form.

```
end if
```

This statement marks the end of the conditional code that either sets an error message or stores a value in the Order Form depending on whether a value for the specified form field exists.

Each of the subsequent **ship-to** fields is processed in the same way as the **ship-to-name** field.

```
REM -- bill to:
if Request.Form("_bill_to_copy").Count > 0 then
```

The Address Form page (ORDERFORM.ASP) contains a check box that the shopper can select to specify that the billing address is the same as the shipping address. If this check box is selected when the shopper submits the form, the NAME attribute of the field that is passed to the XT_ORDERFORM_PREPARE.ASP template is set to **_bill_to_copy**. In this statement, the **Count** property returns the number of **_bill_to_copy** fields in the form. If the number is greater than 0 (that is, if the **_bill_to_copy** field exists in the form), then the subsequent statements (only one of which is shown below) are run to set the **bill-to** properties of the Order Form to the same values as the corresponding **ship-to** properties.

```
if Not IsNull(orderForm.ship_to_name) then ⏎
   orderForm.bill_to_name = orderForm.ship_to_name
```

If there is a value for **ship_to_name** on the Order Form, then **bill_to_name** is set to that value.

```
else
   bill_to_name = page.RequestString("bill_to_name", null, 1, 100)
```

If there is no form field whose NAME is **_bill_to_copy**, then the **Request-String** function retrieves the value of the **bill_to_name** form field passed from the ORDERFORM.ASP template, converts it to a string, and validates it against the specified parameters. The *null* parameter specifies that if no value is available for **bill_to_name**, the default value is Null, resulting in display of an error specified by the next group of statements. (The *null* parameter essentially makes this a required field, because an error is generated if no value has been entered.) The 1 and 100 parameters specify the minimum and maximum permissible number of characters in the string.

```
if IsNull(bill_to_name) then
errorFields("bill_to_name") = "bill to name must be a string ⏎
   between 1 and 100 characters"
OrderFormPrepareArgs = false
```

If the value of the **bill_to_name** field is Null, then the specified error string is inserted into the **bill_to_name** property of the *errorFields* object, and the value of the *OrderFormPrepareArgs* variable is set to false. The *errorFields* object is created later in this template.

```
else
    orderForm.bill_to_name = bill_to_name
```

If there is a value for the **bill_to_name** field, the value of **bill_to_name** is stored on the Order Form.

```
end if
```

This statement marks the end of the conditional code that either sets an error message or stores a value in the Order Form depending on whether a value for the specified form field exists.

Each of the subsequent **bill-to** fields is processed in the same way as the **bill-to-name** field.

```
end if
```

This statement marks the end of the conditional processing that sets values in the Order Form depending on whether the **Same As Shipping Address** check box is selected on the Address Form page.

```
end function
```

This statement marks the end of the first function declaration.

```
function OrderFormPrepare(byVal orderFormStorage, byVal ⤾
    shopperID, byVal page, byRef errorFields)
```

This section of the template declares the **OrderFormPrepare** function and its arguments. The arguments pass the *orderFormStorage* object, the shopper ID, the **Page** object, and the *errorFields* object.

```
REM -- retrieve Order Form from storage:
on error resume next
```

This statement turns off error handling to ensure that the next statement will not generate an error. This is necessary because in VBScript, the **Set** statement expects an object, but the following **Set** statement could return either an object or Null (which would ordinarily result in an error). Error handling is reinstated immediately following the next statement by the **On Error Goto 0** statement.

```
set orderForm = orderFormStorage.GetData(null, shopperID)
```

The **GetData** method retrieves the Order Form data from the database for the given shopper ID. The **Set** statement assigns the data to the *orderForm* variable name.

```
on error goto 0
```

This statement reinstates error handling that was disabled earlier with the **On Error Resume Next** statement.

```
if IsEmpty(orderForm) then
   OrderFormPrepare = false
   exit function
end if
```

If no Order Form is found, then the *OrderFormPrepare* variable is set to FALSE and the function ends.

```
REM -- retrieve args from form:
success = OrderFormPrepareArgs(orderForm, page, errorFields)
```

This statement runs the **OrderFormPrepareArgs** function defined earlier in this template, passing it the **orderForm** object, the **Page** object, and the **error-Fields** object. If the function fails, *success* is set to FALSE. If the function is successful, *success* is set to TRUE.

```
REM -- commit so address entered so far is kept:
call orderFormStorage.CommitData(null, orderForm)
```

The **CommitData** method updates the existing Order Form data in the database.

```
if not success then
   OrderFormPrepare = false
   exit function
end if
```

If the preceding Success statement is not TRUE (that is, if the function did not complete successfully and therefore did not set the value of success to TRUE), the *OrderFormPrepare* variable is set to FALSE and the function ends.

```
OrderFormPrepare = true
```

This statement sets the *OrderFormPrepare* variable to TRUE.

```
end function
%>
```

This statement marks the end of the function declaration.

Note The execution of the functions occurs in the following statements.

```
<!--#INCLUDE FILE="include/shop.asp" -->
```

This statement includes the SHOP.ASP file, which sets page variables.

```
<%
Set errorFields = Server.CreateObject("Commerce.Dictionary")
```

The **CreateObject** method creates an instance of a **Dictionary** object, and the **Set** statement gives it the variable name *errorFields*. This object will store error strings generated when the functions are executed.

```
success = OrderFormPrepare(MSCSOrderFormStorage, ShopperID, ⤸
    mscsPage, errorFields)
```

This statement runs the **OrderFormPrepare** function defined earlier in this template, passing it the **MSCSOrderFormStorage** object, the shopper ID, the **Page** object, and the **errorFields** object. If the function completes successfully, it sets the value of *success* to TRUE.

```
if success then
    REM -- go to PURCHASE.ASP page:
    Response.Redirect MSCSPage.SURL("purchase.asp")
end if
```

If the function completed successfully and the value of *success* is set to TRUE, then the **Redirect** method causes the browser to attempt to connect to the specified URL. The **SURL** method generates a secure URL to the PURCHASE.ASP template (handled by a secure port). If the function did not complete successfully, then the processing of this template continues by including the ERROR.ASP template.

```
<!--#INCLUDE FILE="include/error.asp" -->
```

This statement includes the ERROR.ASP template, which displays any error strings contained in the **errorFields** object. For information, see "The Clock Peddler Error Page" later in this appendix.

Gathering Credit Card Information

When the shopper clicks the **Total** button on the Address Form page, the values of the form elements are sent to the XT_ORDERFORM_PREPARE.ASP template, which processes the form and then displays the Credit Card Information page. On this page, the shopper enters the credit card information. After entering the information, the shopper submits the order and the payment by clicking the **Purchase** button. This is the final step in the actual payment process, analogous to signing the charge slip.

The PURCHASE.ASP template

The PURCHASE.ASP template generates the Credit Card Information page. This section explains the statements that appear in this template. Please use Windows Notepad or another text editor to refer to the PURCHASE.ASP template file while reading this section.

```
<% Response.Buffer = TRUE %>
```

The **Buffer** property indicates whether to buffer the page output (wait to send a response to the client until all the server scripts on the page have been processed or until a **Flush** or **End** statement). The property is set to TRUE, which indicates that no output is sent to the client until all scripts have been processed.

```
<% Response.Expires = 0 %>
```

The **Expires** property specifies the length of time before a cached page expires. If the shopper returns to this page before the cached page expires, the cached page is displayed. This property is set to 0, which specifies that the cached page expires immediately (essentially, the page is not cached). This protects the privacy of the shopper's credit card information.

```
<!--#INCLUDE FILE="include/shop.asp" -->
```

This statement includes the SHOP.ASP file, which sets page variables.

```
<%
on error resume next
```

This statement turns off error handling to ensure that the next statement will not generate an error. This is necessary because in VBScript, the **Set** statement expects an object, but the following **Set** statement could return either an object or Null (which would ordinarily result in an error). Error handling is reinstated immediately following the next statement by the **On Error Goto 0** statement.

```
set mscsOrderForm = MSCSOrderFormStorage.GetData(null, ⤸
    ShopperID)
```

The **GetData** method retrieves the Order Form from the database for the given shopper ID. The **Set** statement assigns the data to the *mscsOrderForm* variable name.

```
on error goto 0
```

This statement reinstates error handling that was disabled earlier with the **On Error Resume Next** statement.

```
if IsNull(mscsOrderForm) or IsEmpty(mscsOrderForm) then
    Response.Redirect mscsPage.SURL("BASKET.ASP")
```

The **IsNull** function returns TRUE if the *mscsOrderForm* variable contains no valid data (which indicates that no items have yet been added to the basket). The **IsEmpty** function returns TRUE if the *mscsOrderForm* variable is uninitialized (that is, if an Order Form was not found). If either is TRUE, the **Redirect** method causes the browser to attempt to connect to the specified URL. The **SURL** method generates a secure URL to the BASKET.ASP template (handled by a secure port).

```
else
```

If the **IsNull** or the **IsEmpty** function returns FALSE (which indicates that the Order Form exists), the following statements are run.

```
mscsPage.RunPlan(mscsOrderForm)
```

The **RunPlan** method invokes the Order Processing Pipeline and processes *mscsOrderForm* through all pipeline components except payment and acceptance.

This ensures that the following two statements correctly set the number of items on the Order Form. (If a product no longer exists in the database but still exists on the shopper's Order Form, running the **RunPlan** method deletes that item from the Order Form.)

```
set orderFormItems = mscsOrderForm.Items
```

The **Items** property returns a list of dictionaries—one dictionary for each item in the *mscsOrderForm* data (each dictionary contains a set of name-value pairs specific to the item). The **Set** statement assigns this list to the *orderFormItems* variable name.

```
nOrderFormItems = orderFormItems.Count
```

The **Count** property returns the number of items in the *orderFormItems* list, then the value is assigned to the *nOrderFormItems* variable name.

```
end if
%>
```

This statement ends the conditional code that either redirects the browser or runs the Order Form through the Order Processing Pipeline, depending on whether the Order Form is empty or not.

```
if mscsOrderForm.[_Basket_Errors].Count > 0 then
    Response.Redirect mscsPage.SURL("BASKET.ASP")
end if
```

The **_Basket_Errors** list on the Order Form contains any shopping basket errors generated in the Order Processing Pipeline when the **RunPlan** method was executed. The **Count** property returns the number of errors. If the number of errors is greater than 0 (that is, if there are errors), then the errors are displayed to the shopper on the Shopping Basket page. The **Redirect** method causes the browser to attempt to connect to the specified URL. The **SURL** method generates a secure URL to the BASKET.ASP template (handled by a secure port).

```
if mscsOrderForm.[_Purchase_Errors].Count > 0 then
```

The **_Purchase_Errors** list on the Order Form contains any purchase errors generated in the Order Processing Pipeline when the **RunPlan** method was executed. The **Count** property returns the number of errors. If the number of errors is greater than 0 (that is, if there are purchase errors), then the following statements are run.

```
Set errorFields = Server.CreateObject("Commerce.Dictionary")
```

The **CreateObject** method creates an instance of a **Dictionary** object, and the **Set** statement gives pit the variable name *errorFields*.

```
index = 1
```

This statement creates a page variable named *index* and sets its value to 1.

```
for each errorStr in orderForm.[_Purchase_Errors]
   errorFields(index) = errorStr
   index = index + 1
next
```

The **For Each...Next** statement iterates through each error string in the **_Purchase_Errors** list on the Order Form, storing each string in the *errorFields* object.

```
OrderFormPurchase = null
```

If there are purchase errors, the *OrderFormPurchase* variable is set to Null.

```
REM -- display error and not the rest of the page:
%>
<!--#INCLUDE FILE="include/error.asp" -->
```

This statement includes the ERROR.ASP template, which displays any error strings contained in the **errorFields** object. For more information, see "The Clock Peddler Error Page" later in this appendix.

```
<%
    Response.end
```

The **end** method stops processing of this .ASP template and returns the current result (that is, displays the errors).

```
end if
```

This statement ends the conditional code that displays purchase errors.

```
<!--#INCLUDE FILE="include/header.asp" -->
```

This statement includes the HEADER.ASP template, which generates the header at the top of the page.

```
Your purchase will cost <% = MSCSDataFunctions.Money↵
   (mscsOrderForm.[_total_total]) %>.
```

The **[_total_total]** property returns the total amount of the order (set by the Order Total stage of the Order Processing Pipeline). The **Money** method formats the expression as money and displays the value on the page in the introductory sentence. The **Money** method formats the value appropriately according to the following entry in the \SHOP\GLOBAL.ASA file: *MSCSDataFunctions.Locale = &H0409*, which specifies the locale code for the United States.

```
<% = MSCSDataFunctions.Money(mscsOrderForm.[_oadjust_subtotal]) %>
```

The **[_oadjust_subtotal]** property returns the subtotal of the order (set by the Order Price Adjust stage of the Order Processing Pipeline). The **Money** method formats the expression as money and displays the value on the page. The **Money** method formats the value appropriately according to the following entry in the

GLOBAL.ASA file: *MSCSDataFunctions.LocaleMoney = &H0409,* which specifies the locale code for the United States.

```
<% = MSCSDataFunctions.Money(mscsOrderForm.[_tax_total]) %>
```

The **[_tax_total]** property returns the amount of tax on the order (set by the Tax stage of the Order Processing Pipeline). The **Money** method formats the expression as money and displays the value on the page. The **Money** method formats the value appropriately according to the following entry in the GLOBAL.ASA file: *MSCSDataFunctions.LocaleMoney = &H0409,* which specifies the locale code for the United States.

```
<% = MSCSDataFunctions.Money(mscsOrderForm.[_shipping_total]) %>
```

The **[_shipping_total]** property returns the shipping charge on the order (set by the Shipping stage of the Order Processing Pipeline—the Clock Peddler store uses a flat shipping rate of $19.95 on all orders). The **Money** method formats the expression as money and displays the value on the page. The **Money** method formats the value appropriately according to the following entry in the GLOBAL.ASA file: *MSCSDataFunctions.LocaleMoney = &H0409,* which specifies the locale code for the United States.

```
<% = MSCSDataFunctions.Money(mscsOrderForm.[_total_total]) %>
```

The **[_total_total]** property returns the total of the order (set by the Order Total stage of the Order Processing Pipeline). The **Money** method formats the expression as money and displays the value on the page. The **Money** method formats the value appropriately according to the following entry in the GLOBAL.ASA file: *MSCSDataFunctions.LocaleMoney = &H0409,* which specifies the locale code for the United States.

```
<FORM METHOD="POST"
    ACTION="<% = mscsPage.SURL("xt_orderform_purchase.asp") %>">
```

When the shopper clicks the **Purchase** button on the Credit Card Information page, the values that the shopper has entered into the Credit Card Information form are sent to the XT_ORDERFORM_PURCHASE.ASP template. The **SURL** method generates a URL that is handled by a secure port to protect the credit card information.

```
<% = mscsPage.VerifyWith(mscsOrderForm, "_total_total",⤶
    "ship_to_zip", "_tax_total") %>
```

This statement is used to verify that the data on the Credit Card Information page matches the data in the Order Form. The **VerifyWith** method generates a HIDDEN form field for each of the specified arguments. When the form is submitted to the XT_ORDERFORM_PURCHASE.ASP template, the **ProcessVerify-With** method places the values of fields with the name _VERIFY_WITH_ into a dictionary list on the Order Form. When the **RunPurchase** method is run (on the XT_ORDERFORM_PURCHASE.ASP template), the **RequiredTotal** component of the pipeline compares the values for these fields in the database against the fields in the **_verify_with** dictionary on the Order Form. If there is a mismatch (possibly indicating a security breach), an error is displayed to the shopper. This statement generates HIDDEN fields in the form post, as shown in the following example:

```
<FORM METHOD="POST"
ACTION="http://hostname/clockped/xt_orderform_purchase.asp">
   <INPUT TYPE=HIDDEN NAME="_VERIFY_WITH" VALUE="_total_total=5994">
   <INPUT TYPE=HIDDEN NAME="_VERIFY_WITH" VALUE="ship_to_zip=98765">
   <INPUT TYPE=HIDDEN NAME="_VERIFY_WITH" VALUE="_tax_total=0">
   <INPUT TYPE="TEXT" NAME="cc_name" SIZE="70,1" VALUE="<% = ⏎
      mscsPage.Encode(mscsOrderForm.bill_to_name) %>">
```

This statement generates an INPUT field and sets its initial value to the value of the **bill_to_name** entry on the Order Form.

```
<% rem  SET DEFAULTS FOR CURRENT MONTH/YEAR
    imonth = Month(date)
    iyear = Year(date) %>
```

The **date** function returns the current system date. The **Month** function returns a number between 1 and 12 representing the month in the system date, and the **Year** function returns a whole number representing the year. These two values are assigned the variable names *imonth* and *iyear*. These variables are used to set the current month and year as the default values in the **Expiration Date** drop-down lists.

```
<SELECT NAME="_cc_expmonth">
    <% = mscsPage.Option(1, imonth) %> Jan
    <% = mscsPage.Option(2, imonth) %> Feb
    <% = mscsPage.Option(3, imonth) %> Mar
    <% = mscsPage.Option(4, imonth) % Apr
    <% = mscsPage.Option(5, imonth) %> May
    <% = mscsPage.Option(6, imonth) %> Jun
    <% = mscsPage.Option(7, imonth) %> Jul
    <% = mscsPage.Option(8, imonth) %> Aug
    <% = mscsPage.Option(9, imonth) %> Sep
    <% = mscsPage.Option(10, imonth) % Oct
    <% = mscsPage.Option(11, imonth) %> Nov
    <% = mscsPage.Option(12, imonth) %> Dec
</SELECT>
```

The **Option** method creates the <OPTION> tag, setting its VALUE attribute to the first expression. The statement in which the value matches the *imonth* value is then set as the default value to be displayed in the month drop-down list. For example, if the value of *imonth* is 4, the following HTML is generated:

```
<SELECT NAME="_cc_expmonth">
   <OPTION VALUE="1"> Jan
   <OPTION VALUE="2"> Feb
   <OPTION VALUE="3"> Mar
   <OPTION VALUE="4" SELECTED> Apr
   <OPTION VALUE="5"> May
   <OPTION VALUE="6"> Jun
   <OPTION VALUE="7"> Jul
   <OPTION VALUE="8"> Aug
   <OPTION VALUE="9"> Sep
   <OPTION VALUE="10"> Oct
   <OPTION VALUE="11"> Nov
   <OPTION VALUE="12"> Dec
</SELECT>

<SELECT NAME="_cc_expyear">
   <% = mscsPage.Option(1997, iyear) %> 1997
   <% = mscsPage.Option(1998, iyear) %> 1998
   <% = mscsPage.Option(1999, iyear) %> 1999
   <% = mscsPage.Option(2000, iyear) %> 2000
   <% = mscsPage.Option(2001, iyear) %> 2001
   <% = mscsPage.Option(2002, iyear) %> 2002
   <% = mscsPage.Option(2003, iyear) %> 2003
</SELECT>
```

The **Option** method creates the <OPTION> tag, setting its VALUE attribute to the first expression. The statement in which the value matches the *iyear* value is then set as the default value to be displayed in the year drop-down list.

```
<% REM   footer: %>
<!--#INCLUDE FILE="include/footer.asp" -->
```

This statement includes the FOOTER.ASP template, which generates the footer at the bottom of the page.

Placing the Order

When the shopper clicks the **Purchase** button on the Credit Card Information page, the credit card information is sent to the XT_ORDERFORM_PURCHASE.ASP template, where the information is processed. If the action is successful, the Confirmation page is displayed. If an error occurs, the error page is displayed.

The XT_ORDERFORM_PURCHASE.ASP template

This template provides the functionality that adds the shopper's credit card information to the **orderFormStorage** object. Note that the first part of the template consists of two function declarations. The processing does not actually begin until the **order_id=** statement near the end of the template.

This section explains the statements that appear in this template. Please use Windows Notepad or another text editor to refer to the XT_ORDERFORM_PUR-CHASE.ASP template file while reading this section.

```
<%
function OrderFormPurchaseArgs(byVal page, byRef orderForm,↵
    byRef errorFields)
```

This section of the template declares the **OrderFormPurchaseArgs** function and its arguments. The arguments pass the **Page** object, the Order Form object, and the **errorFields** object.

```
OrderFormPurchaseArgs = true
```

This statement sets the *OrderFormPurchaseArgs* variable to TRUE.

```
REM -- cc info:
cc_name = page.RequestString("cc_name", null, 1, 100)
```

The **RequestString** function retrieves the value of the *cc_name* form field passed from the PURCHASE.ASP template, converts it to a string, and validates it against the specified parameters. The null parameter specifies that if no value is available for *cc_name*, the default value is Null, resulting in display of an error specified by the next group of statements. (The null parameter essentially makes this a required field, because an error is generated if no value has been entered.) The 1 and 100 parameters specify the minimum and maximum permissible number of characters in the string.

```
if IsNull(cc_name) then
    errorFields("cc_name") = "ship to name must be a string ↵
        between 1 and 100 characters"
    OrderFormPurchaseArgs = false
```

If the value of the *cc_name* form field is Null (indicating either that the value was not submitted or that it was not the proper length), then the specified error string is inserted into the **cc_name** property of the **errorFields** object, and the value of the *OrderFormPurchaseArgs* variable is set to FALSE. The **errorFields** object is created near the end of this template, just before the function is executed.

```
else
    orderForm.cc_name = cc_name
```

If there is a valid string of between 1 and 100 characters for the *cc_name* field, the value is stored as **cc_name** on the Order Form.

```
end if
```

This statement marks the end of the conditional code that either sets an error message or stores a value in the Order Form depending on whether a value for the specified form field exists.

```
cc_type = page.RequestString("cc_type", null, 4, 20)
```

The **RequestString** function retrieves the value of the **cc_type** form field passed from the PURCHASE.ASP template, converts it to a string, and validates it against the specified parameters. The *null* parameter specifies that if no value is available for **cc_type**, the default value is Null, resulting in display of an error specified by the next group of statements. (The *null* parameter essentially makes this a required field, because an error is generated if no value has been entered.) The 4 and 20 parameters specify the minimum and maximum permissible number of characters in the string.

```
if IsNull(cc_type) or (cc_type <> "Visa" and cc_type <> "Mastercard") then
   errorFields("cc_type") = "credit card type must be a string between↵
      4 and 20 characters (one of 'Visa' or 'Mastercard')"
   OrderFormPurchaseArgs = false
```

The Clock Peddler store is set up to accept only Visa or Mastercard. Therefore, if the value of the *cc_type* field is Null, or is any value other than Visa or Mastercard, then the specified error string is inserted into the **cc_type** property of the **errorFields** object, and the value of the *OrderFormPurchaseArgs* variable is set to FALSE. The **errorFields** object is created near the end of this template, just before the function is executed.

```
else
   orderForm.cc_type = cc_type
```

If there is a value for the *cc_type* field, the value is stored as **cc_type** on the Order Form.

```
end if
```

This statement marks the end of the conditional code that either sets an error message or stores a value in the Order Form depending on whether a value for the specified form field exists.

```
cc_number = page.RequestString("_cc_number", null, 13, 19)
```

The **RequestString** function retrieves the value of the **cc_number** form field passed from the PURCHASE.ASP template, converts it to a string, and validates it against the specified parameters. The *null* parameter specifies that if no value is available for **cc_number**, the default value is Null, resulting in display of an error specified by the next group of statements. (The *null* parameter essentially makes this a required field, because an error is generated if no value has been entered.) The 13 and 19 parameters specify the minimum and maximum permissible number of characters in the string.

```
if IsNull(cc_number) then
    errorFields("cc_number") = "credit card number must be a ↵
        string between 13 and 19 characters"
    OrderFormPurchaseArgs = false
```

If the value of the *cc_number* form field is Null (indicating either that the value was not submitted or that it was not the proper length), then the specified error string is inserted into the **cc_number** property of the **errorFields** object, and the value of the *OrderFormPurchaseArgs* variable is set to FALSE. The **errorFields** object is created near the end of this template, just before the function is executed.

```
else
    orderForm.[_cc_number] = cc_number
```

If there is a valid string of between 13 and 19 characters for the *cc_number* field, the value is stored as **_cc_number** on the Order Form.

```
end if
```

This statement marks the end of the conditional code that either sets an error message or stores a value in the Order Form depending on whether a value for the specified form field exists.

```
cc_expmonth = page.RequestNumber("_cc_expmonth", null, 1, 12)
```

The **RequestNumber** function retrieves the value of the **cc_expmonth** form field passed from the PURCHASE.ASP template, converts it to a number, and validates it against the specified parameters. The *null* parameter specifies that if no value is available for **cc_expmonth**, the default value is Null, resulting in display of an error specified by the next group of statements. (The *null* parameter essentially makes this a required field, because an error is generated if no value has been entered.) The 1 and 12 parameters specify the minimum and maximum permissible numbers.

```
if IsNull(cc_expmonth) then
    errorFields("cc_expmonth") = "expiration month must be a ↵
        number between 1 and 12"
    OrderFormPurchaseArgs = false
```

If the value of the *cc_expmonth* form field is Null (indicating either that the value was not submitted or that it was not within the acceptable range of values), then the specified error string is inserted into the **cc_expmonth** property of the **errorFields** object, and the value of the *OrderFormPurchaseArgs* variable is set to FALSE. The **errorFields** object is created near the end of this template, just before the function is executed.

```
else
    orderForm.[_cc_expmonth] = cc_expmonth
```

If there is a valid number between 1 and 12 for the *cc_expmonth* field, the value is stored as **_cc_expmonth** on the Order Form.

```
end if
```

This statement marks the end of the conditional code that either sets an error message or stores a value in the Order Form depending on whether a value for the specified form field exists.

```
cc_expyear = page.RequestNumber("_cc_expyear", null, 1997, 2003)
```

The **RequestNumber** function retrieves the value of the **cc_expyear** form field passed from the PURCHASE.ASP template, converts it to a number, and validates it against the specified parameters. The *null* parameter specifies that if no value is available for **cc_expyear**, the default value is Null, resulting in display of an error specified by the next group of statements. (The *null* parameter essentially makes this a required field, because an error is generated if no value has been entered.) The 1997 and 2003 parameters specify the minimum and maximum permissible numbers.

```
if IsNull(cc_expyear) then
    errorFields("cc_expyear") = "expiration year must be a ⏎
        number between 1997 and 2003"
    OrderFormPurchaseArgs = false
```

If the value of the *cc_expyear* form field is Null (indicating either that the value was not submitted or that it was not within the acceptable range of values), then the specified error string is inserted into the **cc_expyear** property of the **errorFields** object, and the value of the *OrderFormPurchaseArgs* variable is set to FALSE. The **errorFields** object is created near the end of this template, just before the function is executed.

```
else
    orderForm.[_cc_expyear] = cc_expyear
```

If there is a valid number between 1997 and 2003 for the *cc_expyear* field, the value is stored as **_cc_expyear** on the Order Form.

```
end if
```

This statement marks the end of the conditional code that either sets an error message or stores a value in the Order Form depending on whether a value for the specified form field exists.

```
end function
```

This statement marks the end of the function declaration.

```
function OrderFormPurchase(byVal page, byVal orderFormStorage, ↵
   byVal shopperID, byRef errorFields)
```

This section of the template declares the **OrderFormPurchase** function and its arguments. The arguments pass the **Page** object, the Order Form Storage object, the shopper ID, and the **errorFields** object.

```
REM -- retrieve Order Form from storage:
on error resume next
```

This statement turns off error handling to ensure that the next statement will not generate an error. This is necessary because in VBScript, the **Set** statement expects an object, but the following **Set** statement could return either an object or Null (which would ordinarily result in an error). Error handling is reinstated immediately following the next statement by the **On Error Goto 0** statement.

```
set orderForm = orderFormStorage.GetData(null, shopperID)
```

The **GetData** method retrieves the Order Form data from the database for the given shopper ID. The **Set** statement assigns the data to the *orderForm* variable name.

```
on error goto 0
```

This statement reinstates error handling that was disabled earlier with the **On Error Resume Next** statement.

```
if IsEmpty(orderForm) then
   OrderFormPurchase = null
   exit function
end if
```

If an Order Form is not found, the *OrderFormPurchase* variable is set to Null and the function ends.

```
REM -- retrieve args from form:
success = OrderFormPurchaseArgs(page, orderForm, errorFields)
```

This statement runs the **OrderFormPurchaseArgs** function defined earlier in this template, passing it the **Page** object, the **orderForm** object, and the **error-Fields** object. If the function completes successfully, the value of success is set to TRUE.

```
REM -- commit so cc info entered so far is kept:
call orderFormStorage.CommitData(null, orderForm)
```

The **CommitData** method updates the existing Order Form data in the database.

```
if not success then
   OrderFormPurchase = null
```

```
      exit function
   end if
```

If the preceding Success statement is not true (that is, if the function did not complete successfully and therefore did not set the value of success to TRUE), the *OrderFormPurchase* variable is set to Null and the function ends.

```
REM -- purchase:
   call page.ProcessVerifyWith(orderForm)
   call page.RunPurchase(orderForm)
```

Three HIDDEN fields with NAME = "_VERIFY_WITH" were passed to this template from the PURCHASE.ASP template. These fields contain the values for **ship_to_zip**, **_tax_total**, and **_total_total**. The **ProcessVerifyWith** method copies these fields to the **_verify_with** dictionary on the Order Form. When the **Run-Purchase** method is run by the next statement, the **RequiredTotal** component of the pipeline compares the values it returns from the database against the fields in the **_verify_with** dictionary on the Order Form. If there is a mismatch (possibly indicating a security breach), an error is displayed to the shopper. The **RunPurchase** method invokes the Order Processing Pipeline and processes the *orderForm* data through all pipeline components, including payment and acceptance, returning the *order_id* if successful.

```
<% if orderForm.[_Basket_Errors].Count > 0 then
   REM -- goto basket to show errors
   Response.redirect Page.SURL("BASKET.ASP")
end if
```

The **_Basket_Errors** list on the Order Form contains any shopping basket errors generated in the Order Processing Pipeline when the **RunPurchase** method was executed. The **Count** property returns the number of errors. If the number of errors is greater than 0 (that is, if there are errors), then the errors are displayed to the shopper on the Shopping Basket page. The **Redirect** method causes the browser to attempt to connect to the specified URL. The **SURL** method generates a secure URL to the BASKET.ASP template (handled by a secure port).

```
if orderForm.[_Purchase_Errors].Count > 0 then
```

The **_Purchase_Errors** list on the Order Form contains any purchase errors generated in the Order Processing Pipeline when the **RunPurchase** method was executed. The **Count** property returns the number of errors. This statement specifies that if the number of errors is greater than 0 (that is, if there are purchase errors), then the following statements are run.

```
index = 1
```

This statement creates a page variable named *index* and sets its value to 1.

```
for each errorStr in orderForm.[_Purchase_Errors]
   errorFields(index) = errorStr
   index = index + 1
next
```

The **For Each…Next** statement iterates through each error string in the **_Purchase_Errors** list on the Order Form, storing each string in the *errorFields* object.

```
OrderFormPurchase = null
exit function
```

If there are purchase errors, the *OrderFormPurchase* variable is set to Null and the function ends.

```
end if
```

This ends the conditional code that stores purchase errors in the *errorFields* object.

```
order_id = orderForm.order_id
```

The *order_id* is returned to the Order Form if the pipeline successfully completes processing of the order. This statement creates a page variable named *order_id* and sets it to the value of **order_id** on the Order Form.

```
REM -- clear out basket:
call orderFormStorage.DeleteData(null, orderForm)
```

The **DeleteData** method removes all data from the *orderFormStorage* object.

```
OrderFormPurchase = orderForm.order_id
```

This statement creates a page variable named *OrderFormPurchase* and sets it to the value of **order_id** on the Order Form.

```
end function
%>
```

This statement marks the end of this function declaration.

Note   The execution of the functions occurs in the following statements.

```
<!-#INCLUDE FILE="include/shop.asp" ->
```

This statement includes the SHOP.ASP file, which sets page variables.

```
Set errorFields = Server.CreateObject("Commerce.Dictionary")
```

The **CreateObject** method creates an instance of a **Dictionary** object, and the **Set** statement gives it the variable name *errorFields*. This object is used to store error strings generated during processing of the functions.

```
order_id = OrderFormPurchase(mscsPage, MSCSOrderFormStorage,
ShopperID, errorFields)
```

This statement runs the **OrderFormPurchase** function defined earlier in this template, passing it the **Page** object, the **MSCSOrderFormStorage** object, the shopper ID, and the **errorFields** object. If the function completes successfully, it sets the value of *order_id* to the value returned by the pipeline.

```
if Not IsNull(order_id) then
    REM -- go to BASKET.ASPpage:
    Response.Redirect mscsPage.SURL("confirmed.asp", "order_id", ⏎
        Cstr(order_id))
end if
```

If there is an *order_id*, then the **Redirect** method causes the browser to attempt to connect to the specified URL. The **SURL** method generates a secure URL to the CONFIRMED.ASP template (handled by a secure port). The URL passes the order ID as an argument to the CONFIRMED.ASP template so it can be displayed to the shopper.

```
    REM -- otherwise show errors:
    %>
    <!--#INCLUDE FILE="include/error.asp" -->
```

If there is no order ID (indicating that the processing of the order failed), this statement includes the ERROR.ASP template, which displays any error strings contained in the *errorFields* object. For more information, see "The Clock Peddler Error Page" on the next page.

Displaying the Purchase Confirmation

When the purchase is completed successfully on the XT_ORDERFORM_PURCHASE.ASP template, the Purchase Confirmation page is displayed to the shopper. The shopper can use the order-tracking number on this page to follow up with the merchant for any subsequent questions about the order.

The CONFIRMED.ASP template

The Purchase Confirmation page is generated by the CONFIRMED.ASP template. This section explains the statements that appear in this template. Please use Windows Notepad or another text editor to refer to the CONFIRMED.ASP template file while reading this section.

```
<% Response.Buffer = TRUE %>
```

The **Buffer** property indicates whether to buffer the page output (wait to send a response to the client until all the server scripts on the page have been processed or until a **Flush** or **End** statement). The property is set to TRUE, which indicates that no output is sent to the client until all scripts have been processed.

```
<% Response.Expires = 0 %>
```

The **Expires** property specifies the length of time before a cached page expires. If the shopper returns to this page before it expires, the cached page is displayed. This property is set to 0, which specifies that the cached page expires immediately (essentially, the page is not cached).

```
<!--#INCLUDE FILE="include/shop.asp" -->
```

This statement includes the SHOP.ASP file, which sets page variables.

```
<!--#INCLUDE FILE="include/header.asp" -->
```

This statement includes the HEADER.ASP template, which generates the header at the top of the page.

```
Your order number is <STRONG><% = Request("order_id") %></STRONG>.
```

The **Request** object extracts the value of the *order_id* argument from the URL. The **Encode** method displays the order ID number on the page.

```
<!--#INCLUDE FILE="include/footer.asp" -->
```

This statement includes the FOOTER.ASP template, which generates the footer at the bottom of the page. Included files are located in the \Clockped\Shop\Include folder.

The Clock Peddler Error Page

Error strings produced during the processing of a store page are stored in the **errorFields** object. When the \SHOP\INCLUDE\ERROR.ASP template is included on the page, it displays each error string in the **errorFields** object.

The ERROR.ASP template

The ERROR.ASP template displays errors generated during the processing of a page. This section explains the statements that appear in this template. Please use Windows Notepad or another text editor to refer to the ERROR.ASP template file while reading this section.

```
<!--#INCLUDE FILE="include/header.asp" -->
```

This statement includes the HEADER.ASP template, which generates the header at the top of the page.

```
<%
for each errorStr in errorFields
    Response.Write "<LI>" & errorFields.value(errorStr)
next
%>
```

This **For Each...Next** statement iterates through each error string in the error-Fields object, applying the **Response.Write** statement to each. The **value** property returns the value (text) of each error string, and the **&** operator concatenates it with the standard HTML <LI> tag. The **Write** method writes the resulting string to the HTTP output and the **Response** object sends the output to the client browser.

```
<% REM    footer: %>
<!--#INCLUDE FILE="include/footer.asp" -->
```

This statement includes the FOOTER.ASP template, which generates the footer at the bottom of the page. Included files are stored in the \ClockPed\Shop\ Include folder.

Processing the order

The Order Processing Pipeline is invoked at three points during the Clock Peddler purchasing process:

1. *Display of the Shopping Basket page.* On the BASKET.ASP template, product data that has been stored in the Order Form storage object is retrieved. The **RunPlan** method invokes the Order Processing Pipeline and processes the Order Form through all pipeline components except payment and acceptance. This processing returns the adjusted item prices and subtotals. The tax and shipping amounts (which are based on the address) are not yet returned because the address information has not yet been entered.

2. *Display of the Credit Card Information page.* On the PURCHASE.ASP template, the **RunPlan** method is again used to process the Order Form through all pipeline components except payment and acceptance. This processing sets properties on the Order Form object that are then used on the generated page to display the subtotal, tax, shipping charge, and total of the order to the shopper.

3. *Placing of the order.* On the XT_ORDERFORM_PURCHASE.ASP template, the **RunPurchase** method invokes the Order Processing Pipeline and processes the Order Form through all pipeline components, including payment and acceptance, returning the *order_id* if successful.

The Clock Peddler store's pipeline configuration file specifies which components of the Order Processing Pipeline are used. To examine the pipeline configuration for the Clock Peddler store, type the following URL: *http://host-name/ClockPed_mgr/default.asp*.

On the Clock Peddler Manager page, click the Configure OPP button. You can double-click any component to see its parameters. If no optional component is specified for a particular stage, that stage's default component (if any) is run. The following list shows the stages of the Clock Peddler pipeline and the components used in each stage.

Product information stage This stage gets information about the product (such as its name, description, and so on) from the database. In the Clock Peddler store, the QueryProdInfo component runs the **product** query to retrieve data about the product from the database. The Sku added to the item dictionary on the Order Form by the **AddItem** method is used as the lookup key in the database. (The SQL text of the **product** query is stored in the **Content** object in the \SHOP\GLOBAL.ASA file.)

Merchant information stage This stage gets information about the merchant from the database. The Clock Peddler store does not use this stage.

Shopper information stage This stage gets information about the shopper. In the Clock Peddler store, the DefaultShopperInfo component extracts the shopper ID from the **MSCSShopperManager** object and stores it in the Order Form.

Order initialization stage This stage initializes the order, setting initial name-value pairs.

Order check stage This stage validates the order.

Item price adjust stage This stage calculates adjusted pricing (price times quantity, sale pricing, and so on) for the items in the order.

Order price adjust stage This stage adjusts the total price of the order (can reflect promotions or discounts).

Shipping stage This stage calculates the shipping charge for the order. In the Clock Peddler store, the FixedShipping optional component specifies a fixed shipping charge (**_shipping_total**) of $19.95 that is applied to every order.

Handling stage This stage calculates the handling charge for the order. In the Clock Peddler store, the DefaultHandling default component sets the handling charge (**_handling_total**) to zero (0).

Tax stage This stage calculates the tax on the order. In the Clock Peddler store, the SimpleUSTax optional component specifies a simple flat tax of 8 percent on any order shipped to Pennsylvania (the physical location of the Clock Peddler store) and 0 percent on orders shipped to any other state.

Order total stage This stage calculates the total amount due on the order. In the Clock Peddler store, the DefaultTotal default component sets the **_total_total** property to the sum of **_oadjust_subtotal**, **_shipping_total**, **_tax_total**, and **_handling_total**.

Inventory stage This stage verifies that every item ordered is in stock.

Payment stage This stage approves credit card payments. The Default Payment component sets the payment authorization type (**_payment_auth_code**) to *FAITH*, which bypasses any authorization checks (so demonstration purchases can be completed). In a real store, this component would most likely be replaced by a third-party authorization component.

The ValidateCCNumber component performs a checksum test on the credit-card number (for the most widely used cards) to ensure that its format is correct.

Accept stage This stage accepts the order.

Appendix H

Hexadecimal Codes for Countries[1]

Many of the methods implemented in the Commerce Server components take locale variables as optional parameters. These variables are represented by unique hexadecimal codes, which are listed in the table below.

Additionally, Commerce Server defines a group of optional application-level locale properties that you can initialize to the values listed below. For a list of these variables, see the "Commerce Server Components Reference Documentation" section in Appendix F.

For a list of locales and language IDs in the National Language Support API (NLSAPI) Functional Specification, see the Microsoft Developer Network (MSDN) compact disc. Appendix A of the specification lists locales and language IDs. Following is an extract of this information listing only the locale IDs. This list is continually growing and further locale support can be added to any future product.

---

1. Material for this appendix, documentation available under \docs\component.doc after installation of the companion CD for this book, is extracted from material provided by the Microsoft Site Server documentation group.

Primary language	Locale name	ID
Albanian	Albania	(0x041c; SQI)
Arabic (16)	Saudi Arabia	(0x0401; ARA)
Arabic (16)	Iraq	(0x0801; ARI)
Arabic (16)	Egypt	(0x0C01; ARE)
Arabic (16)	Libya	(0x1001; ARL)
Arabic (16)	Algeria	(0x1401; ARG)
Arabic (16)	Morocco	(0x1801; ARM)
Arabic (16)	Tunisia	(0x1C01; ART)
Arabic (16)	Oman	(0x2001; ARO)
Arabic (16)	Yemen	(0x2401; ARY)
Arabic (16)	Syria	(0x2801; ARS)
Arabic (16)	Jordan	(0x2C01; ARJ)
Arabic (16)	Lebanon	(0x3001; ARB)
Arabic (16)	Kuwait	(0x3401; ARK)
Arabic (16)	U.A.E.	(0x3801; ARU)
Arabic (16)	Bahrain	(0x3C01; ARH)
Arabic (16)	Qatar	(0x4001; ARQ)
Basque	Basque	(0x042D; EUQ)
Byelorussian	Byelorussia	(0x0423, BEL)
Bulgarian	Bulgaria	(0x0402, BGR)
Catalan	Catalan	(0x0403; CAT)
Chinese (4)	Taiwan	(0x0404; CHT)
Chinese (4)	PRC	(0x0804; CHS)
Chinese (4)	Hong Kong	(0x0C04;CHH)
Chinese (4)	Singapore	(0x1004; CHI)
Croatian	Croatian	(0x041a, SHL)
Czech	Czech	(0x0405; CSY)
Danish	Danish	(0406; DAN)
Dutch (2)	Dutch (Standard)	(0x0413; NLD)
Dutch (2)	Belgian (Flemish)	(0x0813; NLB)
English (6)	American	(0x0409; ENU)
English (6)	British	(0x0809; ENG)
English (6)	Australian	(0x0c09; ENA)
English (6)	Canadian	(0x1009; ENC)
English (6)	New Zealand	(0x1409; ENZ)
English (6)	Ireland	(0x1809; ENI)
Estonian	Estonia	(0x0425, ETI)
Farsi	Farsi	(0x0429; FAR)

Primary language	*Locale name*	*ID*
Finnish	Finnish	(0x040b; FIN)
French	French (Standard)	(0x040c; FRA)
French	Belgian	(0x080c; FRB)
French	Canadian	(0x0c0c; FRC)
French	Swiss	(0x100c; FRS)
French	Luxembourg	(0x140c; FRL)
German	German (Standard)	(0x0407; DEU)
German	Swiss	(0x0807; DES)
German	Austrian	(0x0c07; DEA)
German	Luxembourg	(0x1007; DEL)
German	Liechtenstein	(0x1407; DEC)
Greek	Greek	(0x0408; ELL)
Hebrew	Israel	(0x040D; HEB)
Hungarian	Hungarian	(0x040e; HUN)
Icelandic	Icelandic	(0x040F; ISL)
Indonesian	Indonesia	(0x0421; BAH)
Italian (2)	Italian (Standard)	(0x0410; ITA)
Italian (2)	Swiss	(0x0810; ITS)
Japanese	Japan	(0x0411; JPN)
Korean	Korea	(0x0412; KOR)
Latvian	Latvia	(0x0426; LVI)
Lithuanian	Lithuania	(0x0427, LTH)
Macedonian	Macedonia	(0x042f; MKD)
Norwegian (2)	Norwegian (Bokmal)	(0x0414; NOR)
Norwegian (2)	Norwegian (Nynorsk)	(0x0814; NON)
Polish	Polish	(0x0415; PLK)
Portuguese (2)	Portuguese (Brazilian)	(0x0416; PTB)
Portuguese (2)	Portuguese (Standard)	(0x0816; PTG)
Rhaeto-Romanic	Rhaeto-Romanic	(0x0417; RMS)
Romanian (2)	Romania	(0x0418; ROM)
Romanian (2)	Moldavia	(0x0818; ROV)
Russian	Russian	(0x0419; RUS)
Russian	Moldavia	(0x0819; RUM)
Serbian	Serbian	(0x081a; SHC)
Slovak	Slovak	(0x041b; SKY)
Slovenian	Slovenia	(0x0424, SLV)
Sorbian	Germany	(0x042e; SBN)
Spanish (3)	Spanish (Traditional Sort)	(0x040a; ESP)

Primary language	Locale name	ID
Spanish (3)	Mexican	(0x080a; ESM)
Spanish (3)	Spanish (Modern Sort)	(0x0c0a; ESN)
Swedish	Swedish	(0x041D; SVE)
Thai	Thailand	(0x041E; THA)
Turkish	Turkish	(0x041f; TRK)
Ukrainian	Ukraine	(0x0422, UKR)
Urdu	Urdu	(0x0420; URD)

Using MFC to Create Order Processing Components[1]

This appendix provides a tutorial designed to help the developer create order processing components. It is aimed at the developer who

■ Understands the basic architecture of the Order Processing Pipeline and its components (See Chapter 2, the "Order Processing Pipeline" section.)

■ Is proficient in C++

■ May or may not have experience with Microsoft Foundation Class (MFC) library

---

1. Material in this appendix was provided by Subbaro Vedula of Microsoft.

- Has a working knowledge of OLE and COM programming
- Wishes to change, customize, or extend Commerce Server order processing stages with custom components

OVERVIEW OF ORDER PROCESSING COMPONENT REQUIREMENTS

The following sections describe the steps required to create order processing components. These steps include the following:

1. Implement a basic OLE in-process server. (Chapter 5 discusses these interfaces in the "COM Interfaces" section.)

2. Add the skeleton for the required interfaces.

3. Implement the **IPipelineComponent** interface.

4. Implement the **IPersistStreamInit** interface (or **IPersistPropertyBag**) if the component has any persistent configuration data.

5. Implement **ISpecifyPropertyPages** and OLE property pages if the component is to be configured from the Pipeline Editor.

For more information, see the chapter "Writing a Custom Order Processing Component" in the Commerce Server SDK documentation.

Step 1: Implement the Basic OLE In-Process Server

This tutorial uses MFC (Microsoft Foundation Classes) as the core for the OLE In-process Server. MFC is widely known and provides a rapid means of developing OLE components. The tutorial uses the Microsoft Visual C++ Application Wizard to get started.

To implement the OLE in-process server,

1. Start VC++ and click New from the File menu. Then select Project Workspace as the item you want to create.

2. Choose MFC Wizard (DLL) as the project type and enter the project name and location. Call this component *MinMaxShip*.

3. Enable OLE automation support and click Finish. This will create a skeleton project.

4. Now add the class that implements your Min-Max Shipping component. To do so, use the Class Wizard tool. Choose View, Class Wizard to bring up the Class Wizard window.

5. Click Add Class. Add a new class named ***CMinMaxShipping***. The base class in MFC that implements an OLE server is called CCmdTarget, so choose that as the base class. The class will support OLE Automation, which enables its properties to be exposed to script languages such as VB and VBScript. This support is needed to allow configuration of the component from the Active Server Pages Pipeline Editor.

6. Finally, the object must be OLE createable, so enter a unique ProgID. You now have a basic OLE in-process server.

7. Add properties to the object that will allow you to configure it. Class Wizard makes this easy. Click Class Wizard from the View menu to bring up the Class Wizard window.

8. Select the CMinMaxShipping class under Class Name.

9. Now click the OLE Automation page tab where you can add properties.

10. Click Add Property. Add a property called **MinShipping** that will be of type 'long.'

11. After you recompile the component, you can test it in VB or VBScript again, with the following code:

```
Set MinMaxShip = CreateObject("Tutorial.MinMaxShipping")
MinMaxShip.MinShipping = 1000 '10 dollars
Debug.Print MinMaxShip.MinShipping

Output:
  1000
```

Step 2: Add the Skeleton for the Required Interfaces

To add the skeletons,

1. First add the skeleton for **IPipelineComponent** (required), **IPersistStreamInit** (optional), and **ISpecifyPropertyPages** (optional).

    For a detailed description of how to implement interfaces on MFC classes, see the Microsoft Developers Library CD. You can use the embedded class method that is described there and has built-in support with MFC.

2. In the header file for your class, MinMaxShipping.h, add the following to **CMinMaxShipping**:

```
include "pipecomp.h"
class CMinMaxShipping : public CCmdTarget
{
```

```
...
protected:
BEGIN_INTERFACE_PART(PipelineComponent, IPipelineComponent)
    STDMETHOD (Execute) (IDispatch* pdispOrder,
IDispatch* pdispContext, ULONG ulFlags);
    STDMETHOD (ValuesRead) (ULONG* cNames, LPVARIANT* ppNames);
    STDMETHOD (ValuesWritten) (ULONG* cNames, LPVARIANT* ⏎
        ppNames);
    STDMETHOD (EnableDesign) (BOOL fEnable);
END_INTERFACE_PART(PipelineComponent)

BEGIN_INTERFACE_PART(PersistStreamInit, IPersistStreamInit)
    STDMETHOD (GetClassID) (CLSID *pClassID);
    STDMETHOD (IsDirty) (void);
    STDMETHOD (Load) (IStream *pStm);
    STDMETHOD (Save) (IStream *pStm, BOOL fClearDirty);
    STDMETHOD (GetSizeMax) (ULARGE_INTEGER *pcbSize);
    STDMETHOD (InitNew) ();
END_INTERFACE_PART(PersistStreamInit)

BEGIN_INTERFACE_PART(SpecifyPropertyPages, ⏎
    ISpecifyPropertyPages)
STDMETHOD(GetPages) (CAUUID * pPages);
END_INTERFACE_PART(SpecifyPropertyPages)
...
};
```

3. In the MINMAXSHIPPING.CPP file, add the following skeleton implementations for the three interfaces:

```
/////////////////////////////////////////////////////////////////
// IPersistStreamInit
ULONG CMinMaxShipping::XPersistStreamInit::AddRef()
{
    METHOD_PROLOGUE(CMinMaxShipping, PersistStreamInit)
    return pThis->ExternalAddRef();
}

ULONG CMinMaxShipping::XPersistStreamInit::Release()
{
    METHOD_PROLOGUE(CMinMaxShipping, PersistStreamInit)
    return pThis->ExternalRelease();
}
STDMETHODIMP
CMinMaxShipping::XPersistStreamInit::QueryInterface(
    REFIID iid, void FAR* FAR* ppvObj)
{
    METHOD_PROLOGUE(CMinMaxShipping, PersistStreamInit)
    return (HRESULT)pThis->ExternalQueryInterface(&iid, ppvObj);
```

```
}

STDMETHODIMP CMinMaxShipping::XPersistStreamInit::↵
    GetClassID( CLSID* pCID )
{
return E_NOTIMPL;
}

STDMETHODIMP CMinMaxShipping::XPersistStreamInit::IsDirty()
{
return E_NOTIMPL;
}


STDMETHODIMP CMinMaxShipping::XPersistStreamInit::↵
    Load(IStream* pStm)
{
return E_NOTIMPL;
}

STDMETHODIMP CMinMaxShipping::XPersistStreamInit::↵
    Save(IStream* pStm, BOOL fClearDirty)
{
return E_NOTIMPL;
}

STDMETHODIMP CMinMaxShipping::XPersistStreamInit::↵
    GetSizeMax(ULARGE_INTEGER* pcbSize)
{
return E_NOTIMPL;
}

STDMETHODIMP CMinMaxShipping::XPersistStreamInit::InitNew()
{
return E_NOTIMPL;
}


/////////////////////////////////////////////////////////////
// ISpecifyPropertyPages

ULONG CMinMaxShipping::XSpecifyPropertyPages::AddRef()
{
    METHOD_PROLOGUE(CMinMaxShipping, SpecifyPropertyPages)
    return pThis->ExternalAddRef();
}

ULONG CMinMaxShipping::XSpecifyPropertyPages::Release()
{
```

```
        METHOD_PROLOGUE(CMinMaxShipping, SpecifyPropertyPages)
        return pThis->ExternalRelease();
    }


STDMETHODIMP
CMinMaxShipping::XSpecifyPropertyPages::QueryInterface(
    REFIID iid, void FAR* FAR* ppvObj)
{

    METHOD_PROLOGUE(CMinMaxShipping, SpecifyPropertyPages)
    return (HRESULT)pThis->ExternalQueryInterface(&iid, ppvObj);
}

STDMETHODIMP CMinMaxShipping::XSpecifyPropertyPages::⏎
    GetPages(CAUUID * pPages)
{
return E_NOTIMPL;
}

//////////////////////////////////////////////////////////////////
// IPipelineComponent

ULONG CMinMaxShipping::XPipelineComponent::AddRef()
{
    METHOD_PROLOGUE(CMinMaxShipping, PipelineComponent)
    return pThis->ExternalAddRef();
}

ULONG CMinMaxShipping::XPipelineComponent::Release()
{
    METHOD_PROLOGUE(CMinMaxShipping, PipelineComponent)
    return pThis->ExternalRelease();
}

STDMETHODIMP
CMinMaxShipping::XPipelineComponent::QueryInterface(
    REFIID iid, void FAR* FAR* ppvObj)

{
    METHOD_PROLOGUE(CMinMaxShipping, PipelineComponent)
    return (HRESULT)pThis->ExternalQueryInterface(&iid, ppvObj);
}

STDMETHODIMP
CMinMaxShipping::XPipelineComponent::Execute(IDispatch*⏎
    pdispOrder,
            IDispatch* pdispContext, ULONG ulFlags)
{
```

```
return E_NOTIMPL;
}




STDMETHODIMP CMinMaxShipping::XPipelineComponent::↵
    EnableDesign(BOOL fEnable)
{
return E_NOTIMPL;
}
```

Step 3: Implement IPipelineComponent

For a detailed description of the **IPipelineComponent** interface, see the documentation for IPipelineComponent in "Order Processing Pipeline Interfaces" in Appendix F As a brief overview, the component will be called from the Order Processing Pipeline through **IPipelineComponent::OrderExecute**. It will be passed details about the order in the Order Form object. The component may read properties from the Order Form, perform any needed calculations, and then write properties back to the Order Form. In the C language, you must manipulate the Order Form interfaces, though they are intended to be integrated with Visual Basic. To make this task easier, you can use a few helper functions included with the companion CD's SDK tutorial, which may later be used in building other components. Include the following code in MINMAXSHIPPING.CPP:

```
#include "computil.h"
```

Here is the implementation for **IPipelineComponent::Execute**:

```
STDMETHODIMP CMinMaxShipping::XPipelineComponent::↵
    Execute(IDispatch* pdispOrder,
            IDispatch* pdispContext, ULONG ulFlags)
{
    METHOD_PROLOGUE(CMinMaxShipping, PipelineComponent)

    HRESULT hr = S_OK;
    IDictionary* pdictOrder = NULL;
    ISimpleList* plistItems = NULL;
    IDictionary* pdictItem = NULL;
    long nItems, iItem;
    int nShipping, nMaxShipping;
    if (pdispOrder == NULL)
        return E_INVALIDARG;

    nMaxShipping = pThis->m_nMinShipping;

    if (SUCCEEDED(hr = pdispOrder->QueryInterface↵
        (IID_IDictionary, (void**)pdictOrder)))
```

```
              if (SUCCEEDED(hr = GetListItems(pdictOrder, &plistItems)))
                if (SUCCEEDED(hr = GetNumItems(plistItems, &nItems)))
                  {
                  for (iItem = 0; iItem < nItems; iItem++)


                    {
                    if (FAILED(hr = GetNthItem(plistItems, ↵
                      iItem, &pdictItem)))
                      goto Out;
                    if (SUCCEEDED(GetDictValue(pdictItem, ↵
                      L"shipping", &nShipping)) &&
                          nShipping > nMaxShipping)
                        nMaxShipping = nShipping;
                    }
                  hr = PutDictValue(pdictOrder, L"_total_shipping", ↵
                    nMaxShipping);
                  }

Out:
    if (pdictOrder)
        pdictOrder->Release();
    if (plistItems)
        pdictOrder->Release();
    if (pdictItem)
        pdictOrder->Release();
     return hr;
}
```

Step 4: Implement IPerisistStreamInit

In **IPersistStreamInit**, you must read from and write the configuration data to a stream. See the OLE documentation for a discussion of this interface. Your implementation is fairly straightforward. Add the following code to your file:

```
STDMETHODIMP CMinMaxShipping::XPersistStreamInit::↵
    GetClassID( CLSID* pCID )
{
    if (!pCID) return E_INVALIDARG;
    return GetClassID(pCID);
}


STDMETHODIMP CMinMaxShipping::XPersistStreamInit::IsDirty()
{
    METHOD_PROLOGUE(CMinMaxShipping, PersistStreamInit)
    return pThis->m_fDirty;
}
```

```
STDMETHODIMP CMinMaxShipping::XPersistStreamInit::↵
   Load(IStream* pStm)
{
   METHOD_PROLOGUE(CMinMaxShipping, PersistStreamInit)
    if (!pStm)
      return E_INVALIDARG;

   HRESULT hr = pStm->Read(&pThis->m_nMinShipping,↵
      sizeof(pThis->m_nMinShipping), NULL);
      if (SUCCEEDED(hr))
      pThis->m_fDirty = FALSE;

   return hr;
}

STDMETHODIMP CMinMaxShipping::XPersistStreamInit::↵
   Save(IStream* pStm, BOOL fClearDirty)
{
   METHOD_PROLOGUE(CMinMaxShipping, PersistStreamInit)
   if (!pStm)
      return E_INVALIDARG;

   HRESULT hr = pStm->Write(&pThis->m_nMinShipping, ↵
      sizeof(pThis->m_nMinShipping), NULL);

   if (SUCCEEDED(hr) && fClearDirty)
      pThis->m_fDirty = FALSE;

    return hr;
}

STDMETHODIMP CMinMaxShipping::XPersistStreamInit::↵
   GetSizeMax(ULARGE_INTEGER* pcbSize)
{
   METHOD_PROLOGUE(CMinMaxShipping, PersistStreamInit)
    if (!pcbSize) return E_INVALIDARG;
    pcbSize->QuadPart = sizeof(pThis->m_nMinShipping);
    return S_OK;
}

STDMETHODIMP CMinMaxShipping::XPersistStreamInit::InitNew()
{
    METHOD_PROLOGUE(CMinMaxShipping, PersistStreamInit)
   pThis->m_nMinShipping = 0;
   pThis->m_fDirty = FALSE;
   return S_OK;
}
```

Step 5: Implement ISpecifyPropertyPages and Property Page

To implement the **IspecifyPropertyPage** interface, all you need to do is return the CLSID for your property page. First create a CLSID. Use GUIDGEN.EXE to create one. The one generated for this property page is:

```
// {F3A35359-851F-11D0-BE93-00A0C90DC855}
static const GUID CLSID_MinMaxShippingPpg =
{ 0xf3a35359, 0x851f, 0x11d0, { 0xbe, 0x93, 0x0, 0xa0, 0xc9, ⏎
  0xd, 0xc8, 0x55 } };
```

Include the code above for the implementation of **IspecifyPropertyPage** in your component project file.

CLSIDs are universally unique and must also change with versions.

Note Do not reuse this CLSID for any other component that you may build. Your component will not work properly.

The implementation of **ISpecifyPropertyPages::GetPages** is given below:

```
STDMETHODIMP CMinMaxShipping::XSpecifyPropertyPages:: ⏎
 GetPages(CAUUID * pPages)
{
    if (!pPages)
      return E_INVALIDARG;

    pPages->cElems = 1;
    pPages->pElems = (GUID*) CoTaskMemAlloc(1 * sizeof(GUID));

    if (!pPages->pElems)
      {
        pPages->cElems = 0;
        return E_OUTOFMEMORY;
      }

    memcpy(pPages->pElems, &CLSID_MinMaxShippingPpg, ⏎
      sizeof(GUID));

    return S_OK;
}
```

To implement the property page, use MFC's base class for this type of property page: **COlePropertyPage**. Currently the Class Wizard does not allow you to create property pages that derive from **COlePropertyPage**. You can borrow the skeleton implementation from an OLE control created with the OLE Control Wizard or include the code below:

```
class CMinMaxShippingPpg : public COlePropertyPage
{
    DECLARE_DYNCREATE(CMinMaxShippingPpg)
    DECLARE_OLECREATE_EX(CMinMaxShippingPpg)

public:
    CMinMaxShippingPpg();

    //{{AFX_DATA(CMinMaxShippingPpg)
    enum { IDD = IDD_MINMAXSHIPPING_PPG };
    long    m_nMinShipping;
    //}}AFX_DATA

    //{{AFX_VIRTUAL(CMinMaxShippingPpg)
    protected:
    virtual void DoDataExchange(CDataExchange* pDX);
    //}}AFX_VIRTUAL

protected:

    //{{AFX_MSG(CMinMaxShippingPpg)
        // NOTE: the ClassWizard will add member functions here
    //}}AFX_MSG
    DECLARE_MESSAGE_MAP()
};
```

And the following is the actual implementation code.

```
IMPLEMENT_DYNCREATE(CMinMaxShippingPpg, COlePropertyPage)

IMPLEMENT_OLECREATE_EX(CMinMaxShippingPpg, ⏎
    "Tutorial.MinMaxShippingPpg.1",
0xf3a35359, 0x851f, 0x11d0, 0xbe, 0x93, 0x0, 0xa0, 0xc9, ⏎
    0xd, 0xc8, 0x55);

BEGIN_MESSAGE_MAP(CMinMaxShippingPpg, COlePropertyPage)
    //{{AFX_MSG_MAP(CMinMaxShippingPpg)
        // NOTE: the ClassWizard will add message map macros here
    //}}AFX_MSG_MAP
END_MESSAGE_MAP()

BOOL CMinMaxShippingPpg::CMinMaxShippingPpgFactory::⏎
    UpdateRegistry(BOOL bRegister)
{
    if (bRegister)
        {
        RegisterCATID(CLSID_MinMaxShipping, ⏎
            CATID_MSCSPIPELINE_COMPONENT);
        RegisterCATID(CLSID_MinMaxShipping, ⏎
```

```
                    CATID_MSCSPIPELINE_SHIPPING);
            RegisterName(CLSID_MinMaxShipping, L"MinMax Shipping");
            RegisterThreadingModel(CLSID_MinMaxShipping, L"both");

            return
    AfxOleRegisterPropertyPageClass(AfxGetInstanceHandle(),
                m_clsid, IDS_MINMAXSHIPPING_PPG);
            }

        else
            return AfxOleUnregisterClass(m_clsid, NULL);
    }

    CMinMaxShippingPpg::CMinMaxShippingPpg() :
        COlePropertyPage(CMinMaxShippingPpg::IDD, ⤶
            IDS_MINMAXSHIPPING_PPG)
    {
        //{{AFX_DATA_INIT(CMinMaxShippingPpg)
        m_nMinShipping = 0;
        //}}AFX_DATA_INIT
    }

    void CMinMaxShippingPpg::DoDataExchange(CDataExchange* pDX)
    {
        //{{AFX_DATA_MAP(CMinMaxShippingPpg)
        DDP_Text(pDX, IDC_MINSHIPPING, m_nMinShipping, ⤶
          _T("MinShipping"));
        DDX_Text(pDX, IDC_MINSHIPPING, m_nMinShipping);
        DDV_MinMaxLong(pDX, m_nMinShipping, 0, 2000000000);
        //}}AFX_DATA_MAP
        DDP_PostProcessing(pDX);
    }
```

Having developed all interfaces and included all the code, you can compile the object and register it via the Register Control command on the Tools menu, or enter *regsvr32 minmaxship.dll* from a command prompt. You can create an instance of the component from Visual Basic with the following code:

```
Set MinMaxShip = CreateObject("Tutorial.MinMaxShipping").
```

Microsoft IIS, NT, and SQL: Server Tools Supporting Site Server Operations

This appendix covers tricks of the masters—tools included with the NT, IIS, and SQL Server products that are critical to installing, developing, operating, and maintaining Site Server Enterprise Edition in the NT, IIS, and SQL Server environments. This appendix also covers ODBC tools and techniques that help in connecting to non–SQL Server databases. These tools and techniques are critical for getting a Site Server installation up and running, and they help you with operational and ongoing maintenance issues.

The information in this appendix also helps you with the installation and operations of the evaluation CD in the back of the book. This appendix covers the following topics:

- NT server tools and techniques

- IIS tools and techniques

- SQL Server tools and techniques

- ODBC tools and techniques

NT SERVER TOOLS AND TECHNIQUES

This section explains how you can use Windows NT utilities to monitor or configure NT-based servers and services. The NT Control Panel has several applications that configure and monitor all NT-based servers and services, including: Network application, Services application, and ODBC application. To access these applications, click Start-Settings-Control Panel. These applications are discussed below (see Figure J-1).

Figure J-1. *Control Panel applications.*

NT Control Panel Applications

The Network application in the control panel configures your Transmission Control Protocol/Internet Protocol (TCP/IP) settings, including IP address, subnet mask, and default gateway. Double-click TCP/IP Protocol in the Network Protocol listing to display the TCP/IP Properties dialog box. Click the DNS tab to configure DNS settings, such as host name, domain names, and DNS servers, to resolve names.

To start Network application in NT Server version 4.0

1. Click the Start button and point to Settings.

2. Double-click the Network icon.

3. Select the Protocols tab. (Commerce Server uses both protocols: TCP/IP for connection to the Internet, and Named Pipes for the database connection.)

4. To add Named Pipes (NetBEUI) protocols from this panel, click the Add button.

5. Select Named Pipes (NetBEUI) protocol.

6. Click OK.

The Services application in the Control Panel starts, stops, and pauses the WWW, gopher, and FTP services. (You can also use Internet Service Manager to start, stop, and pause IIS and Site Server services individually.) Use the Startup button to specify whether the service starts automatically when your server restarts. If you have a security reason, you can also use this dialog box to override the account used by the WWW service as set by default in the Service property sheet of Internet Service Manager. You should change this setting only if it is part of your security strategy; otherwise, use the default settings in the Log On As box.

The ODBC application manages database connections and drivers, including trace and debug facilities. This application is useful in viewing and editing Site Server's ODBC connections.

The Add/Remove Programs application can remove or upgrade each and every software application package installed on the NT platform. You may upgrade, remove, or reinstall Site Server installation using this application.

The Devices application installs and removes hardware devices including any system devices such as disks, sound, and video devices needed for your specific server installation.

The System Properties application manages system metrics, performance settings, and profiles. The properties and metrics change the performance of the system, for example, adding additional system pages to avoid bottlenecks and allowing background tasks to run at a higher or lower priority. Please refer to NT documentation before changing these settings. Typically these changes are performed based on performance monitoring. Performance Monitor is discussed later in this section.

NT Web Service Tools

NT also provides a number of tools to configure and monitor all NT-based servers and services, including Windows Explorer, User Manager for Domains, Event Viewer, and Performance Monitor. To access these tools, click Start-Programs-Administrative Tools. These tools are discussed below.

Windows Explorer

Use Windows Explorer to set directory and file permissions on Windows NT File System (NTFS) drives. Use the Permissions item in the Security dialog box to set permissions for access to your Web and Site Server resources. Setting directory and file permissions is an important part of securing your Web site. File access control is not available on file allocation table (FAT) file systems. You can convert your file system to NTFS with the CONVERT.EXE utility. See the Windows NT documentation for more information.

Site Server file level (Web page level) security is integrated with the NT File System (NTFS). You can use Access Control Lists to protect Commerce Server pages.

To change the protection of a store page in Commerce Server,

1. Start the NT explorer from Start, Programs, NT Explorer.

2. Locate the page of interest under stores/*storename*/.

3. Right-click on the page of interest.

4. Select Properties from the drop-down menu.

5. Select the Security tab.

6. Click the Permissions button.

7. Add or remove the permissions for the user of your choice. Commerce Server users logged in anonymously are using IUSR_*machinename* for login name.

User Manager for domains

User Manager is a tool that you can use to manage security for a Windows NT Server computer. With User Manager, you can create and manage user accounts, create and manage groups, manage the security policies, and manage servers individually or as members of a domain.

To start User Manager in NT Server version 4.0,

1. Click the Start button and point to Programs.

2. In the Programs menu, click Administrative Tools.

3. Then click User Manager.

Figure J-2 depicts the User Manager for the computer *showbiz1*.

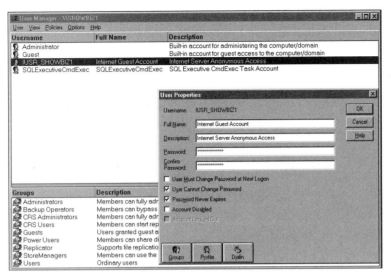

Figure J-2. *User Manager's user properties window.*

Event Viewer

You can view Microsoft Site Server event logs, operational status, and errors through the NT Event Viewer. You can use Event Viewer to view and manage System, Security, and Application event logs. Event Viewer can notify administrators of critical events by displaying pop-up messages, or by adding event information to log files. The information allows you to better understand the sequence and types of events that led up to a particular state or situation.

To start Event Viewer in NT Server version 4.0,

1. Click the Start button and point to Programs.

2. In the Programs menu, click Administrative Tools.

3. Then click Event Viewer.

Event Viewer indicates the severity of the event logged in the Event Detail window. The possible severity types are Success, Informational, Warning, and Error. In this view, blue icons are informational messages, yellow icons are warnings, red icons are errors.

Performance Monitor

You can monitor a Web site to analyze the site's use and improve its performance. Windows NT includes a utility called Performance Monitor that measures the performance of Windows NT objects, such as processes, memory, and cache. Each object has an associated set of counters that provide information about the object. With Performance Monitor, you can create charts that provide a snapshot of a service's activity. You can also create logs of the service's performance, prepare reports that provide performance measurements, and generate alerts when a service counter meets a threshold. For more information on using Performance Monitor, see the Windows NT Help system.

IIS automatically installs Windows NT Performance Monitor counters for the WWW, FTP, and gopher services, as well as Internet Information Services Global. You can use these counters with the Windows NT Performance Monitor for real-time measurement of your Internet service use. Please see Appendix L, "IIS Audit Logs and Performance Monitoring." Except where noted otherwise, each counter is available to monitor any of the three services. For example, you can monitor connection attempts for WWW, FTP, or gopher; but you can monitor current CGI requests only for the WWW service.[1]

Figure J-3 depicts the initial window of Performance Monitor.

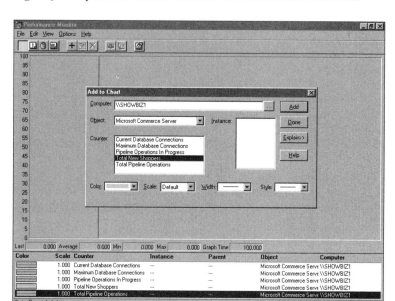

Figure J-3. *Performance Monitor's Add To Chart window.*

Optionally, alerts may be set on any counter or system parameter. Alerts can be powerful in recognizing system problems and reacting to changes in load.

NT Resource Kit

Microsoft Windows NT Resource Kit is a collection of additional tools and applications for managing NT services. The NT Resource Kit is available from Microsoft Press. This section discusses selected NT Resource Kit tools, useful for installation

---

1. The WWW service appears in the Windows NT Performance Monitor as the HTTP Service.

and monitoring of Microsoft Site Server. The NT Resource Kit includes these utilities and more.[2]

APIMON

A profiling tool, APIMON is an application monitor that monitors a running application for all application programming interface (API) calls. APIMON counts and times all API calls. Optionally, it will also monitor page faults caused by the monitored application and report them by API call. APIMON is used as a performance monitor to help tune your application. You can use the data to determine where the hot spots are in your application by examining the APIs with the largest times or counts. You can also look at which APIs the application uses, taking a special look at calls that cause ring transitions to kernel mode or client/server transitions. Large numbers of these calls can cause slow application. APIMON can also generate two types of reports: a report containing all API calls showing their counts and times, and a report showing a trace of all APIs as they occurred in time.

AddUsers for Windows NT

AddUsers is a 32-bit administrative tool that uses a comma-delimited file to create, write, and delete user accounts. AddUsers is most beneficial when the file is maintained in a spreadsheet, such as Microsoft Excel, that will work with comma-delimited files. The format for the comma-delimited file requires headings for users, global groups, and local groups.

You should first execute AddUsers with the /d switch, the dump accounts option, to write the headings, user accounts, local groups, and global groups to a file. Viewing this file should give you a clearer picture of the structure and headings of the comma-delimited file before you use the /c option to create user accounts. You must be a member of the Administrators group on the target computer to add accounts, and a member of the Users group to write accounts.

AppleTalk Network Device Analyzer

Where Site Server coexists in an Apple environment, this GUI utility performs an AppleTalk lookup for registered AppleTalk devices on an AppleTalk network. The user can perform a lookup of all AppleTalk devices, specific Net, Name, Type, partial Name, and Types in the selected zone(s). You can use this utility to find information on the AppleTalk network, such as which systems are routing, which systems have a printer captured, or a list of printers or computers running Windows NT. Each device returns values for their Net, Node, Socket, Name, Type, and Zone. The combinations of Net/Node/Socket or Name/Type/Zone are unique values. The computer that will be executing AppleTalk Network Device Analyzer must have the AppleTalk stack installed. The stack is part of Microsoft's Services for Macintosh.

---

2. Excerpts from *"Overview of Windows NT Resource Kit Tools,"* version 4.00.02 by Microsoft Corporation.

SRVANY

An NT service is similar to a Unix daemon running continuously in the background ready on demand. With SRVANY, you can run any Windows NT application as a service. SRVANY works best with 32-bit applications written for Windows NT. You can use this utility to start 16-bit Windows applications as services, but some 16-bit applications are not able to keep running after a user logs off from the computer. Background tasks are implemented differently on different systems. This tool simplifies the details of implementing a background task, such as background replication or background monitoring tasks.

C2CONFIG.EXE

An excellent tool for security auditors, you can use C2CONFIG.EXE, the Windows NT C2 Configuration Manager, to compare the current security configuration on your Windows NT workstation with C2-level security requirements of the United States government's National Computer Security Center. You can then configure the workstation to conform up to the C2 level.

C2 Configuration Manager displays the Windows NT parameters that the C2 evaluators felt were critical, along with current Windows NT configuration. Selecting one of these items displays more information on the configuration of that item and allows you to change the configuration. C2CONFIG.EXE comes with an .H file that lets users write their own extensions to the application by calling DLLs. C2DLL.TXT is the text file that explains how to do this.

Command Scheduler

Many systems have tasks that run periodically. Use Command Scheduler[3] to schedule commands on a local or remote computer to occur once or regularly in the future. The current scheduled commands for the local computer are displayed by default when Command Scheduler is started. The list of scheduled commands is automatically refreshed, so the display is always current. Scheduled commands are displayed in a format similar to that of the Unix command-line *AT* command. You can run Command Scheduler from within Windows NT or from the command line.

Crystal Reports Event Log Viewer

An excellent tool for the Site Server administrator, the Crystal Reports Event Log Viewer, available only for Windows NT Server, is a full-featured report writer that provides an easy way to extract, view, save, and publish information from the Windows NT system and application and security event logs in a variety of formats. Crystal Reports offers direct access to the event logs of multiple computers. It can open and manipulate existing log files (in read-only mode) and access database files. Enhancements in this version allow more flexibility in filtering and analyzing data contained in the security event log. Crystal Reports allows you to format and

---

3. Similar to the Unix Cron utility.

group information, then export it to a printer, word processor, or spreadsheet. It includes 12 usable reports that quickly provide information from one or multiple computers in a single report. The main components of Crystal Reports are CRW.EXE, the report designer-viewer, and CRPE.DLL, the print engine that generates reports.

DNS server statistics

Another system and network administration tool, the DNSSTAT command-line utility provides a dump of DNS server statistics (queries and responses, database size, caching, memory consumption) on a computer running Microsoft DNS Server. You can also use DNSSTAT to clear these statistics without stopping the DNS server. By default, these statistics are cumulative and are not normally cleared until the computer running Microsoft DNS Server is stopped.

Dump event log

This command-line utility copies event log information from a local or remote NT system into a tab-separated text file for presentation and processing. You can also use it to filter for or filter out certain event types. This tool can answer your support-related questions such as how long was the system operating, and what were any errors encountered.

KILL.EXE

Finally, KILL.EXE[4] is another command-line utility similar to Unix's KILL.[5] You can use it to end one or more tasks or processes. When using KILL, you can specify a process by its process ID number, any part of its process name, or its window title if it has a window. You can use PULIST or TLIST, two utilities included with the Resource Kit, to find the process names and process IDs of currently running processes. With KILL, you can also specify how the process is to be stopped: you can have KILL send it a command telling it to halt itself, or have KILL force the process to end.

These are just a few of the hundreds of useful NT server tools. For a full listing, see NT Resource Kit from Microsoft Press. Now we move on to a discussion of SQL Server tools.

---

4. Similar to kill -# on Unix systems.

5. For those who prefer a graphical interface, Shift Control Delete also allows for killing one or more processes on NT.

IIS TOOLS AND TECHNIQUES

IIS provides a graphical administration tool called Internet Service Manager that you can use to monitor, configure, and control Internet services. Internet Service Manager is the central location from which you can control all of the computers running IIS in your organization. You can run Internet Service Manager on any computer that is running Windows NT Workstation or Windows NT Server and that is connected through the network to your Web server. Internet Service Manager uses the Windows NT security model, so only validated administrators are allowed to administer services, and administrator passwords are transmitted in encrypted form over the network. With remote administration you can administer your Web servers from the server computer itself, from a management workstation on the corporate local area network (LAN), or even over the Internet.

In addition to Internet Service Manager, IIS provides an HTML-based Internet Service Manager that you can run from any Web browser. You can perform the same administration tasks by using either version of Internet Service Manager. In this guide, any reference to Internet Service Manager refers to both versions of the tool unless otherwise noted.

Web Server Connection

You can administer any IIS on your network by connecting to it in Internet Service Manager, including Site Server's WWW server. You can specify a Web server by typing the computer's Domain Name System (DNS) host name, IP address, or NetBIOS name (or computer name). You can also find all the computers on your network that are running Internet Information Server.

To connect to a Web server, from the Properties menu in Internet Service Manager, select Connect to Server. In the Server Name box, type the Web server's host name, IP address, or NetBIOS name.

To connect by selecting a Web server from a list, from the Properties menu in Internet Service Manager, select Find All Servers. From the list of servers displayed, double-click the one you want to connect to.

View Selection

Iinternet Service Manager displays a graphical view of the services running on your servers. You can view a complete report, or you can sort information by the service type or by computer name. Views enable you to tell at a glance which services are running. You can also display or hide services and sort services by their state (running, paused, or stopped).

To select a view, choose Servers View, Services View, or Report View from the View menu. Views are described in the following sections.

To sort information in a view, choose Sort by Server, Sort by Service, Sort by Comment, or Sort by State from the View menu. For example, you should sort by state to quickly see which services are currently running.

To display or hide services, choose the service that you want to display or hide from the View menu (FTP, gopher, or WWW).

Report view

Report view is the default view. Report view alphabetically lists the selected computers, with each installed service shown on a separate line. Click the column headings to sort the entire list alphabetically. Report view is probably most useful for sites with only one or two computers running Internet Information Server.[6]

Servers view

Servers view displays services running on network computers by computer name. Click the plus symbol next to a computer name to see which services that computer is running. Double-click a service name to see its property sheets. Servers view is most useful for sites running multiple Web servers when you need to know the status of the services installed on a specific computer.

Services view

Services view lists the services on every selected computer, grouped by service name. Click the plus symbol next to a service name to see the computers running that service. Double-click the computer name under a service to see the property sheets for the service running on that computer. Services view is most useful for sites with widely distributed Web servers when you need to know which computers are running a particular service.

Services Configuration and Management

You can configure and manage the WWW, FTP, and gopher services by using Internet Service Manager. The following information focuses on the WWW service, the most commonly used service.

You can quickly start, stop, or pause a service from Internet Service Manager. Select the service you want to start, stop, or pause. From the Properties menu, choose Start Service, Stop Service, or Pause Service.

In Internet Service Manager, double-click a computer name or a service name to display its property sheets. Click the tab at the top of each property sheet to display the properties for that category. After setting the properties for the service, click OK to return to the main Internet Service Manager window.

---

6. If you are running other Internet services, such as Network News Transfer Protocol (NNTP) and Simple Mail Transfer Protocol (SMTP), they will be listed in the Report view of Internet Service Manager, along with the WWW, FTP, and gopher services.

The Service property sheet

You use the Service property sheet to control what kind of authentication is required to gain access to your Web site and to specify the account used for anonymous client requests to log on to the server. Most Internet sites allow anonymous logons.

The Directories property sheet

You use the Directories property sheet to specify which directories (folders) are available to users and to create a Web site composed of folders that reside on different computers. You can also designate a default document that appears if a remote user does not specify a particular file, or instead enable directory browsing. Directory browsing means that the user is presented with a hypertext listing of the directories and files so that he or she can navigate through your directory structure.

The Logging property sheet

You use the Logging property sheet to log service activity. Logging provides valuable information about how a Web server is used. You can send log data to text files or to an Open Database Connectivity (ODBC)–supported database. If you have multiple Web servers or services on a network, you can log all their activity to a single database on any network computer.

The Advanced property sheet

You use the Advanced property sheet to prevent certain individuals or groups from gaining access to your Web site. You control access by specifying the IP address of the computers to be granted or denied access.

You can also set the maximum network bandwidth for outbound traffic, to control the maximum amount of traffic on your site. For more information, see the following section.

Network Use Limitation

You can constrain your Internet services by limiting the network bandwidth allowed for all of the Internet services on your Web server. Limiting the bandwidth dedicated to users of Microsoft IIS is especially useful if your Internet line has multiple purposes. Limiting bandwidth allows other operations (such as e-mail and remote logons) to use the same line without being slowed down by too much activity on the Web server.

To change bandwidth in Internet Service Manager,

1. Double-click any service on the computer for which you wish to change the bandwidth usage allowed.

2. Click the Advanced tab.

3. Select Limit Network Use by all Internet Services on this computer.

4. Select the bandwidth desired in kilobytes per second you wish to allow for Internet services.

5. Click Apply.

6. Click OK.

If the bandwidth being used remains below the level you set, client requests for information are answered. If the bandwidth is close to the value you set, client requests are delayed until the network traffic decreases. Delaying responses enables the Web server to smooth out network traffic volumes without actually denying browser requests. If the bandwidth exceeds the level you set, client requests to read files are rejected and requests to transfer files are delayed until the bandwidth equals or falls below the set value.

This concludes our overview of IIS tools and techniques. The next section covers SQL server tools and techniques.

SQL SERVER TOOLS AND TECHNIQUES

The database is an integral part of Site Server. A number of administrative tools are available in the Microsoft SQL Server product, such as Service Manager, the ISQL_W tool, and more. These tools help manage the database end of Site Server and are further discussed below.

Service Manager

Service Manager starts and stops the SQL Server's services.

To start SQL Server Manager in Windows NT Server version 4.0,

1. Click the Start button and point to Programs.

2. In the Programs menu, click SQL Server 6.0 or 6.5.

3. Then click Service Manager.

Using ISQL_W tool

This tool is useful in running your modified SQL schema for the Commerce Server sample stores to build your own store.

To start SQL ISQL_W tool in Windows NT Server,

1. Click the Start button and point to Programs.

2. In the Programs menu, click SQL Server 6.0 or 6.5.

3. Select ISQL_W.

4. Enter the SQL Server's server name and administrator login name and password to log in to the server and click Connect.

   To run a sample store schema file or your modified version,

1. Select a database from the DB drop-down list.

2. In the File menu, select Open.

3. Browse to find the *.SQL file you wish to run.

4. Select the file and click OK.

5. Select Execute from the Query menu. The display changes to show error or completion status.

Enterprise Manager

You use Enterprise Manager to create a device for each store prior to Site Server installation. Consult Site Server product installation documentation in Appendix A for information on the requirements for each store device or database.

   To start the SQL Enterprise Manager tool in Windows NT Server version 4.0,

1. Click the Start button and point to Programs.

2. In the Programs menu, click SQL Server 6.0 or 6.5.

3. Select SQL Enterprise Manager.

   To create a device for your store or a Commerce Server store,

1. From the Manage menu, select Devices.

2. From the toolbar, select New Device.

3. Fill in the name and the size of your new device.

4. Click OK to receive confirmation of successful creation of the new device.

SQL Transfer Manager

If you are using a number of SQL Servers and wish to quickly and easily duplicate the schema for your site from one server to another, the SQL Transfer Manager tool is capable of duplicating your database.

   To start the SQL Transfer Manager tool in Windows NT Server version 4.0,

1. Click the Start button and point to Programs.

2. In the Programs menu, click SQL Server 6.0 or 6.5.

3. Select SQL Transfer Manager.

4. Specify source and destination servers and click Logon.

5. Select source and destination databases and click Transfer to duplicate a complete database from one SQL Server to another.

SQL Trace

SQL Trace is a graphical utility that database administrators and application developers can use to monitor and record database activity for SQL Server 6.5. SQL Trace is installed with the SQL Server software and, optionally, with the 32-bit client software. You can start SQL Trace by choosing the SQL Trace icon from the SQL Server 6.5 program group, or by running SQLTRACE.EXE from the C:\SQL\BINN directory.

With SQL Trace you can display all server activity in real time or create filters to monitor the activities of particular users, applications, or hosts. You can display statements or remote procedure calls sent to any SQL Server 6.5. You can save server activity to disk in an ISQL_W-compatible script or as an activity log. System administrators can audit the use of SQL Server.

To start the SQL Trace in Windows NT Server version 4.0,

1. Click the Start button and point to Programs.

2. In the Programs menu, click SQL Server 6.0 or 6.5.

3. Select SQL Transfer Trace.

4. Specify a filter. A filter is a list of login names, applications, and hosts that you may be interested in tracing. In the New Filter dialog box, enter a filter name and take all defaults.

5. Click the Events tab and select desired SQL events such as connections and disconnection events.

6. Click Add. A real-time display of SQL events appears to help debug and troubleshoot applications.

SQL Trace provides a graphical user interface for the extended stored procedure *xp_sqltrace*. For more information about *xp_sqltrace*, see SQL Server Books Online after product installation from the companion CD.

SQL Server Web Assistant

Occasionally, you might want to publish SQL Server data directly into an HTML page. SQL Server Web Assistant makes publishing data on the Web easy—no HTML or database programming is required for common database table to Web publishing tasks.

Follow these steps to publish the products table of the AdventureWorks database to the Internet.

1. Start SQL Server Web Assistant and log into a database. The database may be local or on a LAN. Please note that in addition to standard documentation provided with SQL Server, this tool also has page-by-page information to help you succeed the first time.

2. Select the database, table, and columns you want to publish on the Web.

3. Choose the publishing frequency you want. You will most likely run this only once. However, you could just as easily choose to publish on a regular interval.

4. Enter the location of publication and optionally provide a link for visiting the store or to the Administration page for product management.

5. Specify a few HTML formatting options, such as limiting the maximum size of the query and the query result page size. A final message appears confirming successful completion. The resulting page is available for browsing.

Please refer to product information supplied with SQL Server installation for variations and full details of all options.

This section covered SQL tools and techniques for Site Server operation and maintenance. The next section covers ODBC tools and techniques.

ODBC TOOLS AND TECHNIQUES

The concept of ODBC is that of universal access to databases with a single interface definition. ODBC is one of many database connectivity options for IIS. The advantages of ODBC are ease of use, speed, and unified access to heterogeneous databases. While ODBC was initially slower than the DBLIB[7] implementation in its introductory phase, performance was improved over time such that for my test database connectivity application, the performance was at a level comparable (plus or minus 5 percent) to my DBLIB implementation of the same code.[8]

---

7. A database connectivity application library well known on NT and Unix databases.

8. I helped develop the Compass project, the tool Microsoft Product Support Services uses to log, track, and resolve customer product issues worldwide using SQL Server. As part of this development effort, a database connectivity service was developed that runs as an NT service and periodically replicates and synchronizes data among databases.

The following paragraphs discuss a number of ODBC-related tools and techniques that help during Commerce Server installation. These tools are especially important if you are going to use a third-party database (other than SQL Server) with Commerce Server. Based on my experience of installing Commerce Server using Oracle and Informix databases, I included the following information to assist you in connecting to your favorite databases.

ODBC Tester

When you are going to install the site system using a database other than SQL Server, you can use ODBCTEST.EXE, a member of the ODBC suite of tools, to verify and debug the connection to the database.

Using ODBC Tester, you can test each and every ODBC data source including full driver compatibility, logon, and table access. For more information on this tool or on ODBC in general, please refer to the Microsoft ODBC SDK available from Developer Support, or refer to one of the two following books: *Inside ODBC* by Kyle Gyger, or *ODBC 3.0 or Higher Programming Reference Manual and SDK Guide*, both available from Microsoft Press.

ODBCPING.EXE

You can use the ODBCPING.EXE utility to check whether ODBC is properly installed by connecting to a server using the ODBC SQL Server Driver. This utility is a 32-bit application that is stored in the \SQL60\BINN directory.

To verify ODBC connectivity, from a command prompt, type

```
odbcping /Servername /login_id /Password
```

where *Servername* is the name of a server you will connect to; login_id is a valid login ID for that server, and *Password* is the password for that login ID. If the ODBC connection is established, this message is displayed:

```
CONNECTED TO SQL SERVER
```

If the ODBC connection cannot be established, this message is displayed:

```
COULD NOT CONNECT TO SQL SERVER
```

This concludes our review of NT, IIS, SQL, and ODBC tools and techniques supporting Site Server.

Appendix K

Site Server Support[1]

In the event that you have a technical question about Microsoft Site Server Enterprise Edition, first look in the Help files or find late-breaking updates and technical information in the README files in this product. If you still have a question, Microsoft offers technical support[2] and services ranging from no-cost and low-cost online information services to annual support plans with a Microsoft technical engineer. Below is a brief description of these services to help you decide which option is right for you. For more information about this and other services available in the United States and Canada, visit the Web site at *http://www.microsoft.com/Support/*.

Note The services and prices listed here are available in the United States and Canada only. Services and prices outside these countries may vary.

ONLINE SUPPORT AT HTTP//:WWW.MICROSOFT.COM/SUPPORT/

Use Microsoft's cutting-edge technology to help you access the most relevant technical information and resources to answer your support questions. Diagnose and solve technical problems. Discuss issues and solutions with other Microsoft customers. Or select technical articles, programming aids, or commonly asked questions from Microsoft technical databases.

---

1. Material for this appendix was provided by Product Support Services of Microsoft.
2. Microsoft technical support is subject to Microsoft's then-current prices, terms, and conditions, which are subject to change without notice.

TECHNICAL INFORMATION SERVICES

To download sample programs, device drivers, patches, software updates, and programming aids, use **Microsoft Download Service (MSDL).** Direct modem access to MSDL is available in the United States by dialing (425) 936-6735. The service is available 24 hours a day, 365 days a year. Connect information: 1200, 2400, 9600, or 14,400 baud; no parity, 8 data bits, and 1 stop bit. In Canada, dial (905) 507-3022. Connect information: 1200 to 28,800 baud, no parity, 8 data bits, and 1 stop bit.

Microsoft FastTips is an automated, toll-free telephone service that gets you quick answers to common technical questions, as well as technical articles by telephone, fax, or mail. To access FastTips or to receive a map and catalog, call (800) 936-4400.

PRIORITY SUPPORT OPTIONS

If you need direct assistance from a Microsoft technical engineer, you can purchase one of the Priority Support Options described below.

To purchase an **annual** contract of Priority incidents, or for more information on Priority, call (800) 936-3500, 6:00 A.M. through 6:00 P.M. Pacific time, Monday through Friday. Technical support is not available through this number.

To purchase **pay-per-incident** support for a fee per incident, call (800) 936-5900, 24 hours a day, 7 days a week. Support fees will be billed to your VISA, MasterCard, or American Express credit card.

Microsoft Technical Support offers special support packages for developers using Microsoft products. To find out about pricing and more information on **Priority Developer Support**, call (800) 936-3500, Monday through Friday, 6 A.M. through 6 P.M. Technical support is not available at this number.

To purchase consulting on an hourly basis, call (800) 936-1565.

PREMIER SUPPORT

Premier Support gives you proactive support planning and problem resolution for Microsoft products, with rapid response times. Includes immediate server-down response, 24 hours a day, 7 days a week; and special consulting and planning services. Premier Support is part of Microsoft Service Advantage, a suite of offerings that combine direct Microsoft services with established Enterprise service partners for a total solution for the Enterprise customer. For more information on Service Advantage and Premier Support, in the United States, please call (800) 936-3200. In Canada, please call (905) 568-0434.

TECHNICAL INFORMATION SUBSCRIPTION PRODUCTS

Microsoft TechNet is the comprehensive CD information resource for evaluating, implementing, and supporting Microsoft business products. A one-year subscription to Microsoft TechNet delivers two CDs every month with over 150 thousand pages of up-to-date technical information. To subscribe to Microsoft TechNet, see your local authorized retailer or call (800) 344-2121.

Microsoft MSDN Network provides comprehensive programming information and toolkits for Internet developers or for those who write applications for Windows, Windows 95, or Windows NT, or use Microsoft products for development purposes. To subscribe to MSDN, call (800) 759-5474.

THIRD-PARTY SUPPORT OPTIONS

Microsoft Solution Providers are independent developers, consultants, and systems analysts who offer fee-based technical training and support, industry knowledge, objective advice, and a range of value-added services to companies of all sizes. For the name of a Microsoft solution provider near you, in the United States, call (800) 765-7768, 6:30 A.M. through 5:30 P.M. Pacific time, Monday through Friday (excluding holidays). In Canada, call (800) 563-9048, 8:30 A.M. through 6:30 P.M. Eastern time, Monday through Friday (excluding holidays).

Microsoft Authorized Support Centers. This select group of strategic support providers offer quality, cost-effective, customizable support services that span the complete life cycle of planning, building, and managing your open environment. For more information on the ASC program, in the United States, call (800) 636-7544, 6:00 A.M. through 6:00 P.M. Pacific time, Monday through Friday (excluding holidays). In Canada, call (800) 563-9048, 8:30 A.M. through 6:30 P.M. Eastern time, Monday through Friday (excluding holidays).

ADDITIONAL INFORMATION

For **customer service** issues on Microsoft products, upgrades, and services, you can call the Microsoft Sales Information Center at (800) 426-9400 in the United States. In Canada, call (800) 563-9048. Technical support is not available at this number.

Microsoft **text telephone** (TT/TDD) services are available for the deaf or hard-of-hearing. In the United States, using a TT/TDD modem, dial (425) 635-4948. In Canada, using a TT/TDD modem, dial (905) 568-9641.

For support offerings outside the United States and Canada, contact the local Microsoft subsidiary in your area. For a listing of worldwide Microsoft subsidiaries, connect to *http://www.microsoft.com/supportnet/InternationalPhoneNumbers.htm.*

Appendix L

IIS Audit Logs and Performance Monitoring[1]

This appendix covers two topics: IIS audit logs that show what the user has been requesting and what pages have been served; and performance monitoring counters that track the timing of the above operations and therefore show the response time the user receives. These topics help with performance monitoring and scaling of Site Server.

IIS AUDIT LOGS

Each of the services contained in Microsoft IIS can be configured to log information about who accessed the server and what information they accessed. This data can help you fine-tune your site, plan for the number of users that regularly gain access to your site, assess content, and audit security.

---

1. Material for this appendix was taken from "Logging Server Activity," Chapter 7 of *Internet Information Server (IIS) Installation and Administration Guide* at C:\WINNT\system32\inetsrv\iisadmin\htmldocs\iisdocs\htm.

The logging feature in IIS has been designed for flexibility in the following areas:

- Choice of data stores: File system or Microsoft SQL Server

- Various log-file formats: Standard format, European Microsoft Windows NT Academic Centre (EMWAC) format, or National Center for Supercomputing (NCSA) Common Log File format

- Location of log files within the system

Creation of New Log Files

In logging to a file, you can create new log files whenever the files achieve a particular size, or whenever the day, week, or month changes. This section explains how to do the following:

- Configure logging

- Read file logs

- Log in to databases

- Convert log files to other formats

Configuring Logging

When you set up Internet Information Server, you can enable logging to see who has been using the server and how many times your online information was accessed.

To configure logging,

1. Determine in which folder the logs will be stored.

2. Specify how often logs are to be rotated (every day, every week, every month, and so on).

3. Select the log tools you want to use to analyze the logs your server collects.

4. In Internet Service Manager, double-click the service to display its property sheets. The Logging property sheet sets logging for the selected information service.

Reading file logs

When logging to a file, the maximum total log line is 1200 bytes. Each field is limited to 150 bytes. To start logging, select the Enable Logging check box on the Logging property sheet. To stop logging, clear the Enable Logging check box. Choose

Log to File to log activity information for the selected information service to a text file.

Log Format Use the Log Format box to select the logging format you want. Click the arrow and choose either Standard format or NCSA format, National Center for Supercomputing Applications (NCSA) Common Log File format.

Automatically open a new log This option generates new logs using the specified frequency. If not selected, the same log file will grow indefinitely.

Log file folder This option sets the folder (directory) containing the log file.

File name This field shows the file name used for logging. If multiple services are configured to log to the same folder, they will use the same file. The service will close the log file and create a new one with a different name in the same folder when the appropriate interval or file size is reached. Log file names are as follows:

- **INETSV1.LOG** if Automatically open new log is not selected

- **INETSVNNN.LOG** (where NNN is a sequentially increasing number) if When file size reaches is selected

- **inMMDDYY.LOG** (where MMDDYY is the month, day, and year when the log file is created) if one of the Daily, Weekly, or Monthly options is enabled

For the Daily, Weekly, or Monthly options, the log file is closed the first time a log record is generated after midnight on the last day of the current log file. The new log file name will include the date of the first day in the log file.

For the When file size reaches option, every time the log file is closed and a new one is created, the sequential number in the file name is incremented.

Log in to databases

When you install Microsoft Internet Information Server, logging to a file is the default method of logging. If you prefer to collect logs in a database, you must install Open Database Connectivity (ODBC) version 2.5 or later. To access the pages, make sure that the WWW service is running, and then in the Internet Explorer Address box, type the local computer name. Alternatively, you can follow the manual procedure described later in this section.

Choose Log to SQL/ODBC Database to log activity information to any ODBC-compliant data source. Set the ODBC Data Source Name (DSN), Table, and specify the user name and password to use when logging to the database. When using ODBC for logging, each field is limited to 255 bytes.

Logging to a database increases the amount of time and resources needed to service WWW (HTTP), FTP, and gopher requests. Therefore, if your site has heavy traffic, you should log to the file system to maximize performance. On the other hand, generating reports from a sequential file is time-consuming, while a database would return the results quickly. The choice depends on your specific needs.

To manually prepare for logging to a database,

1. Create a table that conforms to the sizes of the fields for your database programs, such as Microsoft SQL Server.

2. In Microsoft SQL Server, the sizes of the fields for a table are as follows:

```
CREATE TABLE IIS_AUDIT
ClientHost varchar(255),
username varchar(255),
LogTime datetime,
service varchar(255),
machine varchar(255),
serverip varchar(50),
processingtime int,
bytesrecvd int,
bytessent int,
servicestatus int,
win32status int,
operation varchar(255),
target varchar(255),
parameters varchar(255)
```

You can find these values in the LOGTEMP.SQL file in the Inetsrv folder.

3. Set up a database on your server and create a system Data Source Name (DSN). For Microsoft Access, the system DSN is the file name of your database.

To log to a database,

1. In Internet Service Manager, double-click the service for which you wish to set up the database.

2. Click the Logging tab.

3. Select the Enable Logging check box.

4. Select Log to SQL/ODBC database.

5. In the ODBC Data Source Name (DSN) box, type the system DSN that you added in step 3 of the previous procedure.

6. In the Table field, type the name of the table (not the file name of the table).

7. In the User Name and Password fields, type a user name and password that are valid for the computer on which the database resides.

8. Click Apply and then click OK.

Converting log files to other formats

Internet Service Manager provides a choice between two log formats: the Standard format (Microsoft Professional Internet Services format); and NCSA Common Log File format. In the Log Format box on the Logging property sheet, click the arrow and select the format you want.

If you have created Microsoft IIS log files in Standard format and wish to convert them to either the EMWAC log file format or NCSA Common Log File format, use the Microsoft Internet Log Converter (CONVLOG.EXE). At the command prompt, type **convlog** without parameters to see syntax and examples.

To convert logs to other formats,

1. Add CONVLOG.EXE (in the \Inetsrv folder, by default) to your path.

2. In a command-prompt window, type the convlog command. See the syntax and examples below.

The Syntax is convlog -s[f|g|w] -t [emwac | ncsa[:GMTOffset] | none] -o [output directory] -f [temp file directory] -h LogFilename -d<m:[cachesize]>.

The parameters to convlog are the following:

- -s[f|g|w]: Specifies the service for which to convert log entries

- f = Processes FTP log entries

- g = Processes gopher log entries

- w = Processes WWW log entries

  The default for the -s switch is to convert logs for all services.

- -t [emwac | ncsa[:GMTOffset] | none]: Specifies the destination conversion format (The default is to create output files in EMWAC format.)

- -o [output directory]: Specifies the directory for the converted files (The default is the current directory.)

- -f [temp file directory]: Specifies a temporary directory to hold temporary files created by convlog (The default is C:\Temp or the directory specified by the "tmp" environment variable.)

- -n[m:[cachesize]|i]: Specifies whether to convert IP addresses to computer or domain names (The default is to not convert IP addresses.)

- -m[cachesize]: Specifies to convert IP addresses to computer names. (The default cache size is 5000 bytes. "I" = Specifies to not convert IP addresses to computer names.)

■ -h: Displays Help.

LogFilename: Specifies the name of the log to be converted. Convlog will display the file name for the converted file.

■ -dm:[cachesize]: Converts IP addresses in NCSA log format to computer names or domain names (The default is to not convert IP addresses. The default cachesize is 5000 bytes.)

IIS PERFORMANCE MONITORING

IIS is a service that runs on Windows NT Server. It hosts several other services, such as HTTP Server. IIS keeps track of information applicable to HTTP services it hosts, such as the total bandwidth used by HTTP Server.

Internet Information Services Global Counters

For capacity planning, the most important IIS global counters relate to the IIS cache and to the way IIS limits its use of the server's bandwidth.

The IIS cache holds objects such as frequently accessed HTML pages, database queries, and so on. The cache size is configurable through the IIS Service Manager; it defaults to 3 MB or 10 percent of total physical memory, whichever is larger. When a client requests an object, IIS looks for it in the cache; if found, IIS increments the Cache Hit and Cache Hit % counters; if not found, IIS increments the Cache Misses counter, obtains the object through normal means, adds the object to the cache, and increases the Cache Used counter. If an object in the cache is not "hit" within a time-out period, the object is flushed from the cache, and IIS increments the Cache Flushes counter. The only IIS cache counter that applies to a particular type of object is Cached File Handles; this counter reflects the number of static files that are in the system's cache.

The Async (Asynchronous type) counters are relevant if IIS is configured to limit its use of the server's bandwidth. By default, this feature is disabled because monitoring bandwidth usage consumes CPU time. IIS uses as much of the server's bandwidth as it can. If the feature is enabled, the counters reflect how much of the bandwidth is in use, how many operations are allowed, and how many are currently blocked or rejected due to lack of bandwidth.

HTTP Service Counters

Some of the HTTP Service's counters are self-explanatory:

■ Connection Attempts, Connections/sec, Current Connections, Maximum Connections

■ Files Received, Files Sent, Files Total

■ Total Anonymous Users, Total NonAnonymous Users, Maximum NonAnonymous Users, Maximum Anonymous Users, Current Anonymous Users, Current NonAnonymous Users

Others require some explanation:

Bytes Received/sec, Bytes Sent/sec, Bytes Total/sec These counters reflect the amount of data that the HTTP Server transfers. This is always smaller than the total network traffic, because these counters do not include bytes added by lower-level protocols such as TCP and IP.

Current ISAPI Extension Requests, ISAPI Extension Requests, Maximum ISAPI Extension Requests, Maximum CGI Requests, CGI Requests, Current CGI Requests These reflect the number of times clients cause ISAPI or CGI applications (Web server "extensions") to do work, typically to generate dynamic pages.

Logon Attempts If the client is connecting from a permitted IP address, and a new connection will not exceed the server's configured limit, the client is allowed to log on. Thus, this counter's value is always a subset of Connection Attempts.

Get Requests, Head Requests, Post Requests, Other Request Methods These counters, which track usage of several HTML tags that are often used in forms for data entry, can't help identify performance bottlenecks.

Not Found Errors This number usually indicates the number of invalid links to pages on your server.

Identifying Web server bottlenecks

Identifying Web server bottlenecks is discussed in terms of memory, CPU, and link.

Memory If Cache Used is nearly as large as Cache Size, the system might benefit from a larger cache (especially if Cache Hits % is low). Either increase the system's real memory, increase the percentage of the system's memory devoted to the cache, or decrease the number or size of the objects in the cache (for example, remove large graphics from frequently hit pages).

If Cache Hits % is low, the system might benefit from a larger cache. Cache Hits % often equates to performance; however, sometimes performance problems are a function of the total number of cache misses in a time period, not the percentage of hits or misses.

If the server generates dynamic content, memory bottlenecks can be harder to find because of how the application uses memory. Suspect this type of problem if you add the Memory counter called Available Bytes and its value drops while the server is under a constant load.

Also, note that the cache allows the CPU to work efficiently, so a memory bottleneck may manifest itself as a CPU bottleneck.

CPU Percentage (%) CPU Time is a Processor object, not a IIS or HTTP Service object. This counter indicates how much of the CPU's time is devoted to doing work. If this value reaches 100 percent you should look for ways to reduce the system's load. For example, off-load to other systems responsibilities such as file and print serving and domain controller functions. Remember that CGI applications tend to consume typically three to five times as much CPU time as an ISAPI equivalent.

Under normal conditions, % CPU time should be well below 100 percent so that the system can maintain good performance as usage changes. A good rule of thumb is to keep this value's average below 60 percent.

Each user's connection consumes a small amount of CPU time and memory for setting up internal data structures. Some administrators limit the number of connections to reduce this overhead. As a general rule, you can avoid a bottleneck during peak time by keeping the connection limit above twice the average connection value. This bottleneck is easy to identify: the Connection Attempts plateaus, meaning that it has reached a constant value.

If CurrentConnections is consistently high (in the thousands), the server might benefit from increased CPU time, which can be achieved by migrating to a system with a faster processor, or more processors, or reducing CPU load by removing other processes.

Link If the Bytes/sec counter plateaus, suspect that the server's link is being used at full capacity. As a general rule, expect transfers during peak times to be at least twice as high the average Bytes/sec value.

If you run Internet Service Manager and enable the Limit Network Use By All Internet Services On This Computer feature, then IIS restricts its usage of the bandwidth, and the Measured Async I/O Bandwidth Usage counter indicates how much of the allocated bandwidth IIS is using. If this counter is too high, you may need to increase the allocated bandwidth with the Internet Service Manager application, or change the way IIS uses bandwidth, perhaps by reducing the amount of data sent to clients.

The hardware that links the Web server to the clients can cause bottlenecks. For example, a network adapter driver may be poorly optimized, the adapter's BIOS might have a bug, or the adapter might be defective.

Windows NT Resource Kit, available from Microsoft Press, includes an application for monitoring IIS called Wcat discussed in Chapter 7 under scalability. The following table summarizes performance monitor counters of interest for Site Server performance planning when using the Wcat tool to simulate your environment's scaling requirements.

Counter name	*Description*
Aborted Connections	Total number of connections disconnected due to error or over-the-limit requests made to gopher service
Bytes Received/sec	Rate at which data bytes are received by service
Bytes Sent/sec	Rate at which data bytes are sent by service
Bytes Total/sec	Rate of total bytes transferred by service (sum of bytes sent and received)
CGI Requests	The total number of Common Gateway Interface (CGI) requests executed since WWW service startup; CGI requests invoke custom gateway executables, which the administrator can install to add forms processing or other dynamic data sources
Connection Attempts	Number of connection attempts made to service
Connections in Error	Total number of connections (since service startup) that resulted in errors when processed by gopher service
Connections/sec	Rate at which HTTP requests are currently being handled
Current Anonymous Users	Number of anonymous users currently connected to service
Current CGI Requests	Current number of CGI requests simultaneously being processed by WWW service (includes WAIS index queries)
Current Connections	Current number of connections to the service (sum of anonymous and nonanonymous users)
Current ISAPI Extension Requests	Current ISAPI extension requests simultaneously being processed by WWW service
Current NonAnonymous Users	Number of nonanonymous users currently connected to a specific (WWW, FTP, or gopher) service
Files Received	Total files received by (uploaded to) service since service startup (WWW or FTP only)
Files Sent	Total files sent by (downloaded from) service since service startup
Files Total	Total files transferred by server since service startup (WWW or FTP only)
Get Requests	Total number of HTTP GET requests received by WWW service; GET requests are generally used for basic file retrievals or image maps, though they can be used with forms
Gopher Plus Requests	The total number of Gopher Plus requests received by gopher service since service startup
Head Requests	Total number of HTTP HEAD requests received by WWW service; HEAD requests typically indicate that a client is querying the state of a document he or she already has to see if it needs to be refreshed

Counter name	Description
ISAPI Extension Requests	Total number of HTTP ISAPI extension requests received by WWW service; ISAPI Extension Requests are custom gateway dynamic-link libraries (DLLs), which the administrator can install to add forms processing or other dynamic data sources
Logon Attempts	Number of logon attempts made by service since service startup
Maximum Anonymous Users	Largest number of anonymous users simultaneously connected to service since service startup
Maximum CGI Requests	Largest number of CGI requests simultaneously processed by the WWW service since service startup
Maximum Connections	Largest number of users simultaneously connected to service since service startup
Maximum ISAPI Extension Request	Largest number of ISAPI extension requests simultaneously processed by WWW service since service startup
Maximum Non-Anonymous Users	Largest number of nonanonymous users simultaneously connected to service since service startup
Not Found Errors	Number of requests that could not be satisfied by service because requested document could not be found; typically reported as HTTP 404 error code to client
Other Request Methods	Number of HTTP requests that are not GET, POST, or HEAD methods; may include PUT, DELETE, LINK, or other methods supported by gateway applications
Post Requests	Number of HTTP requests using POST method; generally used for forms or gateway requests
Total Anonymous Users	Total number of anonymous users that have ever connected to service since service startup
Total NonAnonymous Users	Total number of nonanonymous users that have connected to service since service startup

Select Internet Information Services Global in the Object list box in the Windows NT Performance Monitor Add To Chart dialog box to monitor general-use and cache-use information about Internet Information Server. Counters for this object are the following:

Counter name	Description
Cached File Handles	Current number of open file handles cached by all IIS services
Cache Flushes	Total number of times since service startup that cache has been flushed
Cache Hits	Total number of times since service startup that a file-open, directory-listing, or service-specific object's request was found in the IIS cache

Counter name	Description
Cache Hits %	Ratio of cache hits to all cache requests
Cache Misses	Total number of times since service startup that a file-open, directory-listing, or service-specific object's request was not found in the cache
Cache Size	Configured maximum size of the shared HTTP, FTP, and gopher memory cache
Cache Used	Current number of bytes containing cached data in shared memory cache (includes directory listings, file handle tracking, and service-specific objects)
Current Blocked Async I/O Requests	Current number of asynchronous I/O requests blocked by bandwidth throttling
Directory Listings	Current number of cached directory listings cached by all IIS services
Measured Async I/O Bandwidth Usage	Measured bandwidth in bytes of asynchronous I/O averaged over one minute
Objects	Current number of objects cached by all of IIS services (includes file-handle tracking objects, directory-listing objects, and service-specific objects)
Total Allowed Async I/O Requests	Total asynchronous I/O requests allowed by bandwidth throttling since service startup
Total Blocked Async I/O Requests	Total asynchronous I/O requests blocked by bandwidth throttling since service startup
Total Rejected Async I/O Requests	Total asynchronous I/O requests rejected by bandwidth throttling since service startup

Appendix M

SQL Server Scaling[1]

Microsoft's SQL Server and BackOffice products running on Windows NT Server have evolved to support huge databases and applications. This appendix outlines the history and current power of SQL Server, showing that it scales down to small one megabyte personal databases and scales up to hundred gigabyte databases used by thousands of people. SQL Server achieves this scalability by supporting symmetric multiprocessing (SMP). Beyond that, SQL Server will scale out by partitioning a huge database into a cluster of servers, each storing part of the whole database, and each doing a part of the work. This clustering approach dovetails with the Windows NT Server cluster architecture. Today, Windows NT Server and SQL Server clusters provide high availability—but we are still in the early stages of this product's evolution. Microsoft continues to extend its cluster architecture to accommodate modular growth, as well as to automate configuration, maintenance, and programming.

TECHNOLOGY TRENDS

Technology advances and the wide adoption of computing have had some surprising results. Today, commodity components are the fastest and most reliable computers, networks, and storage devices. Intense competition among microprocessor vendors has created incredibly fast processing chips. Indeed, the most powerful supercomputers are built from such chips. Conventional water-cooled mainframes are moving to this higher-speed technology.

---

1. Material in this appendix was provided by the Microsoft Desktop and Business Systems division. This section is a selection from a series of white papers designed to educate information technology (IT) professionals about Windows NT Server and the Microsoft BackOffice family of products.

Commodity workstations and servers rival and often outstrip the performance of mainframes. The pace of change in this commodity market is so rapid that the low end is years ahead of the installed base of conventional mainframe and minicomputer architectures. Commodity computer interconnects are also making extraordinary progress. Ethernet has graduated to 12 megabytes per second speeds (100 Mbps). Switched 100 Mbps Ethernet gives a hundred-fold speedup in local networks at commodity prices. Asynchronous Transfer Mode (ATM) hardware will soon be ubiquitous for both local and wide area networks. ATM offers a tenfold increase over switched Ethernet.

The entire computer industry uses the same basic 16 megabit DRAM chips that go into PCs. Memory prices for commodity machines are often three to ten times less than the price of the same memory for a proprietary machine.

The highest-performance and most reliable disks are 3.5" SCSI discs. They have doubled in capacity every year, and are rated at a 50 year mean time to hardware failure. Today, the 4 gigabyte disk is standard. Next year it will be replaced by the 8 gigabyte drive for approximately the same price. In 1995, one thousand dollars bought 4 gigabytes of disks. This is a thousand-fold improvement over the disks of 15 years ago. These low prices explain why typical servers are configured with 10 gigabytes to 100 gigabytes of disk capacity today. Such disks cost two thousand to twenty thousand dollars.

Kinds of Growth

As organizations grow and acquire more and more data, they must deal with increased transaction workloads and larger databases. Each major increment presents new challenges. Scalability covers several kinds of growth.

User population and network If the user population doubles, the network and database workload probably does too.

Database size With databases commonly reaching hundreds of gigabytes, operations such as backup, restore, and load all can become bottlenecks.

Transaction complexity Application designers are building more intelligence into applications, relieving users of tedious tasks. Increasingly, applications are used for data mining and data analysis.

Applications As applications become easier and less expensive to build, organizations are using computers in new ways. These new applications increase the load on existing databases and servers.

Numbers of servers Clustered and distributed applications involve many nodes. Scalable systems allow a large number of nodes to be easily managed from a single location.

Scaleup, Speedup, and Scaleout

An ideal system improves linearly; that is, if you double the number of processors and disks, then throughput doubles (linear scaleup) or response time is cut in half (linear speedup). Linear scaling is rarely achieved in practice because it requires that all aspects of the system be perfectly scalable. The overall architecture includes hardware, operating system, database and network software, and the application software.

It is tempting to simplify scalability to a single metric like the number of processors a system can support. It may seem obvious, but many database applications are very I/O-intensive: adding CPUs to an I/O-bound system will not make it faster. SQL Server running on today's typical 4-processor servers can achieve performance comparable to systems running on hardware with 20 processors! Is the second system more scalable because it requires 20 CPUs to achieve the same throughput? Obviously not. Table M-1 shows some benchmarks using many processors. It shows that a 4-processor Compaq running Windows NT Server and SQL Server outperforms many 8-processor and some 20-processor systems.

Table M-1. *Windows NT Server & SQL Server vs. SMP UNIX Solutions on the TPC-C Benchmark.*

Database	Hardware	CPUs	tpmC	$/tpmC	System Cost
SQL Server 6.5	Compaq Proliant 4500/133	4	3643	$148	$537,508
DB2 for Solaris V2	Sun SPARCServer1000E	8	3256	$199	$646,820
Informix Online 7.1	Sun SPARCCenter 2000E	20	3534	$495	$1,751,004
Oracle 7.3	IBM RS6000 / j30	8	3631	$ 289	$1,049,656

The best metric is how well the system scales for your application. That is impossible to know in advance, but you can estimate scalability by examining standard benchmarks and by looking at applications in related industries.

SERVER SCALABILITY

The proliferation of many processors, disks, and networks poses an architectural challenge. What hardware architecture best exploits these commodity components? No single architecture has emerged as a winner, but there is broad agreement that three generic architectures can provide scalability: (1) shared memory, (2) shared disk, and (3) shared nothing. Windows NT Server supports all these architectures, and will evolve in parallel as these architectures evolve.

Computer Architecture Choices: SMP Hardware Systems and Clusters

Traditionally, most scaleup has been through symmetric multiprocessing (SMP): adding more processors, memory, disks, and network cards to a single server. Several vendors have shown that SMP servers can offer a tenfold scaleup over uniprocessor systems on commercial workloads.

At some point, a single node hits a bottleneck. This shows up as diminishing returns or prohibitively expensive hardware. To grow much beyond a factor of ten, application designers have gravitated to a cluster architecture in which the workload and database are partitioned among an array of networks, processors, memories, and database systems. All the truly large systems are built this way. The IBM MVS Sysplex, the DEC VMS cluster, the Teradata DBC 1024, and the Tandem Himalaya series are all clustered systems. Ideally, this partitioning is transparent to the clients and to the application. The cluster is programmed and managed as a single system but it is, in fact, an array of nodes.

Cluster technology dovetails with and leverages distributed system technologies such as replication, remote procedure call, distributed systems management, distributed security, and distributed transactions. The cluster approach has two advantages over increasingly larger SMP systems: clusters can be built from commodity components and can grow in small increments; and the relative independence of cluster nodes gives a natural fail-over and high availability design.

Microsoft Windows NT Server and SQL Server support both SMP and cluster architectures. SQL Server delivers impressive peak performance for both client-server and data warehouse applications. SQL Server and Microsoft Windows NT Server run on 2-way to 32-way SMP hardware systems, although the most common SMP hardware systems are 2-way and 4-way. SQL Server has demonstrated excellent SMP scalability, both on audited benchmarks and in real applications.

Symmetric multiprocessors (SMP)

SMP gives vertical growth from small processors to superservers by adding more processors, disks, and peripherals to a single system. Beyond a certain point, this growth involves replacing existing equipment with a different system model.

Symmetric multiprocessing grows a server by adding multiple processors to a single shared memory. The system grows by adding memory, disks, network interfaces, and processors. SMP is the most popular way to scale beyond a single processor. The SMP software model, often called the shared memory model, runs a single copy of the operating system with application processes running as if they were on a single processor system. Microsoft Windows NT Server and SQL Server are designed to scale well on SMP systems. They can scale to 32 nodes for some applications, but the practical limits for general purpose use today are the following:

- 8 processors

- 4 gigabytes of main memory (2 gigabytes per application)

- 125 disk drives configured as 25 logical disks holding 500 gigabytes with 4 gigabyte disks

- 1 terabyte with 8 gigabyte disks

- 5000 active clients accessing an SQL Server

Typical large servers are half this size or less. With time, SQL Server, Windows NT Server, and hardware technology will improve to support even larger configurations.

Today SMP is by far the most popular parallel hardware architecture. SMP systems are relatively easy to program. These systems also leverage the benefits of industry-standard software and hardware components. SMP servers based on industry-standard Intel and Alpha AXP microprocessors deliver astonishing performance and price/performance for database platforms. Intel markets a 4-way SMP board based on the Pentium Pro (P6) processor. This SMP board is being incorporated in servers from almost every hardware vendor.

As microprocessor speeds increase, SMP systems become increasingly expensive to build. Today there are modest price steps, as a customer needs to scale from one processor to four processors. Going from four to eight processors in an SMP is comparatively inexpensive. Beyond eight processors, prices rise very steeply and the returns diminish.

For example, as can be seen in Table M-2, Compaq can deliver astonishing performance on a standard, widely available 4-processor SMP machine. It is designed using commodity hardware and delivers very cost-effective database support. A 16-processor machine, designed around that same 133 megahertz Pentium chip, delivers only 50 percent more performance, at over four times the cost.

Table M-2. *Diminishing Returns on SMP Performance.*

Database	Hardware	CPUs	tpmC	$/tpmC	System Cost
SQL Server 6.5	Compaq Proliant 4500/133	4 Pentium 133Mhz	3643	$148	$537,508
Oracle 7 v 7.3.2	NCR WorldMark 5100S c/s	16 Pentium 133Mhz	5607	$394	$2,206,688

At the software level, multiple processors concurrently accessing shared resources must be serialized. This serialization limits the practical scalability for individual applications in shared-memory SMP systems. These software bottlenecks in operating systems, database systems, and applications are as significant as the hardware limitations.

Nonetheless, SMP systems are the most common form of scalability. They will be the dominant form of server for many years to come. The appearance of Intel Pentium Pro, DEC Alpha, IBM PowerPC, and SGI MIPS SMP hardware systems gives powerful and inexpensive SMP nodes.

Microsoft provides excellent support for these commodity SMP hardware systems today, and continues to invest in this technology.

Clusters

A cluster is a set of loosely coupled, independent computer systems that behave as a single system. The nodes of a cluster may be single-processor systems, or they can be SMP hardware systems. The nodes may be connected by a commodity network or by a proprietary, very high-speed communications bus. The computers in a cluster cooperate so that clients see the cluster as if it were a single, very high-performance, highly reliable server. Because the cluster is modular, it can be scaled incrementally and at low cost by adding servers, disks, and networking.

Windows NT Server clusters provide horizontal growth, or scaleout, allowing customers to add processing, storage, and network services to a preexisting configuration. A cluster can also be grown using superserver SMP nodes, but usually it is built with commodity components and commodity interconnects. Two interconnects are used for fault tolerance.

Cluster architectures allow you to scale up to problems larger than a single SMP node. Every SMP system has a maximum size: a maximum number of nodes, memory, disks, and network interfaces that can be attached to the system. To go beyond these limits, the software architecture must support a cluster or network of computers cooperating to perform the common task.

All the largest computer systems are structured as clusters. The largest known database, the Walmart system, runs on an NCR/Teradata cluster of 500 Intel processors accessing approximately 1500 disks. Other large databases are supported by

IBM MVS/Sysplex systems, or Tandem Himalaya systems, or Digital VMS cluster systems.

Clusters work by partitioning the database and application among several different nodes (computers). Each node stores a part of the database and each performs a part of the workload. The cluster grows by adding nodes and redistributing the storage and work to the new nodes. This growth and redistribution should be automatic and require no changes to application programs.

Partitioned data is used in centralized systems to scale up capacity or bandwidth. When one disk is too small for a database, the database system partitions it over many disks. This same technique is used if traffic on a file or database exceeds the capacity of one disk. This partitioning is transparent to the application. The application accesses all data on all the disks as though it were on a single disk. Similarly, clients are partitioned among networks to scale up network bandwidth. Clusters generalize this partitioning to spread the computation among cluster nodes. The key challenge is to make this partitioning transparent to the customer so that a cluster is as easy to manage and program as a single system.

Shared disk and shared nothing clusters There are two basic software models for clusters: shared-disk and shared-nothing. In a shared-disk cluster, all processors have direct access to all disks (and data), but they do not share main memory. An extra layer of software called a distributed cache or lock manager is required to globally manage cache concurrency among processors. Digital's VMS cluster and Oracle's Parallel Query Option are the most common examples of a shared-disk parallel database architecture. Since access to data is serialized by the lock or cache manager, the shared-disk cluster has some of the same scalability limitations as shared-memory SMP systems.

The shared-nothing cluster architecture avoids the exotic interconnects and packaging of a scalable shared-disk cluster by connecting each disk to one or two servers. In a shared-nothing cluster, each node has its own memory and disk storage. Nodes communicate with one another by exchanging messages across a shared interconnect. Each node in a shared-nothing cluster is a free-standing computer with its own resources and operating system. Each is a unit of service and availability. Each node owns and provides services for some disks, tapes, network links, database partitions, or other resources. In case of node failure, the disks of one node may fail over to an adjacent node—but at any instant, only one node is accessing the disks.

Proprietary shared-nothing cluster solutions have been available for several years from Tandem, Teradata, and IBM Sysplex. These solutions all depend on exotic hardware and software, and so are expensive.

SQL Server and Windows NT Server clusters will bring scalability and fault tolerance to the commodity marketplace. Microsoft is building clustering technology directly into the Windows NT Server operating system. This technology will work well with commodity servers and interconnects—and it will be able to leverage special hardware accelerators from vendors like Compaq, Digital, and Tandem. Microsoft BackOffice products such as SQL Server, Internet Information Server, and Exchange will be enhanced to take advantage of this clustering support. Many third-party products are also being ported to this architecture. Clusters have several advantages. The most obvious is that they can grow to huge sizes. By building clusters from SMP nodes, you can scale up an application by a factor of ten or a hundred. For example, Digital, Tandem, and Teradata have many 100-node clusters in production today. Other advantages are described below.

Low cost Clusters can be built with high-volume components that are relatively inexpensive. Relatively few high-end SMP machines are sold; relatively few customers will buy a 20-way SMP, so 20-way SMP hardware systems are expensive because the engineering cost is amortized over relatively few units. Inexpensive clusters can be built with commodity 4-way SMP hardware systems. This means they have superior price/performance. In addition, because they are built from commodity components, commodity clusters can grow in smaller increments. You can add disks or nodes or network cards as needed rather than having to buy a huge new box each time you grow.

Availability via fault tolerance By partitioning data and work, clusters provide firewalls that limit the scope of failures. When a node fails, the other cluster nodes continue to deliver service. By replicating data or by allowing storage and network devices to fail-over to surviving nodes, the cluster can provide uninterrupted service.

In summary, clusters have substantial advantages. Microsoft believes that commodity SMP hardware systems will be the building blocks for clusters. Availability, scalability, and economics will demand that large systems be built as arrays of these commodity components. SMP hardware systems will provide vertical growth of nodes from single-processor systems to large SMP hardware systems. Clusters will provide horizontal growth by combining these SMP hardware systems into Windows NT Server clusters.

Transparency Distributed systems techniques are the key to building transparency into clusters. By structuring applications and systems as modules that interact via remote procedure calls, applications become more modular, and they can be distributed among nodes of the cluster. The client calls upon a service by name. The procedure call either invokes the service locally, or uses a remote procedure call if the service is remote.

Parallelism

Software and applications running on an SMP or clusters must use parallelism to benefit from the many disks and processors that these scalable architectures provide. There are two generic kinds of parallelism: pipeline and partition.

Pipeline parallelism breaks a task into a sequence of steps. Each step of the sequence is done in parallel. The result of one step is passed to the next step. An industrial assembly line is a good example of pipeline parallelism.

Partition parallelism breaks a big task into many little independent tasks that can be done in parallel. Having multiple harvesters collect grain from several fields is a typical example of partition parallelism.

SQL Server provides a good example of both partition and pipeline parallelism when reading disks. By stripping data across many disks, each disk can deliver a part of a large data read—that is, partition parallelism. SQL Server exploits 3-deep pipeline parallelism by having one task issue prefetch reads to the disks, while another SQL Server task processes the data and passes it back to the application task.

Windows NT Server parallel processing

Windows NT Server was designed for SMP hardware systems. Windows NT Server is a fully threaded operating system that provides a rich set of synchronization primitives. The shrink-wrapped version of Windows NT Server is enabled for 4-way SMP. Larger SMP hardware systems are not yet a commodity product and so the operating system is generally packaged with the hardware. Companies like Digital, Intergraph, NCR, Sequent, and SGI, who build 8-way and 32-way Windows NT Server-multiprocessors, modify Windows NT Server for their hardware and ship it with the hardware package.

Windows NT Server parallel I/O

Windows NT Server also has built-in disk partitioning. It allows logical volumes to be spread across multiple physical volumes. Each logical volume can be a RAID disc or it can be an individual disk. Windows NT Server has software support for RAID 0 (stripping a logical volume across multiple physical volumes), RAID 1 (disk mirroring or shadowing in which data is replicated on multiple disks), and RAID 5 (a fault-tolerant storage strategy in which disks are organized so that one stores parity for data on the others). RAID 5 is more space-efficient than RAID 1. This software support lets Windows NT Server customers build reliable storage with commodity controllers and disks. RAID also offers partition parallelism since it spreads the data among multiple disks that can be read in parallel.

Windows NT Server can read individual commodity SCSI disks at their rated speed of 8 Mbps and can drive SCSI controllers at speeds of 18 MB/s. By using a PCI-based machine and by striping data across four SCSI controllers, a single commodity Pentium processor running Windows NT Server has been clocked reading a disk array at 60 MB/s. This means that a single Pentium processor can read or write data at 200 gigabytes per hour. These rates are important for data-intensive operations like data loading, backup, data indexing, and data mining.

These are impressive numbers for any computer, but they are especially impressive when using commodity single-processor systems. By using multiple processors and multiple PCI busses, SMP systems can read and write data at even higher speeds and still have power left over to analyze and process the data.

SQL Server Scalability Architecture

SQL Server is designed to make full use of NT's SMP capabilities: threads and the Windows NT Server scheduler. Each Windows NT Server node typically has a single SQL Server address space managing all the SQL databases at that node. SQL Server runs as a main address space with several pools of threads. Some threads are dedicated to housekeeping tasks like logging, buffer-pool management, servicing operations requests, and monitoring the system. A second larger pool of threads performs user requests. These threads execute stored procedures or SQL statements requested by the clients.

SQL Server is typically used in a client/server environment where clients on other machines attach to the server and issue either SQL requests, or more typically, issue stored procedures usually written in the transact-SQL language. Clients may also be colocated at the server node. SQL Server uses a built-in TP-monitor facility, Open Data Services[2], to support large numbers of clients. In practice, this has scaled to 5,000 concurrent clients. Beyond that size, it makes sense to either partition the application into a cluster of nodes, or use a TP monitor to connect clients to SQL Server. All common TP monitors, such as CICS and Encina, Tuxedo, and Top End, have been ported to Windows NT Server and interface with SQL Server.

SQL Server has devoted considerable effort to achieving near-linear speedup on SMP machines. Many benchmarks have demonstrated this. Two notable examples are the DEC Alpha TPC-C benchmark and the Intergraph benchmark.

Benchmarks showing SQL Server SMP scalability on TPC-C

There is no universally accepted way to measure scalability. However, useful information can be gained from Transaction Processing Performance Council (TPC) benchmarks. The TPC is a nonprofit organization that defines industry-standard transaction processing and database benchmarks. Members of the council today include all major database vendors and suppliers of server hardware systems. They have defined a series of benchmarks, TPC-A, TPC-B, TPC-C, and TPC-D.

TPC-C is the current industry-standard benchmark for measuring the performance and scalability of On Line Transaction Processing (OLTP) systems. It exercises a broad cross-section of database functionality including inquiry, update, and queued minibatch transactions. The specification is strict in critical areas such as

---

2. Open Data Services is often used as a front-end process to SQL Server, either for protocol translation (from foreign protocols to ODBC or DB-Library), or as a simple message dispatcher among multiple SQL Servers at multiple nodes.

database transparency and transaction isolation. Many consider TPC-C be a good indicator of "real world" OLTP system performance. The benchmark results are audited by independent auditors and a full disclosure report is filed with the TPC. These reports are a gold mine of information about how easy it is to use the various systems and how much the systems cost.

In laboratory tests, Intergraph Corporation demonstrated the scalability of SQL Server 6.0 running on Intergraph's high-end ISMP6x server (6 100 megahertz Pentium processors with 1 megabyte secondary caches). Compared to SQL Server 4.21a, version 6.0 achieved greater than 80 percent scalability on the debit/credit transaction processing benchmark.

The Intergraph study concludes that SQL Server 6.0 gained much more performance from the additional processors than SQL Server 4.21a, even though both were running the same benchmark, on the same hardware, and on the same operating system. The differences are especially noticeable as the number of processors increases over 4 since the effect is geometric. A single SQL Server and Windows NT Server can support thousands of users accessing a database containing billions of records. Such systems are capable of supporting a user community exceeding 20 thousand, or a much larger community of Internet users who are occasionally connected to the server. Just to give a sense of scale, the largest banks have less than 10 thousand tellers and the largest telemarketing organizations have less than 10 thousand active agents. So in theory, these systems could support the traditional front-office of huge corporations.

Database fail-over and fallback

SQL Server 6.5 offers fault-tolerance and high availability by providing fail-over from one server to another when the first server fails or needs to be taken out of service for maintenance. The fail-over mechanism works as follows: Two Windows NT Servers can be configured as dual servers. The pair must have shared access to an SQL Server database stored on shared disks. One of the SQL Servers is the primary server. It accepts requests from clients and both reads and writes the database. The other (fail-over) SQL Server node may be providing access to other databases, but it is not accessing the database being managed by the primary server. If the primary SQL Server node fails, Windows NT Server at the fail-over node takes ownership of the disks holding the database. It then informs the fail-over SQL Server that it is now primary. The fail-over SQL Server recovers the database and begins accepting client connections. For their part, clients reconnect to the backup server when the primary server fails.

The dual-server fail-over is completely automatic. The whole process of detecting and recovering from failure takes only a few minutes. When the primary server is repaired, it is restarted and it becomes the new backup server. If desired, the SQL Server can fallback to the original server when it is repaired.

Data replication for data marts and disaster recovery

Data replication helps configure and manage partitioned applications. Many applications naturally partition into disjoint sections. For example, hotel, retail, and warehouse systems have strong geographic locality. The applications and databases can be broken into servers for geographic areas. Similarly, customer care and telemarketing applications often have this strong partitioning. Nonetheless, all these applications need some shared global data. They also need periodic reporting and disaster recovery via electronic vaulting.

Data replication helps solve these problems by automatically propagating changes from one database to another. The replication can propagate changes to an SQL Server system at a remote site for disaster recovery. Then, in case the primary site fails, the backup site can recover and offer service.

The same mechanism can be used to allow one site to act as a data warehouse for data capture OLTP systems. The data warehouse, in turn, may publish its data to many data marts that provide decision support data to analysts. Some applications dispense with the data warehouse and have the operational systems publish updates directly to the data marts.

SQL Server's data replication system is both powerful and simple to use. A graphical user interface in SQL Enterprise Manager allows the administrator to tell operational databases to publish their updates and allows other nodes to subscribe to these updates. This publish-distribute-subscribe metaphor allows one-to-one and one-to-many publication. By cascading distributors, the replication mechanism can be scaled to huge numbers of subscribers. Replication is in transaction units: each subscriber sees a point-in-time consistent view of the database.

SQL Server applications routinely publish tens of millions of bytes of updates per hour. Publication can be immediate, periodic, or on demand. Replication is fully automatic and very easy to administer.

Partitioned data and data pipes

SQL Server has always allowed customers to partition their database and applications among SQL Servers running on several nodes. Clients connect to an application at one of the servers. If a client's request needs to access data at another node, the application can either access the data through Transact SQL, or it can make a remote procedure call to the SQL Server at the other node.

For example, each warehouse of a distributed application might store all the local orders, invoices, and inventory. When an item is backordered or when a new shipment arrives from the factory, the local system has to perform transactions that involve both the warehouse and the factory SQL Servers. In this case, the application running on an SQL Server at the warehouse can access the factory data directly, or it can invoke a stored procedure at the factory SQL Server. OLE Transactions and

SQL Server will automatically manage the data integrity between the factory and the warehouse.

Once data and applications are partitioned among multiple SQL Servers in a cluster, there needs to be a convenient and high-performance way to move data among these servers. Data pipes make it easy to ship data between servers by capturing result sets returned by remote procedure calls directly in node-local tables. Many applications can use this approach as an alternative to distributed query.

Distributed transactions: OLE transactions and DTC

Prior to Windows NT Server 4.0, partitioned SQL Server applications had to explicitly manage distributed transactions by calling SQL Server's prepare and commit verbs of the two-phase commit protocol. With the new OLE transactions, applications just declare *BEGIN DISTRIBUTED TRANSACTION* and from that point on, the Distributed Transaction Coordinator of SQL Server (DTC) automatically manages the transaction. DTC is an integral part of Windows NT Server, and one more step towards a full Windows NT Server cluster facility.

The DTC also connects SQL Server to the open transaction standard X/OpenXA. Clients can connect to transaction processing monitors like CICS, Encina, Tuxedo, and Top End which in turn route requests to the SQL Servers. The use of transaction processing monitors is another approach to distributing the application by using the TP monitor to route transactions to the appropriate servers. The TP monitor also allows SQL Server to participate in transactions distributed across many nodes.

SQL Server has a companion product, Open Data Services, that is often used as a front-end process to SQL Server, either for protocol translation (from foreign protocols to ODBC or DB-Library), or as a simple message dispatcher among multiple SQL Servers at multiple nodes.

All these approaches make it relatively easy to partition data and applications among multiple SQL Servers in a cluster.

SERVER MANAGEABILITY

Microsoft provides easy installation of the operating system and database using graphical tools and wizards. SQL Server also includes wizards to set up operational procedures. But because these systems involve thousands of client systems and huge databases, manageability is the real challenge. Managing and operating a computer system have always been major parts of the cost of ownership. When hardware and software prices plummet, the residual management cost becomes even more significant. Loading, dumping, and reorganizing 100 gigabyte databases is a challenge. At the 3 Mbps data rate of most tape drives, it takes a day-and-a-half just to dump a 100 gigabyte database with one tape drive. Defining and managing the security attributes of 5,000 different users is a daunting task. Configuring the hardware and software for 5,000 clients is another time-consuming task.

A scalable system should automate periodic and repetitive system management tasks. Operators should only be involved in exception situations that require administrative decisions. Even those tasks should have a graphical interface assisted by wizards.

The cost of downtime increases with system size. Paradoxically, larger systems have more components and so are more likely to break. Scalable systems must deliver continuous 7 x 24 availability. They must allow online operations (backup, recovery, reorganization, upgrades), and must mask hardware and software failures with automatic fail-over to another server.

Any solution must use cost-effective hardware platforms. Approaches based on specialized architectures are increasingly costly.

Customer experience, magazine reviews, and independent studies have all shown that Windows NT Server and SQL Server can dramatically help reduce support and management costs when compared to non-Microsoft systems.

Scalable SQL Server Management

SQL Enterprise Manager is a breakthrough in managing database servers. It gives administrators a visual way to manage and operate many SQL systems from a single console. The graphical interface has several wizards built in to help set up and automate standard tasks. The key features of the SQL Enterprise Manager are as follows:

- A fully graphical administration interface to control and monitor the operation of many SQL Servers and the clients accessing them

- A job scheduler that runs periodic administrative tasks such as dumps, reorganizations, and integrity checks

- A Distributed Management Objects mechanism that allows administrators to automate exception handling and to automate tasks by writing Visual Basic scripts or letting a wizard write the script (These procedures can use e-mail and a TAPI-based beeper system to report results or notify operators when their attention is needed.)

- An extension mechanism that allows third parties to add new administrative tools

- A fully graphical interface to configure and manage database replication

SQL Enterprise Manager includes wizards to set up routine operations, a wizard to routinely publish Web pages from the database to an Internet or Intranet, wizards to help set up a data replication strategy, and answer wizards that guide the operator through the online manuals.

Utilities to load, dump, recover, check, and reorganize large databases are key to operating a system with huge databases. Backing up a 100 gigabyte database using a single high-performance tape drive will take over 33 hours. By using multiple disks and tapes in parallel, SQL Server and Windows NT Server have shown a sustained dump rate of 20 gigabytes per hour. This benchmark was I/O limited; with more tapes and disks, the dump rate could have been even faster. The actual management of the dumps can be controlled by the SQL Enterprise Manager job scheduler working with commodity tape robots. These dumps can either be done at full speed, or they can be done in the background at a slower rate. By doing incremental dumps and by increasing the degree of parallelism, huge databases can be dumped in a few hours.

Dump Rates for SQL Server

1 Hour	20 GB
5 Hours	100 GB

Index

FARHAD AMIRFAIZ

Farhad "Fred" Amirfaiz is a technology consultant for Microsoft, currently working in the Developer Relations group, where he helps managers and others understand Microsoft Web servers and Web server technologies. Amirfaiz received an electrical engineering degree from the University of Washington with an emphasis in computer architecture, programming, and design in 1982. He continued his education at the University of Arizona, where he received a computer engineering degree with an emphasis in computer networks, and at Stanford University with post-graduate work in distributed operating systems. In 1991, he earned an MBA from the University of Washington with an emphasis in high technology. He worked for IBM for eight years and has also been an independent business consultant. His first love in computing was the IMSAI two decades ago.

The manuscript for this book was prepared and submitted to Microsoft Press in electronic form. Text files were prepared using Microsoft Word for Windows 95. Pages were composed by Labrecque Publishing Services using Corel Ventura 7 for Windows, with text in Garamond and display type in Helvetica. Composed pages were delivered to the printer as electronic prepress files.

Cover Graphic Designers
Greg Erickson and Patrick Lanfear

Cover Illustrator
Robin Bartholick

Interior Graphic Designer
Kim Eggleston

Interior Graphic Artist
John Nelson

Principal Compositor
Curtis Philips

Principal Proofreader
Beverly McGuire

Indexer
Katherine Stimson

IMPORTANT—READ CAREFULLY BEFORE OPENING SOFTWARE PACKET(S). By opening the sealed packet(s) containing the software, you indicate your acceptance of the following Microsoft License Agreement.

MICROSOFT LICENSE AGREEMENT

(Book Companion CD)

This is a legal agreement between you (either an individual or an entity) and Microsoft Corporation. By opening the sealed software packet(s) you are agreeing to be bound by the terms of this agreement. If you do not agree to the terms of this agreement, promptly return the unopened software packet(s) and any accompanying written materials to the place you obtained them for a full refund.

MICROSOFT SOFTWARE LICENSE

1. GRANT OF LICENSE. Microsoft grants to you the right to use one copy of the Microsoft software program included with this book (the "SOFTWARE") on a single terminal connected to a single computer. The SOFTWARE is in "use" on a computer when it is loaded into the temporary memory (i.e., RAM) or installed into the permanent memory (e.g., hard disk, CD-ROM, or other storage device) of that computer. You may not network the SOFTWARE or otherwise use it on more than one computer or computer terminal at the same time.

2. COPYRIGHT. The SOFTWARE is owned by Microsoft or its suppliers and is protected by United States copyright laws and international treaty provisions. Therefore, you must treat the SOFTWARE like any other copyrighted material (e.g., a book or musical recording) except that you may either (a) make one copy of the SOFTWARE solely for backup or archival purposes, or (b) transfer the SOFTWARE to a single hard disk provided you keep the original solely for backup or archival purposes. You may not copy the written materials accompanying the SOFTWARE.

3. OTHER RESTRICTIONS. You may not rent or lease the SOFTWARE, but you may transfer the SOFTWARE and accompanying written materials on a permanent basis provided you retain no copies and the recipient agrees to the terms of this Agreement. You may not reverse engineer, decompile, or disassemble the SOFTWARE. If the SOFTWARE is an update or has been updated, any transfer must include the most recent update and all prior versions.

4. DUAL MEDIA SOFTWARE. If the SOFTWARE package contains more than one kind of disk (3.5", 5.25", and CD-ROM), then you may use only the disks appropriate for your single-user computer. You may not use the other disks on another computer or loan, rent, lease, or transfer them to another user except as part of the permanent transfer (as provided above) of all SOFTWARE and written materials.

5. SAMPLE CODE. If the SOFTWARE includes Sample Code, then Microsoft grants you a royalty-free right to reproduce and distribute the sample code of the SOFTWARE provided that you: (a) distribute the sample code only in conjunction with and as a part of your software product; (b) do not use Microsoft's or its authors' names, logos, or trademarks to market your software product; (c) include the copyright notice that appears on the SOFTWARE on your product label and as a part of the sign-on message for your software product; and (d) agree to indemnify, hold harmless, and defend Microsoft and its authors from and against any claims or lawsuits, including attorneys' fees, that arise or result from the use or distribution of your software product.

DISCLAIMER OF WARRANTY

The SOFTWARE (including instructions for its use) is provided "AS IS" WITHOUT WARRANTY OF ANY KIND. MICROSOFT FURTHER DISCLAIMS ALL IMPLIED WARRANTIES INCLUDING WITHOUT LIMITATION ANY IMPLIED WARRANTIES OF MERCHANTABILITY OR OF FITNESS FOR A PARTICULAR PURPOSE. THE ENTIRE RISK ARISING OUT OF THE USE OR PERFORMANCE OF THE SOFTWARE AND DOCUMENTATION REMAINS WITH YOU.

IN NO EVENT SHALL MICROSOFT, ITS AUTHORS, OR ANYONE ELSE INVOLVED IN THE CREATION, PRODUCTION, OR DELIVERY OF THE SOFTWARE BE LIABLE FOR ANY DAMAGES WHATSOEVER (INCLUDING, WITHOUT LIMITATION, DAMAGES FOR LOSS OF BUSINESS PROFITS, BUSINESS INTERRUPTION, LOSS OF BUSINESS INFORMATION, OR OTHER PECUNIARY LOSS) ARISING OUT OF THE USE OF OR INABILITY TO USE THE SOFTWARE OR DOCUMENTATION, EVEN IF MICROSOFT HAS BEEN ADVISED OF THE POSSIBILITY OF SUCH DAMAGES. BECAUSE SOME STATES/COUNTRIES DO NOT ALLOW THE EXCLUSION OR LIMITATION OF LIABILITY FOR CONSEQUENTIAL OR INCIDENTAL DAMAGES, THE ABOVE LIMITATION MAY NOT APPLY TO YOU.

U.S. GOVERNMENT RESTRICTED RIGHTS

The SOFTWARE and documentation are provided with RESTRICTED RIGHTS. Use, duplication, or disclosure by the Government is subject to restrictions as set forth in subparagraph (c)(1)(ii) of The Rights in Technical Data and Computer Software clause at DFARS 252.227-7013 or subparagraphs (c)(1) and (2) of the Commercial Computer Software — Restricted Rights 48 CFR 52.227-19, as applicable. Manufacturer is Microsoft Corporation, One Microsoft Way, Redmond, WA 98052-6399.

If you acquired this product in the United States, this Agreement is governed by the laws of the State of Washington.

Should you have any questions concerning this Agreement, or if you desire to contact Microsoft Press for any reason, please write: Microsoft Press, One Microsoft Way, Redmond, WA 98052-6399.